WITHDRAWN
FROM STOCK

Ideas and Concepts

Landscape Architecture

george lam / pace publishing ltd

712.2/LAM

Library & Learning Centre
University for the Creative Arts
Farnham

© 2009 by Pace Publishing Limited

editor : george lam (george.lam@beisistudio.com)
design + colour edit : polly leung

pace publishing limited
17/f., north point asia-pac commercial ctr.,
10 north point road,
hong kong
t: +852 28971688
f: +852 28972888
www.beisistudio.com
pace@pacebase.com

While all reasonable efforts have been made to ensure accuracy, Pace Publishing Limited and the publishers do not, under any circumstances, accept responsibility for errors, omissions and representations expressed or implied.
All rights reserved. No portion of "Ideas and Concepts - Landscape Architecture" may be reproduced or transmitted in any form or by any means electronic or mechanical, including photocopying, recording, or any information storage or retrieval system, without prior permission in writing from the publishers.

isbn 978-962-7723-24-0
printed in china

Publisher's Statement

A lot of publications / books are devoted to document design projects which have completed construction. As it may take years from design stage to project completion, the ideas and concepts that were employed in designing these projects might not be considered the most current ones. Some good design projects, for other reasons beyond their design merits, might not be constructed / materialized at all.

This book sets out to document landscape architecture projects that are either unbuilt, under construction, or purely experimental with an intention to bring to readers the current thinking, ideas and concepts in Landscape Architecture.

"Ideas and Concepts - Landscape Architecture" presents 55 designs from 41 design practices and individuals. These designs, if carried out, would spread over 13 countries; and provide readers a glimpse to the current trend, from East to West and from North to South.

Contents

City Planning, Plazas and Streetscapes

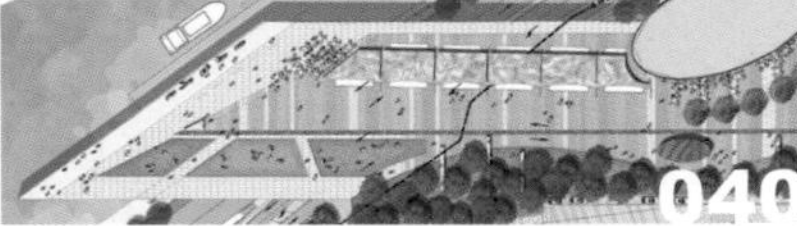

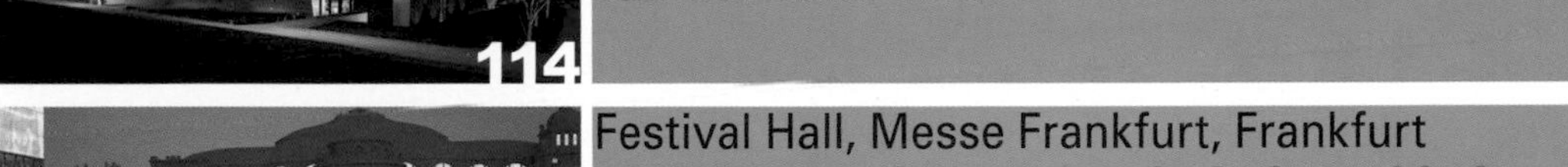

Institutional and Commercial

... contents

Parks, Gardens and Memorials

Residential

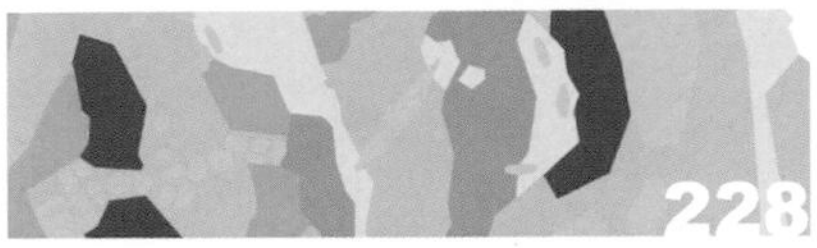

8 Down to Earth Exhibition, Melbourne

"IRRIGATION NATION"

As the majority of our cities remain gripped by drought, the Down to Earth exhibition at the 2007 Melbourne Design Festival, was a free outdoor exhibition that was thematically driven by issues surrounding sustainability and water use. Hassell's installation 'Irrigation Nation' was one of five participants.

Water is the medium with which we bring our domestic landscapes to life, and subsurface irrigation, lurking below the surface, is the vehicle that carries it. Irrigation Nation, a minimalist installation, brought drainage infrastructure to the surface in order to visibly celebrate and abstract the inherent possibilities of the material itself, and provoke a dialogue about future water shortage and use.

The resultant work comprised of an assemblage of metres of ubiquitous slotted agricultural pipe forcing juxtapositions of drainage infrastructure and fluidity, and exposing those conditions of circulation that drip feed our everyday landscapes.

The agricultural pipes were woven and draped over larger pipes to form a rippling and fluid structure which mimicks the formal and physical qualities of water, such as the way it reflects light. A circular mirror inlaid into the sculpture captures the reflection of a nearby building and deflected the glint of afternoon sunlight.

Strategies of repetition and bound volume of the drainage pipe are utilised to create a tactile immersive space and direct the 'flow' of visitors' movements off the adjacent path and through the installation.

Threaded with linear ropes of light, the perforations of the pipe were illuminated by night, shedding light not water out into the exhibition landscape.

©Trevor Mein

(above) Section.
(below) Plan.

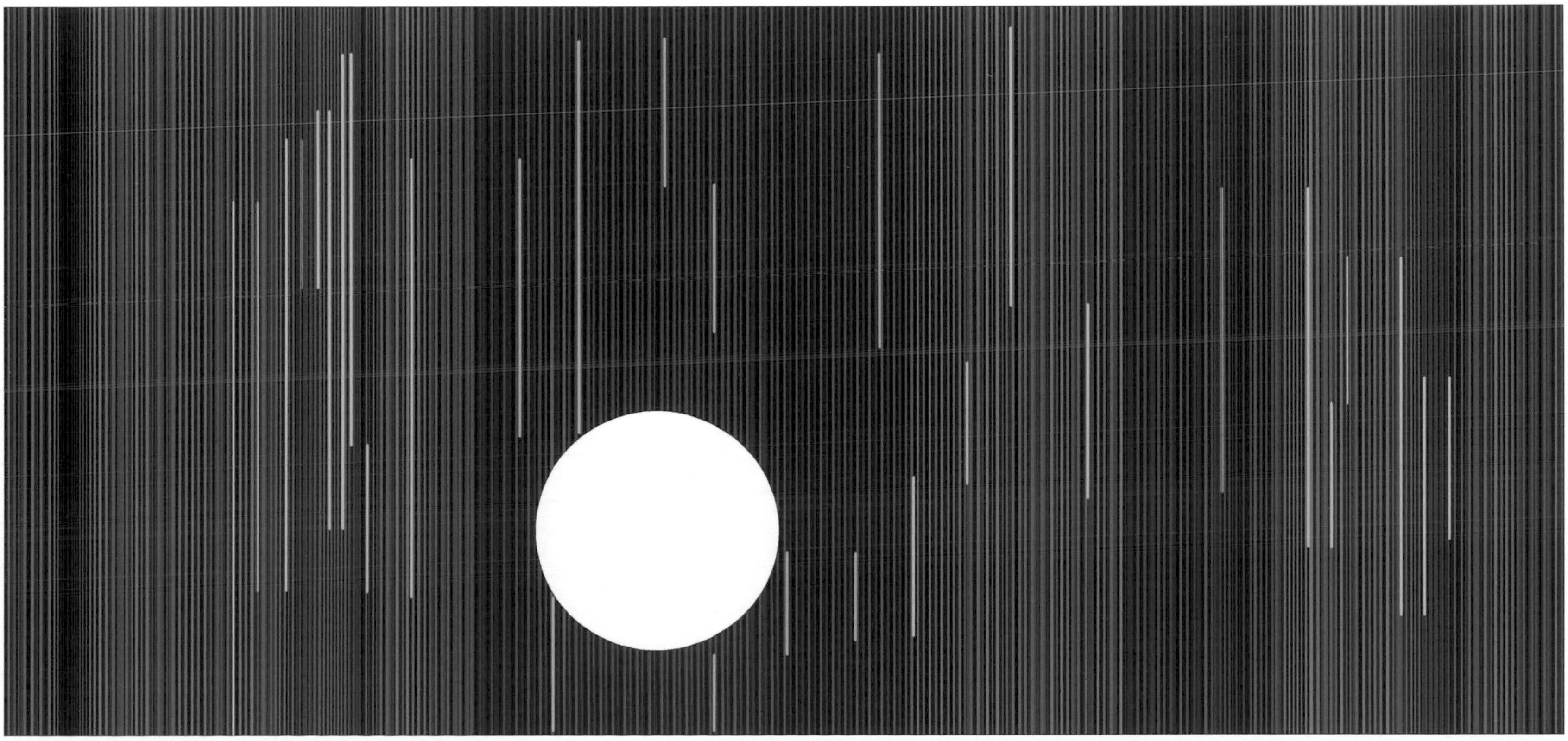

(below) The installation capturing the glint of the afternoon sun.

(right) The mirror represents a small pool and references the capacity of water to reflect the city and sky.

©Trevor Mein

©Trevor Mein

©Trevor Mein

12 Amoeba 1 + 2, Sydney

Design rationale

[amoeba] originates from the Greek 'amoib' meaning change.

Every day our cities change. Our climate changes, there is political change, land uses change, demographics change and there is social change.

Our cities are getting fatter. Sprawling over the landscape faster than ever, they are chewing up surrounding agricultural land and forest. One third of our cities are now covered by road alone. To put the brakes on this urban obesity our cities need to choose a healthier diet, avoiding low-density McMansion style houses on super sized lots at the fringes of the city.

One solution for getting leaner is to recycle leftover space inside our cities for new, more compact housing forms and to downsize the old Aussie back yard. Today we don't need a hills hoist, a cricket pitch and a tool shed for every family. Our future gardens need to be smarter and sexier, use less water, less space, recycle materials and provide better ecologies for our birds and animals. [amoeba] embodies these ideas.

Initially mcgregor + partners developed [amoeba 1], a conceptual idea of a series of mobile gardens built using recycled materials, towed behind a fleet of eco-hybrid cars. The flexible, organic design intended for different formations to materialise. Derelict public spaces could be proposed for resurrection into [amoeba] spaces for transformation into temporary event environments. These self-propagating sustainable gardens, housed in their own mobile organic constructions could host live performances, community activities or music and video events.

In celebrating the Year of the Built Environment, the Sydney Royal Botanic Gardens showcased the 'Gardens of Tomorrow' exhibition. mcgregor+partners proposed [amoeba 2], born from the original theoretical [amoeba 1] concept, which aimed to bring the exhibition out of the gardens and into Sydney's streets and urban landscapes.

On the 28th October [amoeba 2] appeared in Martin Place for one day. It consisted of 132 [amoeba 2] cells each representing some 100,000 tires discarded every year in the states of New South Wales. The nucleus of each cell was made from a new Australian soil replacement technology, Stratum Green, made up of 100% shredded recycled tyres into which grew the sacrificial lawn. On the [amoeba] cells sat some disused sprinklers donated by the gardeners of Sydney. By donating their rusty old sprinklers, each gardener pledged to support [amoeba] by using less water in their environment and promised to change their garden to Australian native plants.

[amoeba 2] was then dismantled at night and its cells reappeared in the Sydney Botanic Gardens a day later as an exhibit in the Australian Institute of Landscape Architects 'Gardens of the Future Exhibition'. [amoeba 2] again confronted the public materialism as two piles of tyres conveying a story of the waste materials and junk our throwaway society generates. The tyres were arranged in unloved heaps to contrast with the arcadian beauty of the Botanic Gardens site. These materials would typically end up in landfill polluting the earth from where they came.

Alongside the tyres lay the remnant circular grass tiles organised on the lawn in a perfect grid as memorial shadows of the [amoeba 2] event held in Martin Place the day before. Again the idea being that the turf returned to the earth in its final conclusion completing the circle to remind us that constructed beauty still must result in waste. Future gardens have to consider conservation of valuable resources and through understanding the generation of our own waste we can reflect upon the appropriateness of our actions as designers.

The flexible, organic design allowed for different formations to materialise into various randomly selected urban spaces. These self-propagating sustainable gardens, housed in mobile organic constructions could host live performances, community activities or music and video events.

[amoeba 1 + 2] asks us to question our everyday contributions because, change can be good or change can be bad, and the future of our young city is up to us.

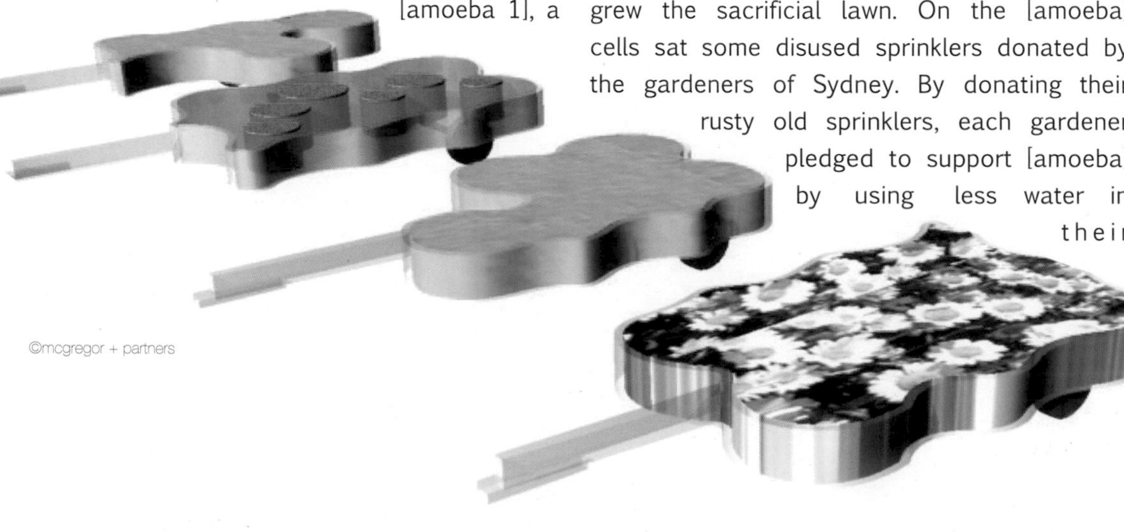

©mcgregor + partners

client / owner
Australian Institute of Landscape Architects

location
Martin Place & Royal Botanical Gardens, Sydney, Australia

©mcgregor + partners

©mcgregor + partners

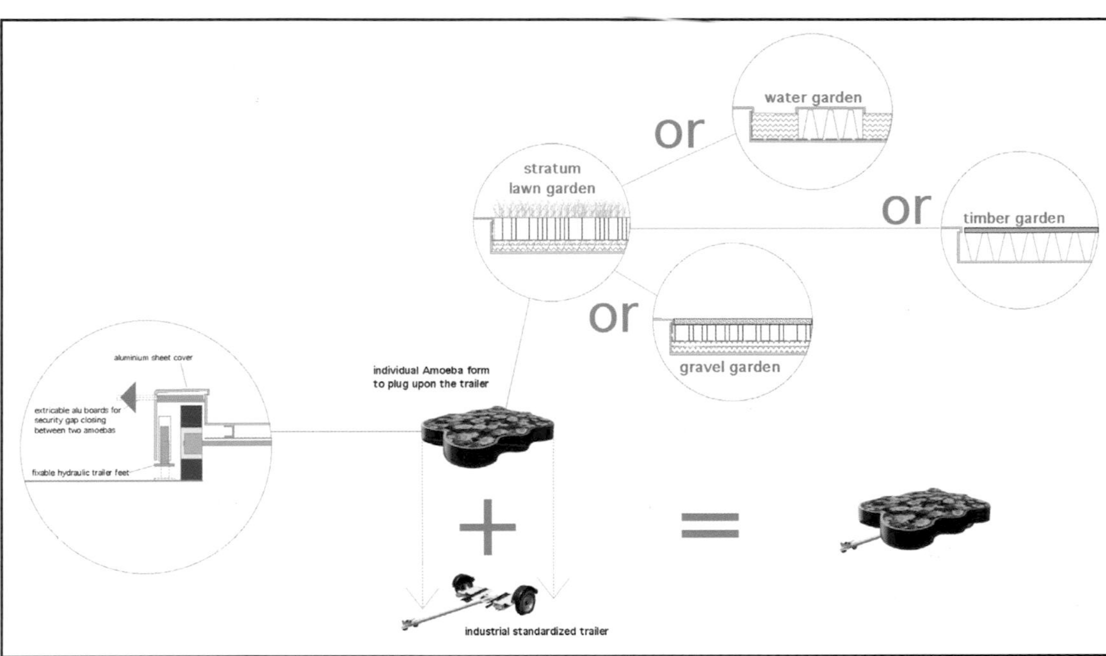

©mcgregor + partners

©mcgregor + partners

(left) Amoeba 1: Collection.
(top) Amoeba 1: Space Alfa.
(abovo) Amoeba 1: Space Delta.
(right top) Amoeba 1: Expressions.
(right) Amoeba 1: Tyres with prius flower.

(top) Amoeba 1: Space Charlie.
(left) Amoeba 1: Space Foxtrott.

AMOEBA UNIT WITH TIMBER SEAT

LEGEND

01 STEEL FRAME
FOR STRATUM FILLING H 150-250MM
ON STEEL PLATE
FIXED WITH SCREWS ON TYRE

02 ECO COLOUR PAINTED SURFACE

03 STANDARD TRUCK TYRE C 300/1055MM

04 TIMBER SEAT 50MM
ON STEEL CONSTRUCTION

1055

660

300

1:10@A3

mcgregor+partners

OCTOBER 2004_A

AMOEBA YEAR OF THE BUILT ENVIRONMENT_FUTURE GARDENS

DETAIL PLAN|02

©mcgregor + partners

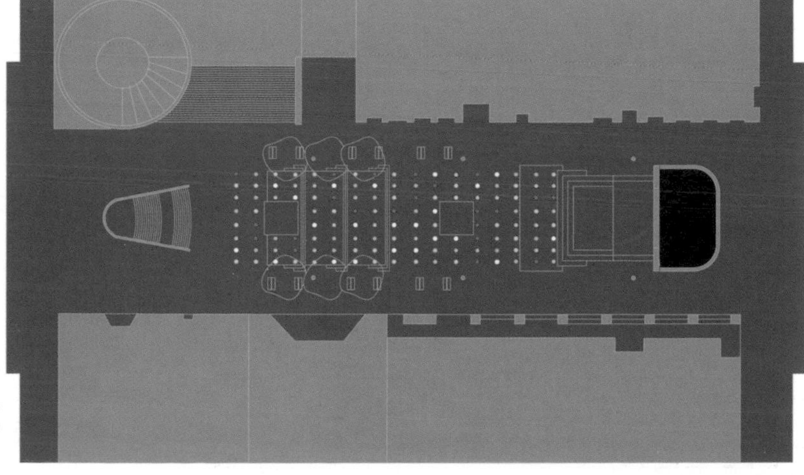

©mcgregor + partners

(top) Amoeba 2:Detail – Martin Place.
(left) Amoeba 2: Plan – Martin Place.

Amoeba 2: Arial view - Martin Place.
(opposite page, top left) Amoeba 2: Kid with tyre - Martin Place.
(opposite page, top right) Amoeba 2: Sprinkler on tyre - Martin Place.
(opposite page, bottom) Amoeba 2: Flowers - Martin Place.

©Simon Wood

©mcgregor + partners

©Simon Wood

©Simon Wood

(left) Amoeba 2: Tyre stack - Royal Botanical Gardens.
(below) Amoeba 2: Stratum on grass - Royal Botanical Gardens.
(right) Amoeba 2: Tyre dump - Royal Botanical Gardens.

©Simon Wood

©Simon Wood

Back to the city — Trojan, Newcastle

Background

Surrogate Trojan was conceived as part of the three week Back To the City [http://www.backtothecity.com.au] exhibition held in Newcastle in February 2008. Back to the City was a temporary public art exhibition and symposium convened by the University of Newcastle S_Lab and the Newcastle Region Art Gallery to celebrate the culture of the port city. Adrian McGregor collaborated with Richard Goodwin and Russell Lowe on their exhibit, Trojan.

This project takes as its starting point the arrest of three Greenpeace activists in 2003 who blockaded the wharf trying to prevent an international grains trader sneaking 57,000 tonnes of GE canola seed to its Newcastle plant.

Placed directly opposite the grain silos on Newcastle harbour, a shipping container was filled with a bed of non GE canola seed; its interior fitted out as theatre for contemplation with a short film [http://www.russelllowe.com/trojan_download.htm] revealing the harbour's complicity in the movement of these Trojans. The project interrogates the role of the urban harbour within broader national environmental concerns.

The exhibit was awarded the 'back to the city prize for best installation'.

Project description

When three Greenpeace activists were arrested on 6th December 2006 for blockading the floating dock at Kooragang Island the rest of Australia took notice for a day.

They were trying to prevent an international grains trader sneaking 57,000 tonnes of Canadian Genetically Modified [GM] canola seed to its Newcastle plant. Unfortunately they failed and the grain was shifted silently around Australia to produce margarine, mayonnaise, canola oil and animal feed, ultimately ending up on Australia's dinner tables.

Recent announcements in Victoria and NSW that the genetically engineered (GE) crops moratorium will be lifted threaten more than just the income of Australia's farmers and food companies. There is irrefutable evidence that GE foods are unsafe to eat.

Jeffrey M. Smith, Executive Director of Institute for Responsible Technology Iowa, USA, documented 65 health risks of GE food. There are thousands of toxic or allergic-type reactions in humans, thousands of sick, sterile, and dead livestock, and damage to virtually every organ and system studied in lab animals.

According to Jeffrey the only human feeding study conducted on GE foods found genes had transferred into the DNA of gut bacteria and remained functional. This means that long after we stop eating a GE food, its protein may be produced continuously inside our intestines.

Furthermore Jeffrey notes, lab animals fed GE crops had altered sperm cells and embryos, a five-fold increase in infant mortality, smaller brains, and a host of other problems. Documents made public by a lawsuit revealed that scientists at the US Food and Drug Administration warned that gene-spliced foods might lead to allergies, toxins, new diseases and nutritional problems.

As vessels slip silently in and out of the port we give little thought to their hidden cargo. Like the Trojan Horse of antiquity, these surrogate mother ships spawn an invasion to which most of us remain oblivious. Marching on in multitudinous armies they subversively invade our peace.

Yes, the US has upheld a law allowing living material to be patented and corporations are racing to cash in. We are set to reap a withering disaster of our food bio-diversity systems and our health. GE/GM food has no legal requirement for testing on humans before it enters our supermarkets. This country has no food labelling laws to warn consumers about the mutant, invading genes. We are the guinea pigs of the food giants.

©Murray McKean

collaborators
landscape architects: Adrian McGregor
mcgregor+partners;
art, architecture: Richard Goodwin & Russell Lowe

location
Newcastle, Australia

awards
Back to the city prize for best installation

©Murray McKean

(left) Night Trojan with people.
(above) Trojan with movie.
(below) Trojan night view.

©Murray McKean

©Murray McKean

(above) Movie watchers.
(right) Series - Composite.

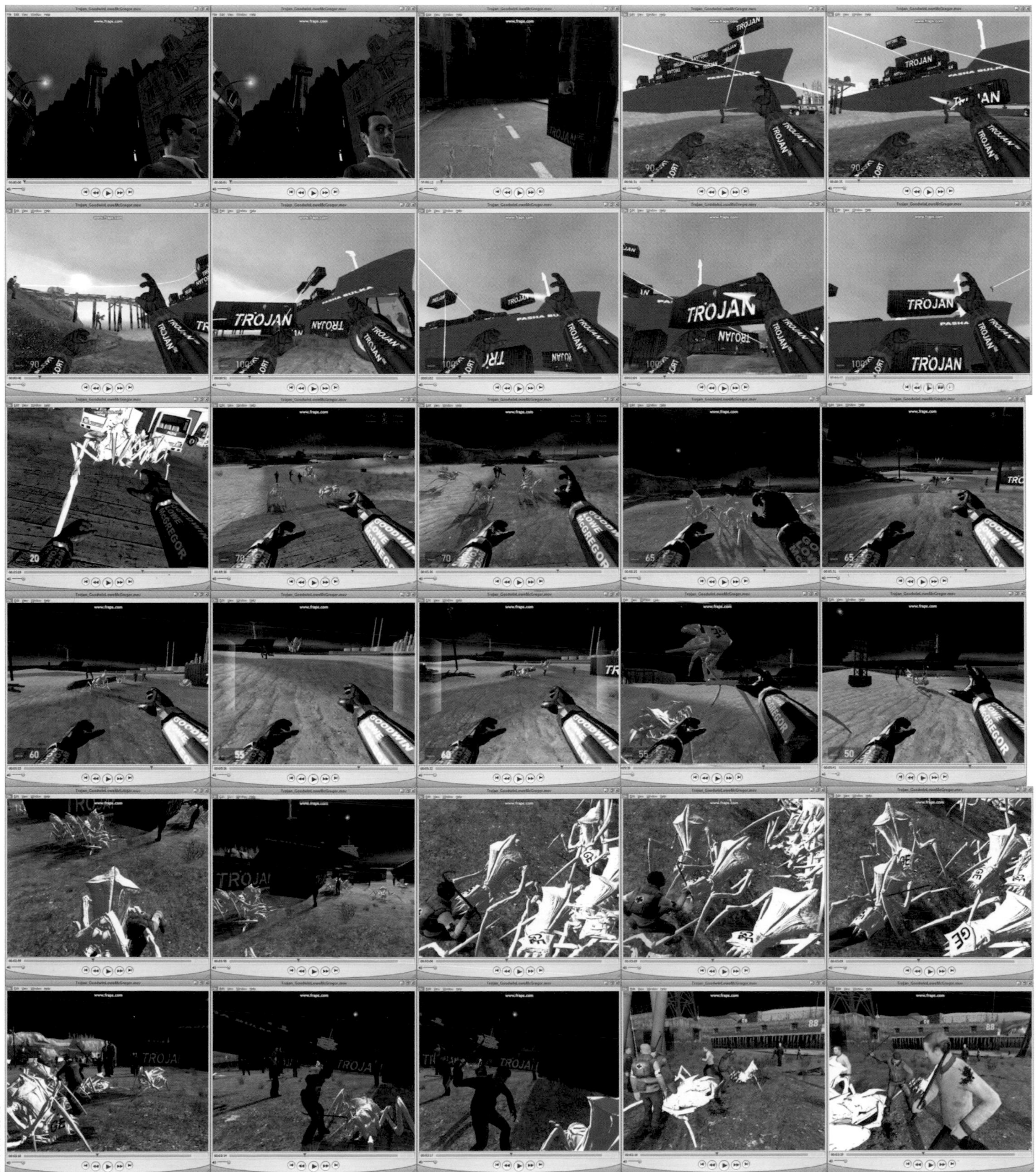

©Russell Lowe

Overhead 400kv Electricity Transmission Towers — Vertical and Horizontal Formation

Lattice electricity transmission towers that pepper the world are well established, albeit resented, artefacts in our landscapes. They are generally perceived as anthropomorphic — with 'spread legs, outstretched arms and heads' and as such are emotionally linked to giants. A 1993 UK Alternative Tower Design Report quoted people's perceptions of lattice towers with comments ranging from 'unobtrusive' through 'familiarity' to 'a large monstrosity'.

Facing the prospect of landscape protection policies forcing new power lines to be buried underground at a substantial capital cost, the UK NGC (previously National Grid Company) decided to procure visually attractive designs for its transmission towers. NGC cost analysis showed that even if a new type of a tower were to be several times more expensive than the traditional ones, if such a new visually attractive tower enabled new power lines to run above ground it would still offer substantial savings if compared with underground installations. Our low and tall towers were among the winners in an invited NGC competition, with some of the UK's big architecture names also on the initial short list recommended by the RIBA.

With full appreciation of the fact that high voltage electricity transmission towers are unlikely to ever seamlessly blend with landscape, and be unconditionally accepted by the general public, we have narrowed our alternatives to two principal solutions. We have developed two diametrically different tower designs; both of them inspired by botany and plant morphology. Both 'grow' from a single stalk that links their foundations with their power cable carrying section, like a trunk of a tree which links its canopy with its roots.

The tall design is intended for locations near human habitation and addresses the health concerns linked to electromagnetic fields. The design offers a unique vertical cable arrangement, with cables placed in one vertical plane. Passing underneath this power line takes virtually a second. Use of colour would enhance the art-in-the-landscape aspect of the design. The straw or crochet needle-like organic form of this tower is made up of a 'stalk' fabricated from four standard section steel or stainless steel tubular elements, a pre-cast concrete base, allowing it to be sculpted without additional cost, and the head carrying the lightening conductor. The intention was to make the head in carbon fibre composite, taking advantage of mass production economies.

The lower design addressed situations where minimal visibility was the issue. The design offered the lowest possible cable arrangement reducing the prominence of power lines in the landscape. Use of colour would further enhance the art-in-the-landscape aspect of the design. The soft, unthreatening, playful and organic form of this tower is made up of three standard section steel or stainless steel tubular elements, a pre-cast concrete base, allowing it to be sculpted without additional cost, and two 'horns' carrying both power cables and lightening conductors. The intention was to make the 'horns' in carbon fibre composite, taking advantage of mass production economies.

We carried out a £100K study for the NGC, involving form design, electrical and structural engineering. The primary aim of this project was to demonstrate that high voltage transmission towers can be designed so as to offer pleasing aesthetic qualities while being based on sound structural and electrical engineering. And if designed with sensitivity and creativity, the towers can indeed, enhance their context through their sculptural qualities. Tests have to be carried out to establish whether there are any long time effects of carbon fibre being placed in an electromagnetic field.

(right) Low tower in landscape context.
(below) Low tower — elevation and base.

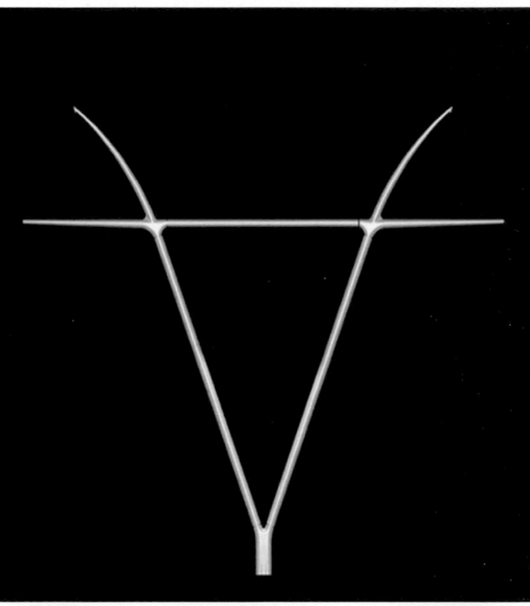

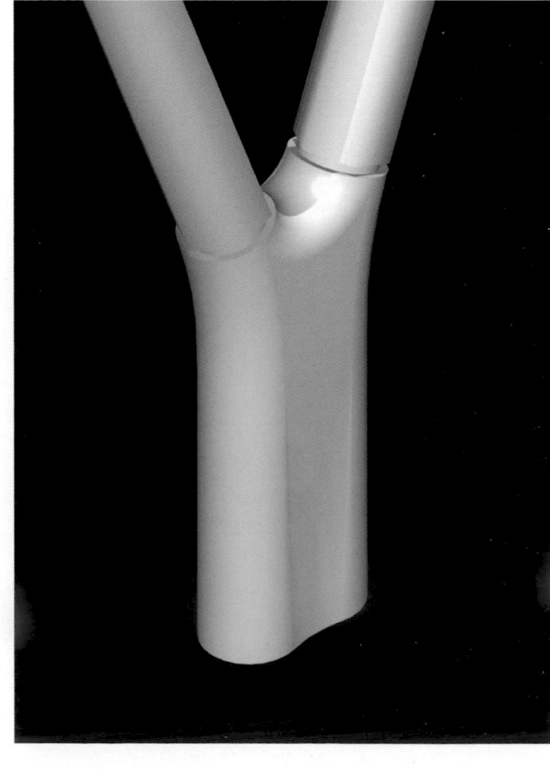

client / owner	other key consultants	location	awards
NGC, UK	Balfour Kilpatrick Ltd Flint & Neill Partnership	Sites of visually protected landscape	A winner in an invited design competition

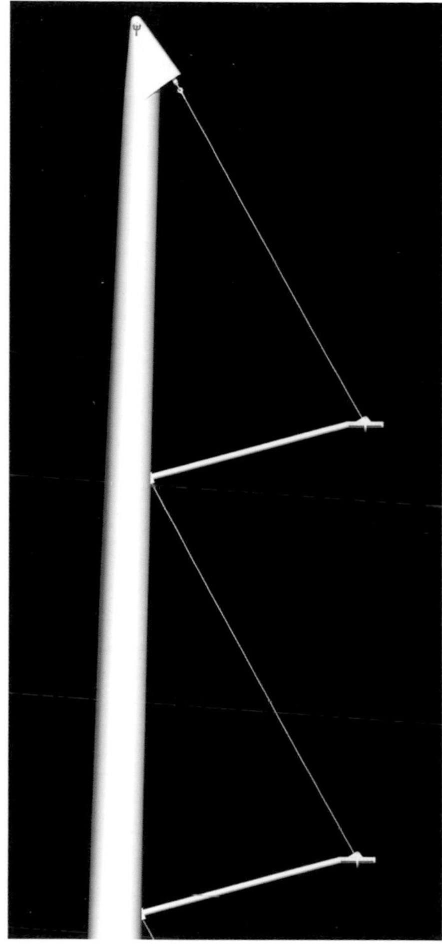

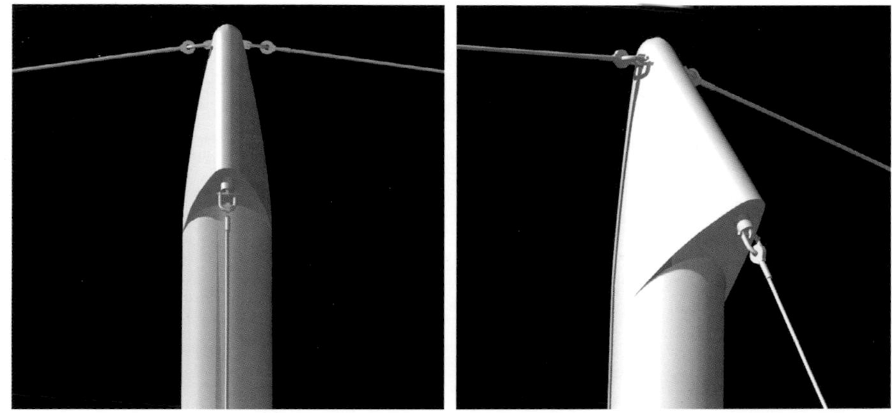

(far left) Tall tower – elevation.
(left) Tall tower in landscape context.
(above) Tall tower – cable suspension.
(top right) Tall tower – head.
(right) Tall tower – colour schemes.

City Planning, Plazas and Streetscapes

Toronto Central Waterfront Innovative Design Competition, Toronto

The Toronto Waterfront is in the process of renewal from industrial uses to mixed use residential neighbourhoods. The Toronto Waterfront Revitalization Corporation (TWRC) has been the catalyst of this renewal, with the planning and now construction of several key precincts underway. The Toronto Central Waterfront competition was conceived to provide an overall strategy to bind together these separate neighborhoods into a cohesive whole, giving a distinct overall strength and identity to the heart of the waterfront renaissance.

The West 8 + DTAH winning proposal advocates design of the urban waterfront on a civic scale, big enough to accommodate Toronto's aspirations. Key to the success of the waterfront is a reconnection with the city — this prompted the proposal to explore not only the removal of barriers such as the Gardiner Expressway, but also the nature of the north-south streets that terminate at the lakefront. The intention is to understand these lines of culture that connect the waterfront to its hinterland, and to celebrate them where they kiss the water's edge.

A 18 metre promenade flanked with native trees, a series of boardwalks, graceful timber bridges over the slips and a floating waterfront of pontoons connect and expand the water's edge condition. This creates a "new" shoreline and public space that is able to accommodate diverse activities, ecologies and special events on a civic scale. Two lanes of traffic on the waterfront's lakeside boulevard — Queens Quay — are permanently closed to allow the construction of a generous recreational trail to energize the esplanade. Finally, the vision includes a bold plan to bridge the lakeshore boulevard linking the Harbourfront Village to Toronto's most recognizable icon – the CN Tower.

The impact of the competition sent a wave of excitement through the city that focused the energy of Torontonians in imaging the future of their waterfront. West 8 + DTAH are currently working with the TWRC on the design and implementation of the Central Waterfront proposal.

(right) Proposed timber pedestrian bridge crossing at the Yonge Slip between Harbour Square Park and the new Ferry Terminal.
(bottom right) Aerial site plan of proposed central waterfront scheme.
(bottom) View from the inner harbour towards the city showing proposed floating Maple Leaf boardwalk in morning mist.

client / owner

Toronto Waterfront Revitalization Corporation

key consultants

Team Lead: du Toit Allsopp Hillier in joint venture with West 8, Rotterdam;
Environmental: Schollen and Company inc.
Structural/ Civil/ Traffic: Arup;
Structural Engineering/ Sustainability: Halsall Associates Ltd;
Architect: Diamond and Schmitt Architects Incorporated;
Industrial Design: David Dennis Design

location

Toronto, Canada

(left) View of Queens Quay pedestrian promenade and Martin Goodman Trail at Music Garden.

(bottom left) Perspective view of Queens Quay looking south-west at Harbourfront Centre (Simcoe Street).

(bottom) Axonometric view of the integrated waterfront parts; primary waterfront (18m row), Floating waterfront, and Queens Quay Boulevard and slip ends.

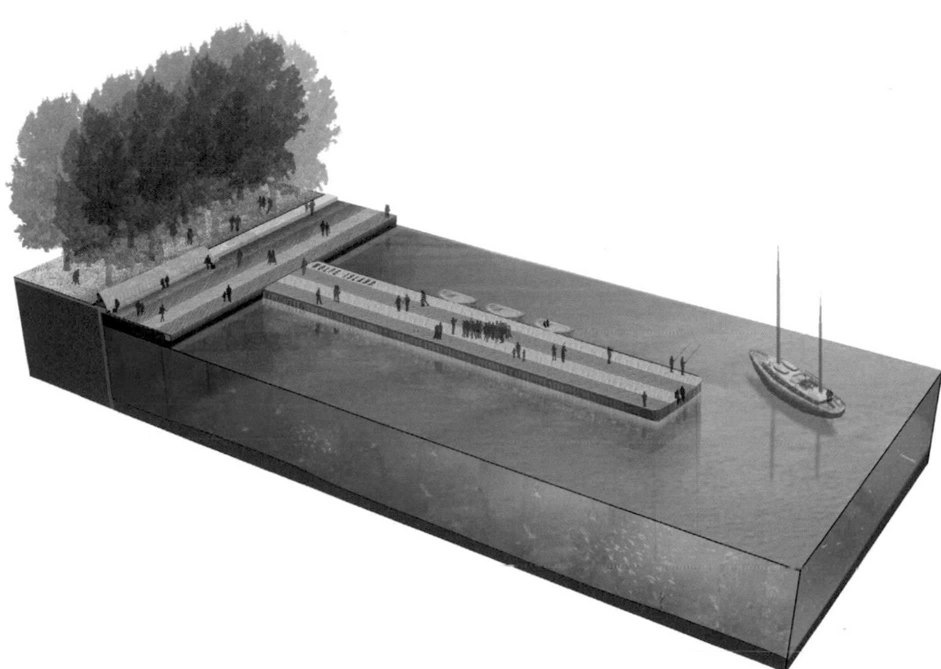

(top) Impression of the powerful impact of the proposed green foot below the skyline of Toronto.
(top right) Axonometric view of proposed 18 metre public row with native tree esplanade and floating pontoon.
(bottom) Overall view of model in BCE place.
(bottom right) People gather around the model at the exhibition in BCE Place, Toronto.

Kaohsiung Waterfront Master Plan — Floating Hills, Living Islands, Kaohsiung

The Kaohsiung water's edge is the first in Taiwan to be revitalized from a former industrial brownfield port to a mixed-use recreational space. The large 64-hectare site has a shoreline of about 6.8 kilometers that extends the length of the central city core of Kaohsiung.

&Co's master plan was called Floating Hills — Living Islands, and was a strategy for reconnecting the people of Kaohsiung with their harbour. The strategy included connecting the existing street network to a series of parks and open spaces that created a continuous open waterfront. A variety of housing types were developed in a block system that created living villages, centred around principal roads. Views to the sea were created and protected by arranging diagonal streets and transitional heights in the built form. Living islands were proposed for the inner harbour. These floating islands created a wetland park that provided natural habitat as well as bioremediation for the harbour waters. The topographical proposal creates a striking skyline for the city of Kaohsiung but more importantly, it provides views from the city to the nearby mountains and to the sea, ensuring that everyone can enjoy the waterfront. The island villages create small communities right on the water and define a series of connected open spaces that are interspersed with fantastic urban landmarks.

client / owner	other key consultants	location	awards
City of Kaohsiung, Taiwan, China	Architecture & Design: Sweeny Sterling Finlayson & Co Architects Inc.; Landscape Architecture: PMA Landscape Architects.	Kaohsiung, Taiwan, China	Award of Honour from the City of Kaohsiung

(top) Longitudinal section across harbour mouth.
(left) Day view of Ferry Island.
(below) Night view of Ferry Island.

(top) Axonometric view.
(right) Harbour view.
(below) Master plan.

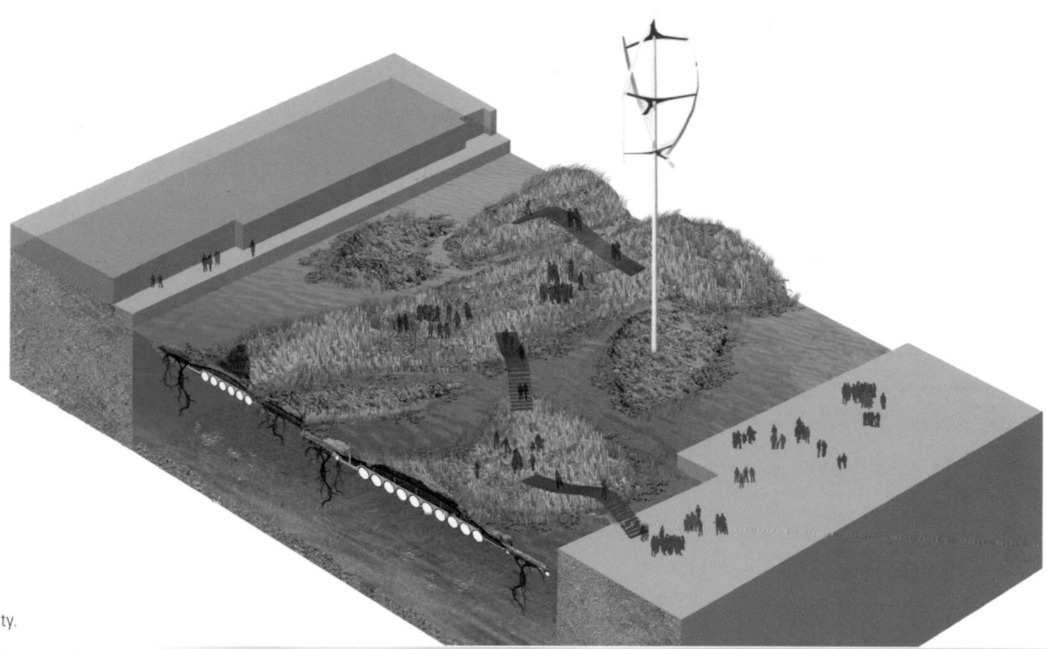

(right) Axonometric view of floating islands.
(left) Tower Podium to West City.
(below right) View from channel back to the city.

Park City, Moscow

Moscow is currently experiencing a large economic boom in the commercial business sector, and a rapid change in character. This has led to an increased demand for high class residential and commercial developments in the city.

Park City is a residential led mixed-use development that will create a live/work environment where people can make use of new retail and leisure facilities without having to get into the car. The character and quality of the proposed public realm will be a key component in creating this vision for Park City.

The Site: The 15 hectare site is situated on the Moscow River with impressive views to the emerging Moscow International Business City, the White House parliament building and the skyline of the historic centre, including the Kremlin.

History: The site contains several valuable historic buildings which will play an important role in establishing a sense of character for the new quarter.

The Badayev brewery was built in several stages from 1876-1899, 1904-1910 and later in 1970-1972 by prominent Moscow Architects August Yegorovich Weber and Roman Ivanovich Klein. At the time the enterprise not only provided buildings associated with the brewing process, but also barracks for workers, canteens and other welfare buildings.

The buildings of the Sacco and Vanzetti pencil factory date from 1926 to the 1970s. The founders, Nicola Sacco and Bartolomeo Vanzetti were two Italian born anarchists, who were executed in Boston in 1926.

Proposals

Character Zones: There are two key axial relationships proposed; the main boulevard, focusing on the historic Hotel Ukraine and the 'diagonal', which relates to the facades of the historic buildings. These two axes form the framework of the public realm with the creation of two new public squares, a grand boulevard, residential gardens and a linear park.

Grand Boulevard: Dramatic avenues of large trees will form a strong address along the central boulevard and will act as a major pedestrian route from Pencil Square to Amber Plaza. Raised lawns underneath the trees will provide areas for informal sitting whilst south facing spill out areas for cafes will be created to catch the sun and best aspect at street level.

Upstand walls and careful placement of street furniture, bollards and lighting will serve to control parking from the pedestrian realm and provide a strong street identity. Ease of orientation and way-finding is an integral part of the development, with well lit and clearly identifiable routes enhancing the experience across the site.

Amber Plaza: Hinging between the main boulevard and the linear park, this plaza will be a major meeting place which will also serve as a prestigious forecourt address for the existing historical buildings.

Courtesy of TBC

Hard landscape materials such as paving, walls, seating and street furniture have been designed to be capable of withstanding abrasive conditions resulting from cleaning equipment, sweepers, grit and salt.

Linear Park — 'The Diagonal': The linear park forms a diagonal connection from Amber Plaza to the River and is inspired by the existing brewery buildings and the strong industrial character of the site. A story of the heritage and history will be reinterpreted through the hard landscape, artwork in the ground plane and reuse of industrial objects and materials within the parkland.

Species will be carefully selected for their suitability to the harsh winter climate and long periods of snow cover. A combination of evergreen trees and Birch will create a forest oasis in the city, reflective of the vast forest areas on the city outskirts.

Conclusion

The landscape and public realm proposed for Park City hopes to create a neighbourhood that will make a distinct and positive contribution to both the immediate area and to the wider contact, a memorable place in which to live, work and play.

Courtesy of Edward Freeman

client / owner
ZAO Park City Investment

other key consultants
Masterplan Architect: Kohn Pedersen Fox Associates
Building Architects: Arcovento, Brisac Gonzalez, Kohn Pedersen Fox Associates, Leo A Daly, Mosproekt-2, Nabil Gholam, Rafael Vinoly Architects, Swank Hayden Connell Architects
Structural Engineers: Waterman Group
M & E Engineers: Buro Happold

location
Moscow City Centre, Russia

(opposite page, left) Badayev Brewery from the 1800s to the1900s.

(opposite page, right) Existing condition of brewery façade. Industrial artifacts to be retained.

(right) Park City site on the banks of Moscow River. In the distance Hotel Ukraine and The White House parliamentary building can be seen.

(bottom) Landscape and Public Realm masterplan .

Courtesy of Daria Sibiryakova

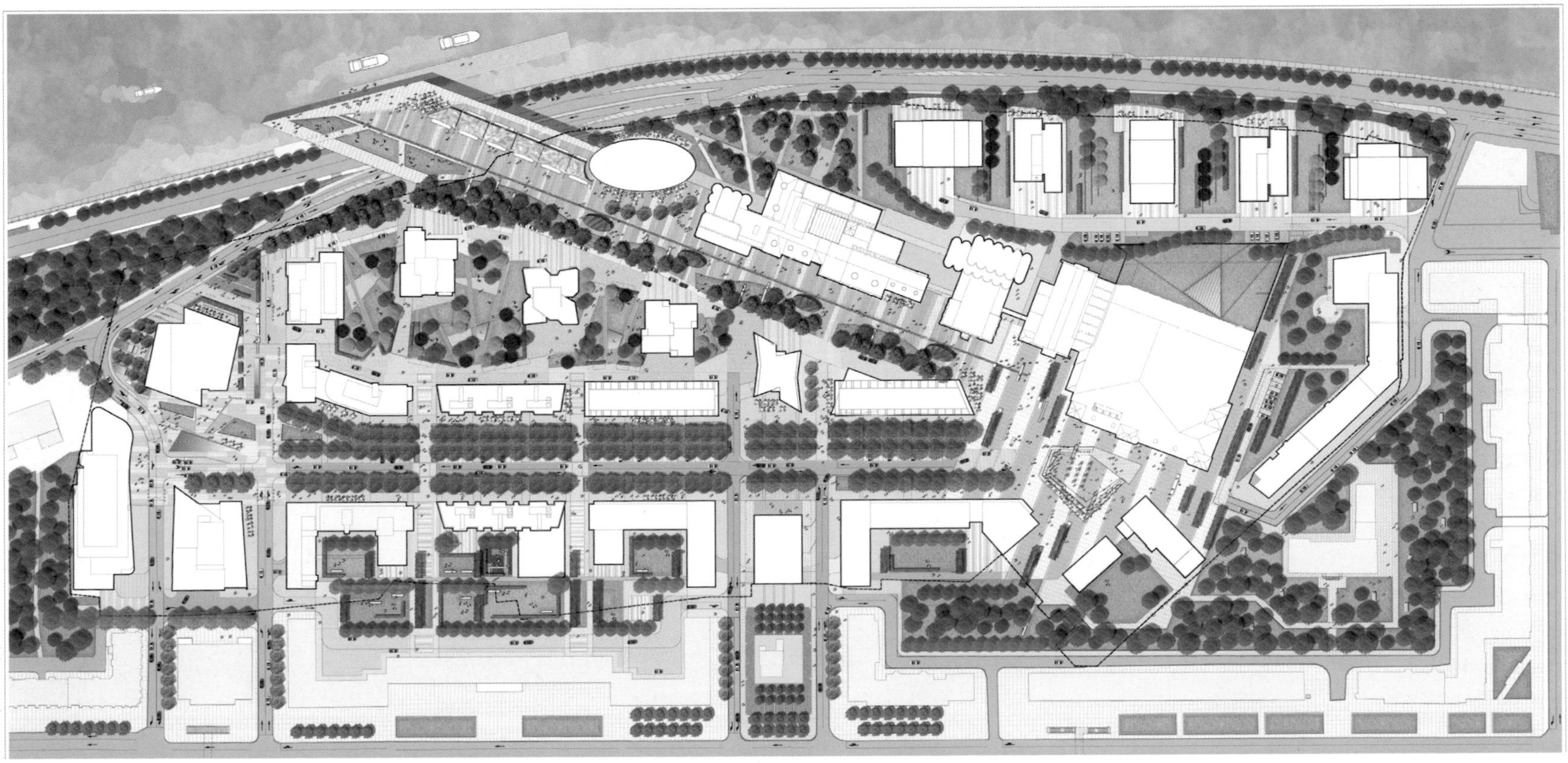

Courtesy of Lovejoy London

Courtesy of Daria Sibiryakova

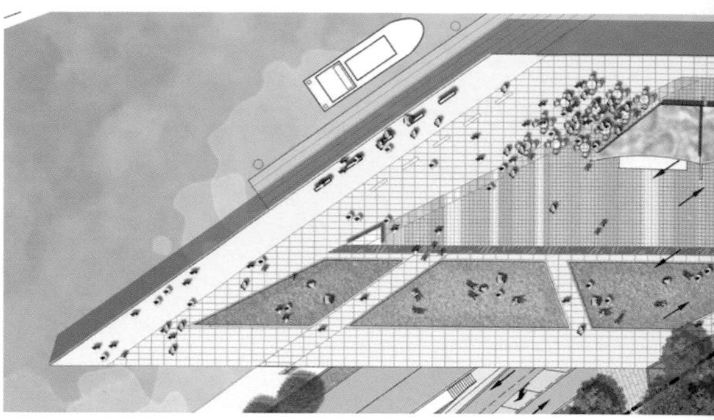

(left) Landscape character zoning.
(top) Linear Park 'The Diagonal' Plan.
(bottom left) Schematic Model for the Park City site.
(bottom) Rendering – Linear Park.

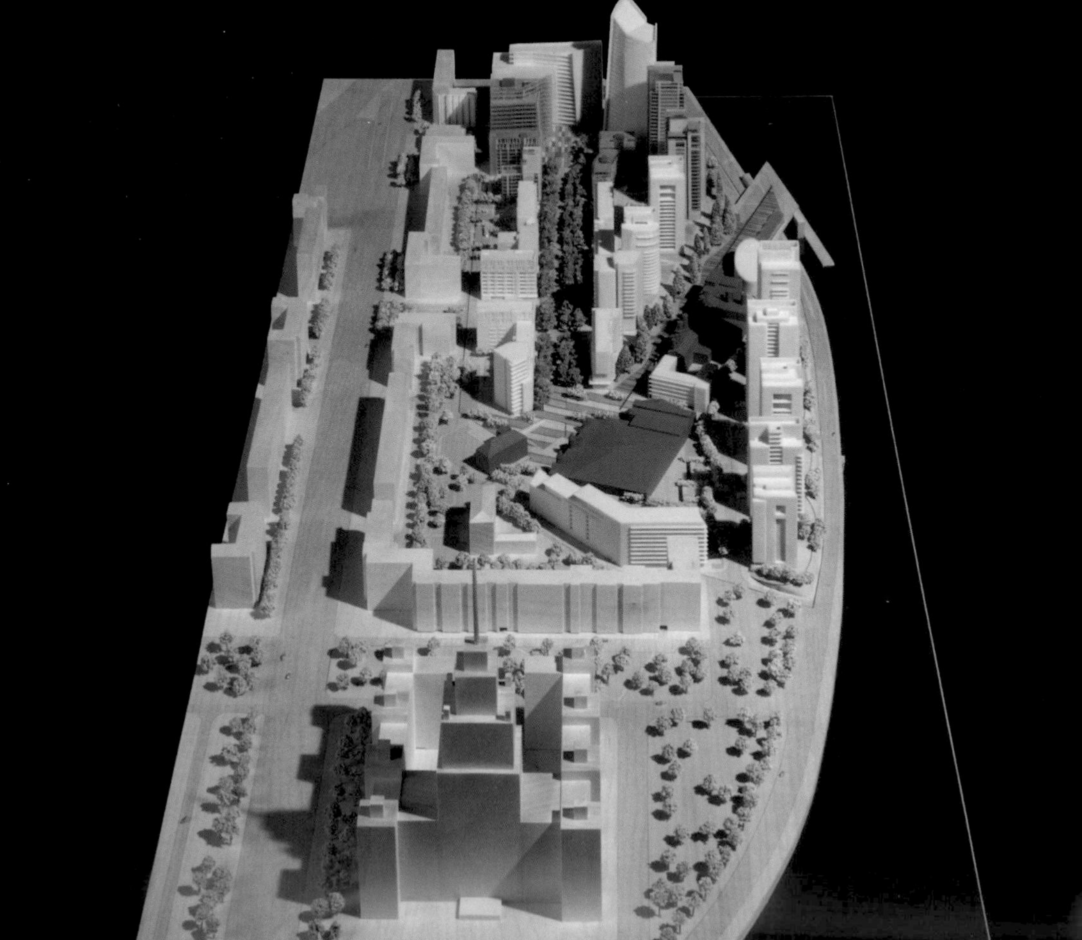

Courtesy of Kohn Pedersen Fox

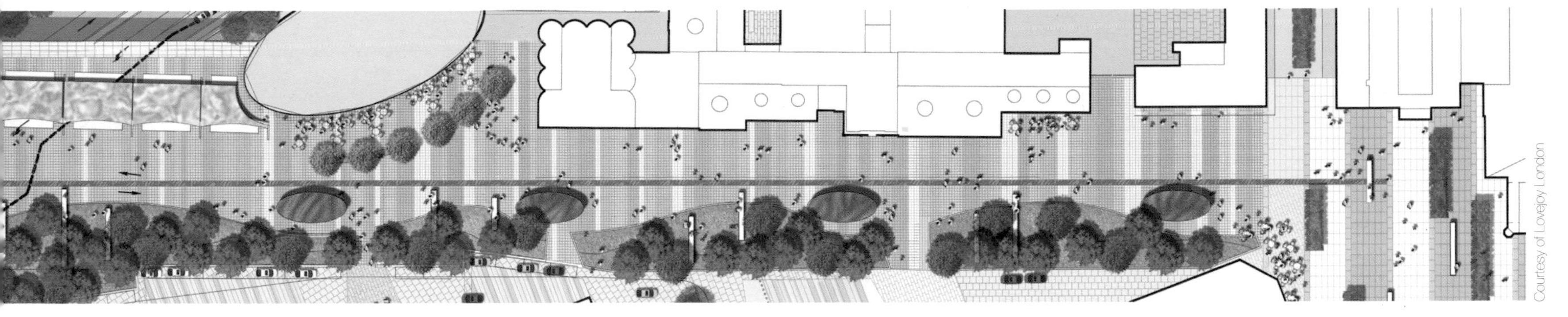

Courtesy of Lovejoy London

Courtesy of Swank Hayden Connell/Crystal

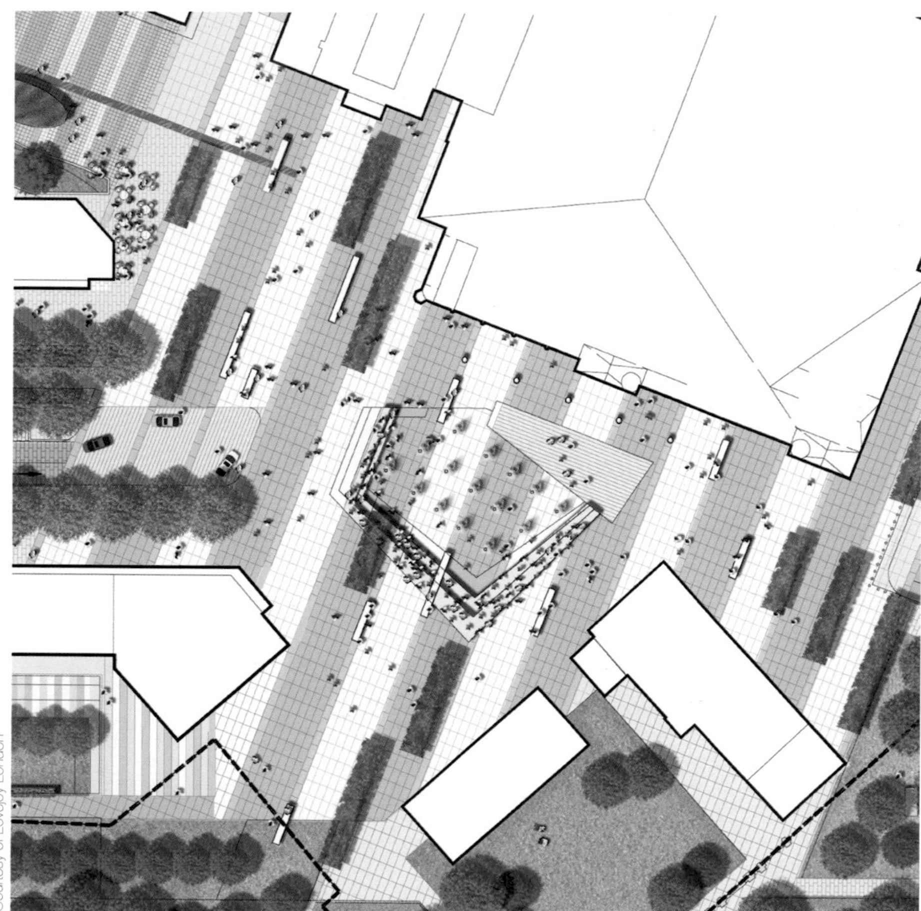

Courtesy of Lovejoy London

(left) Amber Plaza plan.
(bottom) Rendering – Amber Plaza.
(right) Landscape Materials Vocabulary.

Courtesy of Swank Hayden Connell/Crystal

Courtesy of Lovejoy London

New Centre of the City, Reem Island, Abu Dhabi

The Overall Development Concept

This project is planned as a world class development project and will comprise an important part of the future development on Al Reem Island, which is promoted as the new centre of the city of Abu Dhabi.

The overall vision is: **"A world class project that not only meets the demands of a successful real estate development but creates an urban framework for a community ... in which they live, work, shop, learn and relax in an inspiring, safe and unique environment in the centre of the new Abu Dhabi."**

The landscape and open spaces will be a significant feature in achieving this vision. They will provide passive and active recreation opportunities, as well as set high quality and robust aesthetic standard for what is primarily a high rise and high density residential development.

With a planned population of around 60,000 residents the landscape planning of facilities and the design of open spaces will have to cater for a range of user demands. In addition, the landscape of the public areas, including the streetscape and the coast will be an important element in the visual appreciation of this project in Abu Dhabi as a well designed high quality living environment.

LANDSCAPE OPEN SPACE STRATEGY

Design Philosophy

The design philosophy guiding the landscape layout is: **"to provide a high quality landscape aesthetic, based upon the vitality of water, that reflects the coastal, marina and canal elements on Reem Island".**

The main landscape objectives supporting this philosophy are:

- To provide a sequential landscape experience that augments and highlights the major urban centres and marinas of the development;
- To establish a diverse range of landscape features and facilities that will provide variety to the open spaces;
- To create discrete areas of repose and calmness within the hustle and bustle of a high density and high rise urban environment;
- To mitigate the climatic conditions of direct sunlight and reflect glare through the use of planting and shade structures;
- To establish design themes that celebrate the richness in pattern and variety of experiences provided by the association of land and water.

Major Landscape Design Principles:

- Create a unique high quality landscape development with variety of open spaces.
- Highlight the island character of Reem Island to maximise views and recreational opportunities.
- Enhance the character of each zone to make it special and for easy orientation.
- Improve the micro climatic conditions throughout the site for human well-being.
- Ensure accessibility for all including the disabled and mothers with small children.
- Provide a range of recreation facilities that meet the demands of different age and user groups.
- Promote the theme of water as a major decorative design element and climatic ameliorator through out the landscaped areas.
- Ensure that the landscape enhances the development and promotes interaction and integration between buildings, landscape and water.
- Accentuate the identity of each neighbourhood through use of their own typical details, materials, elements and plants.

Open Space and Landscape Plan

Landscape Master Plan

The Landscape Master Plan sets the overall design parameter, which is illustrated in a series of key landscape areas within the open space network.

The master plan shown on page 47 shows the major landscape elements across the site. They have been categorized according to the major functions which they serve.

Major Public Open Spaces: major parks, civil park pocket parks and island parks. Emphasis will be on soft landscape elements and the provision of recreational facilities. These will be landscaped areas to accommodate a variety of passive and active recreational opportunities. It is envisaged these areas will be heavily planted with a range of native and ornamental trees, shrubs and groundcover species.

Pedestrian Areas: canal and marina promenades - forming a linear landscaped feature through the centre of the development, which will comprise predominantly hard landscape with pockets of planting. These pedestrian priority areas will feature hard landscape areas and are primarily for circulation and access through the development. In some cases there will be shared use with vehicles accessing parking or routes for emergency vehicles. Planting will be through ornamental flowering and fragrant species and concentrated to create shade and colour. The softscape and hardscape elements would be complemented and enhanced by landscape lighting.

Landscaped Road Corridor: providing decorative gateways into the development, formal avenue planting along Boulevard, and greenery along residential streets. This will basically involve street tree planting alongside road and within the median strip, where space is available along the utility ROW. Paving and hard landscape elements along the street will be decorative and reflect the neighbourhood character to enhance orientation and a sense of place for residents and visitors.

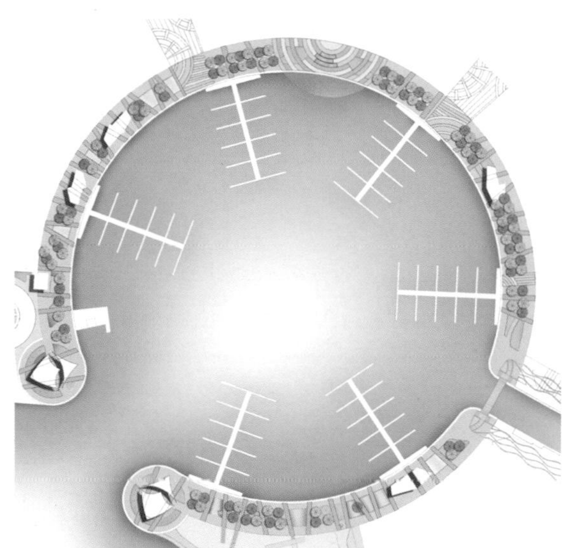

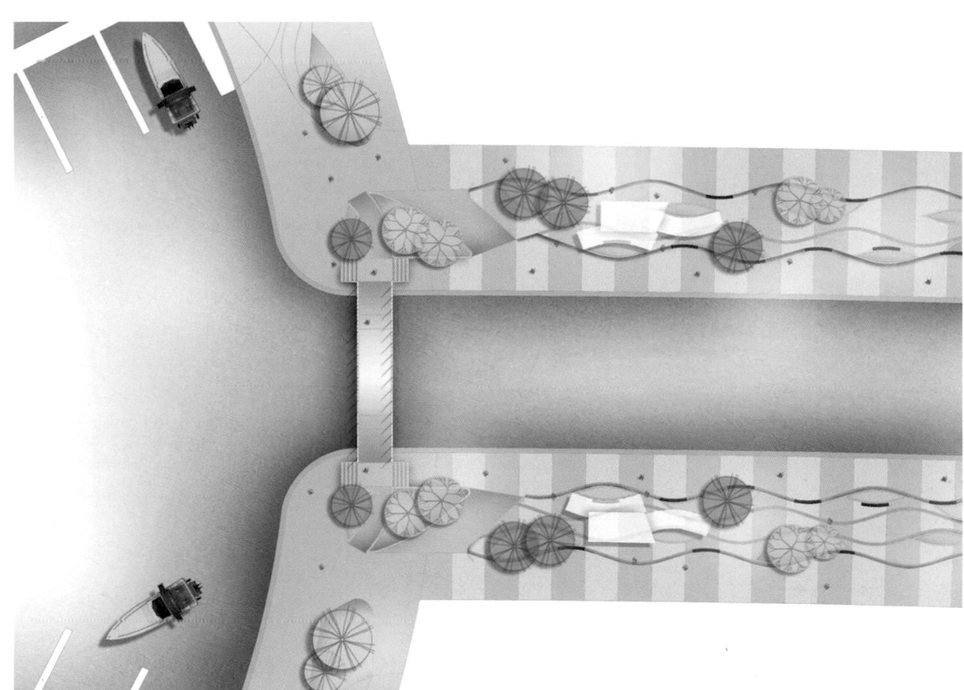

(top left) Marina layout.
(top right) Pedestrian bridge and promenade.
(bottom) Illustrative landscape masterplan.

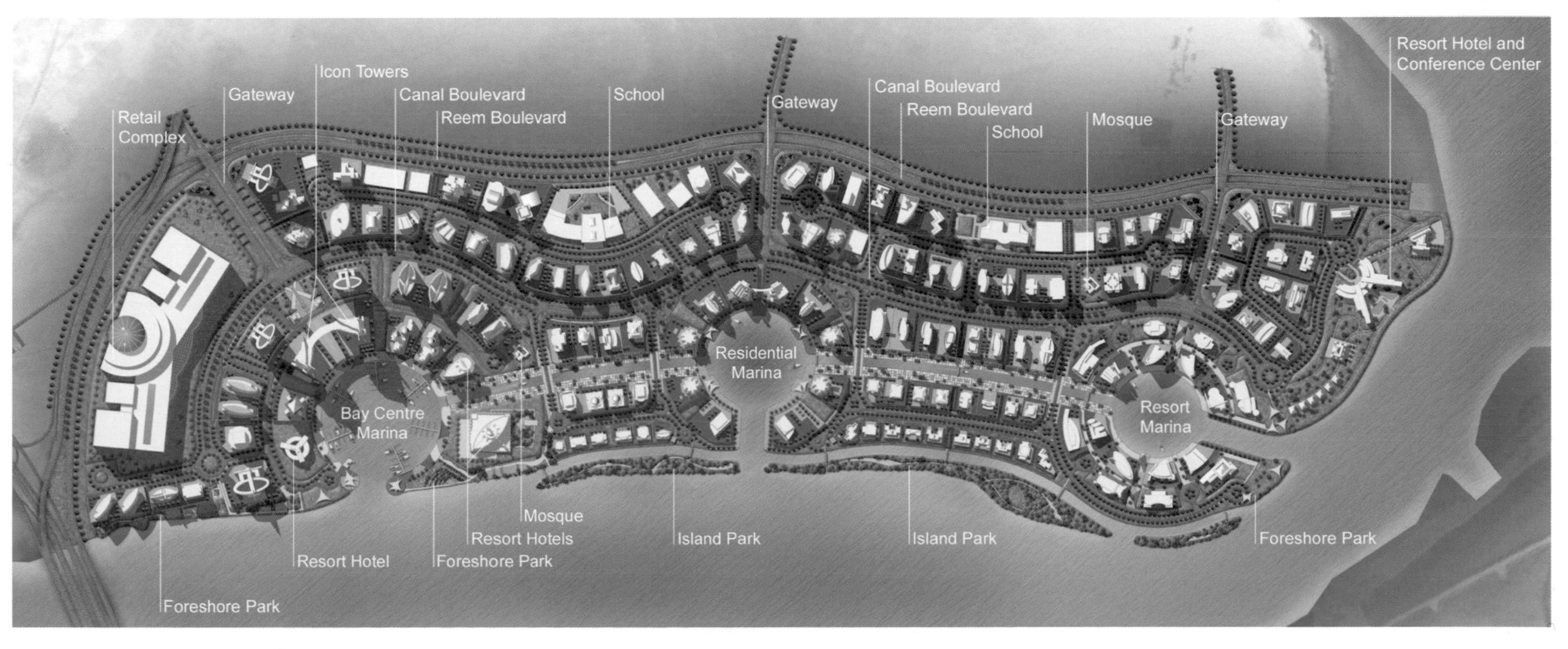

(top) Photo of model.
(bottom) Typical section — canal promenade

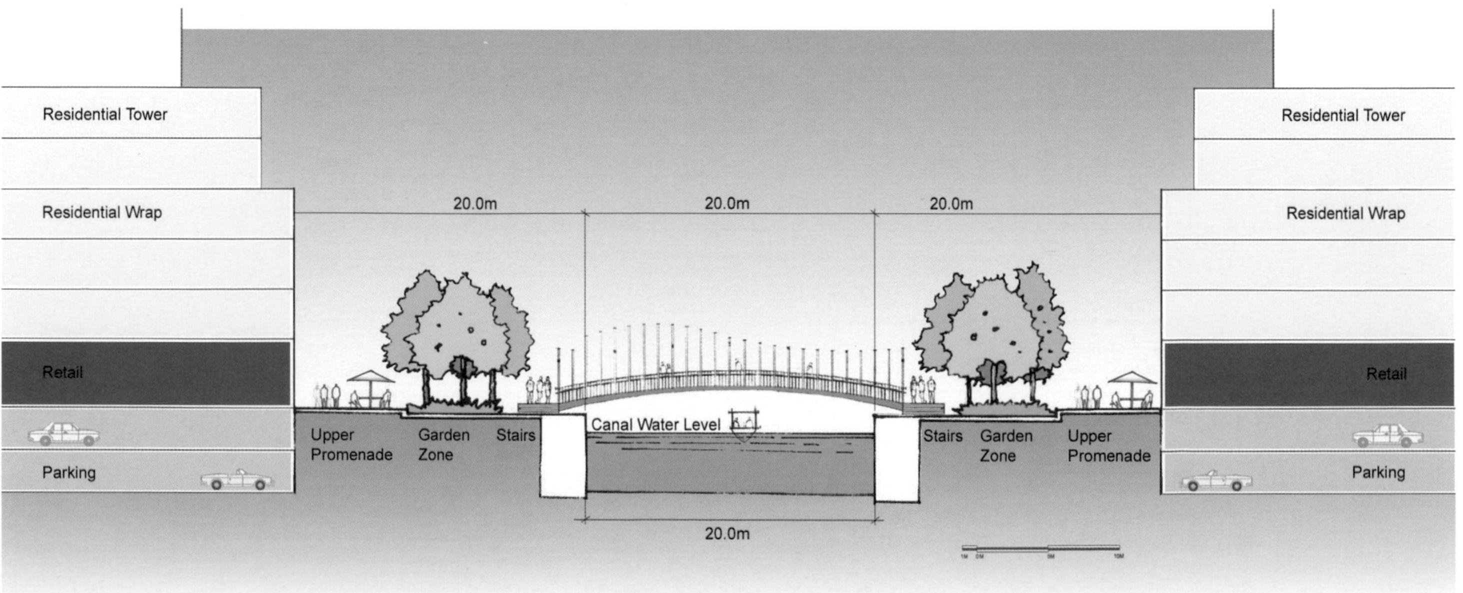

(top left) Fore shore park.
(top middle) Key node marina.
(top right) Bay centre marina.
(bottom left) Artist impression — canal promenade.
(bottom right top) Central park.
(bottom right bottom) Water plaza.

(top) Residential marina at night.
(left) Night impression.
(right top) Gateway to development.
(right bottom left) Water feature on promenade.
(right bottom right) Gateway feature.

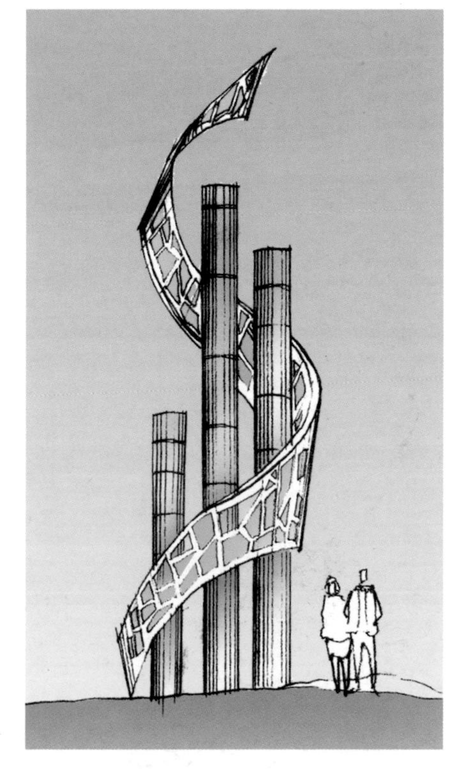

Erie Street Plaza, Milwaukee

The quarter-acre plaza is one of a series of public space activators along the Milwaukee Riverwalk, a three-mile pedestrian corridor that connects downtown Milwaukee to the emerging and redeveloping Third Ward and Beerline Districts.

The plaza is conceived as a flexible field that fosters social and environmental activity and appropriation. It activates and registers environmental cycles of stormwater by collecting runoff to support a reconstituted marsh / wetland, and through the generation of steam that allows for winter activity and the growth of an exotic grove of bamboo, which pulses and glows at night. Socially, the plaza is designed to accommodate a wide array of potential activities, including art festivals, gatherings, concerts, movies, weddings, festivals, farmer's markets, and winter carnivals, as well as less intense, every day activities like boat-watching, fishing, sitting, sunbathing, and simply hanging out.

The subtly folded ground plane directs stormwater to the low marsh and to six collection pits in the bamboo grove; here immersion heaters generate steam that amplify the evergreen qualities of the bamboo and create a respite from cold winter winds. In so doing, the project amplifies and privileges the transitional and ephemeral. Stormwater, steam, marsh grass and bamboo, reflected and projected light all become actors in this civic place; even the intermittent high water of Lake Michigan, present only in 20-year cycles, may inundate the plaza, provoking both reflection and action.

The project included extensive interface with the City of Milwaukee Public Works and Community Development Departments, the Planning and Fine Arts Commissions in Milwaukee, the Wisconsin Department of Natural Resources, and various community groups, abutters, and stakeholders.

client / owner
City of Milwaukee, Wisconsin, USA

other key consultants
Urban Design: Vetter Denk Architecture;
Engineering: Graef Anhalt Schloemer & Associates;
Lighting Design: Light THIS!

location
Milwaukee, Wisconsin, USA

awards
First Place, Erie Street Plaza International Design Competition

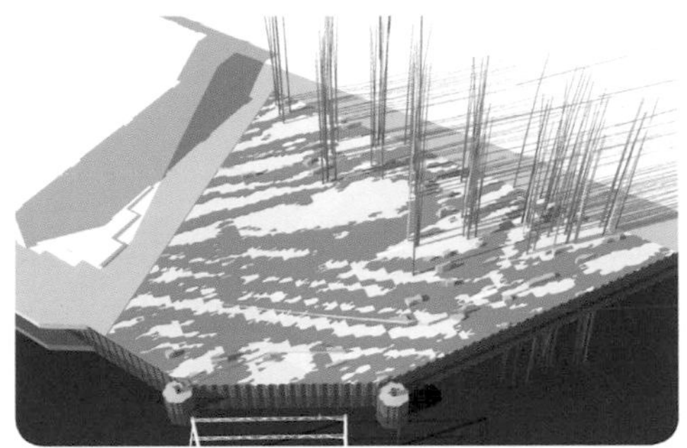

baby boom play park

super active amphitheater

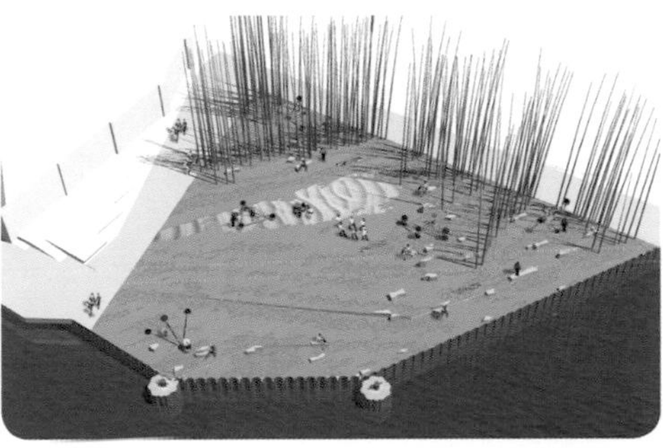

winter carnival grounds

global warming water world

festival plaza

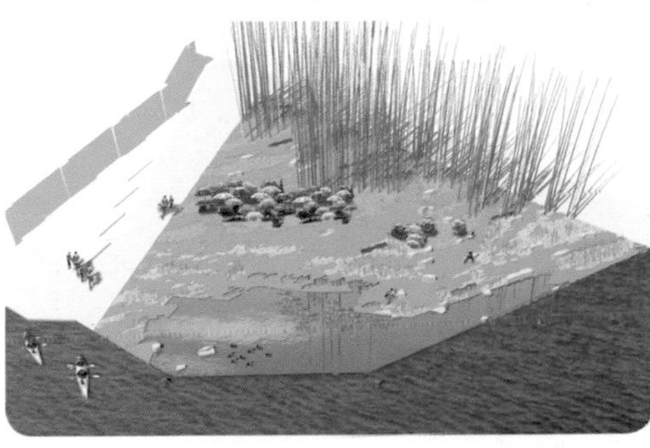

global cooling ice park

(left) Overview of proposed plaza, which terminates the downtown Riverwalk (from the left) and inaugurates the Lake Shore Parks system along the shipping channel (to the right).

(right) Long-term evolutions are future possibilities for the plaza that play off of potential environmental, social, and administrative changes, and dramatize the plaza's flux conditions.

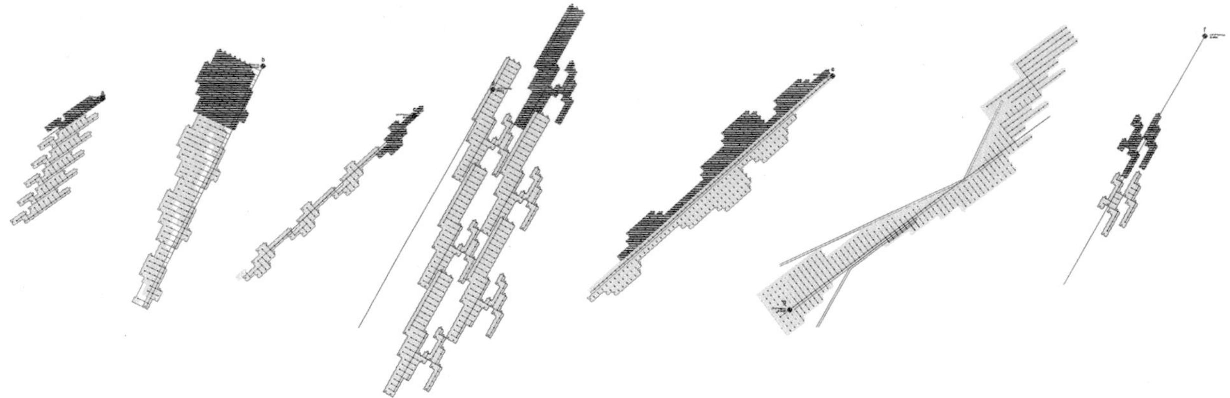

(top left) Paver layout strings for the flexible field, which are calibrated to produce the desired performative and visual effects.

(bottom left and below) The flexible field, a hybridized plaza-green that can be used for a wide array of both individual and group activities, far more than a plaza or green alone could.

(right) Study models for luminous fiberglass benches, which are scattered erratically throughout the plaza in order to offer a range of choices for seating: in groups or alone, in sun or in shade.

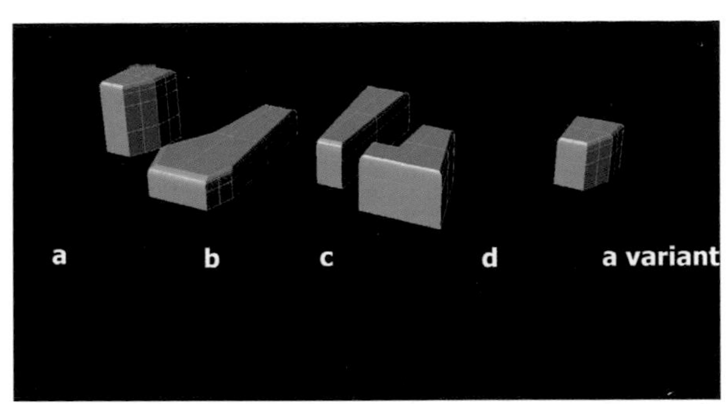

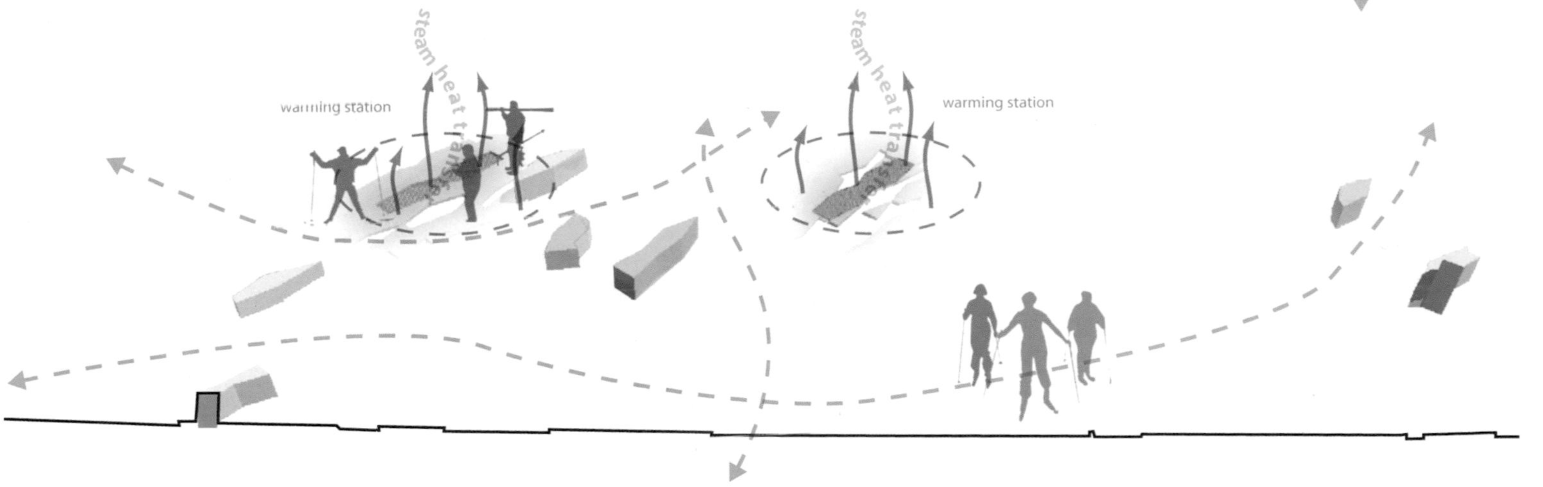

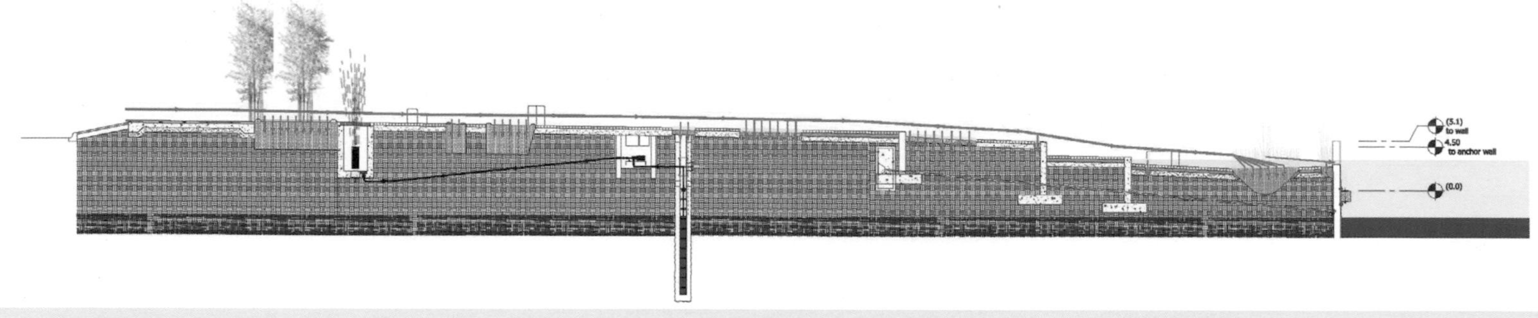
(5.1)
to wall
4.50
to anchor wall
(0.0)

(top left) Refined hydrologic cycle, which taps clean groundwater resources to generate steam in the bamboo grove, while simultaneously allowing the entire plaza to function as a stormwater filter, which cleans runoff and allows it to re-charge the groundwater.

(middle left) The steel marsh, at the lower end of the plaza gradient, is tucked behind the existing bulkhead wall to protect it from industrial and recreational boat wake; the slits in the wall allow the marsh to be flooded on a 20-year cycle.

(bottom left) The radiant grove, in which steam from below warms cold cross-country skiers and renders the bamboo evergreen; year-round, the bamboo grove glows at night, reinforcing the plaza's otherworldliness.

(top and middle right) Views of the plaza to and from the Milwaukee River.

(bottom right) Site context, with downtown Milwaukee to the left and the project site at the bend in the river in the foreground.

HafenCity, Hamburg

The business district of HafenCity (Wharf district) accommodates a large variety of architectures. The public domain, as its connecting element, has to bind the heterogeneity of this new part of the city together.

The former quays stretch out as a continuous open band between the functional traffic of the wharves and the peaceful tides of the waterside. The basic pattern of the public domain is interspersed with distinctive spatial structures like plazas and parks. Beyond this, the light sculpture confers on HafenCity a singular, recognizable sign. The tracing of the quay edges evokes a recollection of its historical use as a seaport. The vertical split between the two main levels, the old seaport and the new wharf level, is a structural element following the quay edges. It brings unity to the band of light and the promenade, and wraps around HafenCity.

client / owner
Freie und Hansestadt, Hamburg

other key consultants
Lighting: Hans Peter Kuhn

location
Hamburg, Germany

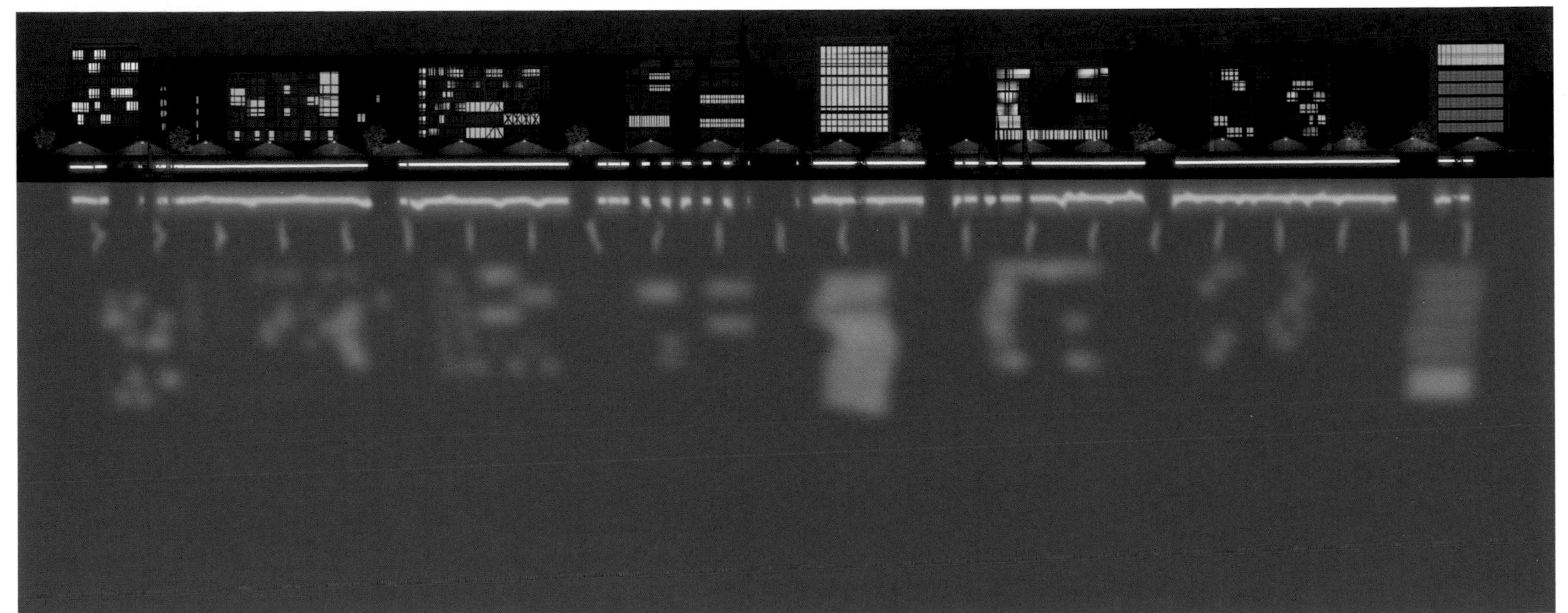

(left top) Plan of HafenCity and its relationship with neighbouring area.
(left) Master plan of HafenCity.
(this page) The light sculpture by Hans Peter Kuhn runs around the wharves, emphasizing the line between water and land as the most distinguishing element of this site.

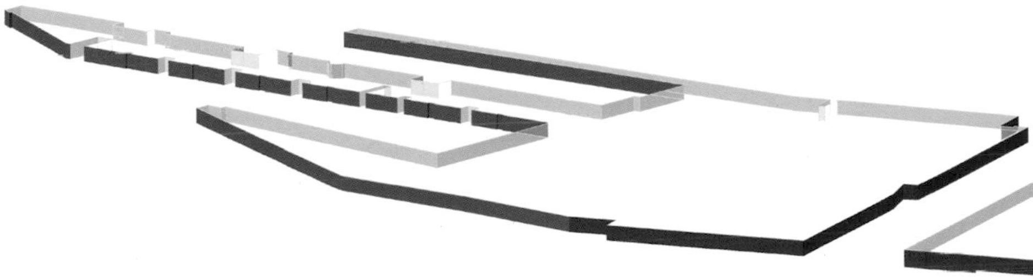

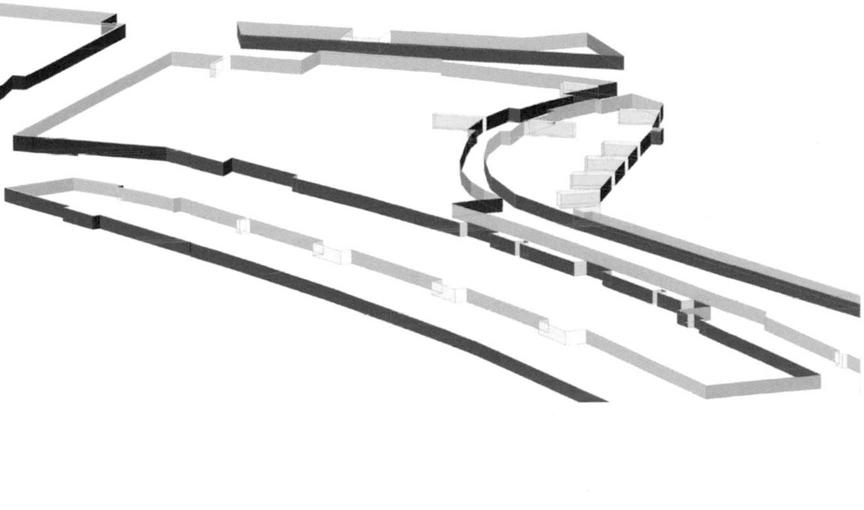

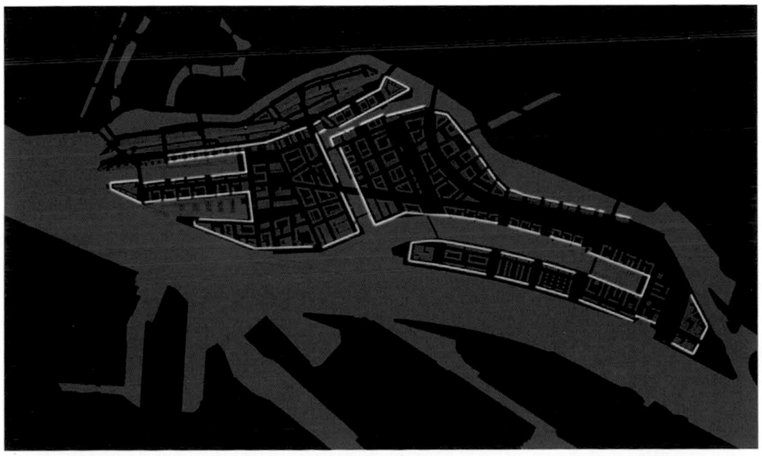

(left and below) The 3 meter high continous wall bridges the difference in height between the former port level and the new flood safe level.

(left bottom) Ramps and stairways facilitate the access to different levels.

(right) Open space

Lao Shan Centre Plaza, Qingdao

ASPECT Studios and Woods Bagot collaborated on the design of a series of urban spaces along a new spine within Qing Dao's new civic district. The spine contains 5 public squares which knit together a series of public and commercial buildings spanning from the mountains to the sea.

The design for the Qing Dao Squares is generated from 3 main ideas:

1. The movement and expression of water through the spine to the sea.
2. The connection between the squares via strong large urban gestures which promote movement and amenity (built canopy connectors and tree planting).
3. Knitting and weaving the squares to provide cross connections using strong paving design and the expression of landscape elements which integrate the buildings on either side of the squares.

The design caters for the distinctive spaces occurring throughout the site which (in order from the highest point down to sea level) are: The Government Square, Exhibition Square, Museum Square, Retail Square (main study area) and the Entertainment Square.

Each square is defined by a sculptural marker which informs the public about local cultural events and creates a clear pedestrian link from surrounding streets.

A shade canopy builds on the notion of drawing the greater public into each space. The canopy provides easy, all weather access throughout the different squares and creates an urban boulevard through the entire site. The urban boulevard is further promoted by linear tree planting along the entire spine which links all five squares along the north south axis.

Water is a reoccurring theme throughout the five squares and each square features a different water theme as its centre piece. The themes change according to each square's program and reflect the notion of water's journey from the mountains to the sea.

Lightweight glass structures lit from within appear along the entire span with each one serving a different purpose according to its location along the spine.

Vibrant paving design, in ground lighting and sculptural elements unite the five squares as one and emphasize that each square functions not just as a single space but part of an exciting new urban plaza in Qing Dao.

A more focused study took place for the retail square which forms the address and public open space to the proposed retail towers designed by Woods Bagot. The retail square is the social hub of the urban boulevard and is flanked by the new Qing Dao Opera House (under construction). Retail features at ground level and the basement retail is accessible by a series of wide staircases that provide generous connections between upper and lower levels. Large garden spaces on the lower level are crossed on the plaza level via a series of lightweight bridge structures which create interest by providing viewing opportunities from above and below. The bridges are lit at night and are key circulation devices for the retail square above.

The illuminated glass retail boxes are flanked by community stages which can support a number of performance uses. Retail pods located under the canopy connector help to activate the square whilst the canopy structure itself provides sheltered access throughout the site. Water jets and strip lighting create interest on the ground plane whilst the graphic paving design draws the public directly into key retail entry points.

Large sculptural elements guide the public on the opera house side of the plaza and large crowd gathering areas have been purposely created to cater for larger events at this venue.

The landscape design for the Qing Dao Lao Shan Centre Plaza provides an inspiring public open space and retail experience and forms an integral part of a wider spine of urban spaces within the New Qing Dao CBD.

(right) Plan.

client / owner
Qingdao Laoshan District Government, China

other key consultants
Woods Bagot

location
Qingdao, China

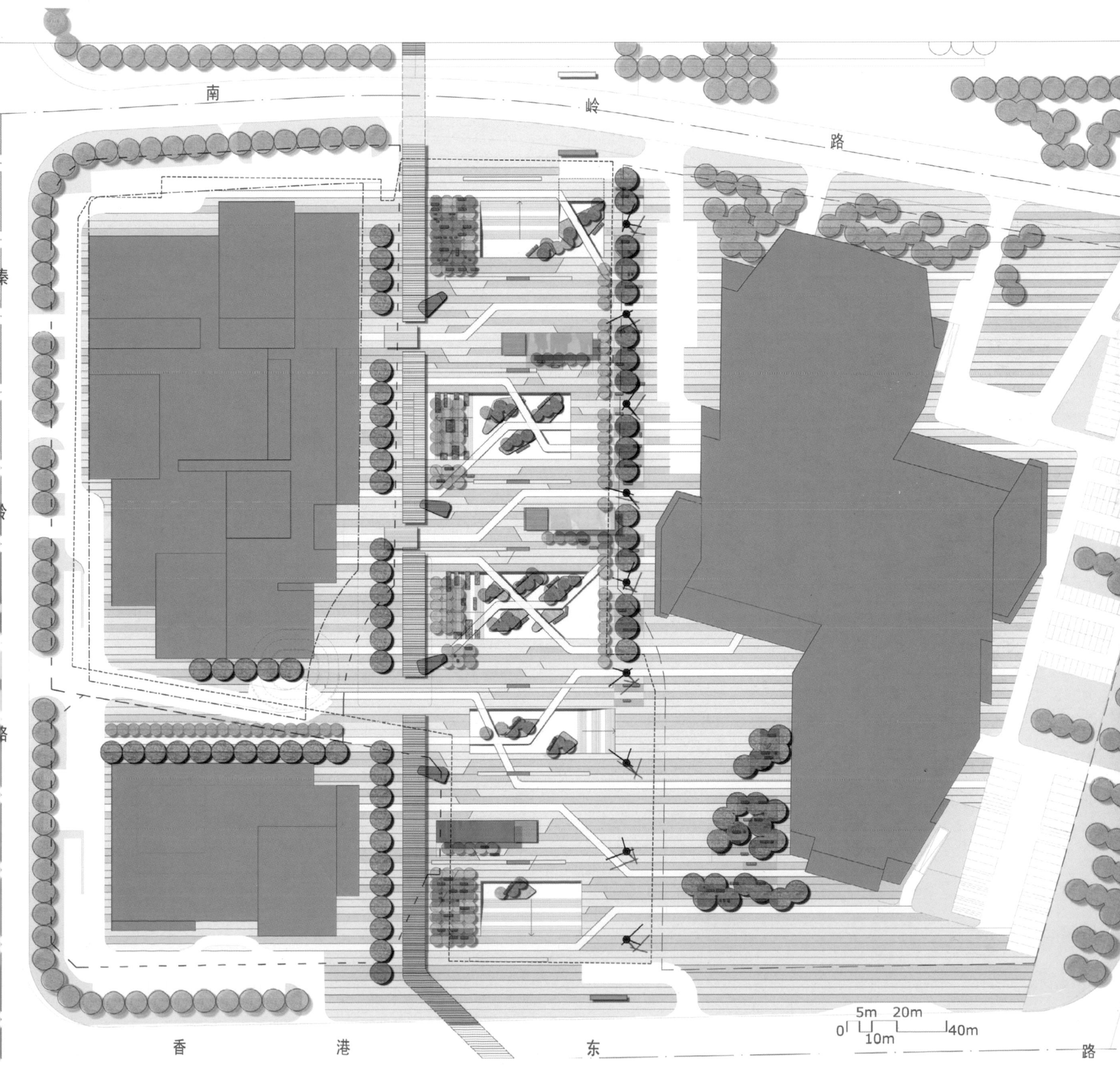

(left top) Commercial plaza.
(left) Sculpture.
(top) Bird's-eye-view.
(right) Canopy.

Bury Mount and the Mill Stream, Towcester

The Brief: The re-design of an area of public greenspace surrounding a 17th Century Scheduled Ancient Monument by the name of Bury Mount. The brief called for re-development of this space to provide a high quality open civic/events space situated directly adjacent to Eaton Neston Park — a historic parkland and The Mill Stream — an ancient watercourse bordering the park.

Located in the centre of the mediaeval town of Towcester — Northamptonshire, Bury Mount is the remnant of a Norman Motte and Bailey castle built in the 11th Century. The castle was born as a symbol of power, and as a watch tower, defending the town and the manor.

Bury Mount exists today as a simple landform; a grassed mount.

Despite the original placement of the mount as a feature to control two major junctions in the town, nowadays it is disconnected from and misunderstood by the local community.

Planet Earth was pre-selected out of over 30 other to submit proposals to re-design the space surrounding Bury Mount. Planet Earth's design is an innovative interpretation of the Mount's physical, geographical and historic context. The mount forms the key source of inspiration for the design which seeks to re-instate Bury Mount as the heart of Towcester and the Community.

The Concept: 'The Mount needs a Plane'
Following research concerning other similar historical 'mount' landscape features, a striking connection was discovered. Each mount sits within an open plane of land, uncluttered, extensive and complementary its form and verticality. When considering Bury Mount sitting within its own landscape 'plane' it became apparent that the plane could be as vast and expansive as the

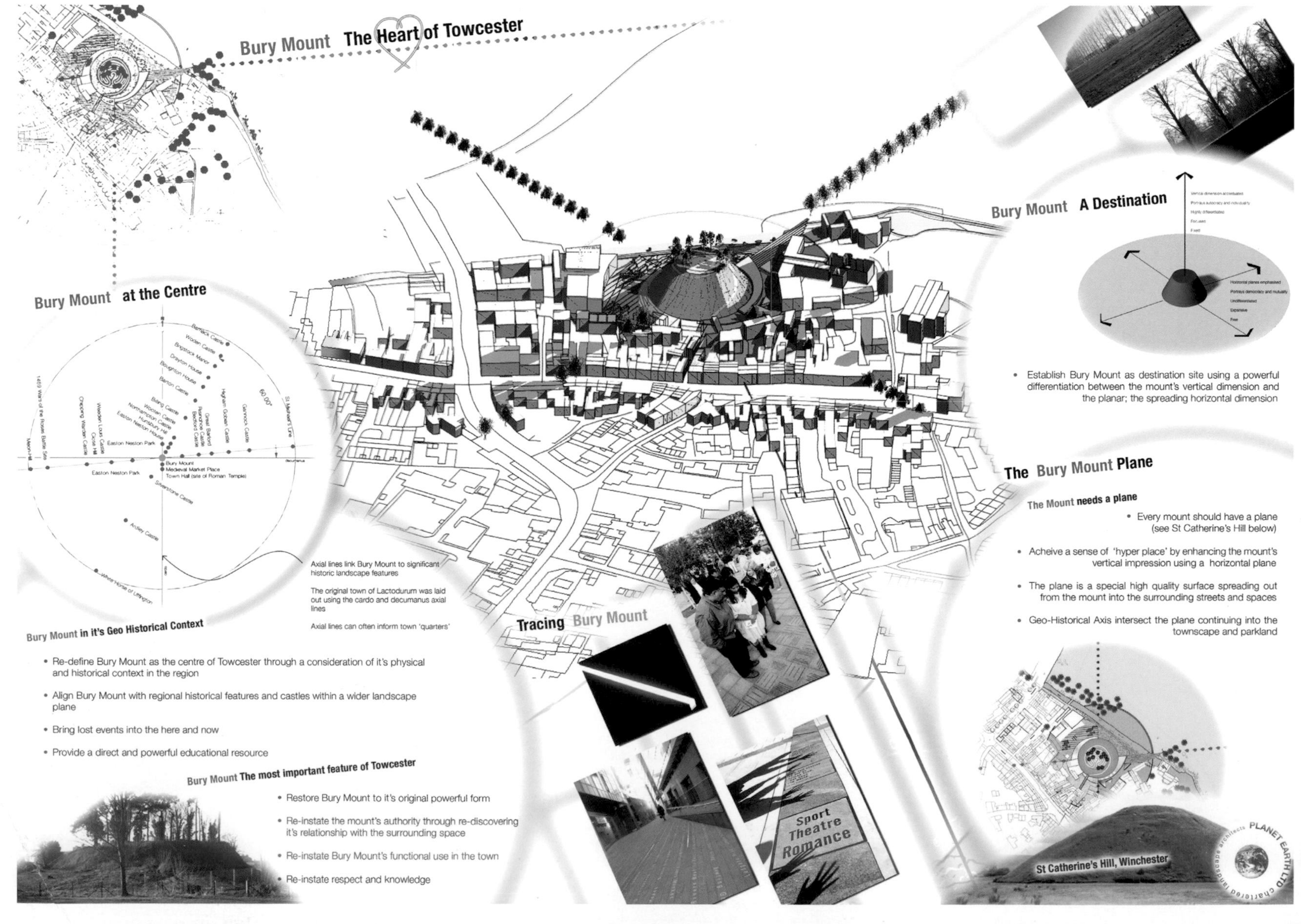

client / owner
Urban Delivery on behalf of South Northamptonshire Council, UK

other key consultants
Quantity Surveyors: LG Consult

location
Towcester, Northamptonshire, UK

awards
Shortlisted Competition Entry

land allowed. Bury Mount was mapped at the centre of a wide 80km radial plane and surprising alignments with other historic landscape features along various axes were established.

Preceding this, a more localised 80m plane around the mount was considered. This 80m radial plane covers both urban and rural open space. Where the plane exists within an urban environment, a high quality paved surface would distinguish the plane as a civic/events space. This surface then tapers out where it meets a rural edge and the plane becomes an area of open parkland. It envisaged the planes would evolve and change around the mount to further assist the urban to rural transition.

The axis connecting Bury Mount with the wider landscape can be viewed as intersecting lines in the ground plane and lines of trees and furniture. The axis act as a physical reference extending through the town indicating the location of the mount and its plane and also as an educational reference featuring ground inscriptions informing local history. These axes also act as divisions to the plane creating different character areas which relate to the use of neighbouring buildings.

It is understood that a moat formerly existed around the mount and that this once formed part of the same body as the Mill Stream, the bordering river. In order to control access to the Mount, and create life and activity in the plane, a moat is re-instated around the base, changing in character as it moves around the plane and through each character area.

(opposite page) Shows Bury Mount and the Plane within the context of the Town and Parkland. Shows the axis extending into the landscape and the 'line of light' leading visitors to the summit of the mount.

(below) Shows all elements of the Plane such as the moat and water rill which acts as a radial gateway into the plane. The wetlands form the northern quarter of the plane whilst re-uniting the moat and the mill stream. Movable seating allow de-clutter of the the plane for open events space.

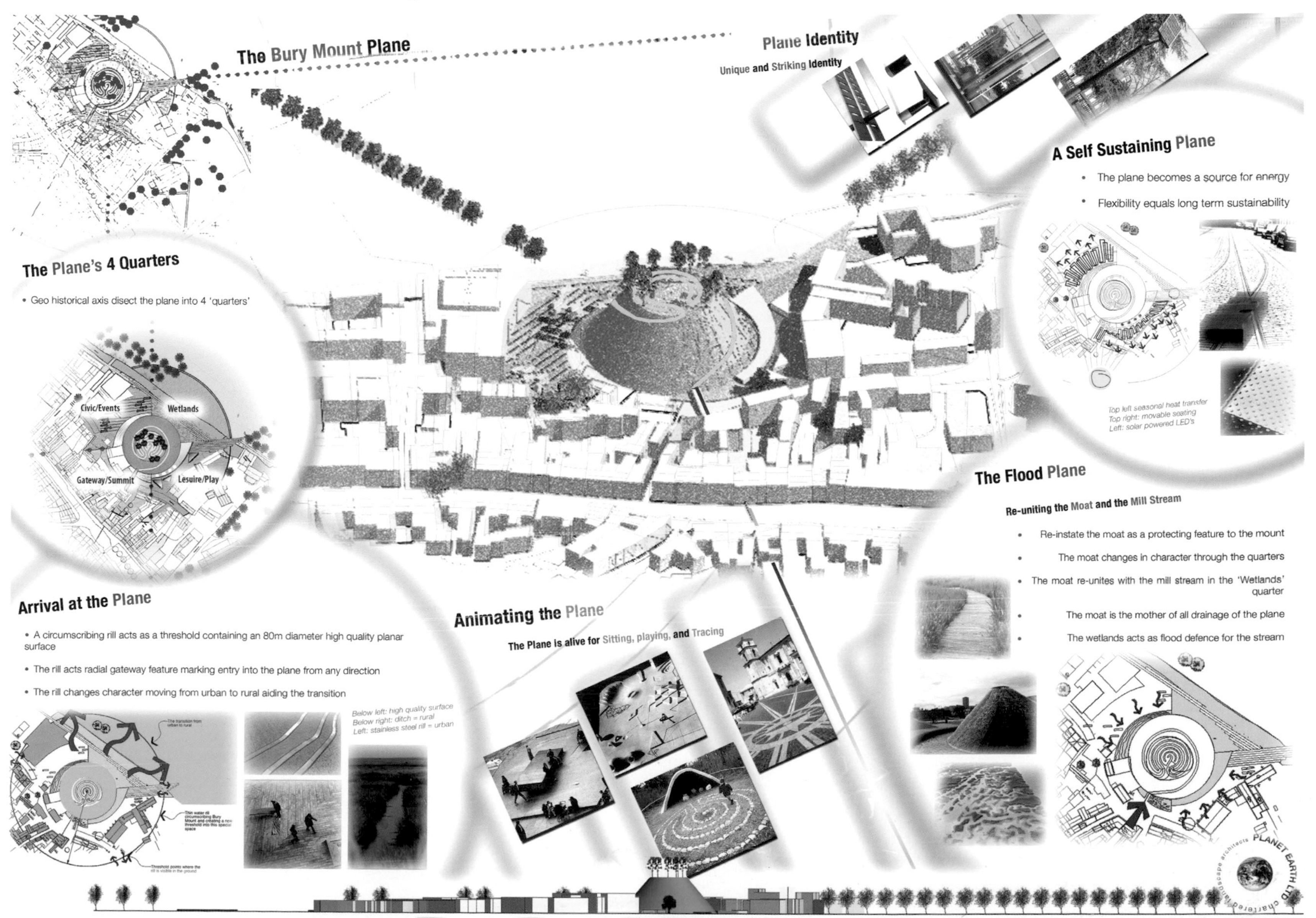

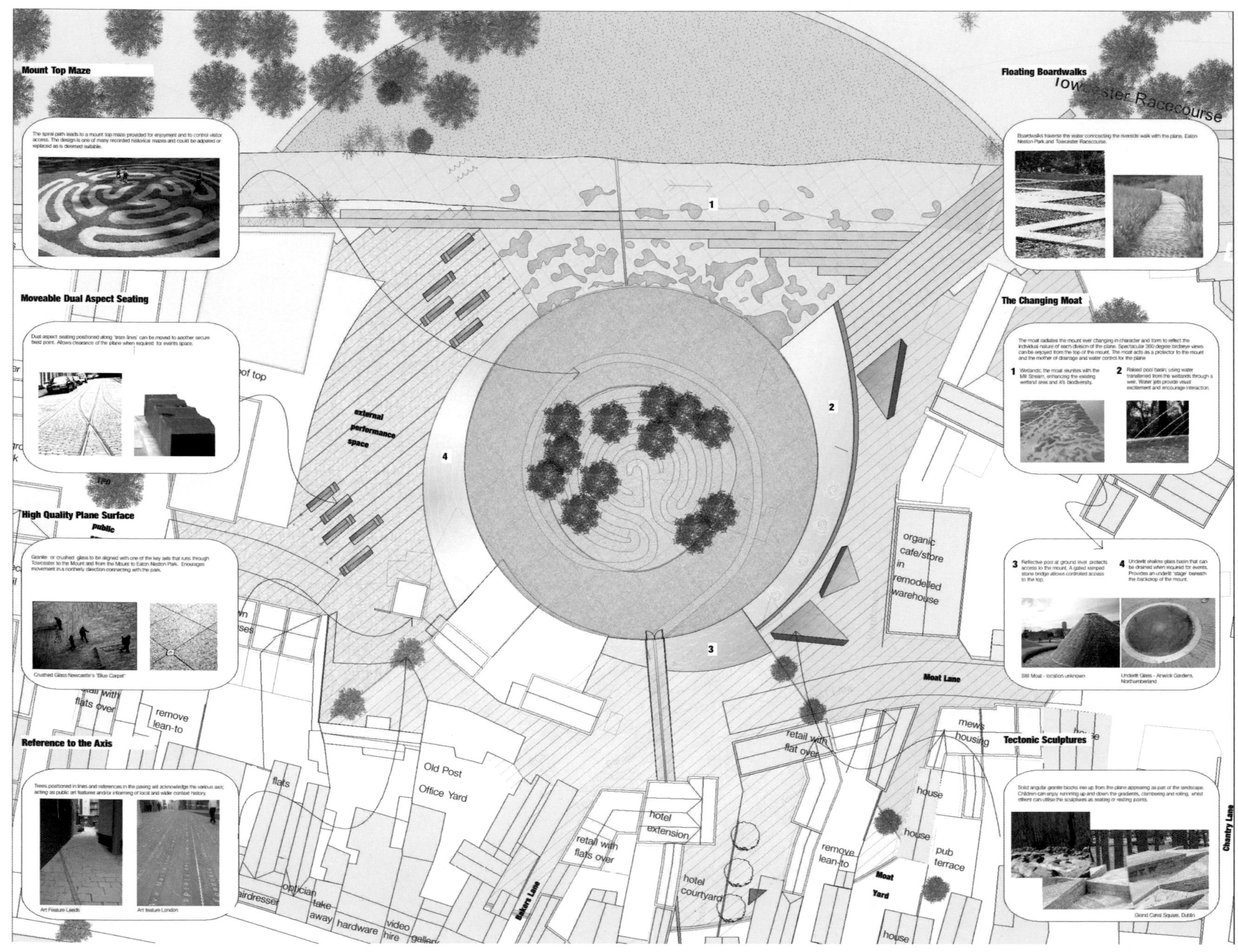
Mount Top Maze
The spiral path leads to a mount top maze provided for enjoyment and to control visitor access. The design is one of many recorded historical mazes and could be adpated or replaced as is deemed suitable.
Moveable Dual Aspect Seating
Dual aspect seating positioned along 'tram lines' can be moved to another secure fixed point. Allows clearance of the plane when required for events space.
High Quality Plane Surface
Granite or crushed glass to be aligned with one of the key axis that runs through Towcester to the Mount and from the Mount to Eaton Neston Park. Encourages movement in a northerly direction connecting with the park.
Crushed Glass Newcastle's 'Blue Carpet'
Reference to the Axis
Trees positioned in lines and references in the paving will acknowledge the various axis; acting as public art features and/or informing of local and wider context history.
Art Feature Leeds
Art feature London
Floating Boardwalks
Towcester Racecourse
Boardwalks traverse the water connecting the riverside walk with the plane, Eaton Neston Park and Towcester Racecourse.
The Changing Moat
The moat radiates the mount ever changing in character and form to reflect the individual nature of each division of the plane. Spectacular 360 degree birdseye views can be enjoyed from the top of the mount. The moat acts as a protector to the mount and the mother of drainage and water control for the plane
1 Wetlands; the moat reunites with the Mill Stream, enhancing the existing wetland area and it's biodiversity.
2 Raised pool basin; using water transferred from the wetlands through a weir. Water jets provide visual excitement and encourage interaction.
3 Reflective pool at ground level protects access to the mount. A gated ramped stone bridge allows controlled access to the top.
4 Underlit shallow glass basin that can be drained when required for events. Provides an underlit 'stage' beneath the backdrop of the mount.
Still Moat - location unknown
Underlit Glass - Alnwick Gardens, Northumberland
Tectonic Sculptures
Solid angular granite blocks rise up from the plane appearing as part of the landscape. Children can enjoy running up and down the gradients, clambering and rolling, whilst others can utilise the sculptures as seating or resting points.
Grand Canal Square, Dublin
Chantry Lane
external performance space
organic cafe/store in remodelled warehouse
Moat Lane
retail with flat over
mews housing
house
pub terrace
Moat Yard
remove lean-to
hotel courtyard
hotel extension
retail with flats over
Old Post Office Yard
flats
Bakers Lane
take away
hardware
video hire
optician
hairdresser
remove lean-to
flats over
public

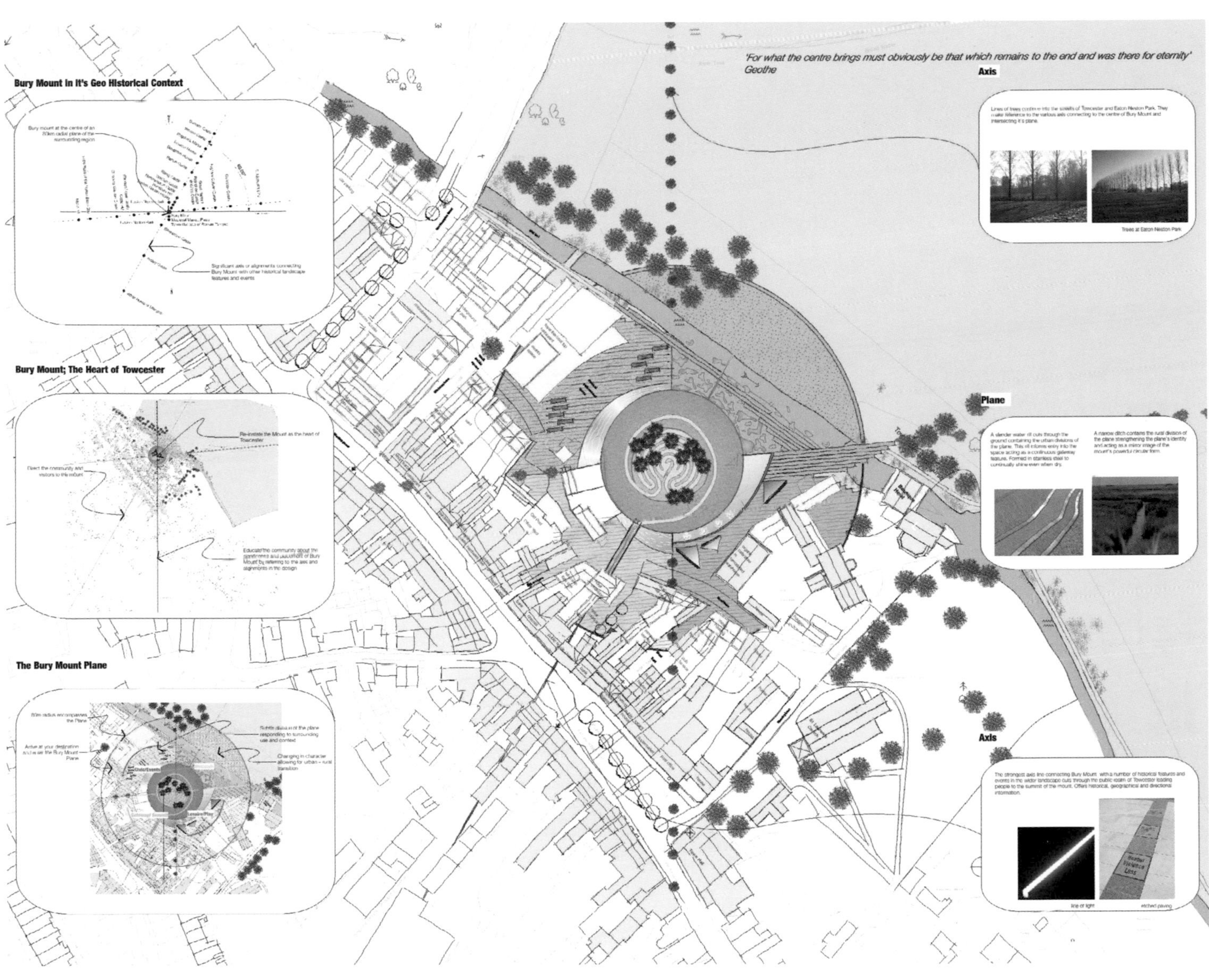

(left) Materials and features of the plane.
(above) Summary of the design and the concept.

After Maximus, Rome

After Maximus is a memorial to the innocents who died in Rome's original Circus Maximus where everything from public executions to wild animal fights took place for hundreds of years. The elongated earthen mound, augmented by grass, stone and cypress trees, was inspired by the ancient landscape mounds such as those that crowned the tombs of Emperors Hadrian and Augustus. An over-scaled alter anchors one end of the site where one can leave offerings to the deceased. Tension builds over the length of the site and culminates between soaring stone walls that finally open to light and repose in the deep, grassy bowl. David Meyer developed this visionary design for the 25 acre site while spending a year working in Rome on his Rome Prize fellowship.

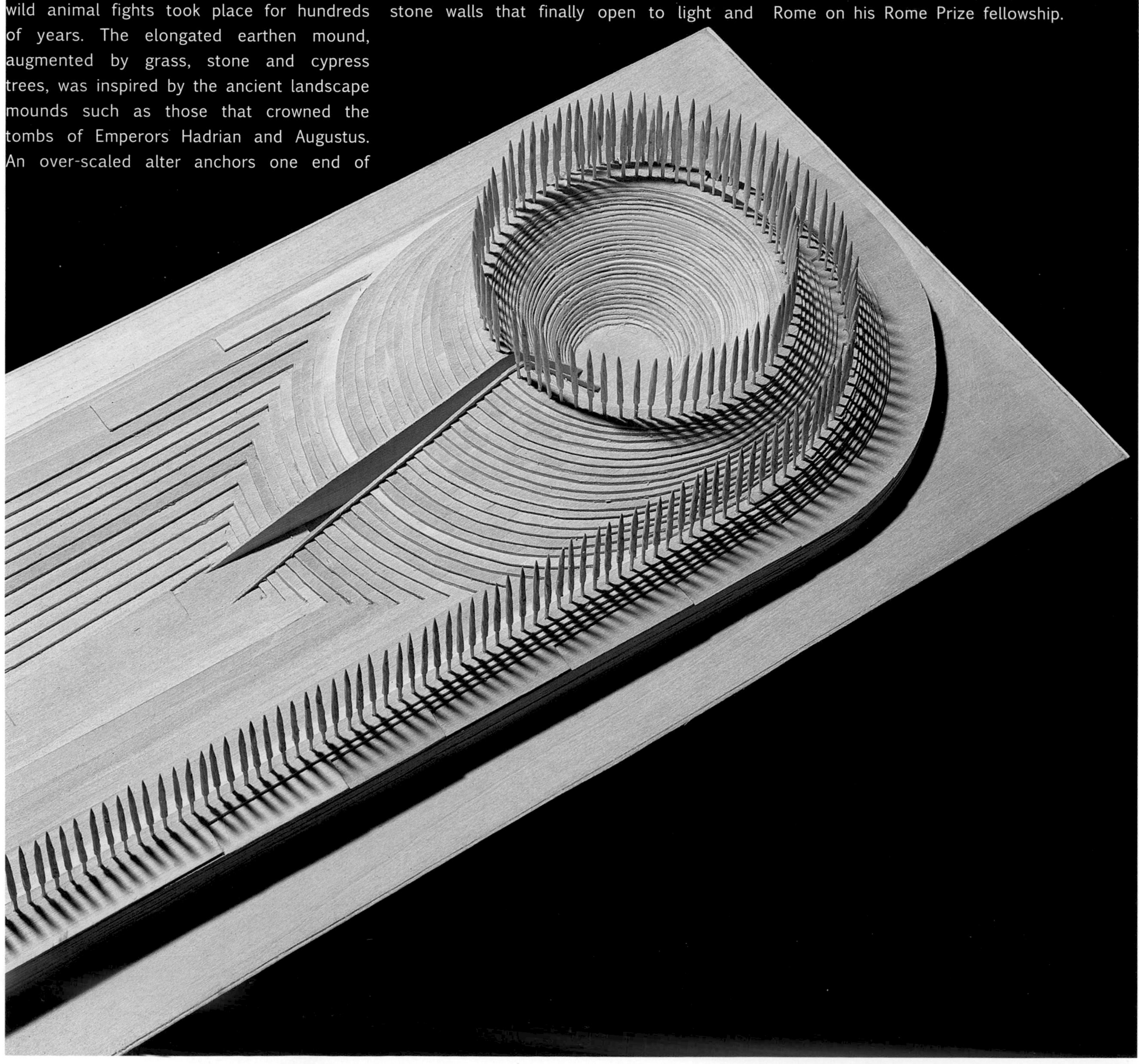

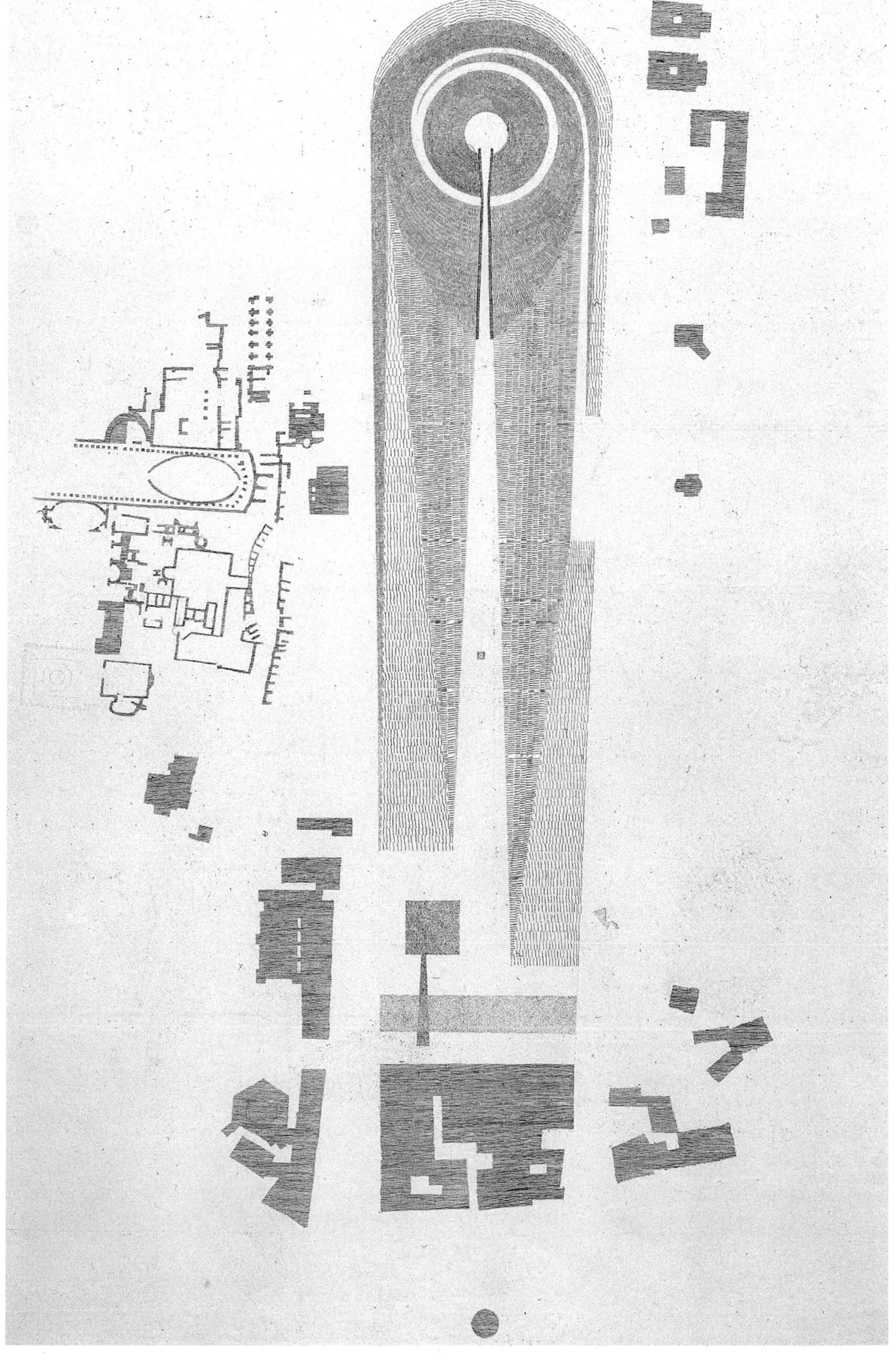

(left) Site model detail of the earthen mound.
(right) Site plan and context plan.

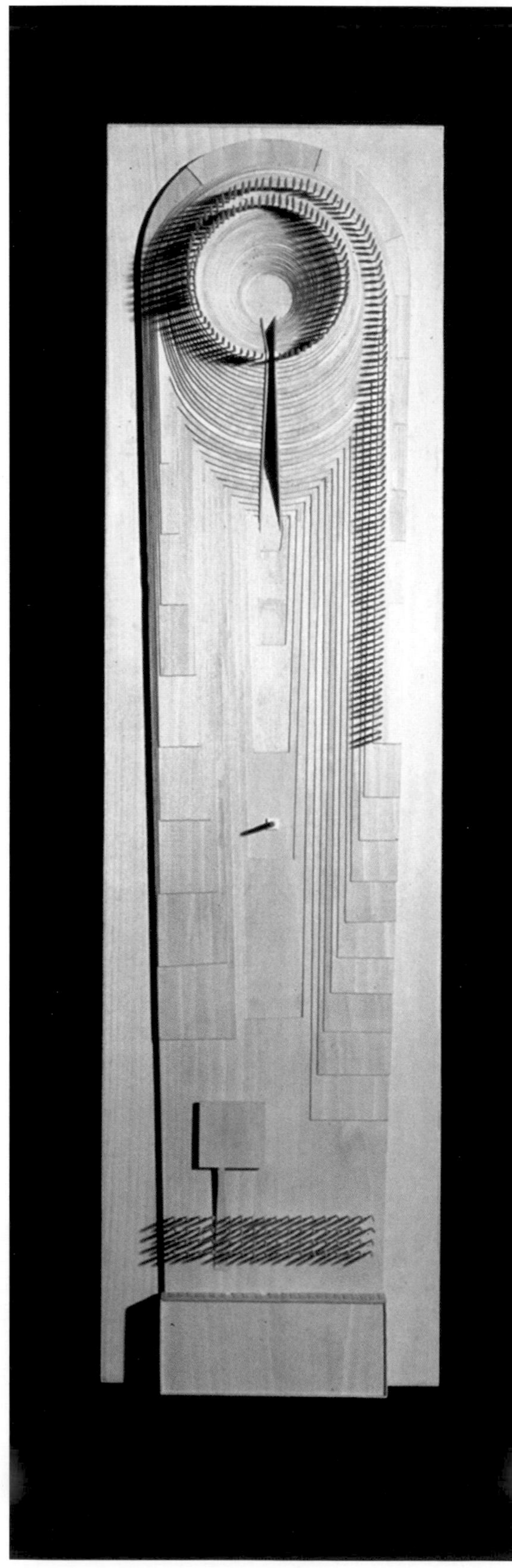

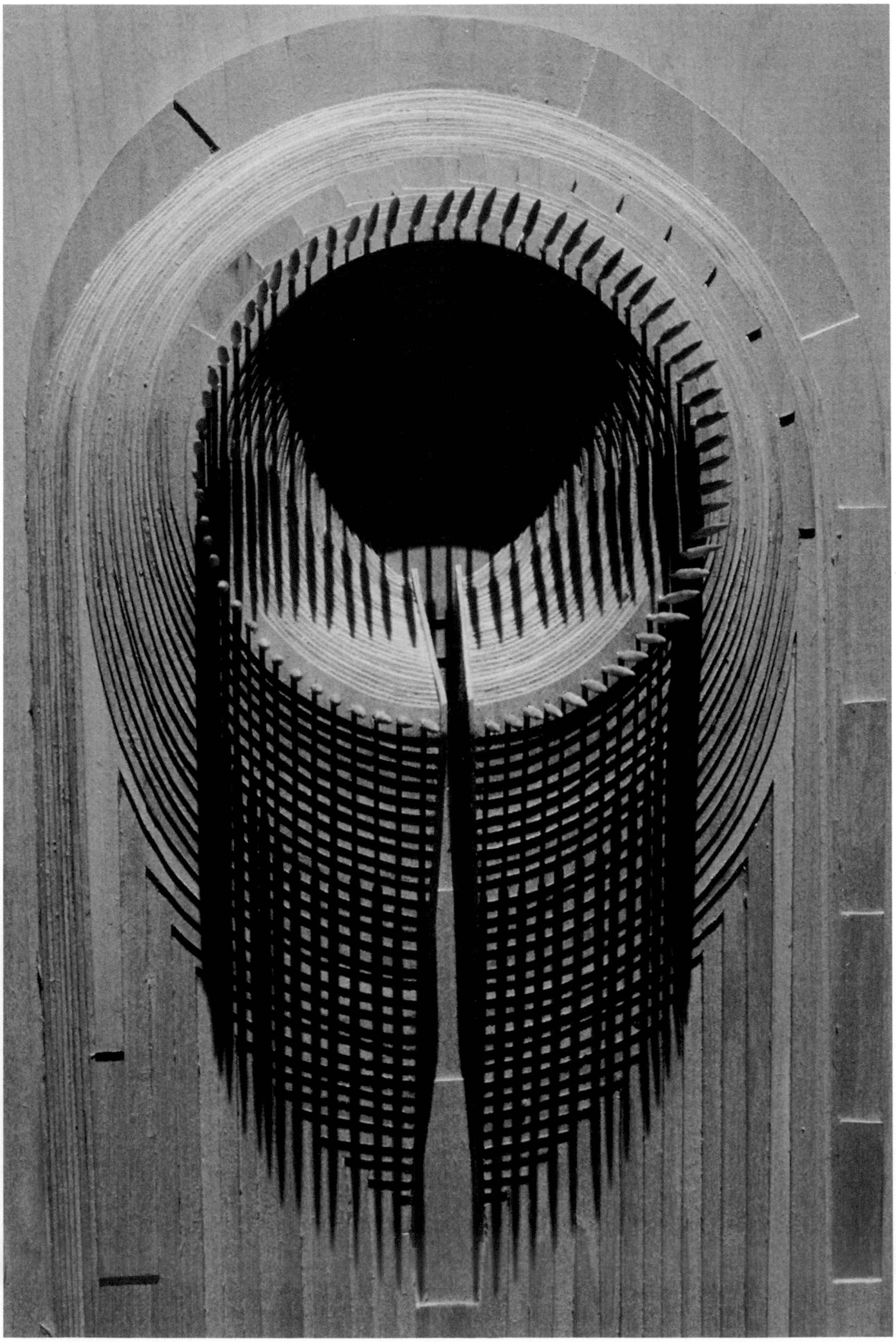

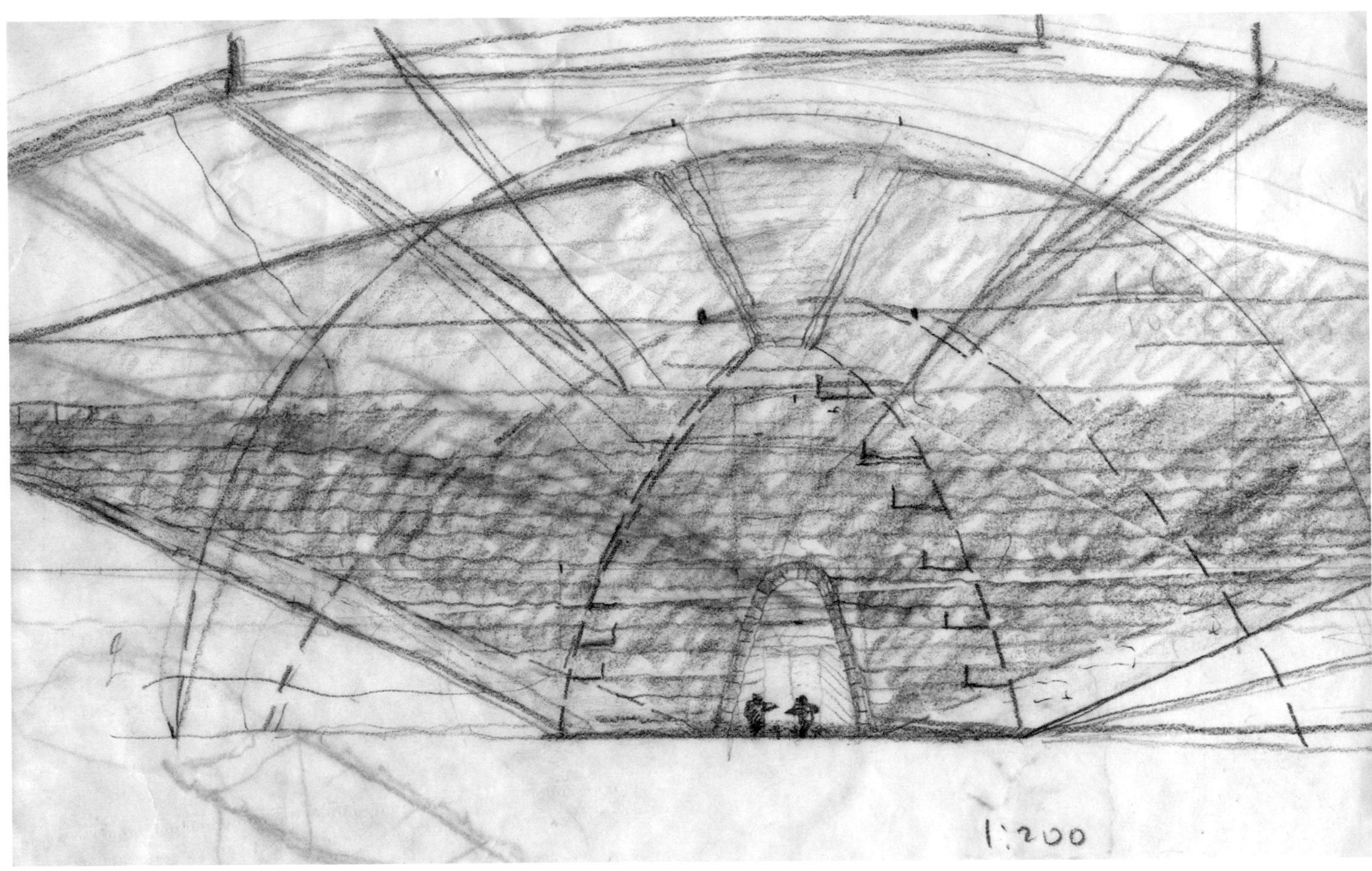

(opposite page, left) Site model overall view.
(opposite page, right) Site model view of dramatic shadows at the earthen mound.
(top) Conceptual study.
(below) Section through earthen bowl and stone slot.

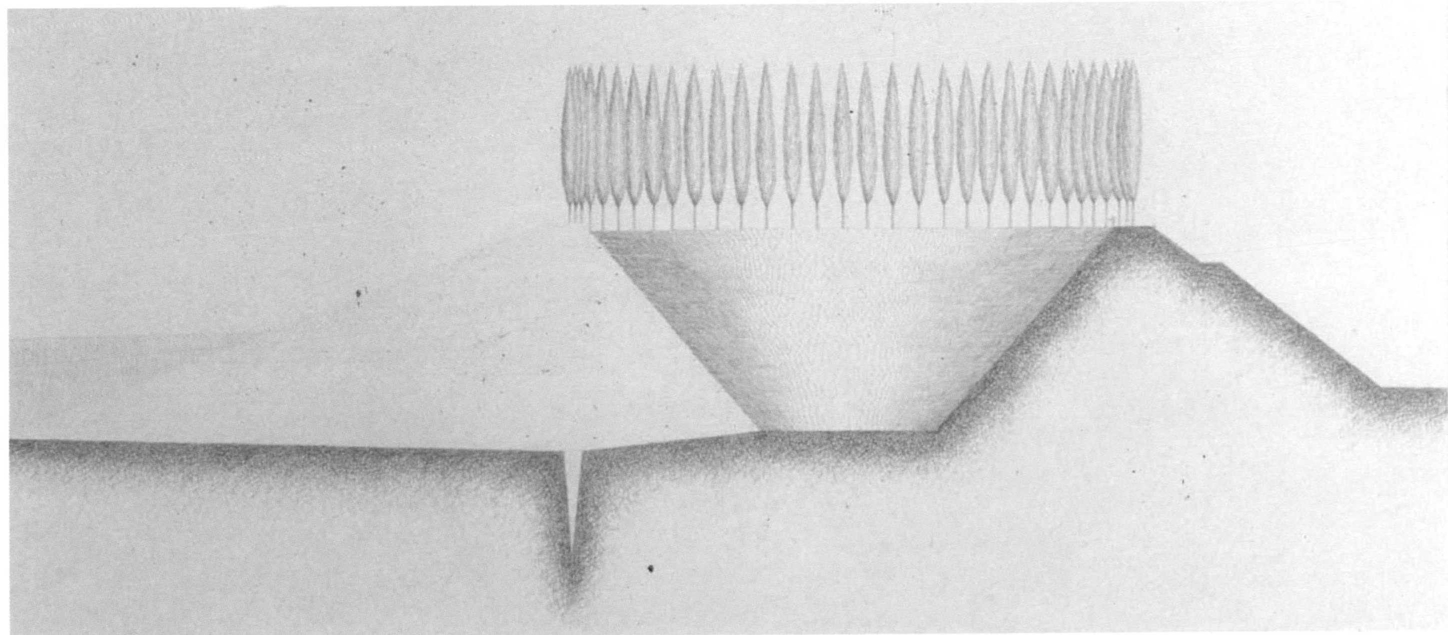

74 Whistler's Mountain Square, Whistler

Whistler Village, a mountain resort, is undertaking a renewal and enhancement program as it ramps up to host the Olympic and Paralympic Winter Games in 2010. After other areas of the village have been upgraded, attention has turned to Mountain Square as showing the greatest need for renewal.

The Mountain Square design approach draws upon many factors: site history, analysis data, site uses, snow management, structural limitations on slab, private stakeholder concerns, client factors, past design proposal process outcomes, site context, local geography, artistic collaboration and unique feature opportunities.

The design team includes Tom Barratt Ltd. Landscape Architects, with collaborating artists Robert Studer and Jill Anholt.

An early proposal for Mountain Square was a plaza sized 'Worldclock'. This concept grew out of the Worldclock idea, designed to simulate the earth's rotation of one revolution every 24 hours, and tell the time in 200 major cities worldwide.

The final proposal for Mountain Square looked the edges and gateways into the plaza and reducing its wide expanse to create a usable and attractive space. The Landscape Architect and Artists worked together to explore an imbedding meaning as well as expression of art in the landscape.

Design concepts for the Black Tusk warming station envisioned an outdoor fireplace and recycled SLAB glass reflection wall.

Glowing Track elements formed from textured (recycled) laminated glass inset into the paving and lit from below with linear LED lighting would create glowing dynamic elements within the ground surface. The colourfully lit tracks could be created in varying forms & patterns evocative of the many winter activities such as cross country skiing. These lit tracks would draw/lead one into Mountain Square, defining various areas of activity within the plaza, and also potentially as a wayfinding device.

Along edges, or where there is a potential for gathering areas, the tracks would lift from out of the paving surface to provide dynamic glowing seating elements for visitors to the plaza.

Within the centre area of Mountain Square, glowing elements in the plaza surface would reach dynamically upwards into the air, projecting light into the sky. The sky tracks would be not only a reference to air-borne winter events such as ski jumping, but would also give form metaphorically to ideals of the strive for human excellence and achievement in sport. The projecting lights would create a highly visible marker for Mountain Square that could be seen from far away locations elsewhere in Whistler.

Tracks of varying shapes and patterns would carve into existing or newly formed walls found in building and planter edges. The carved track impressions would be lined with tactile wood material and then lit from above with LED cove lighting and be physically warmed by solar powered radiant heating elements placed within. Passersby could place their hands into the glowing Warming Tracks when they are cold.

The final edge to Mountain Square opens into an alleyway between the Hilton and Carleton Lodge. This is an area that see crowds of kids gather prior to their ski lessons each morning. In keeping with contemporary culture and the interests of modern kids, the character of dynamic snowboard graphics would be inlaid in lower, double tiered style seating/planter walls created along the edges of the walkway. These graphics could be created in recycled glass and be lit from behind, thus tying it into the language of the lit glass tracks throughout the plaza.

The design solution may be intuitive and abstracted in some cases, but is factually founded in local history, geography and social factors, that work together to create a fresh dynamic plaza experience.

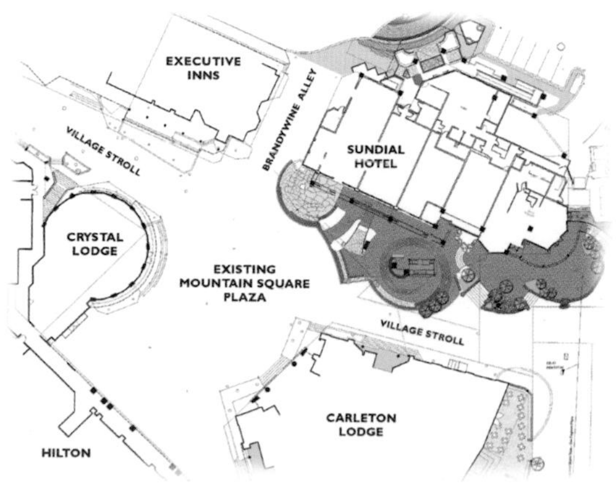

client / owner

Resort Municipality of Whistler, Canada

other key consultants

Consulting Engineers: Read Jones Christofersen; Parks Planner: Kevin McFarland, Resort Municipality of Whistler

location

Whistler, British Columbia, Canada

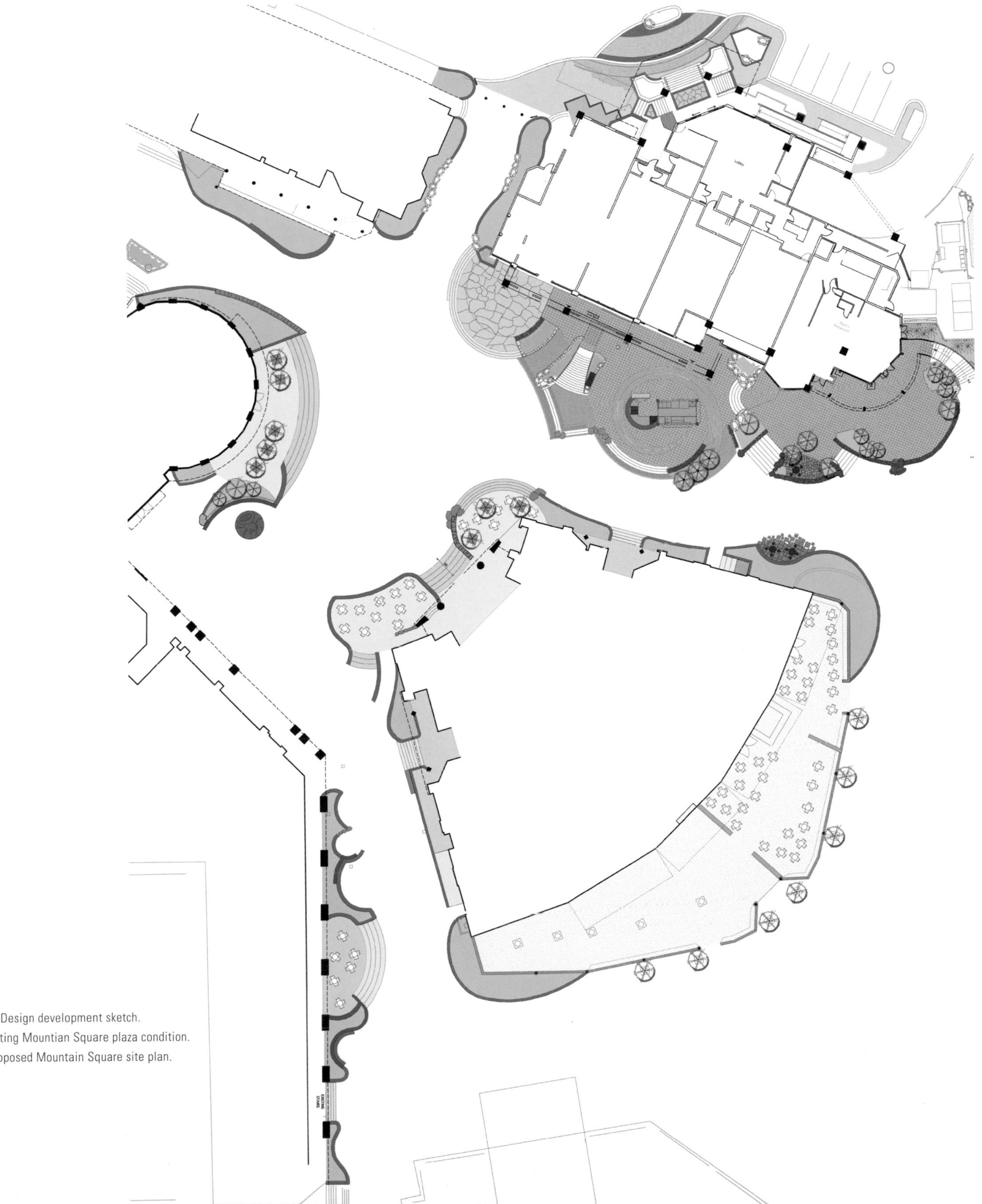

(left top) Design development sketch.
(left) Existing Mountian Square plaza condition.
(right) Proposed Mountain Square site plan.

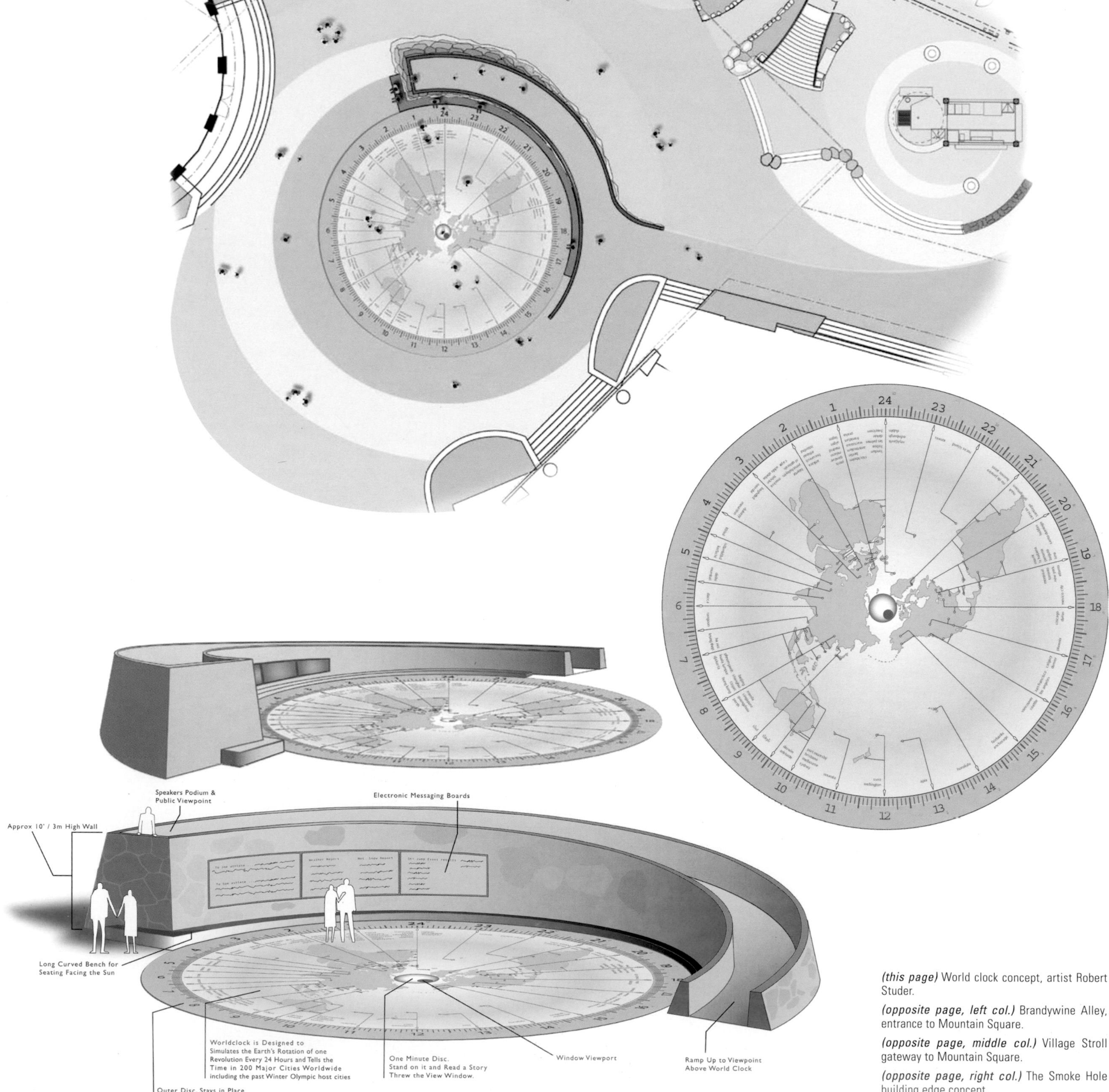

(this page) World clock concept, artist Robert Studer.

(opposite page, left col.) Brandywine Alley, entrance to Mountain Square.

(opposite page, middle col.) Village Stroll gateway to Mountain Square.

(opposite page, right col.) The Smoke Hole building edge concept.

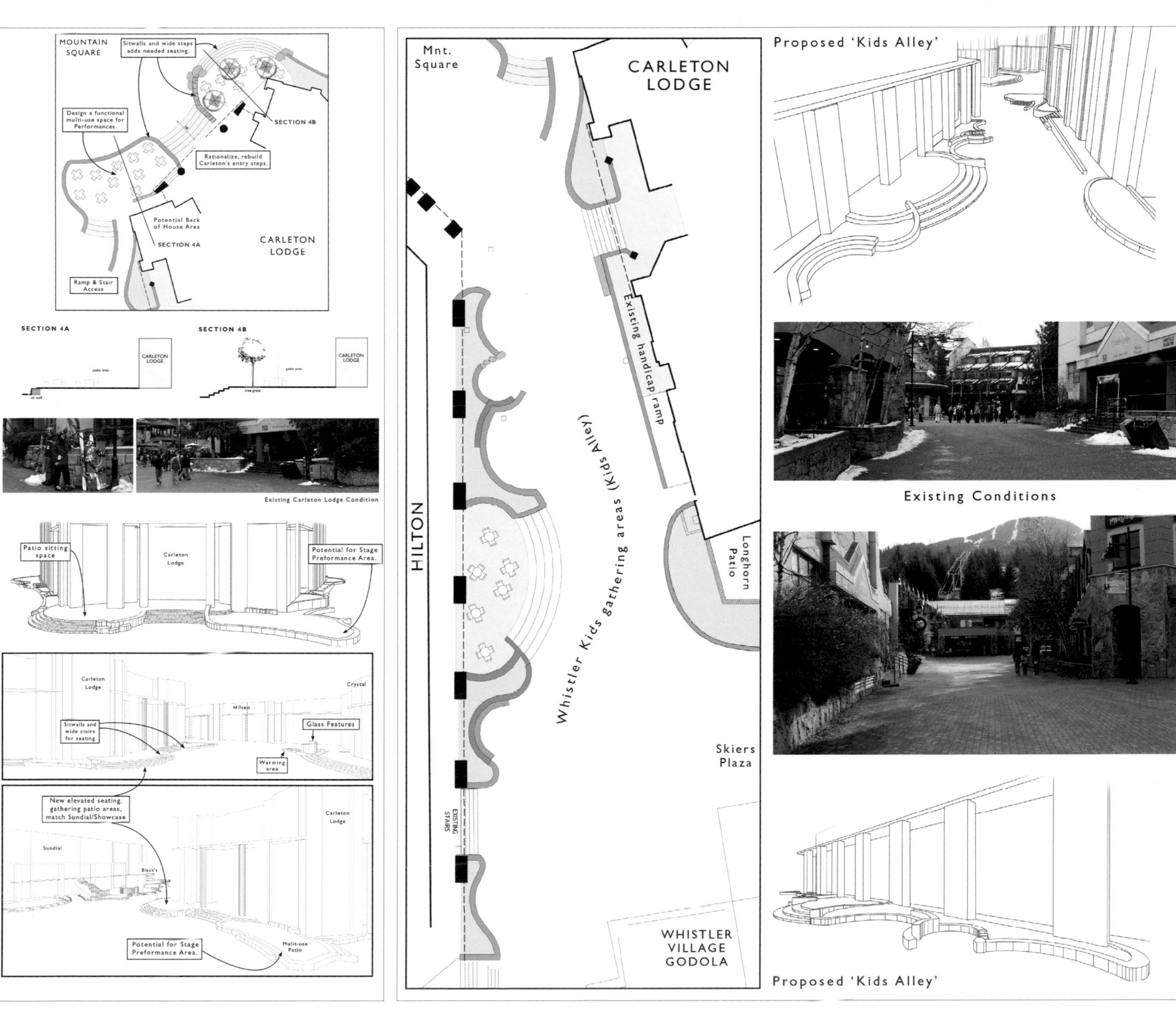
MOUNTAIN SQUARE
Sitwalls and wide steps adds needed seating.
Design a functional multi-use space for Performances.
SECTION 4B
Rationalize, rebuild Carleton's entry steps.
Potential Back of House Area
SECTION 4A
CARLETON LODGE
Ramp & Stair Access
SECTION 4A
SECTION 4B
Existing Carleton Lodge Condition
Patio sitting space
Carleton Lodge
Potential for Stage Preformance Area.
Carleton Lodge
Crystal
Sitwalls and wide stairs for seating
Glass Features
Warming area
New elevated seating, gathering patio areas, match Sundial/Showcase
Carleton Lodge
Sundial
Potential for Stage Preformance Area.
Mulit-use Patio
Mnt. Square
CARLETON LODGE
HILTON
Existing handicap ramp
Whistler Kids gathering areas (Kids Alley)
Longhorn Patio
EXISTING STAIRS
Skiers Plaza
WHISTLER VILLAGE GODOLA
Proposed 'Kids Alley'
Existing Conditions
Proposed 'Kids Alley'

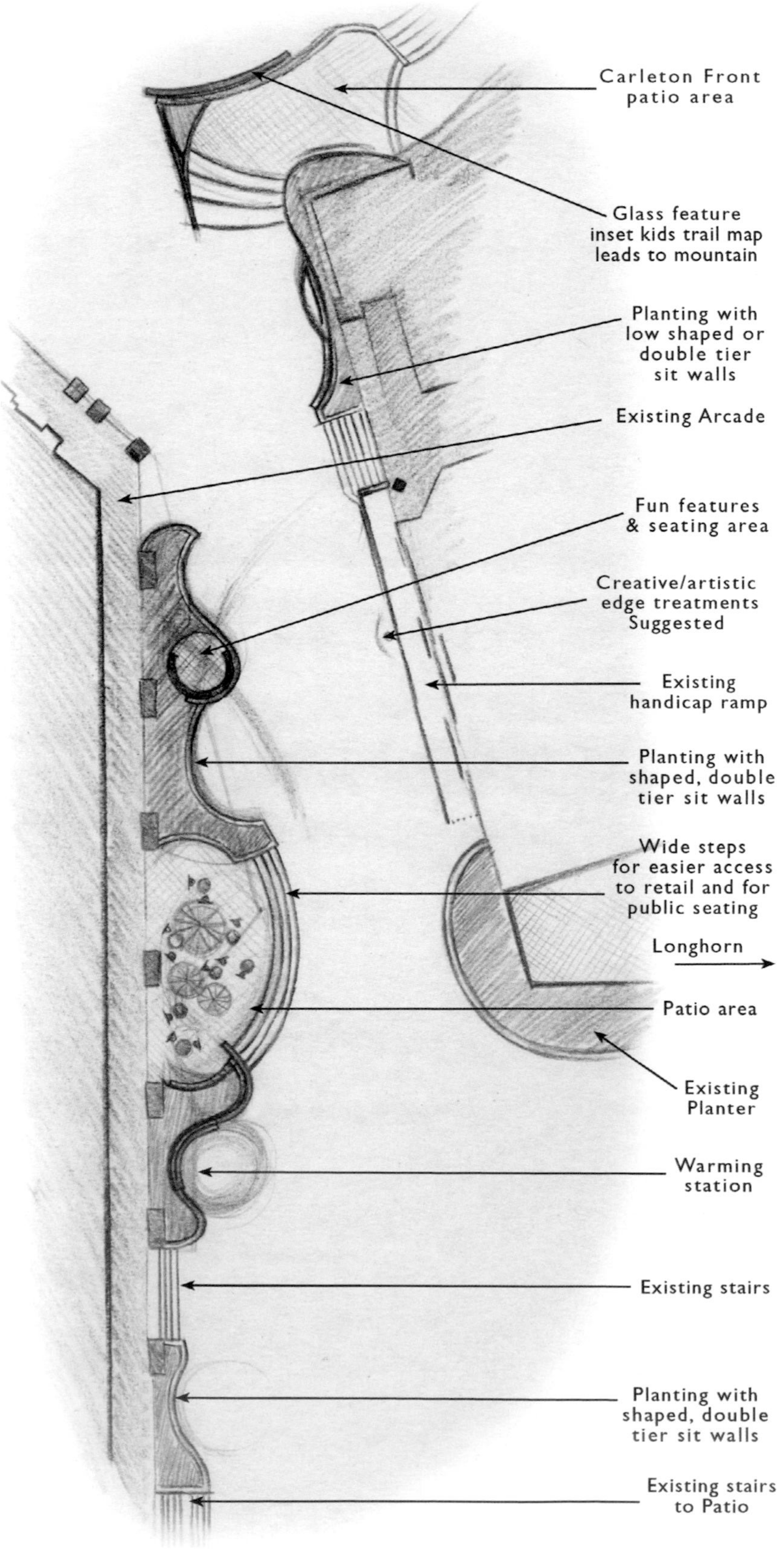
Carleton Front patio area
Glass feature inset kids trail map leads to mountain
Planting with low shaped or double tier sit walls
Existing Arcade
Fun features & seating area
Creative/artistic edge treatments Suggested
Existing handicap ramp
Planting with shaped, double tier sit walls
Wide steps for easier access to retail and for public seating
Longhorn
Patio area
Existing Planter
Warming station
Existing stairs
Planting with shaped, double tier sit walls
Existing stairs to Patio

vibrantly coloured ceramic and glass elements are inlaid in concrete
snow sneen neige
boarder graphics and multilingual words for 'snow' contemporize kids area benches

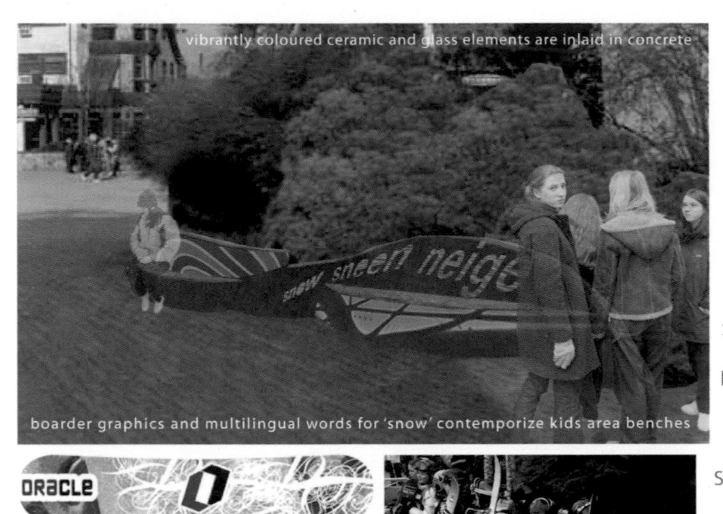

bore
snijeg
snih
sneen
hank
neige
Schnee
havazik
neve
Sneeuw
sno✓
sneg
nieve
snö

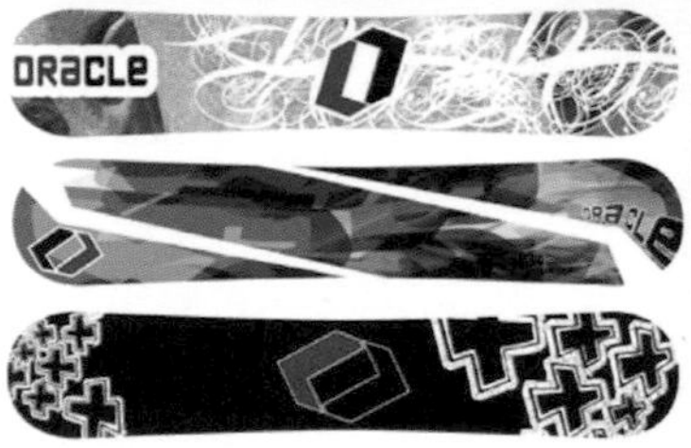
ORACLE

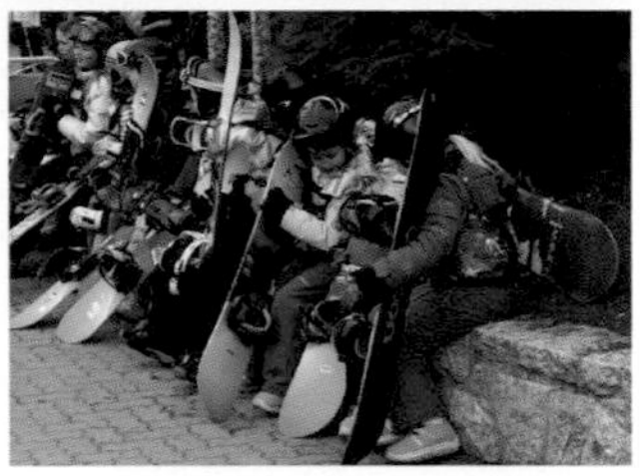

lower seat walls work well
lower edges makes for easier & safer seating for little people
lower seat walls work well
burton
group seating and meeting areas needed
Forms should follow function

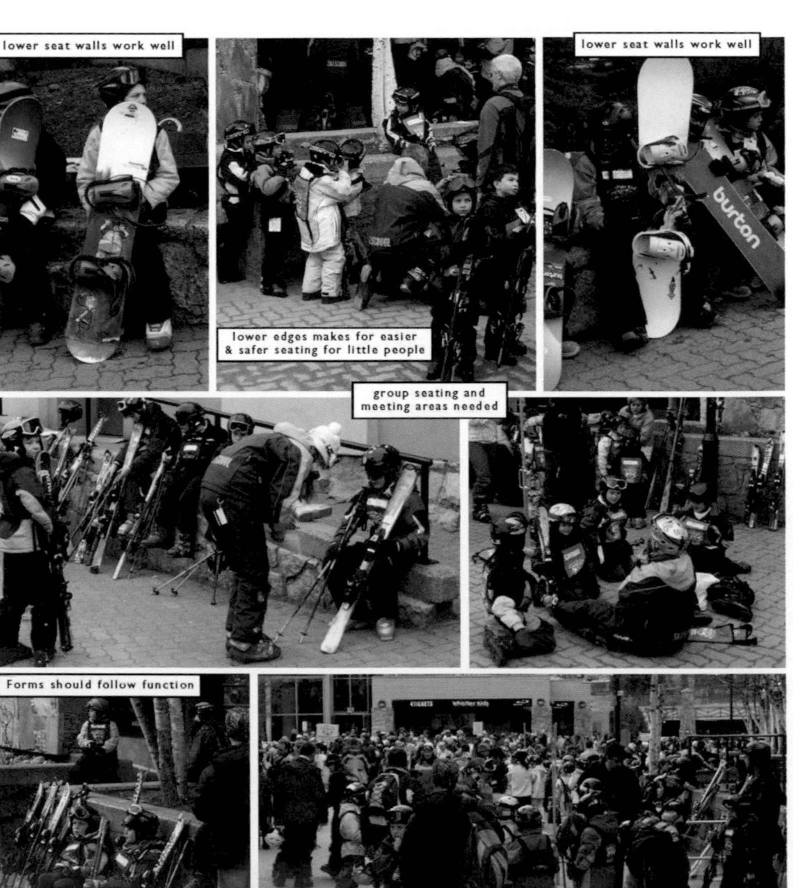

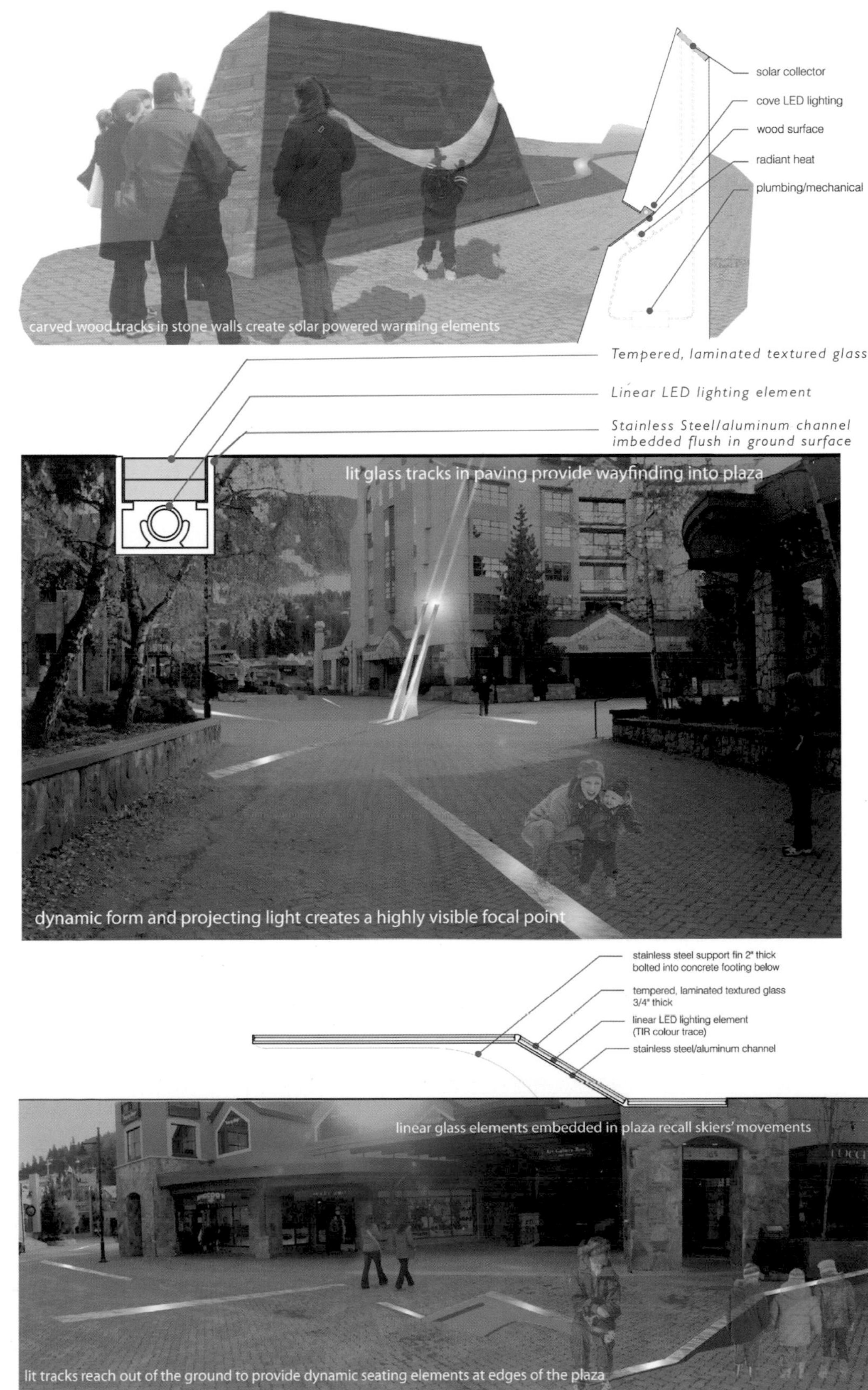

(far left) Kids alley conceptual sketches and development, artist Jill Anholt.

(left top) Kids alley benches.

(left bottom) Kids alley chaos.

(top) Artist concept warming tracks.

(middle) Artist concept sky tracks.

(bottom) Artist concept glowing tracks, artist Jill Anholt.

Greenlinks, Detroit, Michigan

DETROIT, MI - Plans are underway to bring a sustainable, livable environment to this city with the Corktown-Mexicantown Greenlinks project. The concerted efforts of urban architects, McIntosh Poris Associates and 511 Design are to bring in an extensive network of bicycle and pedestrian pathways that will connect the city's blighted areas to the widely-anticipated West Riverfront development.

With a $100,000 grant from the Community Foundation for Southeastern Michigan, the project developed by the Greater Corktown Development Corporation will provide nearly 15 miles of landscaped pathways. These will include 7.3 miles of bicycle lanes, 3.3 miles of off roads, shared-use routes, and 3.1 miles of signed bicycle routes. The network will ultimately be connected to various greenway links that are being planned in seven other counties in Southeastern Michigan.

The Detroit bicycle lanes will provide a vital link to facilitate the multi-cultural Mexicantown and Hubbard communities to access the city's cultural, civic, business, and entertainment attractions. McIntosh Poris Associates, a local architecture firm that has been taking a critical role in revitalizing Detroit, joined 511 Design in this proactive plan to promote a healthy lifestyle and an environmentally smart transportation system that increases accessibility.

"Greenlinks directly addresses all the issues our firm has envisaged throughout the past decade — urban vitality, livability, density, and mobility," says Michael Poris, AIA, principal of McIntosh Poris Associates. "These are the planning ideas that are at the heart of Detroit. Greenlinks gets people moving again."

The architects' proposed design transforms some of Detroit's bleakest, most under utilized roads and passages into vibrant corridors that will be landscaped, repaved, planted, and supplemented with appropriate bicycle lanes, pathways, and signages. The target area which fronts the Detroit River is bounded by West Grand Boulevard to the west, Martin Luther King Boulevard to the north, and the Lodge Freeway to the east.

(left) Final development showing infrastructure improvements, bike lane routes, signage routes, Southwest Detroit Riverfront Greenway, parks, and schools.

(right top) A bridge connecting 14th Avenue across the rail right-of-way would extend the importance of 14th Avenue as a bicycle commuting route.

(right bottom) Vernor Highway bike lane.

client / owner
Greater Corktown Development Corporation

other key consultants
511 Design

location
Detroit, Michigan, USA

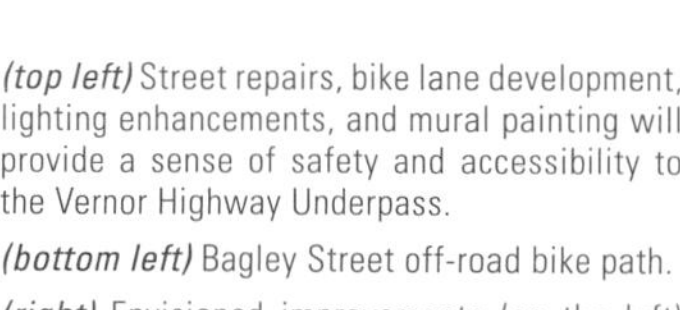

(top left) Street repairs, bike lane development, lighting enhancements, and mural painting will provide a sense of safety and accessibility to the Vernor Highway Underpass.

(bottom left) Bagley Street off-road bike path.

(right) Envisioned improvements (on the left) and as-is conditions (on the right) of several areas in the Greenlinks plan, including (from top to bottom) Ash Street signage route, Bagley Street signage route, Lafayette Boulevard bike line, Martin Luther King Boulevard off-road bike path, and Michigan Avenue bike lane.

Redevelopment of "Spielbudenplatz" Hamburg

A public space with two faces

The Spielbudenplatz by the Reeperbahn connects and harmonizes the tension between Hamburg's world-famous boulevard of iniquity, and a booming and innovative district of offices, apartments, and nocturnal entertainment. For this reason, the longitudinal square presents two distinctly different faces to the public. Its daytime appearance is simple and modern while at night it will turn into a stage for after-dark activities. It reflects and amplifies the exotic life around it.

The plans envisage a gently concave thoroughfare, a shallow arch reminiscent of a corset tracing a body line. Roofing canopies are positioned directly above the points where the surface of the Platz descends into the underground car park, giving an impression of a garment bursting at the seams. This lends the Platz an appealing plasticity. At night, the lighting from the surrounding streets, buildings, and advertisements are reflected in the gleaming, polished asphalt surface.

The district is in a constant state of flux. Plans therefore provide for an unencumbered area free of fixed edifices, superstructures or installations, an open stage that challenges people to experiment and dream, to take possession of it and turn it to whatever purpose they see fit.

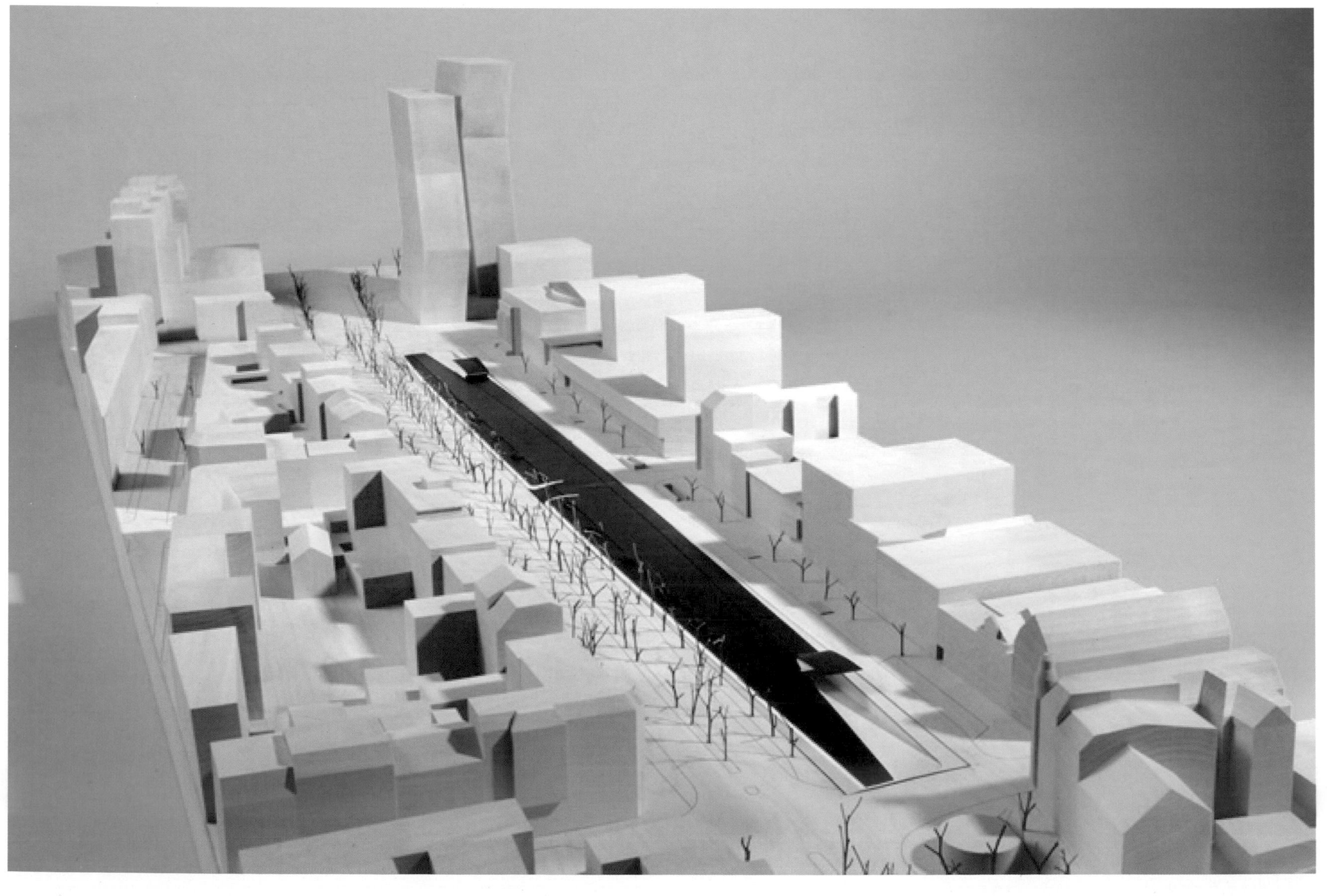

client / owner
Free and Hanseatic City of Hamburg

other key consultants
Architect: Peter von Klitzing

location
Hamburg, Germany

awards
4th prize, International Design Competition 2004

(left) The design model.
(above) Spielbudenplatz by day.
(below) Plan and sections.

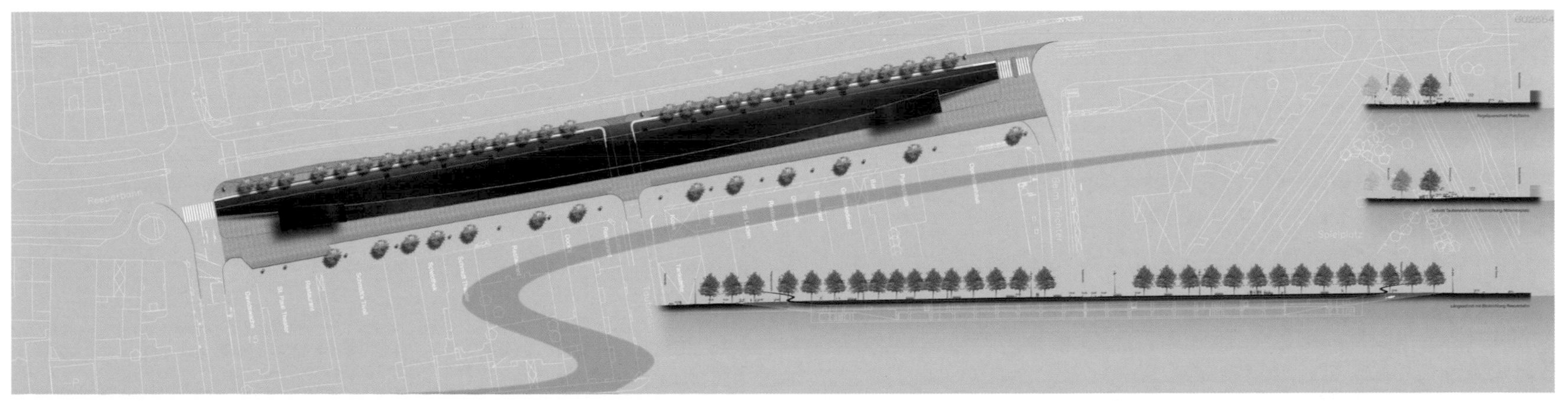

Nachtbild

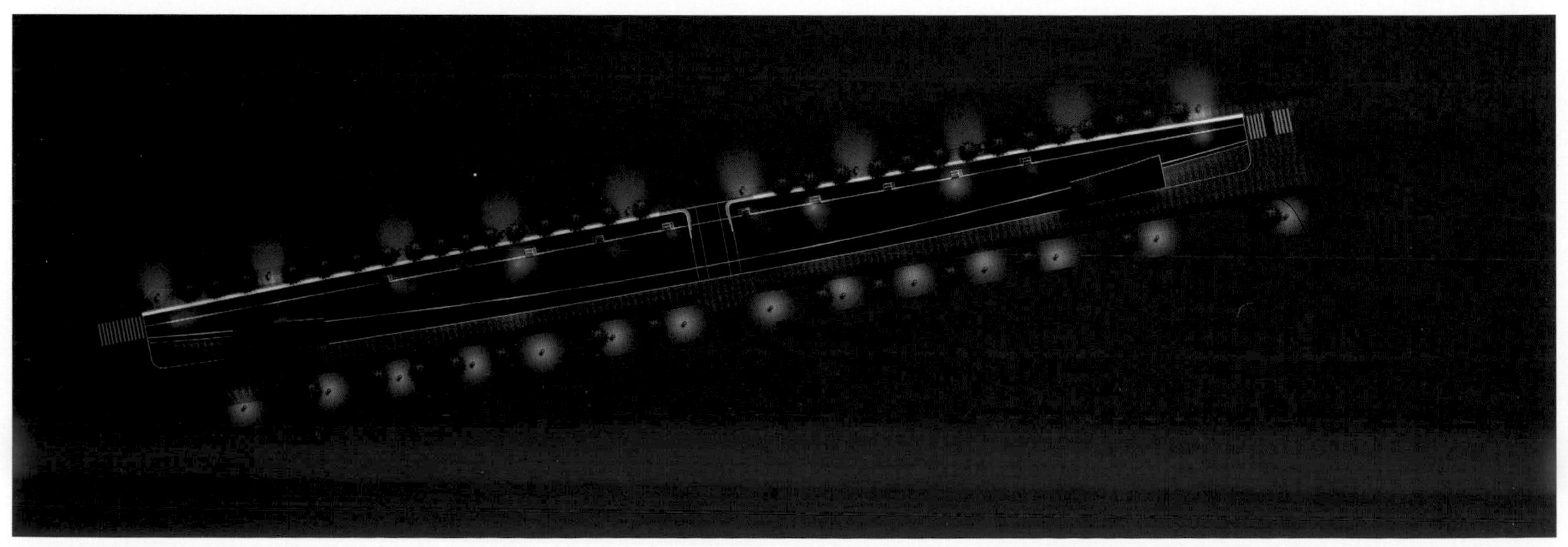

(left) Spielbudenplatz by night.
(left bottom) Aerial view by night.
(right) Night reflections on polished asphalt.
(below) Street furniture and railings, various perspectives.

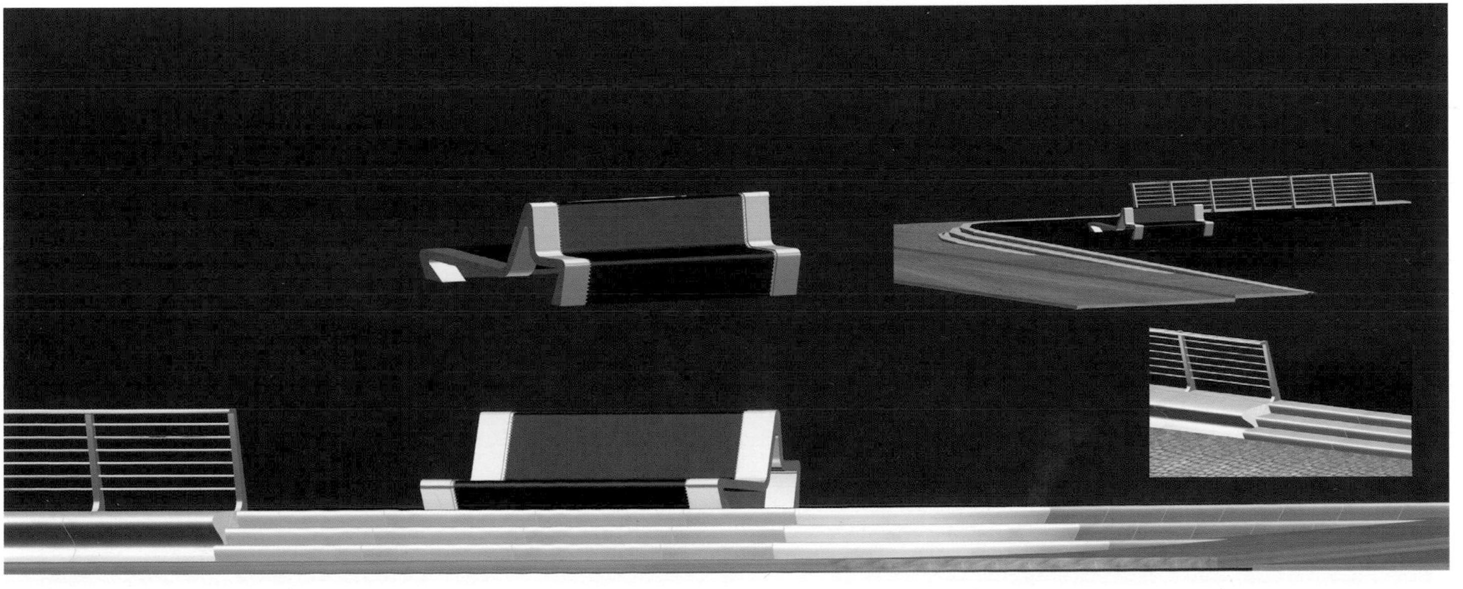

Tram Spaces and Places — Mornington Crescent, London

This is a fascinating multilayered project — a new means of transport used as an agent of urban change. We won it in a limited competition involving 5 high profile design offices. It involved pedestrian movement studies and urban analysis/design for an area of some 18km^2, extending 500 metres either side of the proposed Cross River Tram route. The analysis pin-pointed locations where the new tramline could act as a catalyst for local urban improvements. A series of demonstration projects is to be realised along the route ahead of the construction of the tramline. The London Cross River Tram will emulate European systems and models praised by the National Audit Office in a recent report, which highlighted the fact that co-ordination with existing transport services and integration into urban areas was a critical factor in their success. TRAM SPACES AND PLACES funding comes from the European Commission regeneration fund INTERREG IIIB set up to promote common approaches to transport issues. It is matched by funding from the Cross River Partnership.

Mornington Crescent, one of the most neglected public areas in Camden Town, was singled out as one of the locations where the new London tramline could bring about change. This proposal is intended as an indication of what could be achieved in this location, that has suffered years of neglect, in terms of public domain regeneration through the introduction of kerb/sign free shared drive/walk surface solutions combined with de-cluttering of the streetscape.

Camden Council advised that a 1998 count at Mornington Crescent indicated traffic flows of between 20,000 and 25,000 cars per day. This was before the London Congestion Charge was introduced. These figures are directly comparable with locations like Drachten or Amsterdam in Holland, where successful kerb/sign free shared drive/walk surface solutions have been deployed. As a result of the traffic congestion charging in Central London the flows at Mornington Crescent could in fact now be even lower. We have consulted our ideas with Prof John Adams, Ben Hamilton-Baillie and Koop Kerkstra from Drachten.

client / owner	other key consultants	location	awards
Camden Borough Council / Cross River Tram Partnership	Intelligent Space Partnership	Camden, London, UK	Winner of an invited competition

Our design proposal draws inspiration from the work and life of Richard Cobden whose statue stands, presently forlorn, in the middle of the traffic island at Mornington Crescent. The present urban clutter with railings, lights and roads signs is removed and so created shared street surface becomes the canvas for an artwork. Its pattern symbolically represents the free flowing Free Trade ideals, of which Cobden was the creator, and his love Peace and Cosmopolitanism that led him to deplore any survival of the colonial system. Stainless steel objects symbolize corn 'kernels' of his Anti-Corn-Law-League. These artifacts are placed in strategic positions where they also act as direction markers and separators for vehicular traffic.

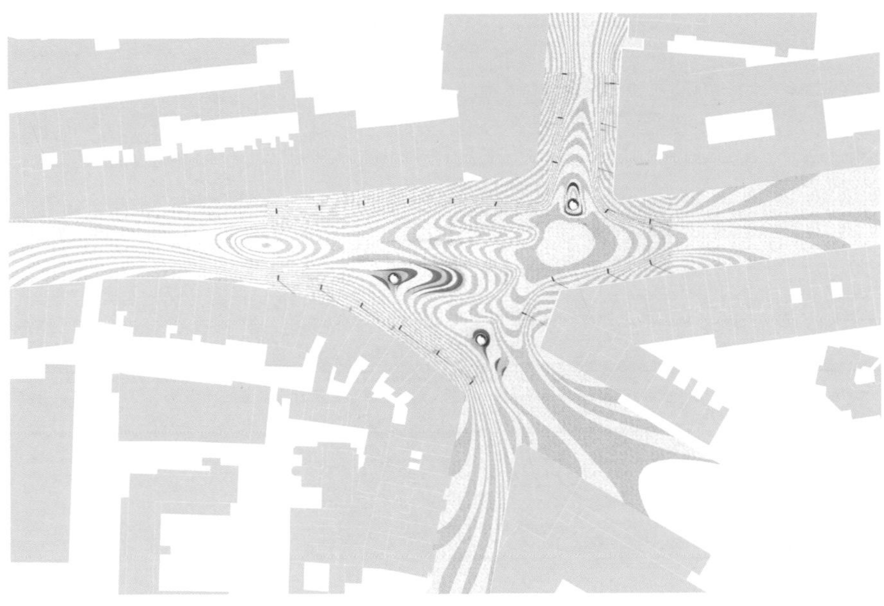

(left) General view of proposal.

(top) Plan showing art work at shared street/ pavement level.

(below) Close-up of proposal showing stainless steel 'kernels'.

(bottom) Tram Route map with 500m/500m project zone.

(right) View of existing Mornington Crescent.

(bottom right) Aerial view of existing Mornington Crescent.

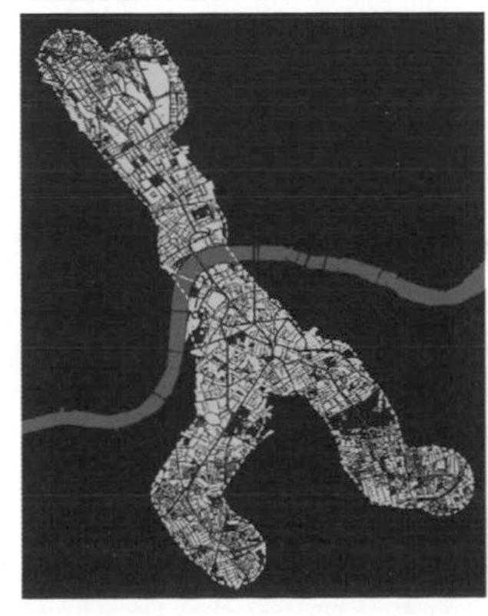

Rhine Boulevard, Koblenz

As part of the 2011 German Federal Garden Show, the river banks along the Rhine and Moselle will be redesigned in the urban area of Koblenz. The new design aims at improving the connection between the city and its two rivers.

In between the river park at the 'Deutsches Eck', a tourist attraction — the new 'antipole' called Rhine Boulevard is located in front of the city palace stretching over a length of 1.8 kilometres. A 110m long broad staircase will help disseminate visitors over a wider area at the river bank. The planned promenade will be developed as an inner city open space built on a consistent design language using conforming furnishings and structures, and a uniform surface material.

The functional areas for the different types of traffic (tourist buses, bikes, delivery trucks, pedestrians) will be separated but conveniently inter-connected. The surface will be covered with large pavers at a minimum length of 120cm and a width of 40-60cm in a variety of patterns. The pavers are natural stones inlaid on a concrete mounting plate.

The central part of the boulevard is characterized by old sycamore trees complemented by new tree plantings. The ground will be built with crushed natural stone as a water-bound paving.

client / owner	other key consultants	location	awards
BUGA Koblenz 2011 GmbH, Germany	Von Canal Architekten, Koblenz	Koblenz, Germany	1st Place, National competition

(left) Steps at the river bank.
(top) Rhine boulevard between castle and "Deutsches Eck".
(below) Boulevard with old sycamore trees.

Institutional and Commercial

Monash University Caulfield Campus Landscape Masterplan, Melbourne

The continuing development of the Monash University's Caulfield Campus (Melbourne, Australia) proposes the reoccupation of the campus grounds, improving connections and creating a series of open spaces which address the increasing urbanization of the site as a place for learning and living.

The concept proposes a dynamic landscape that reflects the diversity and creativity of the academic and social life of the campus.

The landscape is comprised of 3 key spaces.

The Common Lawn provides a central space which will become the heart of campus life. Capable of sustaining large events and a space for relaxation in quiet times, the concept offers a balance between flexibility for large groups and the needs of a more individual appreciation of the designed environment.

The new Ceremonial Entry is an important new focus and will essentially be an extension of the Common Lawn, a promontory of campus space leading to the public realm outside the campus. A grassed agora will provide a focal space for special events, gathering and performances.

The Eastern Courtyard is a more contemplative/ intimate space for smaller scale university activities. A 'sculptural landscape' provides a diversity of spaces for relaxation, outdoor teaching and exhibition of student artwork.

(bottom) Landscape concept – Campus Context.
(right top) View of the Eastern Courtyard from walkway above.
(right bottom) Landscape concept plan – Eastern Courtyard.

client / owner
Monash University, Australia

location
Monash University Caulfield Campus, Melbourne, Australia

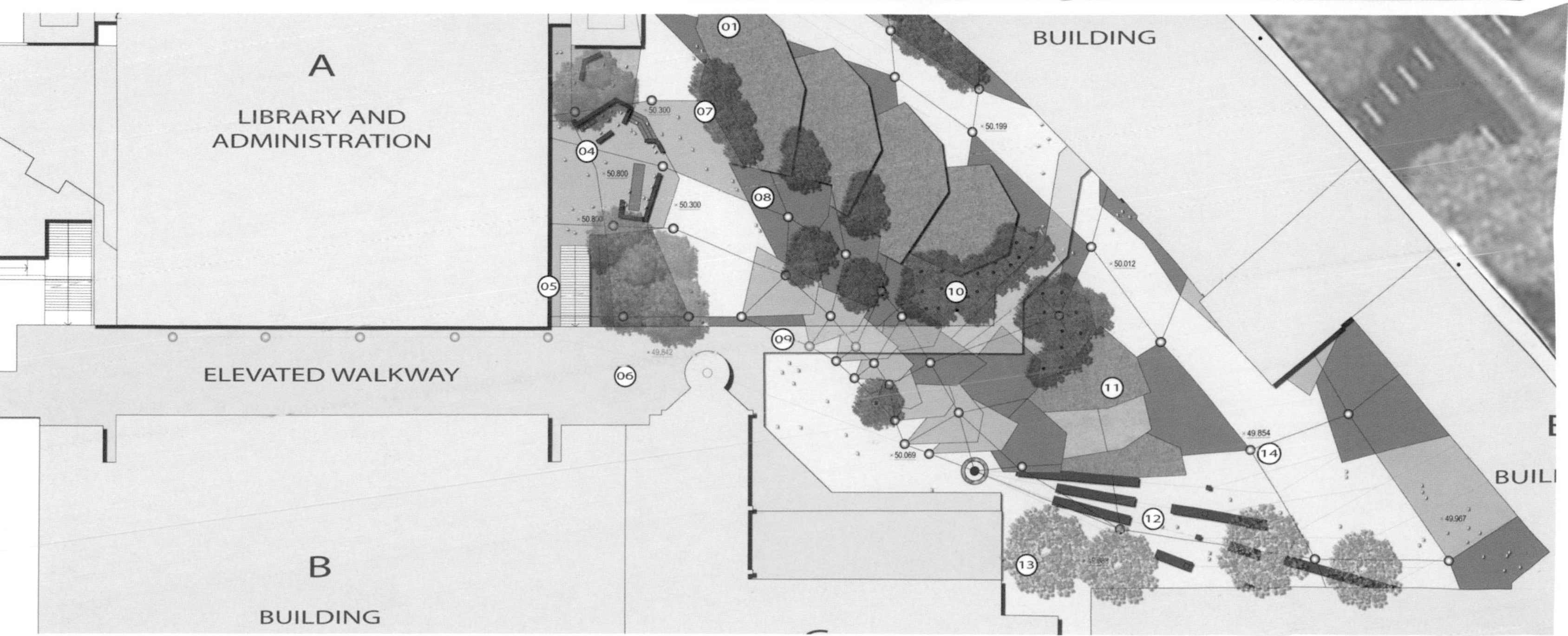

(top) View north west towards library and overhead walkway.

(bottom) View towards the Fine Arts Building.

(right) View of Ceremonial Entrance and Green Agora.

(left top) View of Common Lawn towards Library.

(left bottom) View of Common Lawn from overhead walkway.

(right) Landscape concept plan – The Common Lawn and Ceremonial Entrance.

(bottom) View of grass steps and Green Agora.

Deakin University Rainforest Courtyard, Melbourne

In response to Deakin University's mission statement of 'Relevant', 'Responsive', 'Innovative' and 'Progressive', the Rainforest Courtyard uses the Voronoi tessellation to generate spatial reality. Embedding the theme of bio-diversity the courtyard becomes a Victorian temperate rainforest emerging from a graphical ground plane of patterned concrete and artificial terrain objects.

(bottom) Architectural Concept Roof Plan.

(right) View of Rainforest Courtyard towards the cluster of taut fabric pillars.

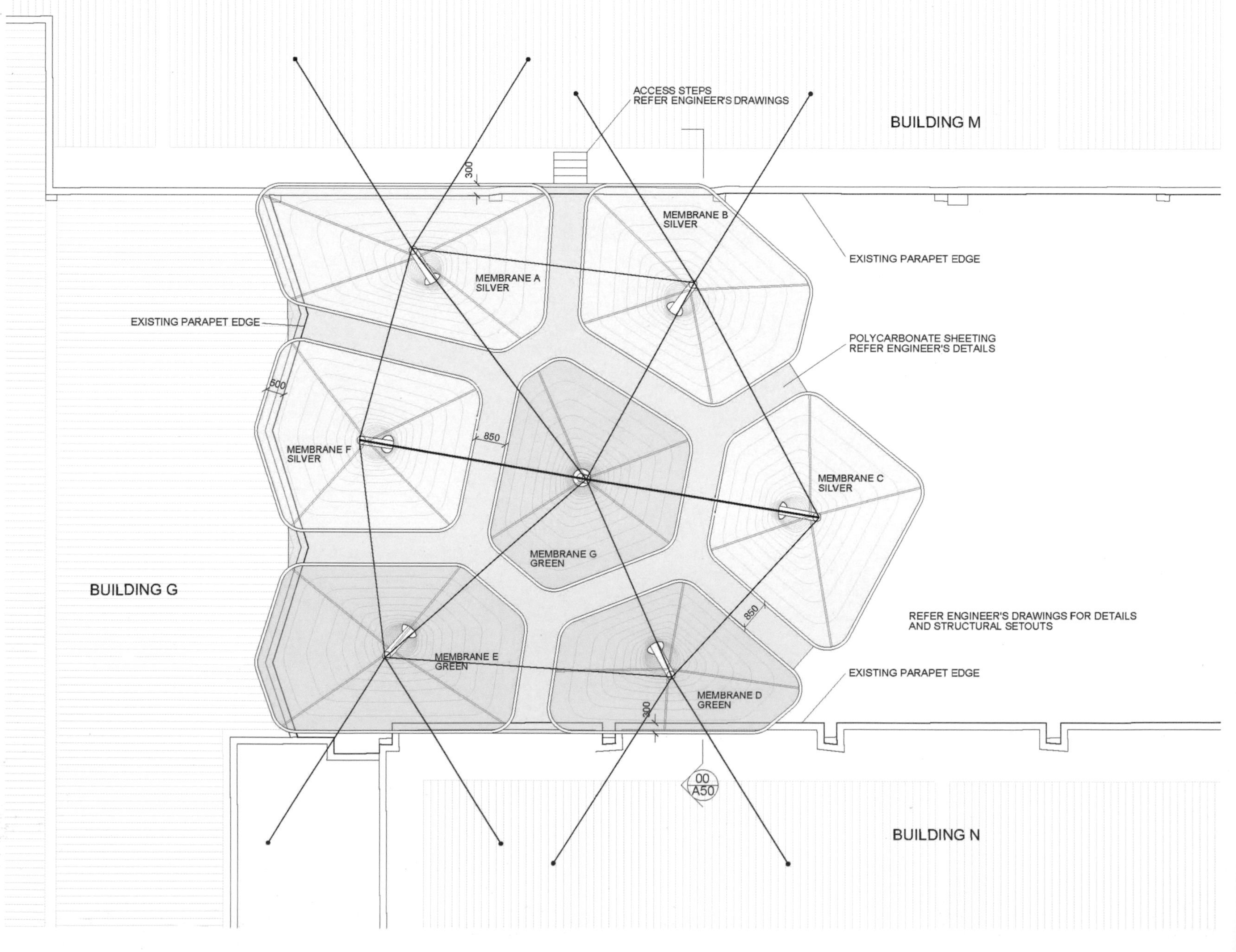

client / owner
Deakin University, Australia

other key consultants
Minifie Nixon Architects

location
Deakin University Burwood Campus, Melbourne, Australia

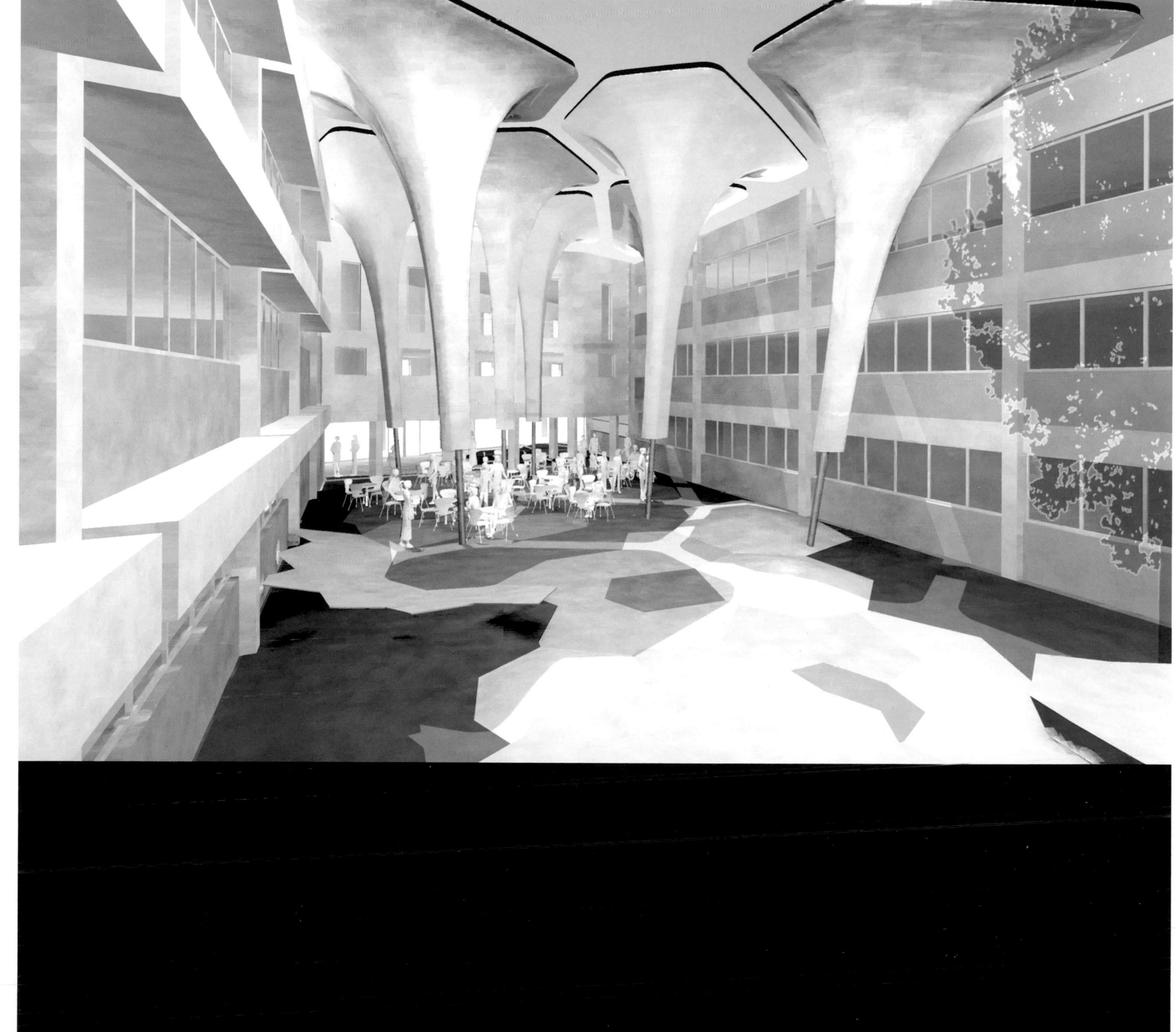

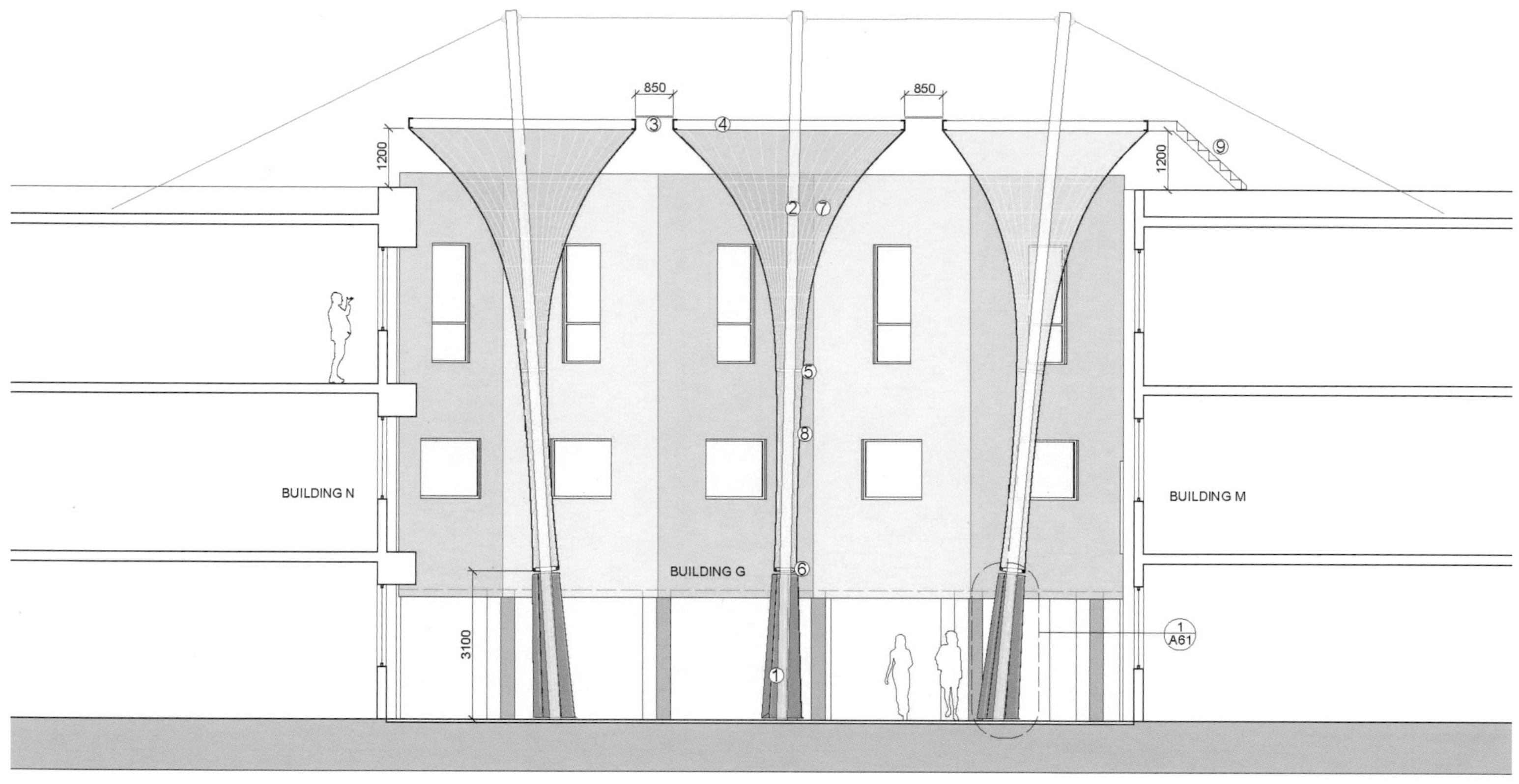
850
850
1200
1200
BUILDING N
BUILDING G
BUILDING M
3100
1
A61

(left top) Architectural Concept Section.
(left bottom) Landscape Concept Plan.
(right) View of partially shaded café space under taut fabric pillars.

University of British Columbia (University Boulevard Competition), Vancouver

The winning competition entry for the University of British Columbia's University Boulevard weaves disparate areas of the campus into a unified whole to create a vital nexus of community. It is an urban design solution that successfully integrates social and academic realms, buildings and landscapes. Memorable places nurture interaction, connect to climate and context, and project the campus into the global conversation.

The University Boulevard is a landscaped promenade paved with a rich woven pattern inspired by the artistic weaving of native cultures. A central rill reinforces the visual axis — a silver thread — while collecting the abundant rainwater. Under the elms, carpets of native grasses create rain gardens and places for interaction. The eastern extension of University Boulevard rises up to meet the central axis of the campus and becomes an ecological demonstration of water collection and purification using native species and creative civil engineering practices to deal with the significant amount of storm water that is characteristic of the Vancouver area. A fountain at the intersection of the Main Mall acts as the source, linking University Boulevard to the historic campus center. The existing bosque of oaks becomes a more accessible eave of trees, paths, and activities.

The major open spaces converge at University Square where the weaving of paths and districts is celebrated. A new "lantern" entry to the University bookstore combines with granite seat walls, new sloping north and south knolls, and a richly detailed paving to define an inviting yet flexible plaza. Secondary spaces are arranged to create quiet, informal paths and courtyards. These spaces, combined with green roofs and roof gardens, provide a hierarchy of social spaces from public through private uses.

©Olin Partnership

©Olin Partnership

(top right) Perspective of ecostream.
(right) Section/elevation of ecostream.

client / owner
University of British Columbia

other key consultants
Moore Ruble Yudell Architects & Planners

location
Vancouver, British Columbia, Canada

awards
American Institute of Architects, National Honor Award for Regional and Urban Planning 2006; Royal Architectural Institute of Canada Urban Design Award 2006.

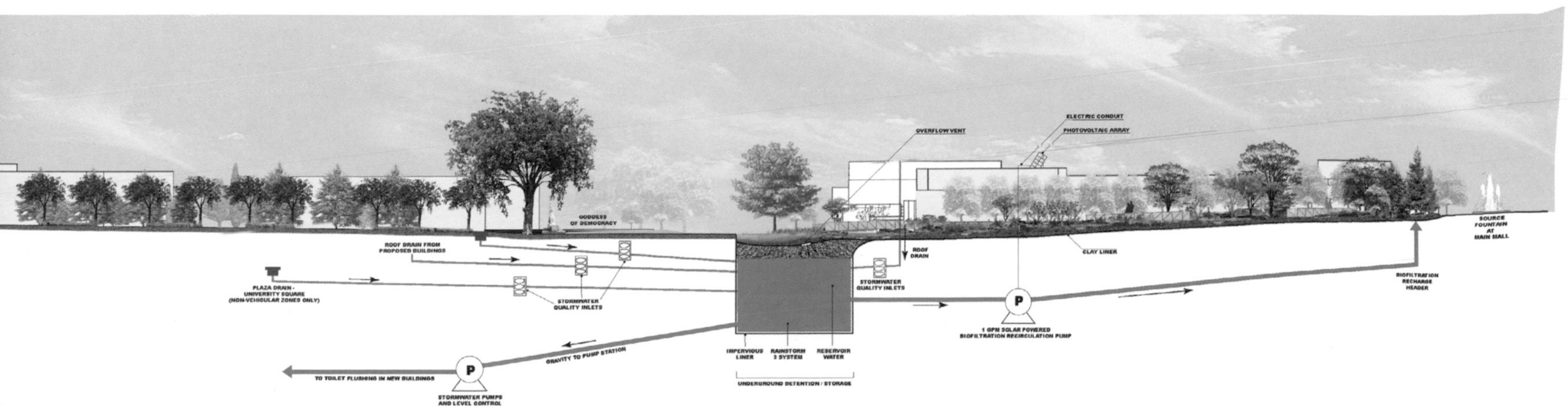

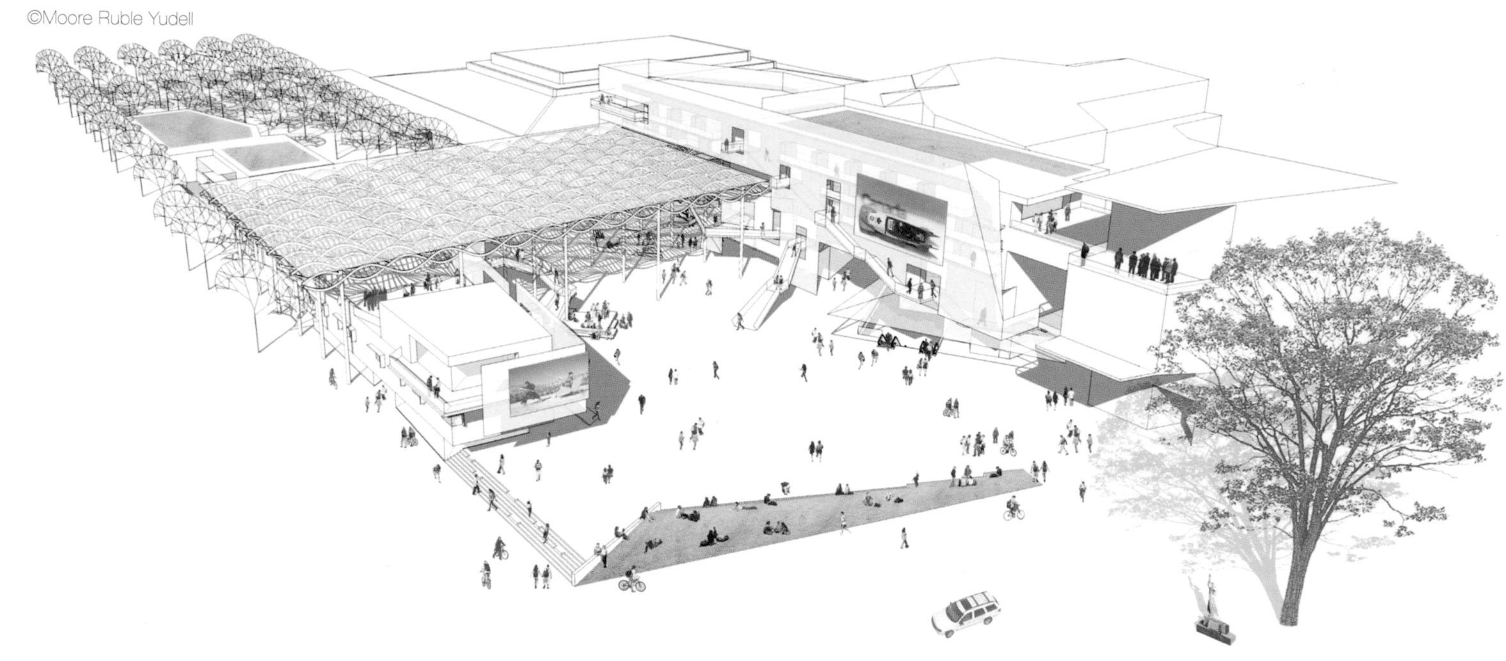

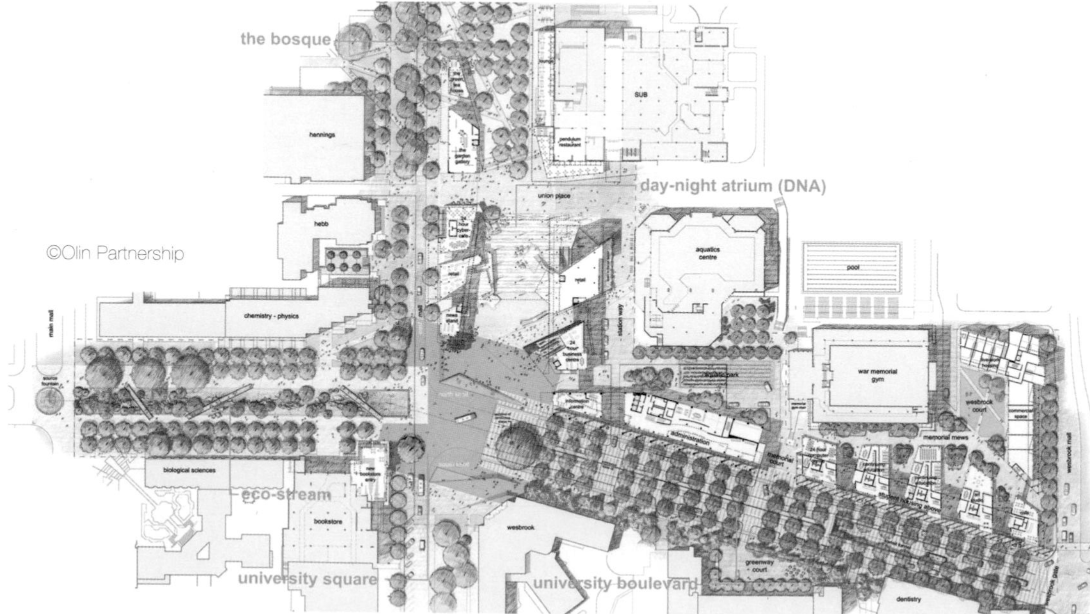

(top) Aerial perspective of University Square.
(left) University of British Columbia site plan.
(top right) View northeast to University Square.
(right) University Square meeting point.

©Moore Ruble Yudell

©Moore Ruble Yudell

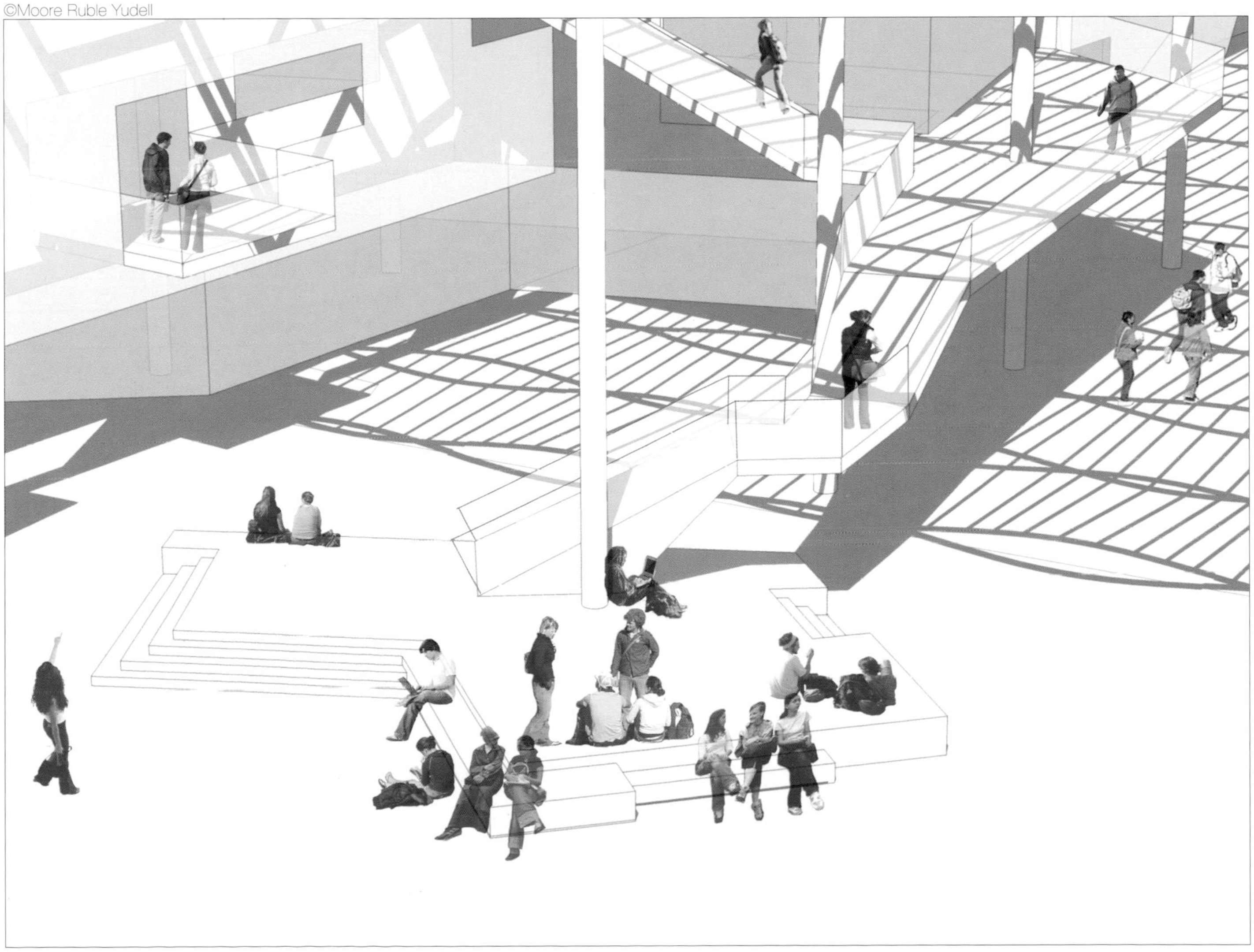

Ducie High School, Manchester

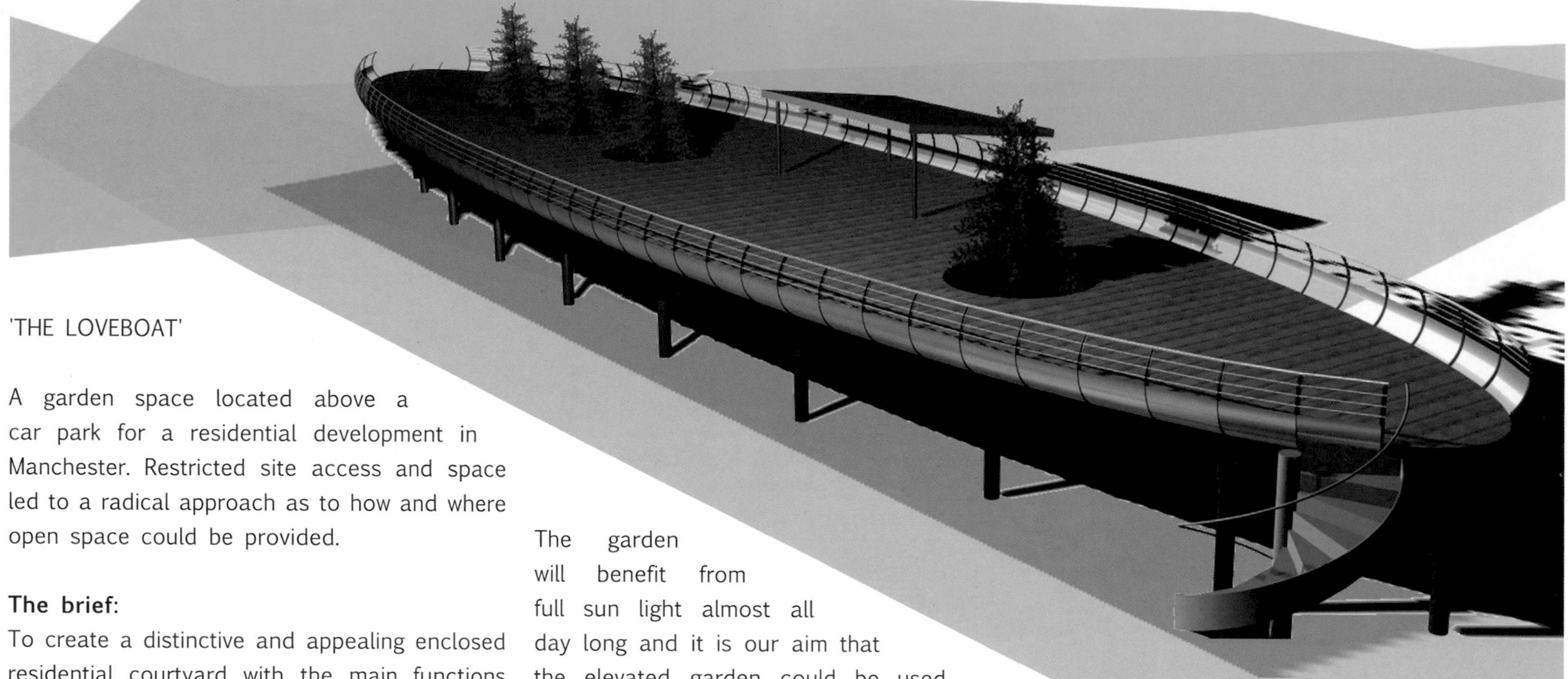

'THE LOVEBOAT'

A garden space located above a car park for a residential development in Manchester. Restricted site access and space led to a radical approach as to how and where open space could be provided.

The brief:
To create a distinctive and appealing enclosed residential courtyard with the main functions being amenity and parking. Due to planning obligations, an area of open amenity space for residents was required.

The design:
The courtyard was to be generally hard paved with good quality materials that provide texture and quality to the whole scheme. Clear, safe and easy vehicular and pedestrian circulation within the courtyard can be achieved through the manipulation of the paving materials.

In the centre of the courtyard a very unusual elevated garden sits above the proposed car parking to provide a feature of stunning visual interest and veritable amenity value.

The raised garden will be a valuable outdoor space for residents, used for relaxing and meeting. The use of high quality materials, bespoke features and specimen planting will create an attractive yet functional garden space which will also provide a stunning point of visual interest from the surrounding apartments.

The garden will benefit from full sun light almost all day long and it is our aim that the elevated garden could be used throughout the day time and evening. This can be achieved and encouraged through the installation of strategically placed lights that will enhance the key features and create a feeling of safety and comfort. The night scene will be a very important element to the scheme and therefore lighting will provide both aesthetic and functional illumination to ensure the garden deck and adjacent parking are appropriately lit.

The deck itself is made from a simple steel structure with self draining safety surfacing, used in a range of shapes and colours. The space is enclosed by a marine style steel railing, which has an adjacent raised planter, interrupted by timber seating. This planter will provide an environment from which specimen climbers will be encouraged to grow up, over and through the railing in order to drape over the deck sides. The establishment of these climbers will soften the transition between the lower parking and the elevated deck area. Simple clipped hedges run though the centre of the deck creating smaller individual spaces within the garden.

On the northern edge of the site a belt of evergreen trees provide shelter from the prevailing wind and offer a visual screen between the existing properties and the proposed development. Within the courtyard, the planting of trees and shrubs create focus and calm through the use of vertical elements.

Through the centre of the site fastigiate trees are positioned in a linear form. Where they meet with the 'Green Deck' they penetrate holes created in the deck to form a canopy above. The position of the trees will help to anchor the 'Green Deck' by providing a visual connection between the two levels.

Overall, the landscape proposal endeavours to accentuate and enhance the quality of the proposed development whilst maintaining the successful function and ergonomics required for a scheme of this nature.

(left) elevation view.
(right) ground view.
(middle & bottom) apartment views.

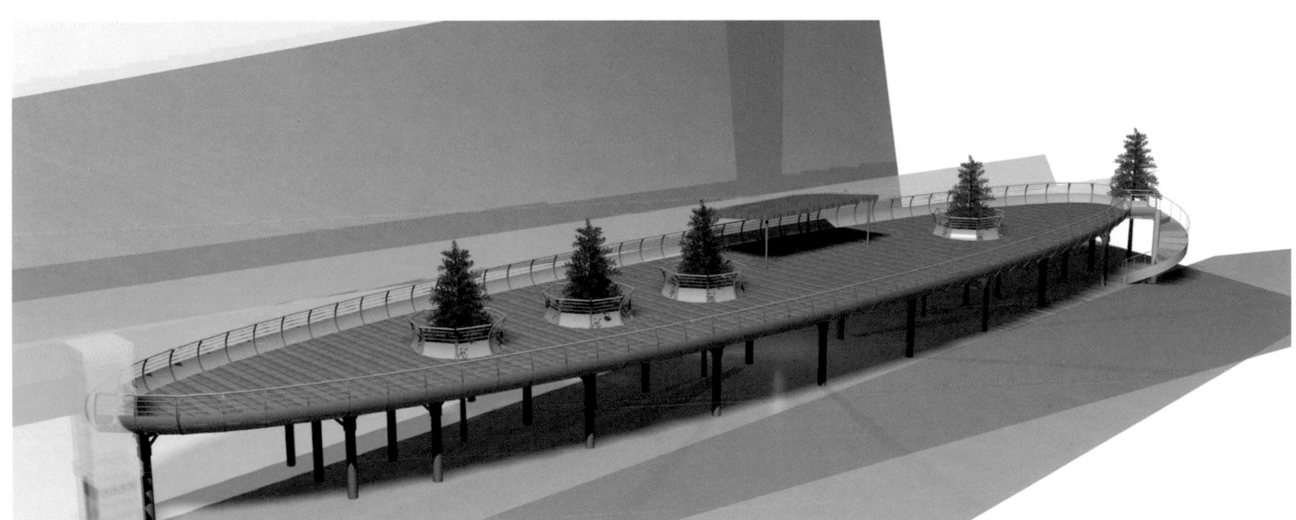

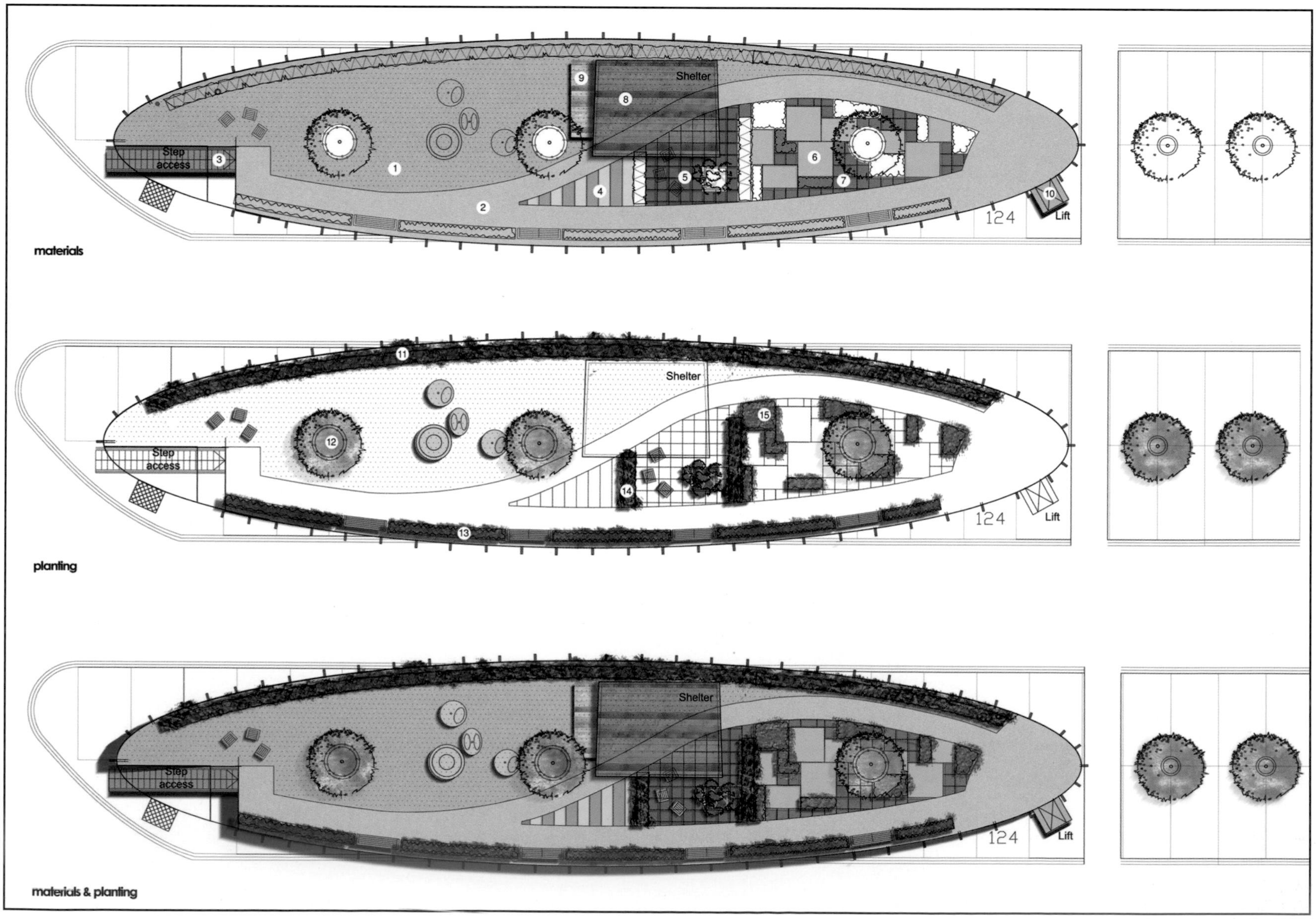

Shelter
Step access
Lift
124

materials

Shelter
Step access
Lift
124

planting

Shelter
Step access
Lift
124

materials & planting

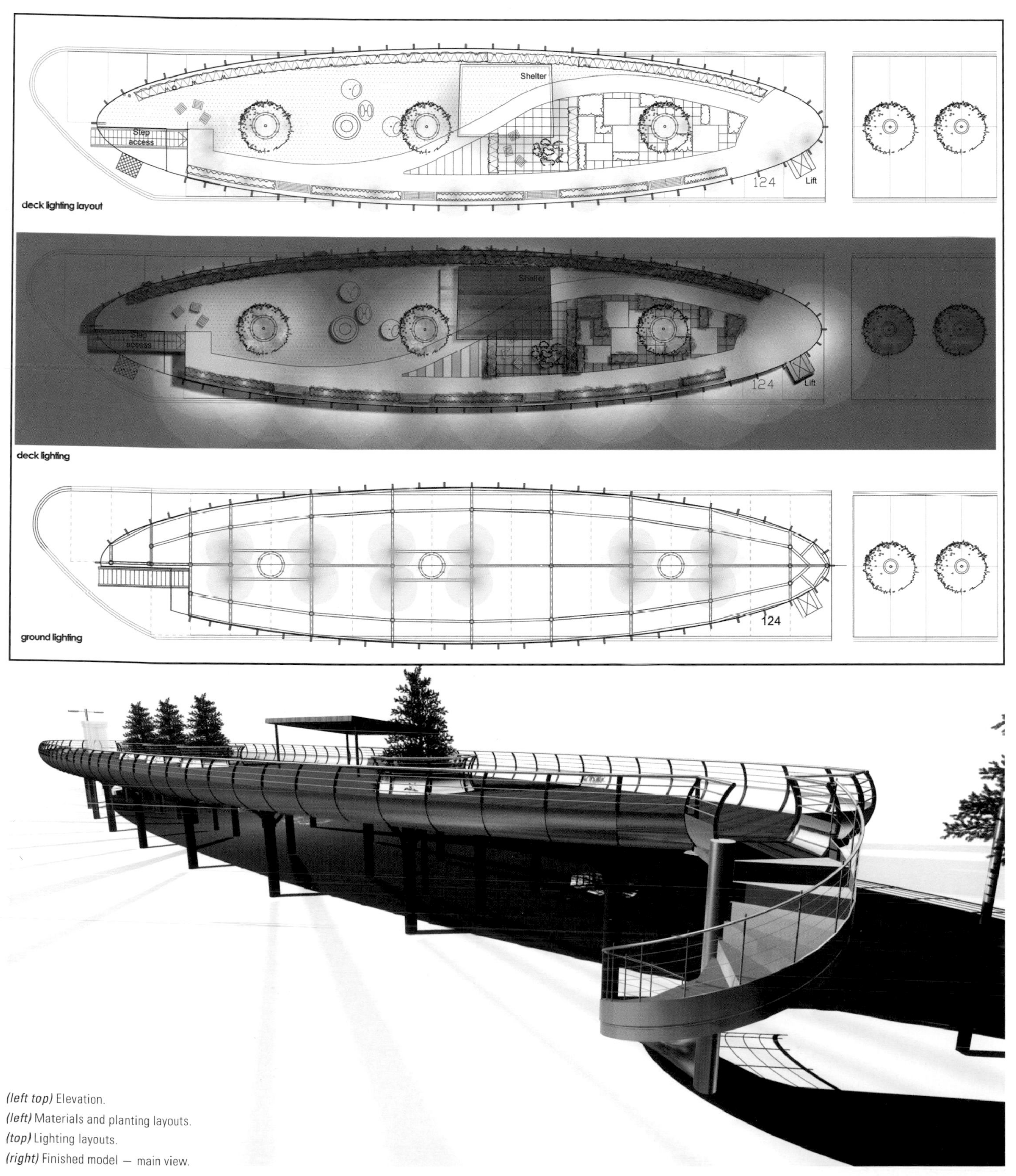

(left top) Elevation.
(left) Materials and planting layouts.
(top) Lighting layouts.
(right) Finished model — main view.

Abbotsford Cultural Centre, Abbotsford

The Abbotsford Cultural Centre is part of a larger 150 million dollar investment into culture and sport for the city of Abbotsford in 2007-2009. The Cultural Centre itself is a museum and classroom to showcase Abbotsford's unique history and to train and teach artists and historians. The building architecture is modern and dramatic with metal wrapped walls and unique LED lighting effects washed onto the façade.

VDZ inc. prepared site development concepts that served to provide outdoor display space for the museum itself. Three major concrete pads are integrated into the museum grounds for display of agricultural equipment or other industrial machines from the city's working history.

The soft landscape is developed to represent significant aspects of Abbotsford's development as a modern city. The south end of the building is planted with large, native trees to represent Abbotsford's beginnings as a timber/lumber centre within the region. The long, articulated bands of planting and cobble represent the city's agricultural heritage. The hard-surfaced plaza areas represent the city's transformation to a modern urban centre of the Fraser Valley. Within the plaza area, a crushed glass 'stream' metaphor is curved through the base plane. This metaphor is representative of the Fraser River Valley. This River system was the primary source of food, transportation, and wealth for the indigenous peoples and subsequent generations of European settlers.

©Hughes Condon Marler

(top) Computer rendering.
(right) Hardscape.
(bottom) Preferred Scheme.
(bottom left) Aerial view, model.
(bottom right) Section AA.

©Hughes Condon Marler

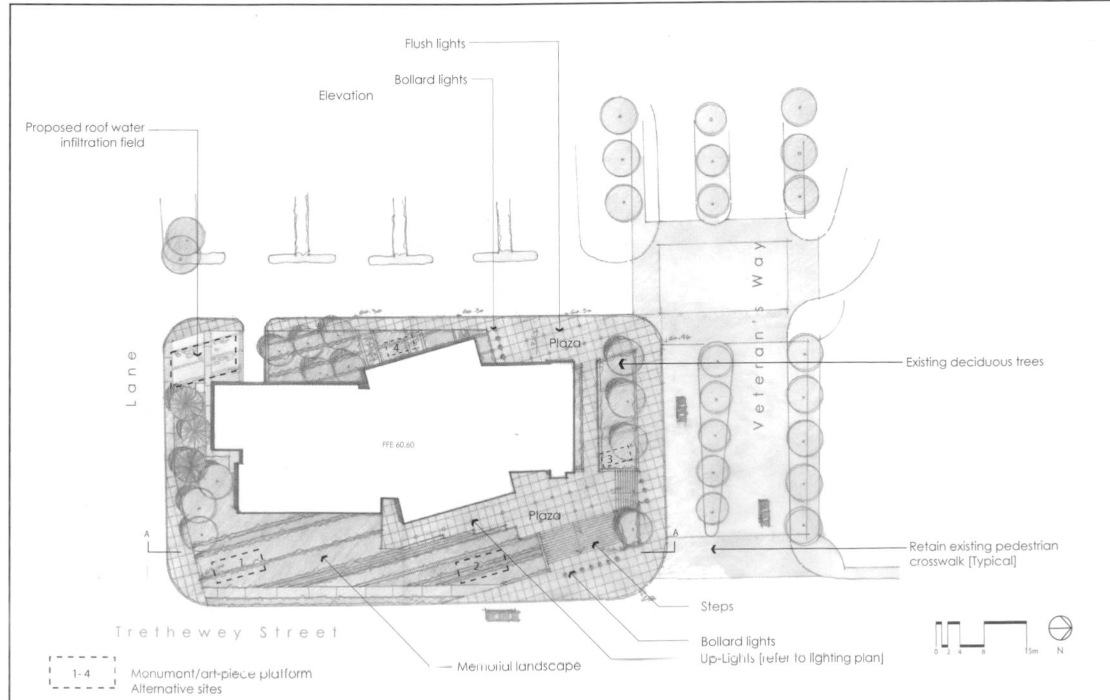

client / owner
City of Abbotsford, BC, Canada

other key consultants
Architects: Hughes Condon Marler; Engineering: SL engineers

location
Abbotsford, British Columbia, Canada

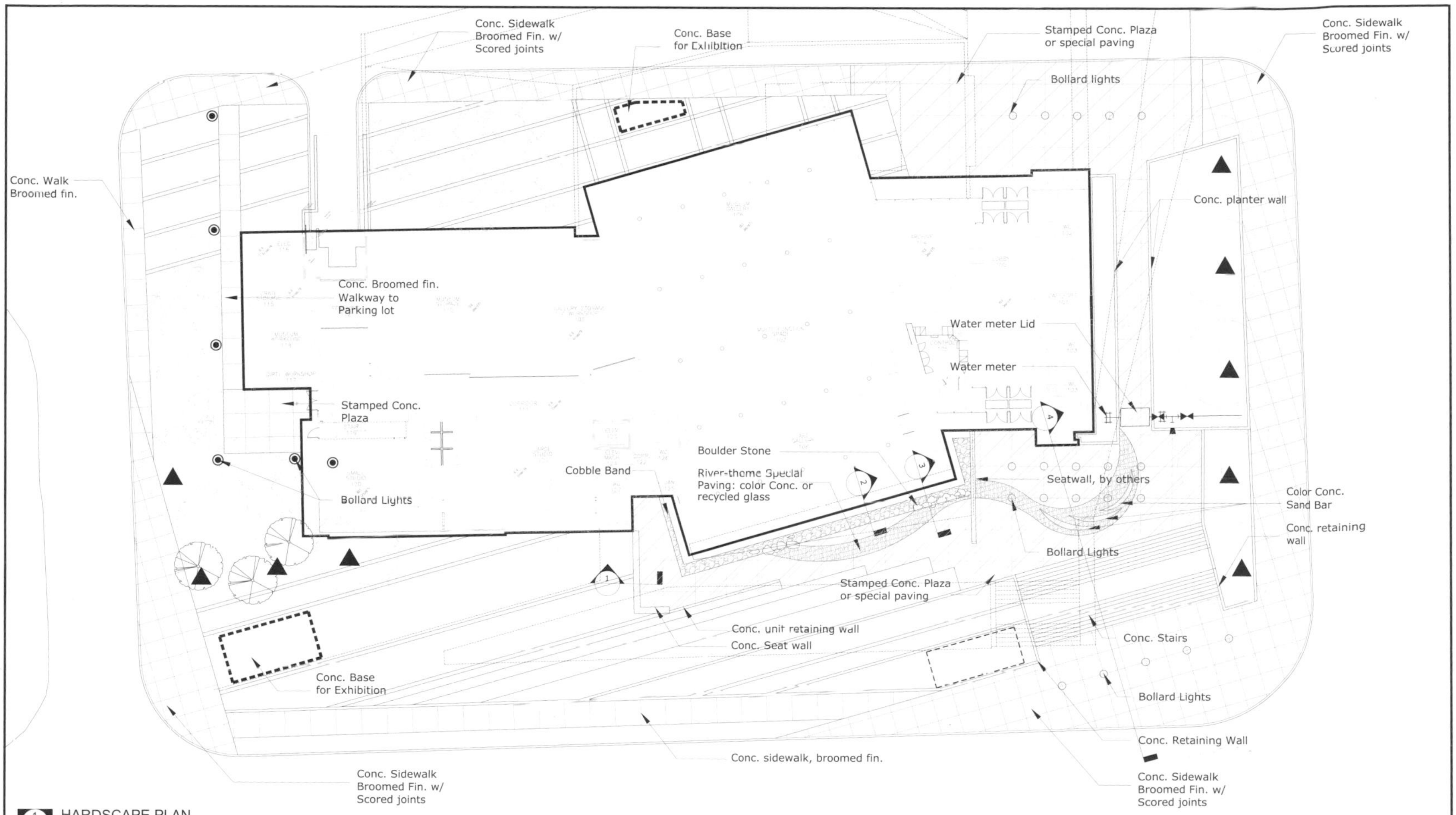

Conc. Sidewalk Broomed Fin. w/ Scored joints
Conc. Base for Exhibition
Stamped Conc. Plaza or special paving
Conc. Sidewalk Broomed Fin. w/ Scored joints
Bollard lights
Conc. Walk Broomed fin.
Conc. planter wall
Conc. Broomed fin. Walkway to Parking lot
Water meter Lid
Water meter
Stamped Conc. Plaza
Boulder Stone
Cobble Band
River-theme Special Paving: color Conc. or recycled glass
Seatwall, by others
Bollard Lights
Color Conc. Sand Bar
Conc. retaining wall
Bollard Lights
Stamped Conc. Plaza or special paving
Conc. unit retaining wall
Conc. Seat wall
Conc. Stairs
Conc. Base for Exhibition
Bollard Lights
Conc. Retaining Wall
Conc. sidewalk, broomed fin.
Conc. Sidewalk Broomed Fin. w/ Scored joints
Conc. Sidewalk Broomed Fin. w/ Scored joints

HARDSCAPE PLAN
SCALE: 1 : 150

	Legend	Material	Quantity
Hardscape		Conc. walk, broomed fin.	853.9 sqm
		Stamped Conc. or special paving	504.1 sqm
		Cobble Paving	50.7 sqm
		Conc. Steps	16 steps, 15linear m
		Recycled Glass	42.8 sqm
		Colored Concrete Sand Bar	3.6 sqm

3.5M HT PEDESTRIAN LIGHT
Callisto Series Model Cal61
by LUMEC *
www.lumec.com

BOLLARD LIGHT
Callisto Series Model CalB2
by LUMEC *
www.lumec.com

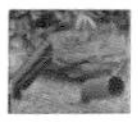

TREE UPLIGHT
Delta Star MR16
by B-K Lighting *
www.bklighting.com

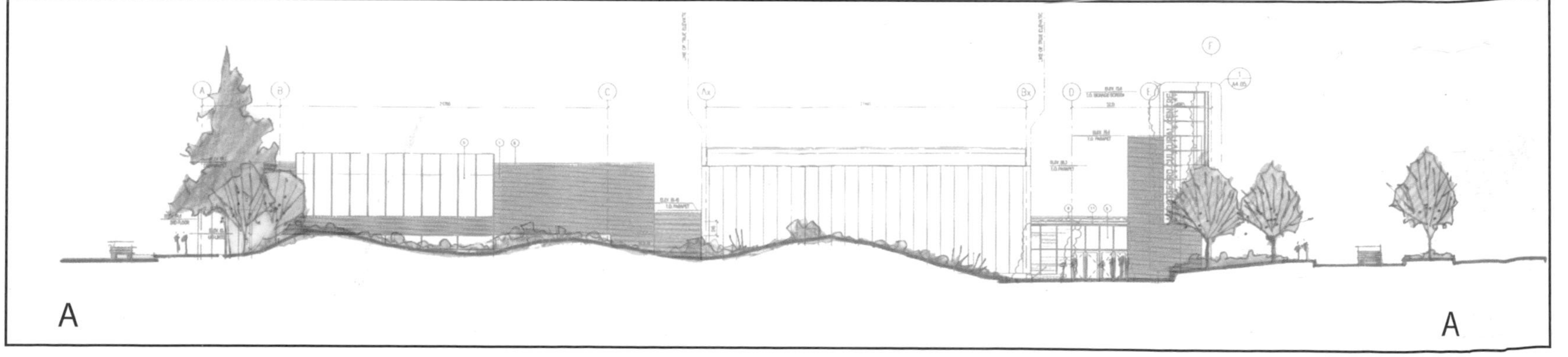

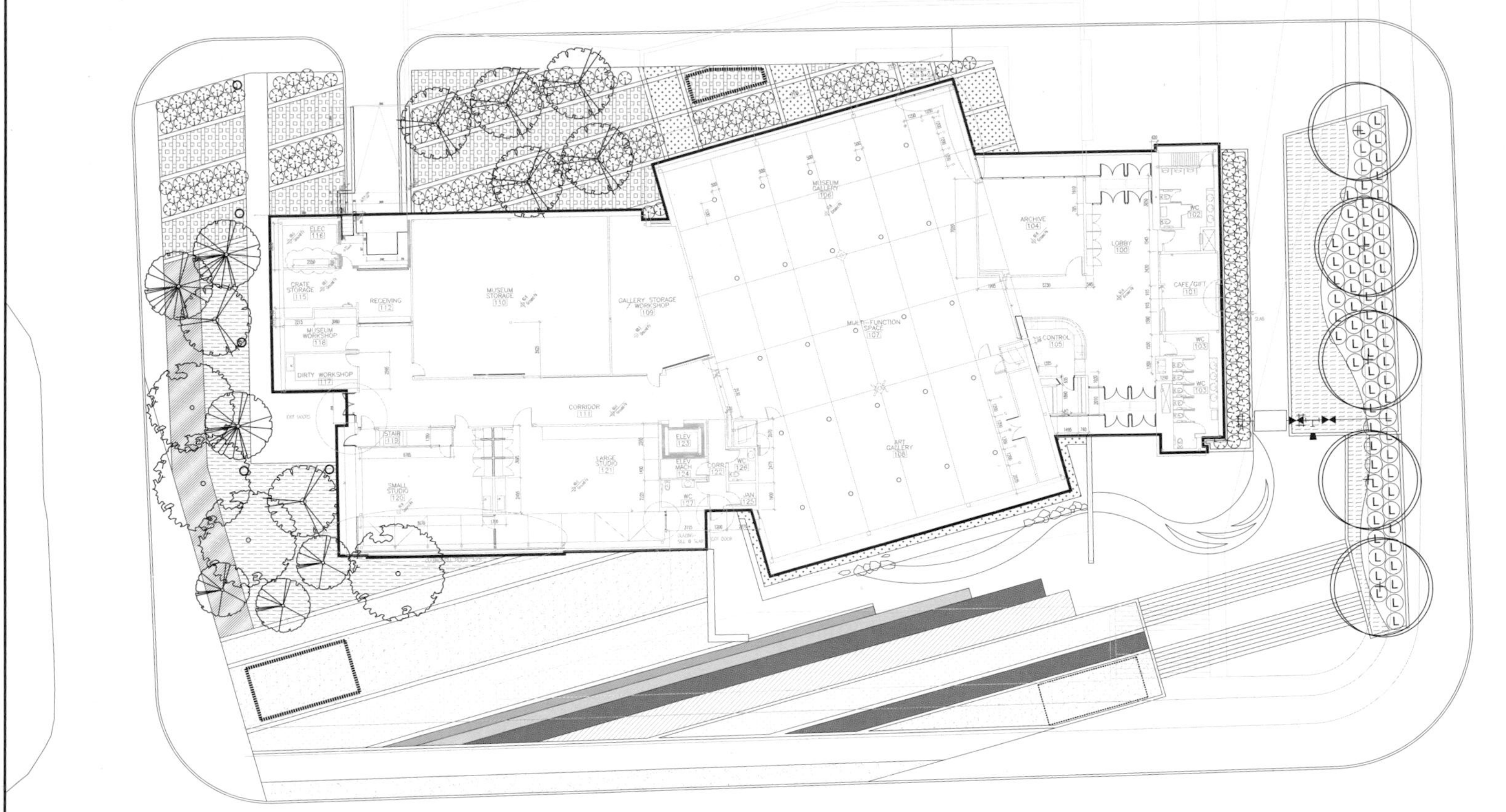

PLANTING PLAN
SCALE: 1 : 150

PROPOSED TREE SCHEDULE

LEGEND	AB	BOTANICAL NAME	COMMON NAME	QTY	SIZE	COMMENT
		Cedrus atlantica glauca	Blue Atlas cedar	4	6'-8'	Conifer 1
		Picea gluaca hudsonii	White Spruce	3	9'	Conifer 2
		Abies concolor candicans	Candicans white fir	7	6'	Conifer 3
		exist. tree	exist. tree	5	NA	
		Heritage Rhododendron	Heritage Rhododendron	3	NA	

PROPOSED PLANT SCHEDULE

LEGEND	AB	BOTANICAL NAME	COMMON NAME	QTY	SIZE	COMMENT
		Elymus mollis	American Dunegrass	203.2 m²	#1	low profile plant 1
		Juncus effusus	Common Rush	80.9 m²	#1	low profile plant 2
		Festuca ovina glauca	Blue fescue	196.0 m²	#1	low profile plant 3
		Panicum virgatum	Switch Grass	20.9 m²	#1	low profile plant 4
		Pennisetum varieties	Cane Grass	30.0 m²	#1	low profile plant 5
		Vaccinium ovatum	Evergreen huckleberry	66.9 m²	#1	forest understory
		Cornus canadensis	Bunchberry dogwood	153.5 m²	9cm	forest understory
		Iris pseudacorus L.	Yellow Iris	60.1 m²	#1	Wetland Species
L		Leucothoe axillaris	Coastal doghobble	70	#1	Shrub
		Potentillia fruticosa 'Gold Star'	Potentilla gold star	232	#1	Shrub
		Blechnum spicant	Deer Fern	144.7 m²	#1	Groundcover
		Fragaria chiloensis	Beach Strawberry	90.9 m²	#1	Groundcover

©Hughes Condon Marler

(above) Planting plan.
(left) Computer rendering.
(right top) Recycled glass paving band detail.
(right middle) Stair and planting slope detail.
(right) Iris band and cobble detail.
(far right) Seawall detail.

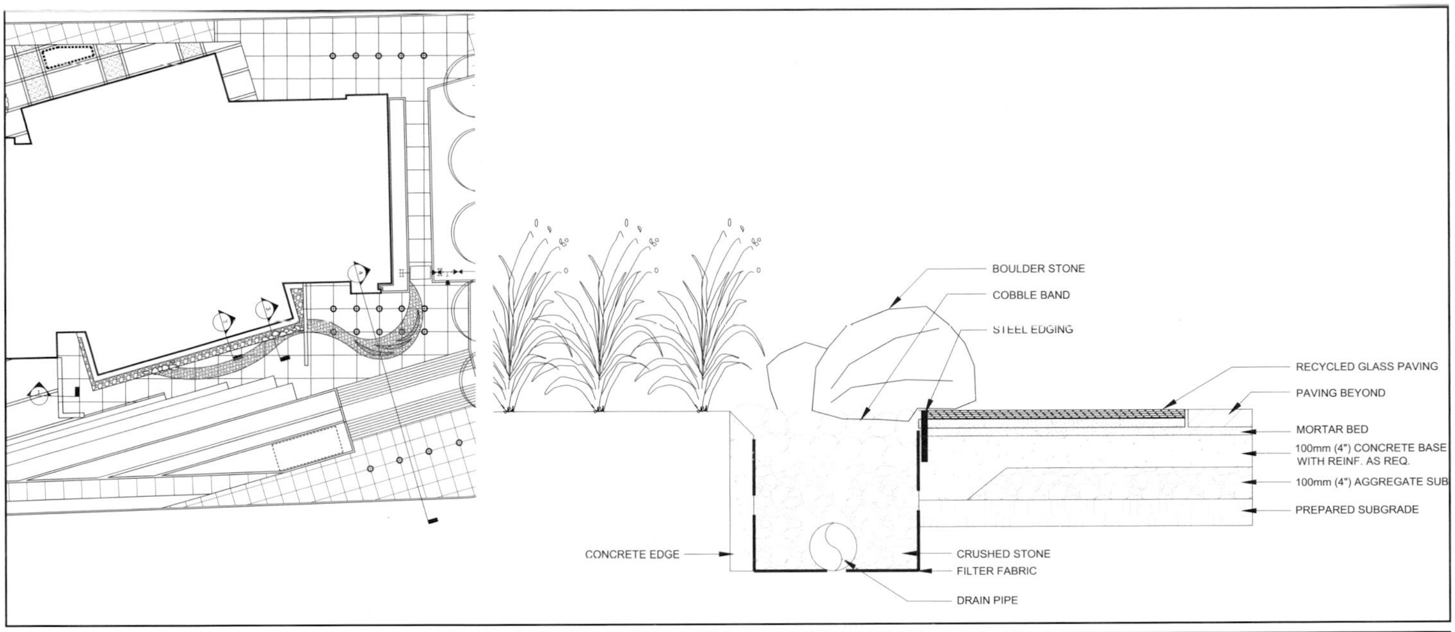

BOULDER STONE
COBBLE BAND
STEEL EDGING
RECYCLED GLASS PAVING
PAVING BEYOND
MORTAR BED
100mm (4") CONCRETE BASE WITH REINF. AS REQ.
100mm (4") AGGREGATE SUB
PREPARED SUBGRADE
CONCRETE EDGE
CRUSHED STONE
FILTER FABRIC
DRAIN PIPE

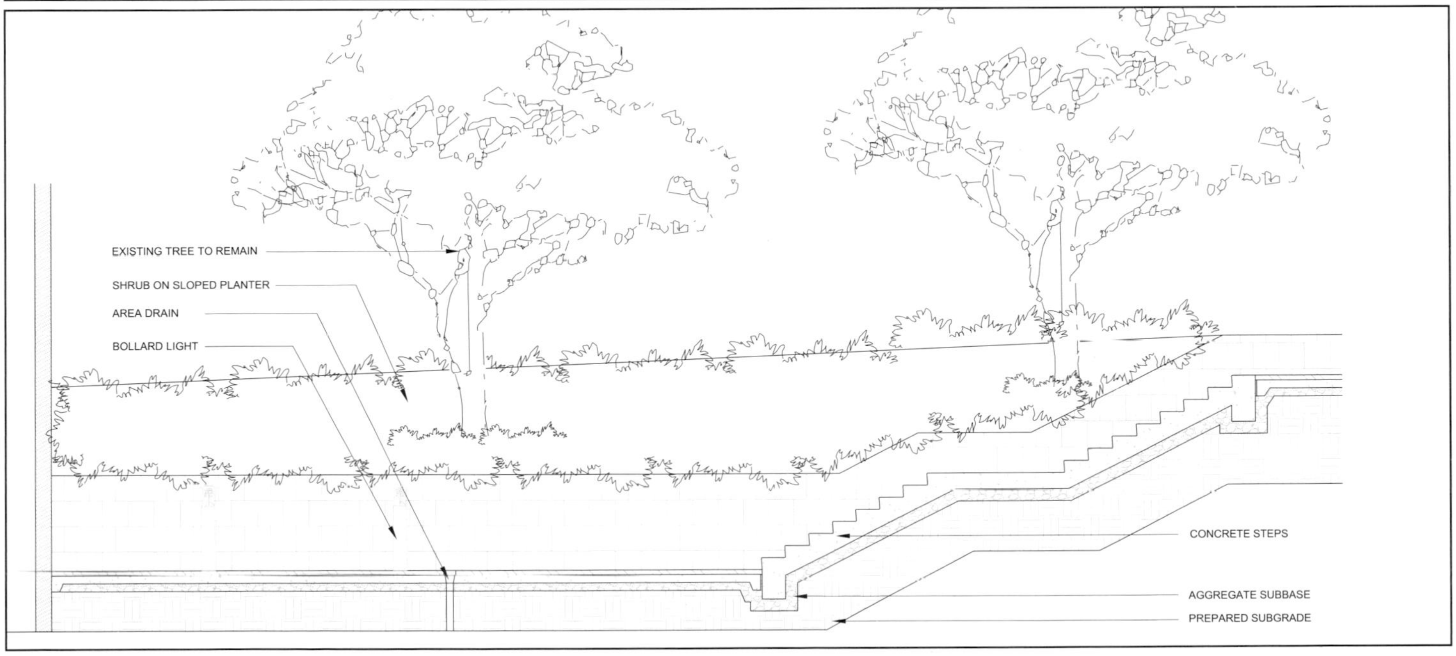

EXISTING TREE TO REMAIN
SHRUB ON SLOPED PLANTER
AREA DRAIN
BOLLARD LIGHT
CONCRETE STEPS
AGGREGATE SUBBASE
PREPARED SUBGRADE

IRIS BAND
COBBLE BAND
55mm (2 ¼") BRICK PAVERS ON 25mm (1') MORTAR SETTING BED WITH 10mm (⅜") MORTAR JOINTS
100mm (4") CONCRETE BASE WITH REINF. AS REQ.
100mm (4") AGGREGATE SUBBASE
PREPARED SUBGRADE
CONCRETE EDGE
CRUSHED STONE
FILTER FABRIC
DRAIN PIPE

TW 61.1
PRECAST CONCRETE CAP
CONCRETE SEATING WALL
CRUSHED STONE
FILTER FABRIC
DRAIN PIPE
55mm (2 ¼") BRICK PAVERS ON 25mm (1') MORTAR SETTING BED WITH 10mm (⅜") MORTAR JOINTS
FG 60.6
100mm (4") CONCRETE BASE WITH REINF. AS REQ.
100mm (4") AGGREGATE SUBBASE
200mm (8") CONCRETE FOOTING
PREPARED SUBGRADE
150mm (6") AGGREGATE SUBBASE

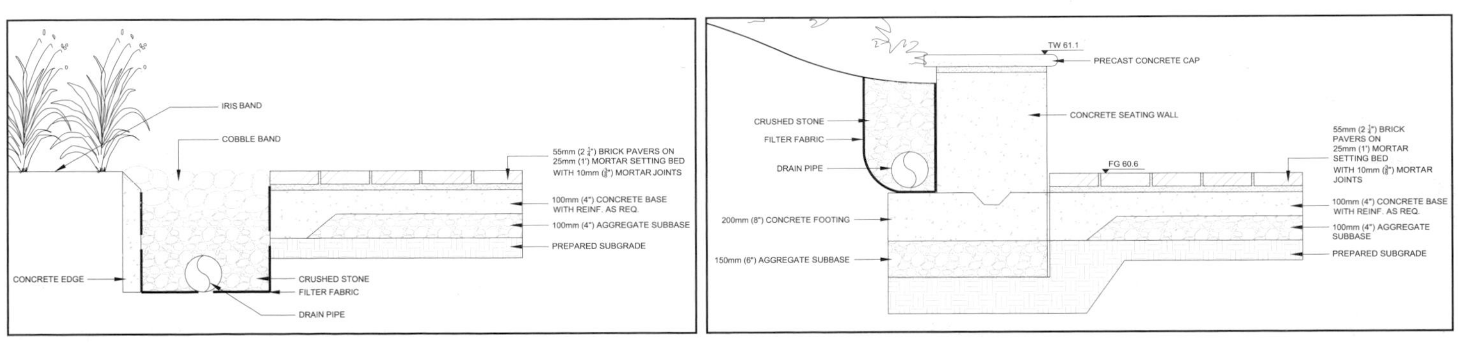

Festival Hall, Messe Frankfurt, Frankfurt

The festival hall designed by Architect Friedrich von Thiersch was inaugurated in 1909 as one of the largest unsupported doomed buildings.

The design and functional areas were based on the prototype of a palace building. Thiersch originally planned to add a garden in the forecourt of the hall which is now adopted by the new design.

By converting the large stone plaza into a garden connected to the hall, the prestigious function of the festival hall is accentuated. Thorough considerations were given to the dimensions, positioning, and shape of the garden to maintain a consistent correlation with the other solitaire buildings in close vicinity.

The result is a garden sculpture with a designated theme of fencing in the fair ground and the garden itself. The form — a flat bowl meeting on four points is a result of transforming spatial structures on the site. It provides access to the corners rising above ground level.

High quality concrete with natural stone supplements suggests a touch of elegance and weight. The inner garden structure shows a pattern which resembles the formal garden parterres. It is fragmented and slightly distorted by the concavity. The structure suggests association with formal palatial gardens but at the same time creates its own identity at the place.

The design includes a plane diversely planted with perennials, seasonal bulbs, annuals and grass lawns. Dwarf trees and ornamental shrubs add vertical emphasis to the place where permanent seating is supplemented by mobile chairs placed sporadically to match the ground pattern.

At night time, an elaborated lighting will put the sculpture on stage lending itself the focal attention to the festival hall.

The garden will be built to celebrate the 100th year anniversary of the festival hall.

(below) Landscape plan.
(right) The garden sculpture with rising corners.

client / owner	other key consultants	location	awards
Messe Frankfurt Venue GmbH & Co. KG, Stadt Frankfurt am Main	TEK TO NIK Architekten, Frankfurt a. M.	Frankfurt am Main, Germany	1st Place, Int'l competition

(left) Garden structure with geometric pattern.
(left bottom and bottom) Lighting concept.

Hargreaves Mall, Bendigo

The Hargreaves Mall is at the heart of Bendigo's City Centre and has an important role in hosting a range of activities including shopping, entertainment and outdoor eating. The Mall has strong links to all areas of the City Centre through Arcades, Laneways and footpaths that provide easy access for pedestrians and cyclists. The plan to construct a new Mall for Bendigo built on the strengths of the existing Mall and aims to create a lively and vibrant place that will attract visitors, residents, investors and innovative businesses.

The new design for the Mall restores a public street feeling to Hargreaves Mall. Our vision is to create a new place where people can meet, shop, rest a while and enjoy city life. Lines of deciduous trees frame each side of the Mall and a wide pedestrian concourse is located down the middle. On each side, broad footpaths with ample space for outdoor eating places are to be provided.

In the centre of the Mall, two iconic kiosks will bring a civic focus to the mall as well as provide public amenities in conjunction with retail and events opportunities.

Hargreaves Mall provides for a great variety of central city experiences including shopping, going to work and meeting other people and friends. The new design allows for an increased number of public and civic uses, particularly during the evening and weekends when the Mall will be the ideal location for dining, entertainment, public exhibitions and street life.

Retailers will have greater profile as a result of clear views along shop fronts on either side and along Hargreaves Street. This will support the retail centre of the City to continue to grow and prosper into the future.

The geology of Bendigo is a very important part of the history of the City and this is recognised in the design through the use of stones such as granite and quartz, and minerals and materials such as gold.

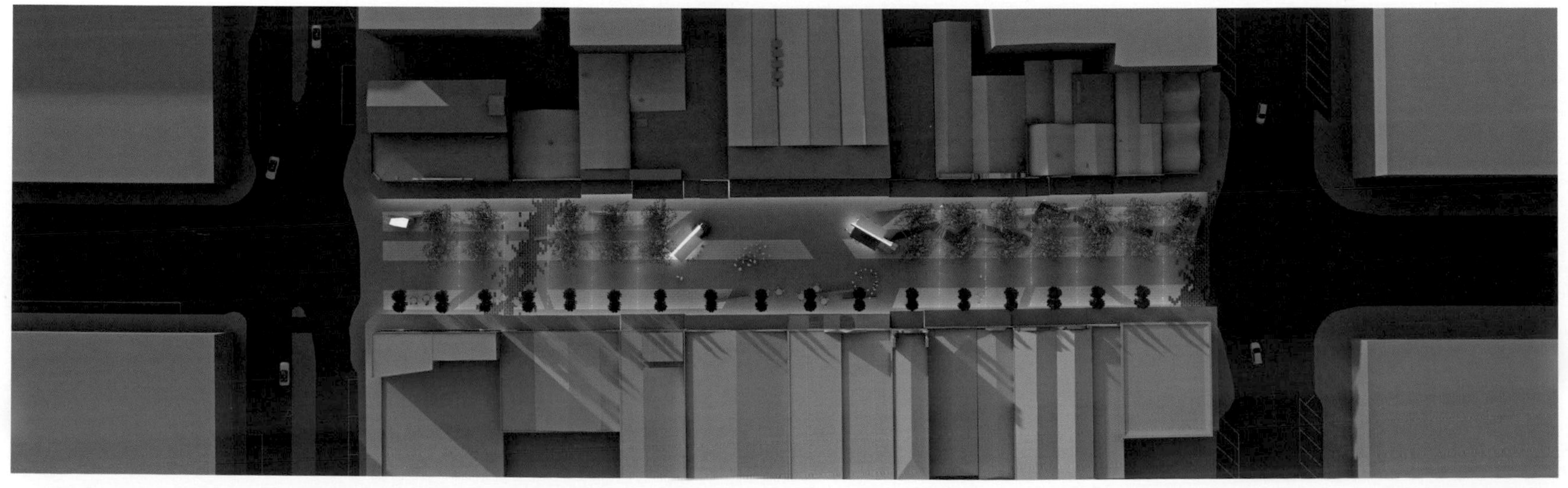

client / owner
City of Greater Bendigo, Australia

other key consultants
Toon Architect Group, ARUP

location
Hargreaves Mall, Bendigo, Victoria, Australia

(left) Bird's eye view of the mall at night. Lights will be hung from cables above the main public space and footpaths. This is a very economical way to provide safety lighting and allows lights to be placed exactly where they are needed. At ground level, small feature lights laid into the pavements or shining on play features will add sparkle and interest, particularly for young children.

(top) Getting around is easy. A wide pedestrian walkway through the centre of the Mall makes getting around easy and opens up views to the Town Hall and Hargreaves Street. This space also provides access for service deliveries and emergency vehicles.

(bottom) Aerial view of central activities space.

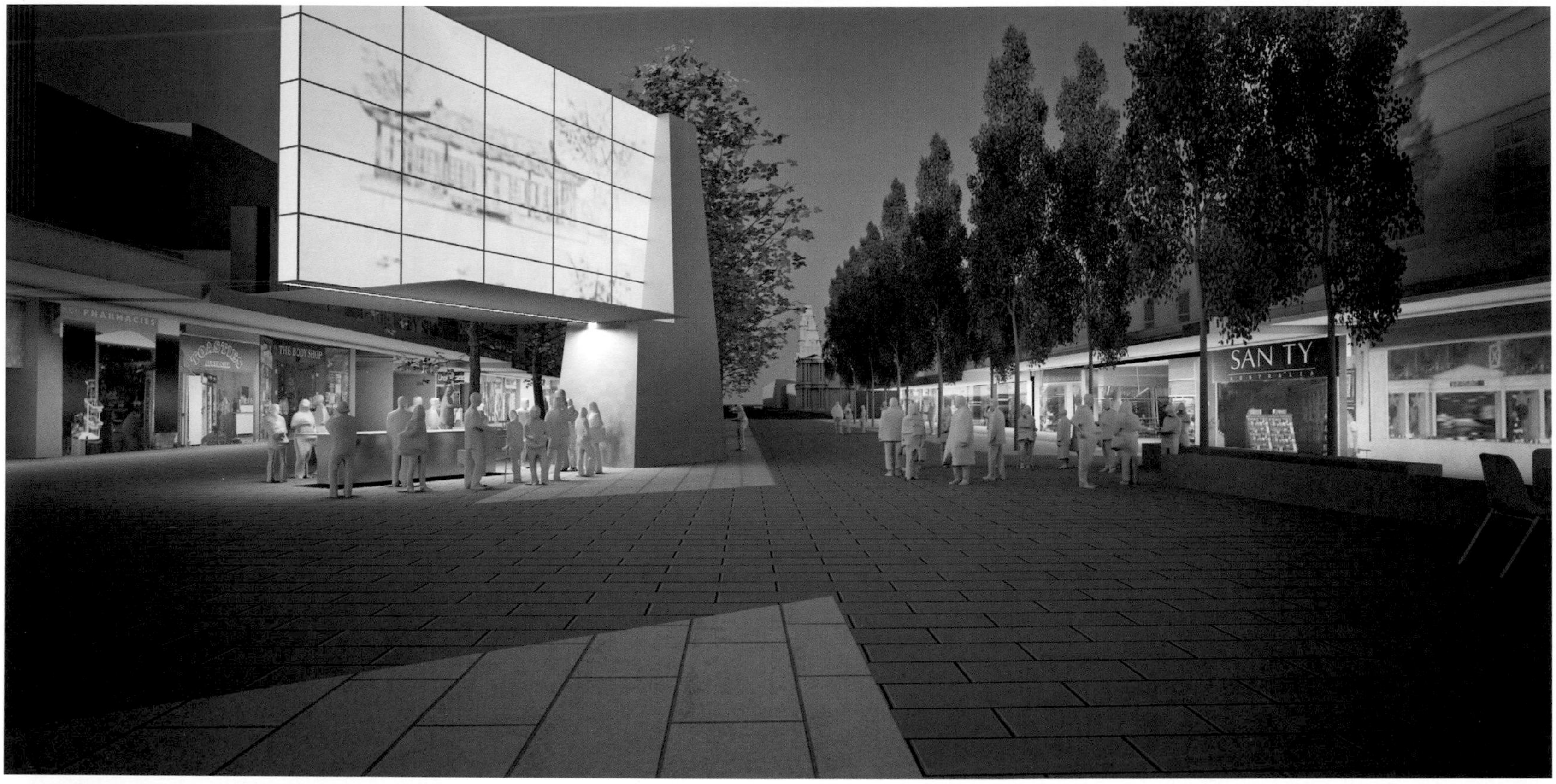
PHARMACIES
THE BODY SHOP
SAN TY

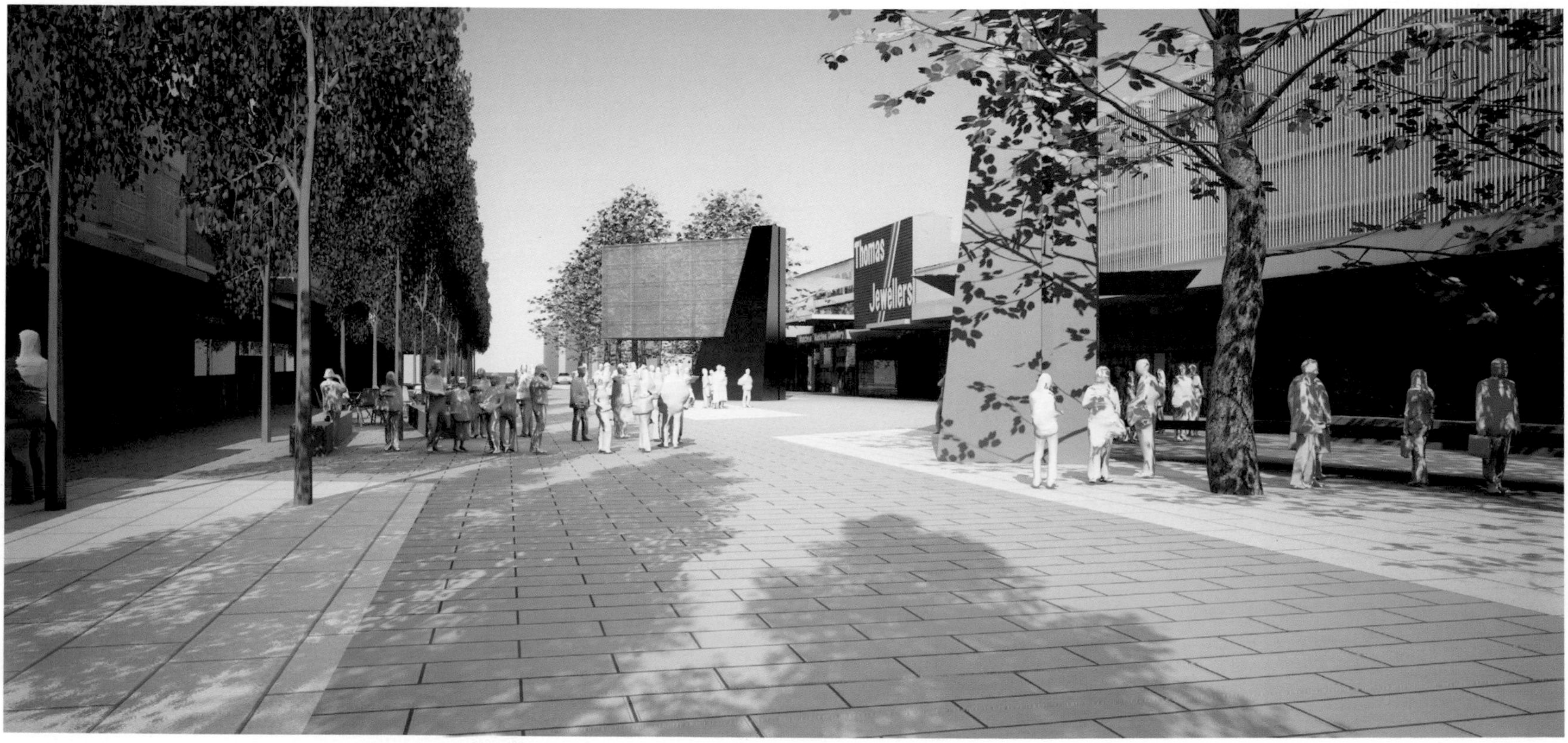
Thomas
Jewellers

(left top) View towards one of the proposed kiosks at night. During the evenings the soft glow of lantern-like light will fill the facade creating a warm and sophisticated ambience. A special highlight could be the transformation of building facades by projecting images or video onto blank walls.

(left bottom) View of the proposed mall towards kiosk. People will enjoy spending more time in the Mall with ample seating and shading providing a great place to meet.

(right) Aerial view of the proposed mall from the west towards the Bendigo Town Hall.

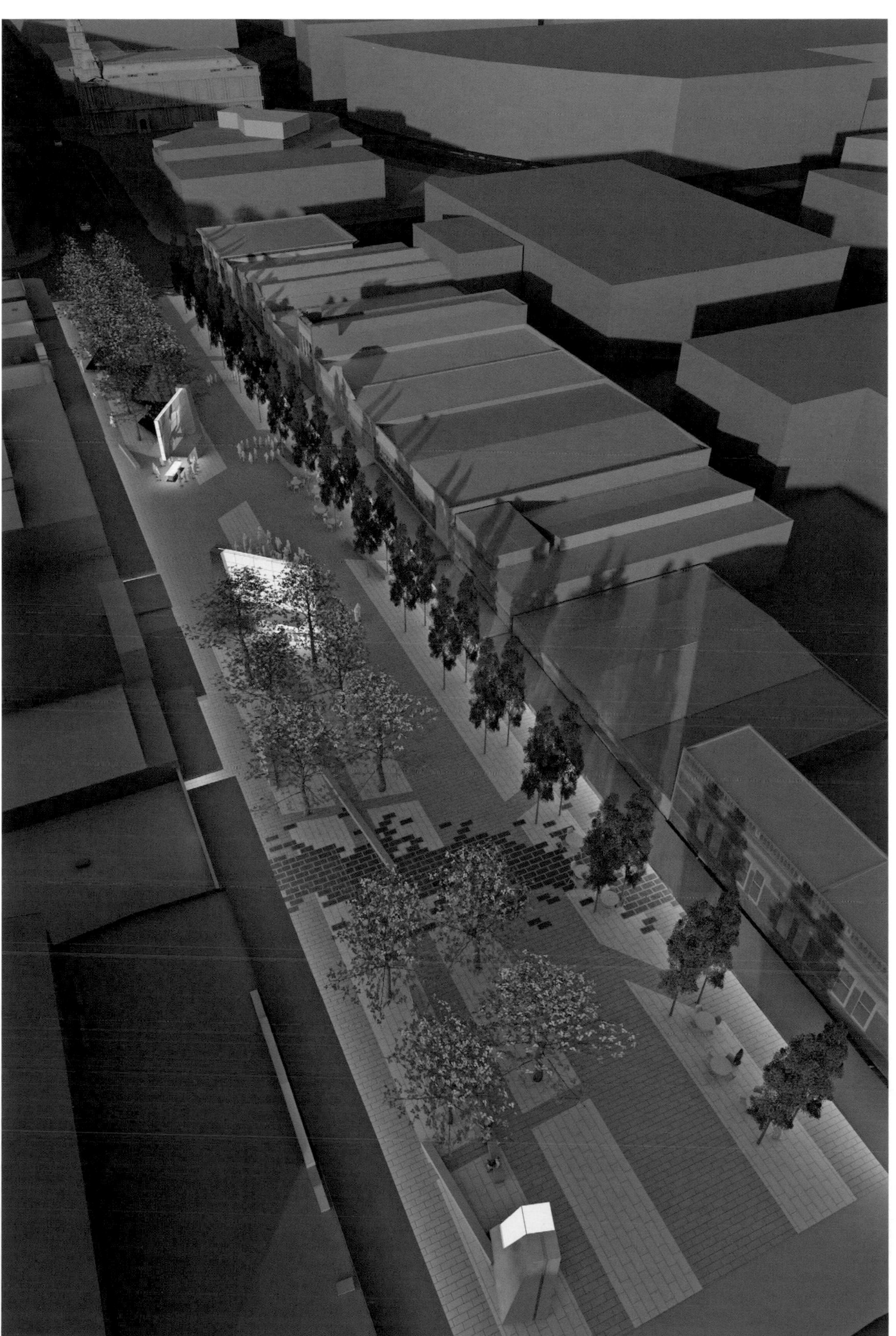

Shenzhen Xichong International Tourism Resort, Shenzhen

In 2005, ASPECT won 2nd place in the international competition for the Xichong International Tourism Resort Planning Competition as one of the 5 short-listed companies from 79 international design companies. The total design area is 1,293 Ha.

The future of this area was considered by ASPECT to be at a critical point with many possible scenarios that could be enacted out. The planning and design competition presented a rare opportunity that could allow Xichong Bay to achieve a broad variety of outcomes that are rich and diverse and yet observe a common goal of sustainability.

The guiding scenario for the future of Xichong Bay is its transformation into a world-class sub tropical resort which remains in harmony with its natural surroundings. The main objective for this proposal is the selection, planning and design of the most appropriate transformation scenarios. The master plan utilises the existing natural elements and agrarian culture to develop the site in a manner which improves its economic prosperity and highlight its natural grandeur. The flexibility of the overall design and approach towards the intertwinding of these two different factors allows the bay to take on a series of guises over time.

ASPECT's proposal seeks to embrace and enhance the magnificent landscape of Xichong in a manner that is sensitive to the environment while increasing the site's economic viability.

Eco-Cove

The intention of the ecological approach is to bring together two main elements: a resort that is secluded and a landscape that has ecological health. A 'cove' represents an image of a place of calm seclusion, protected from the outside world. 'Eco' is about creating a place that improves its ecological well-being over time, and reduces its dependence on the outside world for its water, energy, food and recreation.

Ecological Strategy

A key element underpinning the master plan is a desire to build upon the existing ecological and landscape systems. To enhance, regenerate, repair and improve the natural state of the existing systems with sensitivity to the properties on the site. Increasing the site's biodiversity was seen as a strong attractor to the site potential to draw visitors.

The planning proposal encompassed an entire green strategy for the site, a system which enables physical and economic change for both the locals and visitors. The key to this strategy is the long term change from the environmentally damaging farming practices to ecologically sustainable ones and ensuring the health of the local economy through the employment of locals as part of the resort.

It recognizes increasing productivity gains from well managed intensified farming and looks to provide ecological offsets through wetlands, passive cooling and power generation techniques and retention of productive land and forest resources and improvements to local offshore fisheries and fish nurseries. Furthermore the development model provides social and educational opportunities that foster traditional Chinese family values and has the potential to provide support networks including sustainable employment at all levels that begin to deal with the issues associated with increasing dependency ratios.

Whilst it is recognized that the ecological footprint of the proposal is larger than the projected Xichong ecological footprint of 2050 this is marginal.

Offset benefits, brought about by the development require less demand for outside energy generation, and water resources through local power generation and water harvesting. Passive cooling systems, localized sewerage treatment and harvesting, retention and recycling of water resources all reduce consumption.

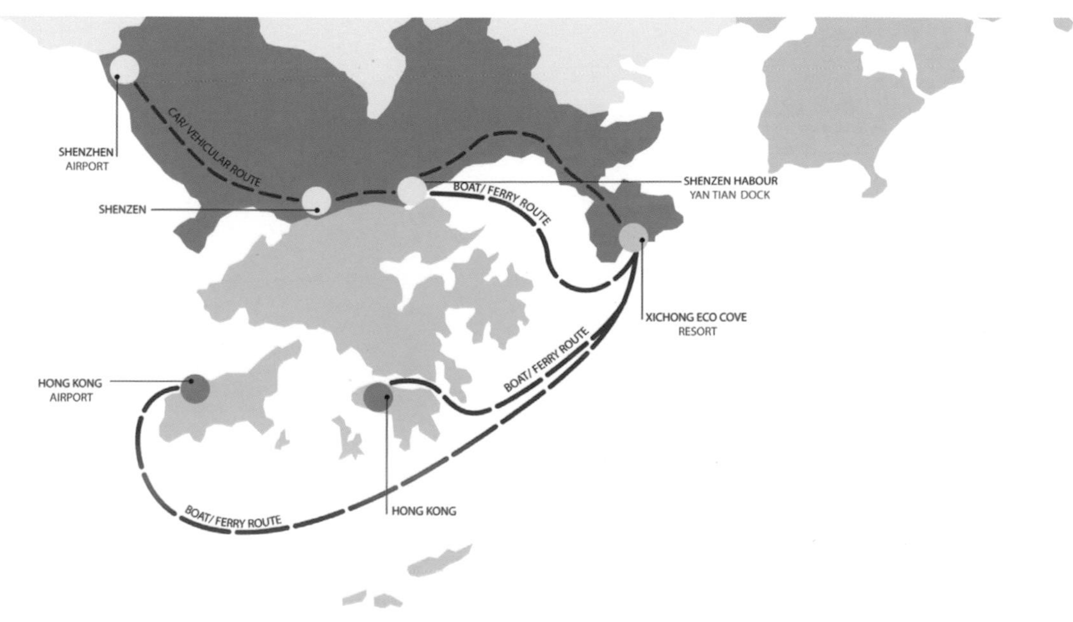

client / owner
Shenzhen Municipal Planning Bureau

location
Shenzhen, China

awards
2nd Place, International Competition

(left) Transportation organization.
(top) Bird's eye views.
(right) Master plan and site analysis diagram.

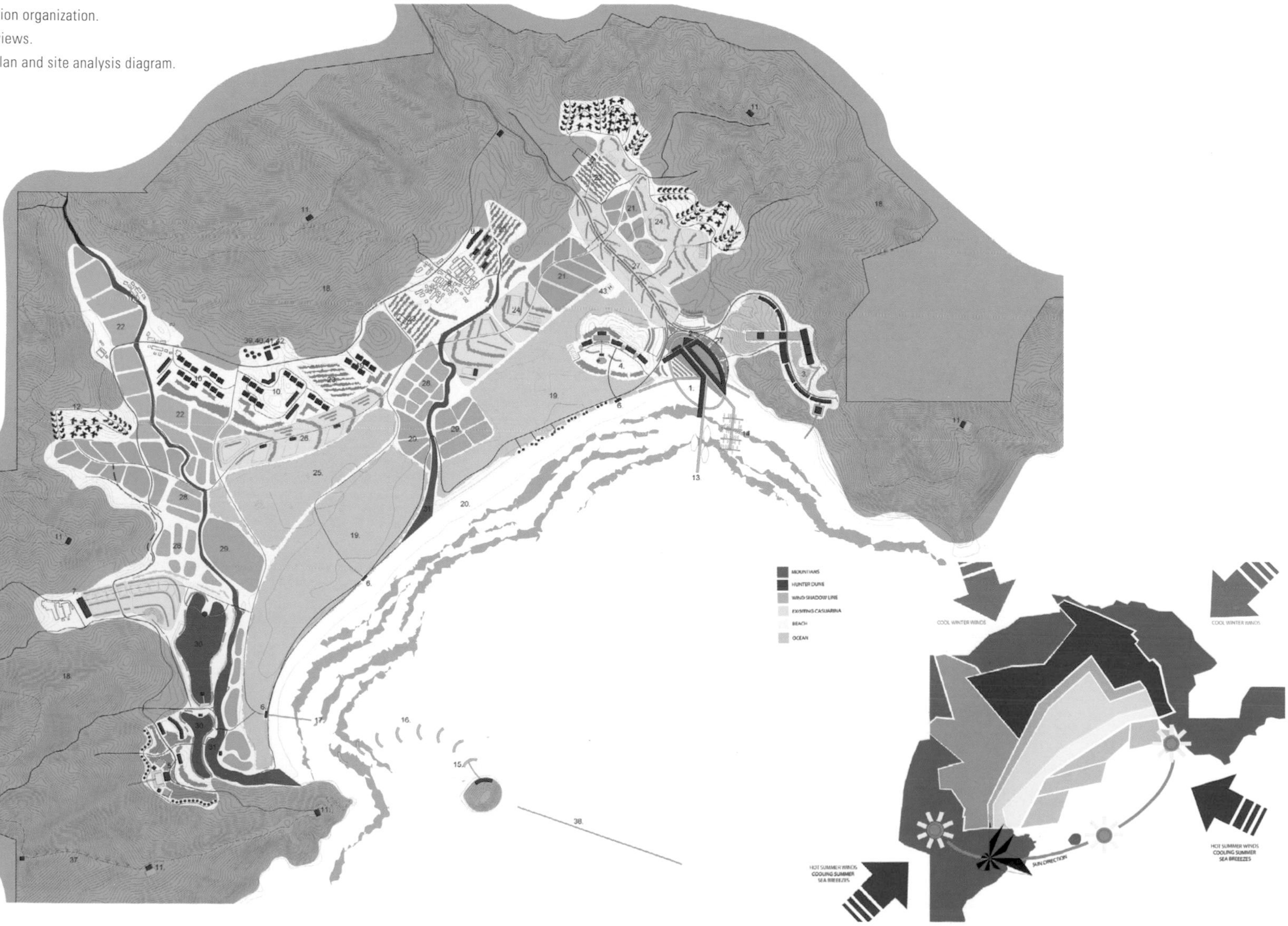

(right) Bird's eye views.
(below) Section illustrating environmental sustainable design principles.

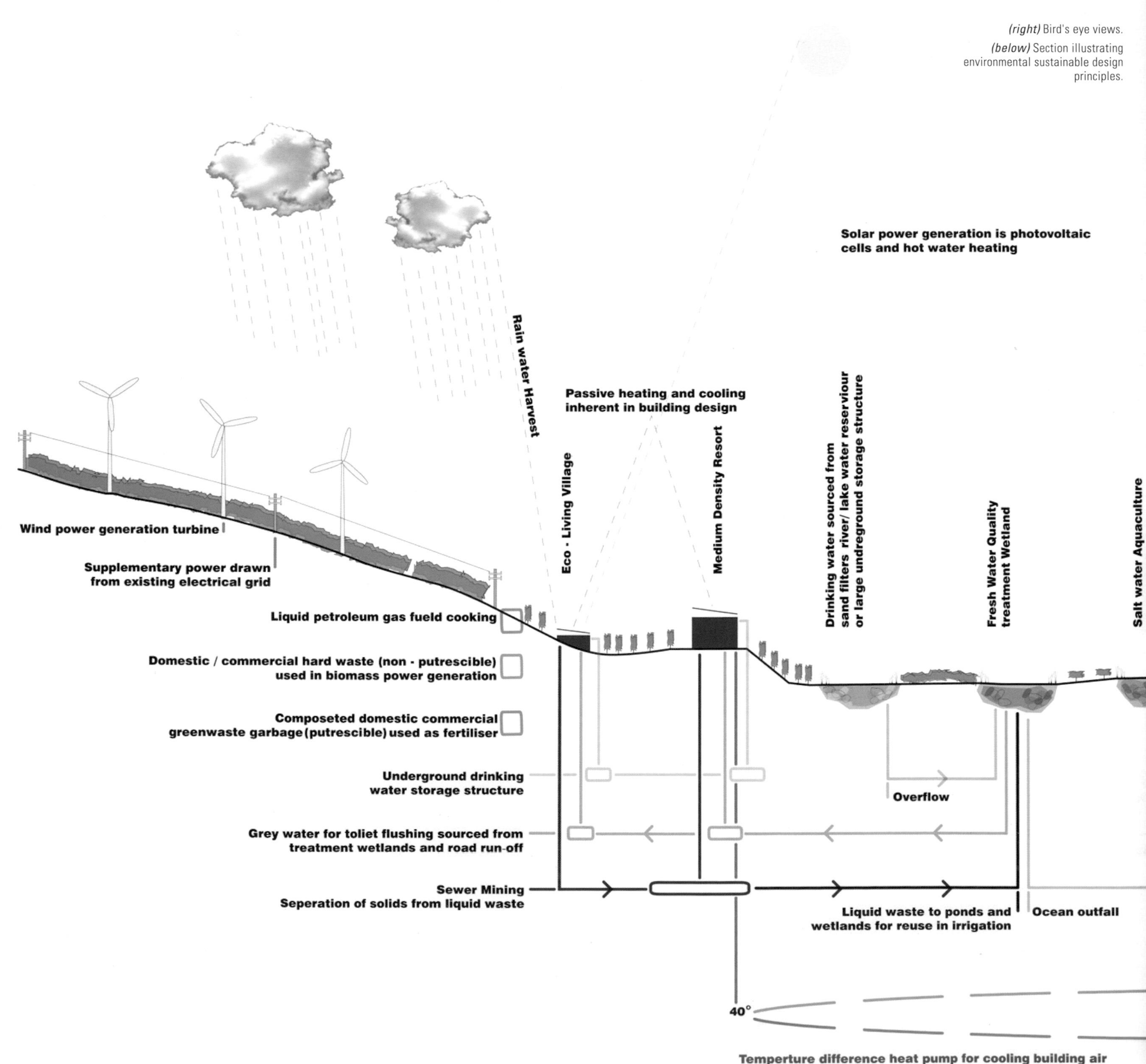

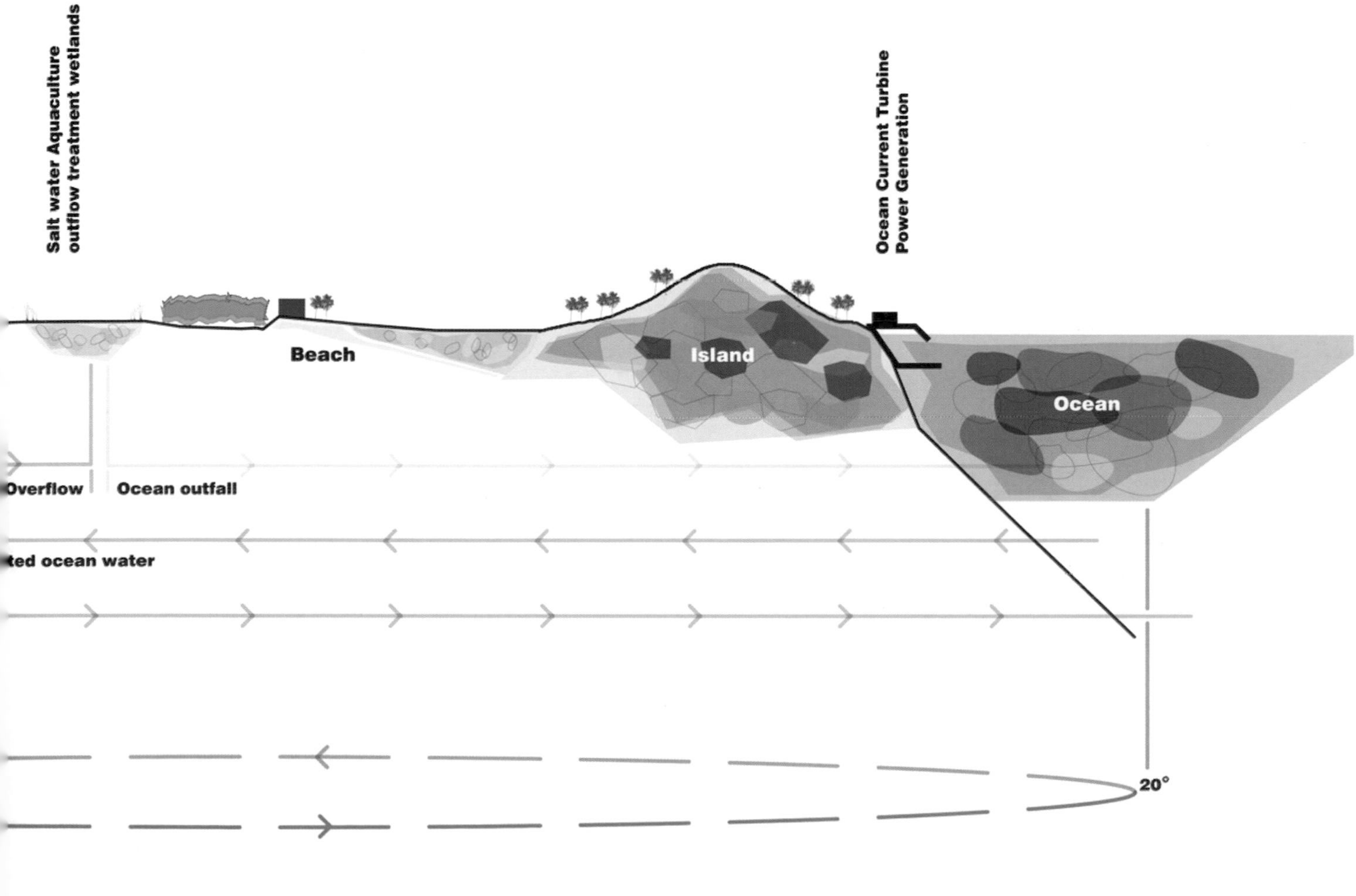

Salt water Aquaculture outflow treatment wetlands

Ocean Current Turbine Power Generation

Beach

Island

Ocean

verflow

Ocean outfall

ted ocean water

20°

International Spa Complex, Torres Novas

The master planning and design for the estate grounds for a large spa complex designed for an international clientele, located outside the town of Torres Novas, 80km to the north of Lisbon. The 70 hectare site is part of a historic estate with a traditional Castello, fine original terraced gardens and parterres, set in land with agricultural and ecological importance that has protected status.

A series of gardens in the immediate vicinity of the new and existing buildings was planned to augment the formality of the original grounds. The additional estate land was to be used for a variety of holistic activities to complement those of the spa. The valley area in particular presented an excellent opportunity to carefully augment the existing features, improve the seasonal waterflow with holding ponds, stocked with local freshwater fish, selectively improve the existing mature trees and re-plant in areas where the excessive shade had inhibited growth and naturalisation.

Formal and informal areas surrounding the spa complex presented us with opportunities for high quality detailing. Terraced seating areas, water features and lush planting well maintained, offered the visitor the ultimate in relaxation and recuperation.

Planning the layout of the estate presented wonderful opportunities to preserve and improve the Castello's formal garden with other distinct areas being linked with a series of paths, steps and cycle ways. The estate offered self contained accommodation in a number of villas and apartments on a hilly area of the land some distance from the main complex. We planned different settings throughout this area to give additional privacy and character for villa guests. The villas were linked to the Spa by walkways wide enough to accommodate buggies and bicycles.

A 'natural' swimming pond (which eliminates the need for chemicals and constant cleaning), flower gardens and the growing of organic vegetables and fruit were to be included. The spa was to re-cycle water, grey water and waste through a 'living' machine located on the site.

Our aim throughout was to respect the regional traditions for wine growing, fruit and nut trees and excellent seasonal produce. We planned the planting of vines, additional fruit trees to create a series of orchards and vegetable growing with a view to producing sufficient organic fruit and vegetables to feed spa guests throughout the season. In addition, extensive liaison and planning with the local regional authorities was required to respect the designated status of the land.

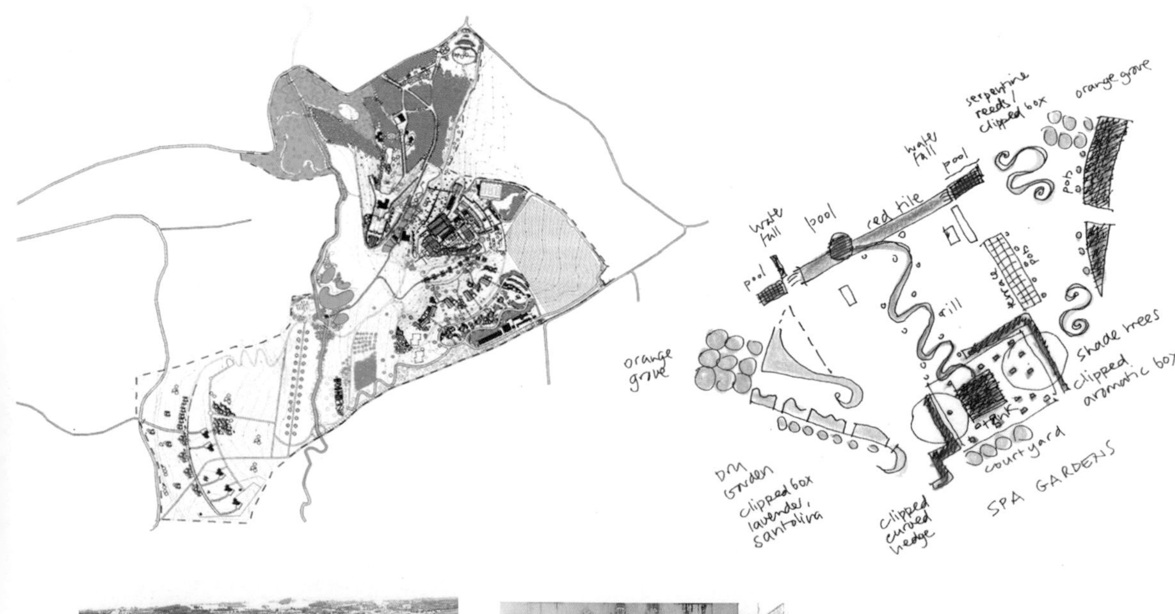

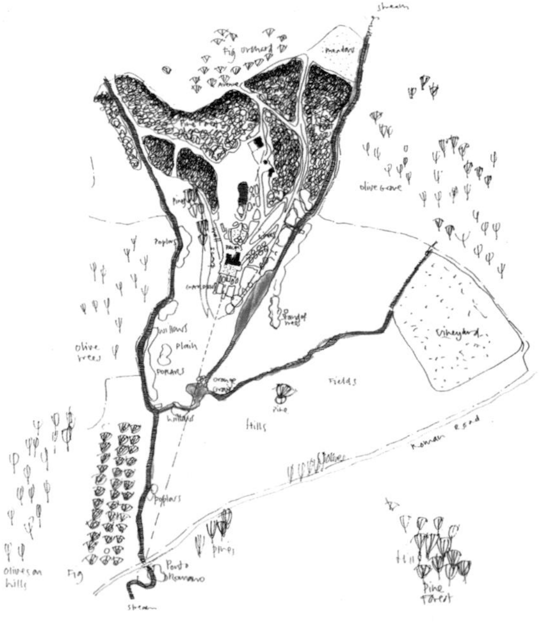

LANDSCAPE CHARACTER

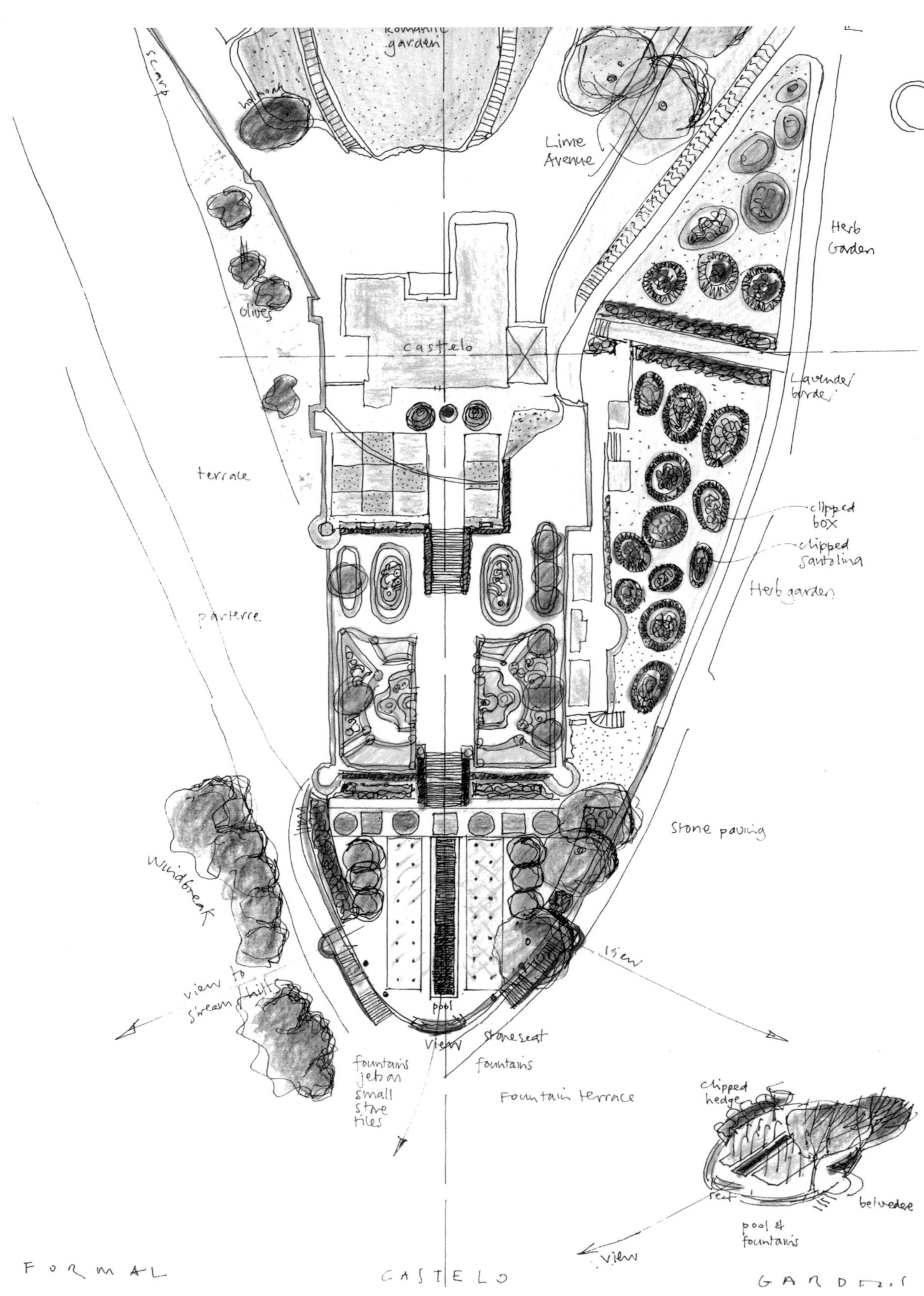

(opposite page, far left) The 70 hectare estate and Castello had been neglected for a number of years.

(opposite page, middle) Spa Gardens stylised plan.

(opposite page, right) Landscape Character.

(opposite page, bottom left) The planning for the use of the estate to accommodate a high quality spa complex kept the character of the land as integral to the development.

(opposite page, bottom right) The formal gardens surrounding the Castello were to be restored.

(right) The formal gardens, once restored were to be used as a formal entertainment area.

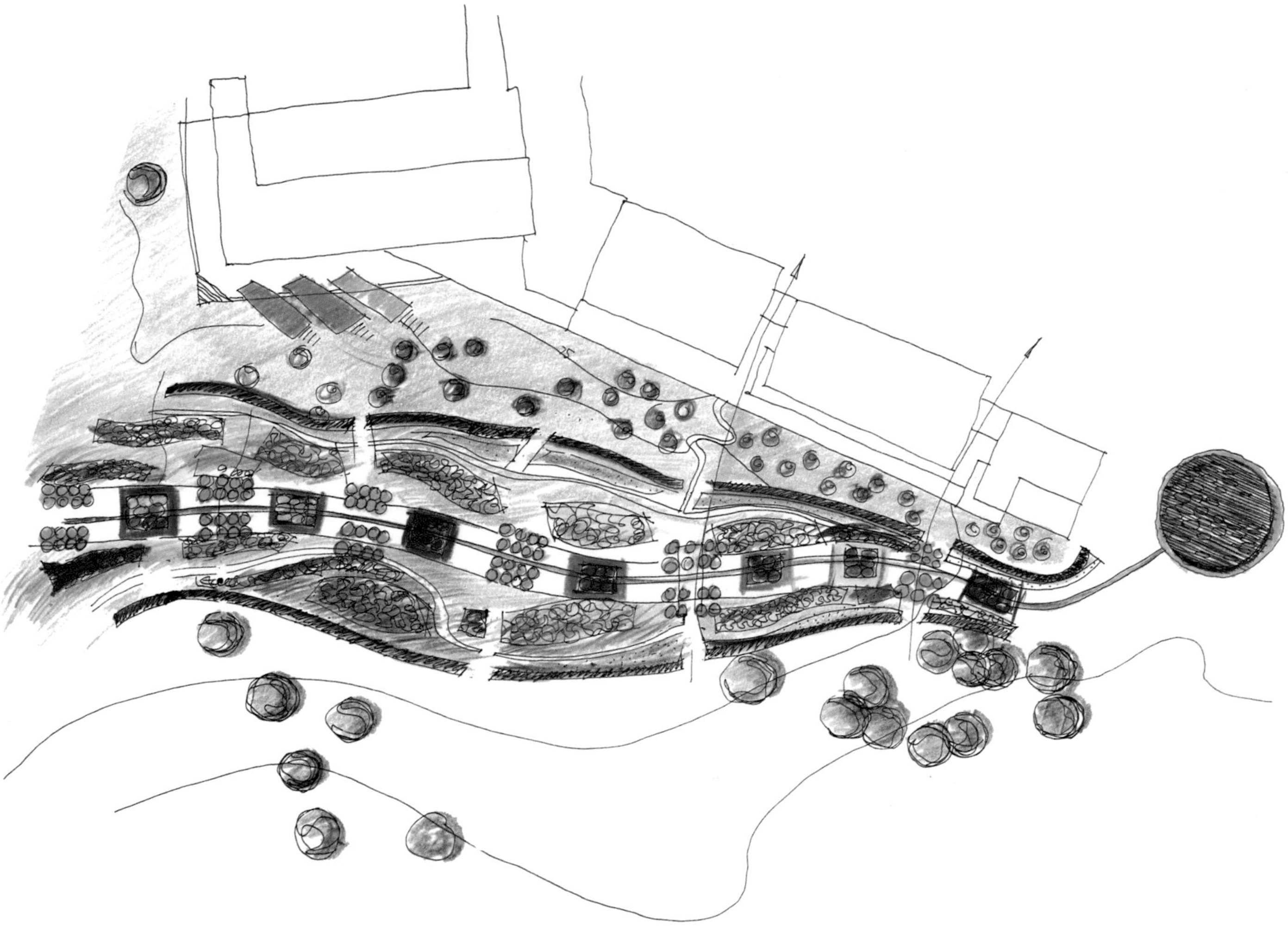

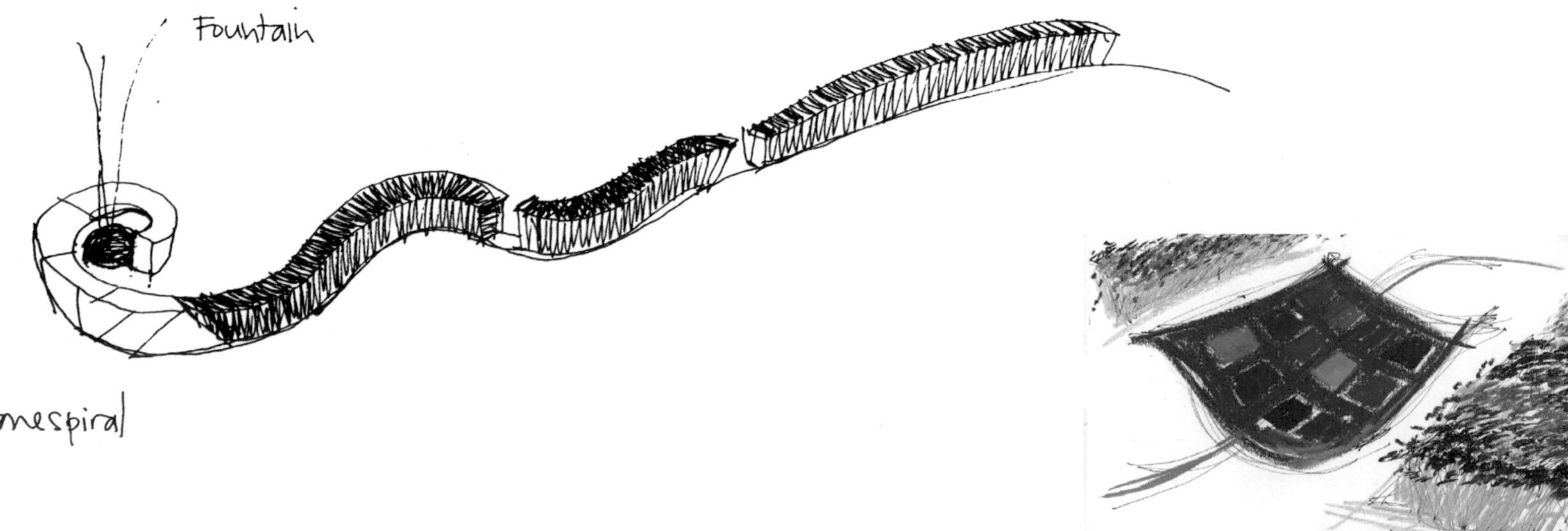
Fountain
Stonespiral

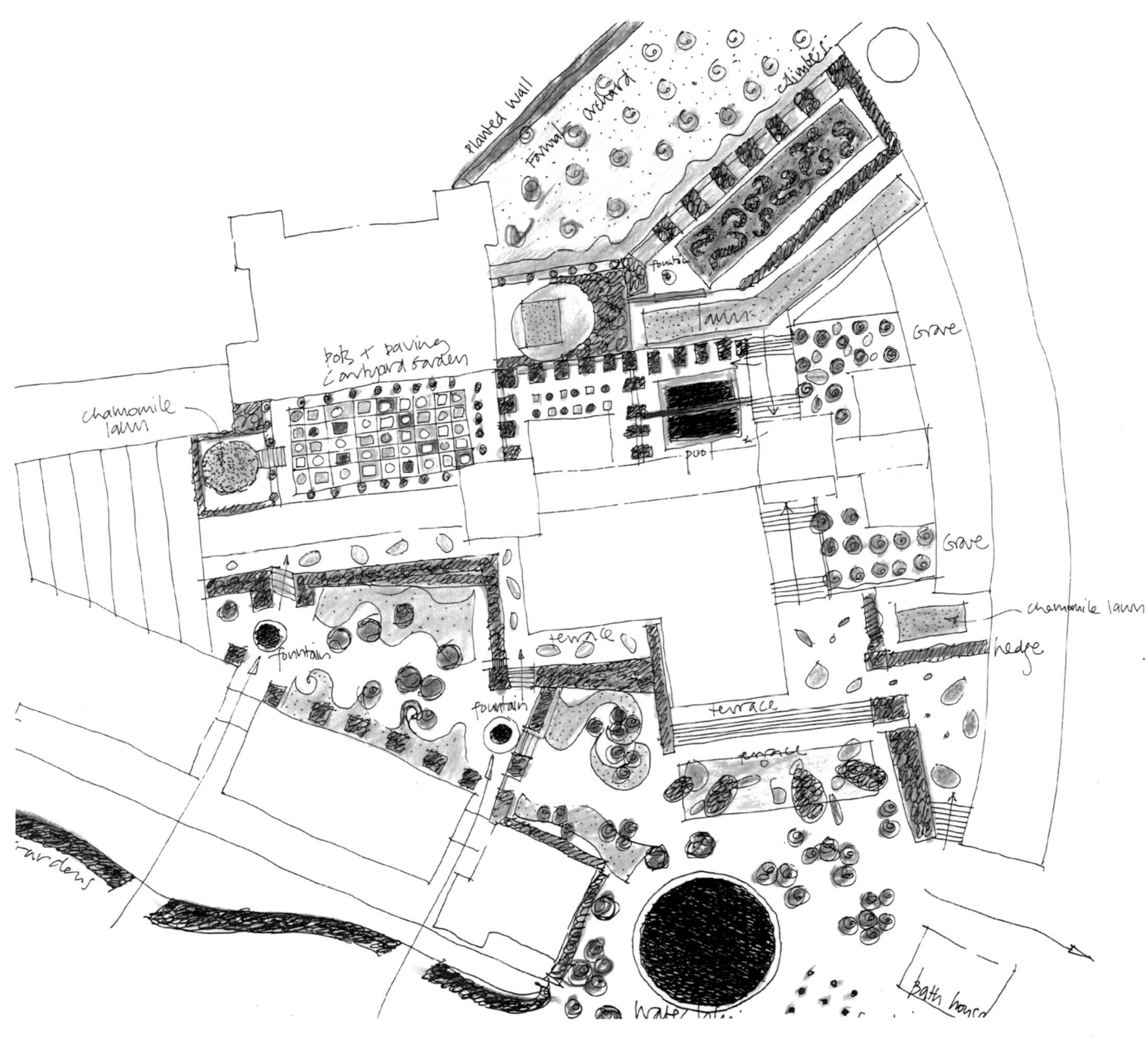

(above) The area immediately surrounding the spa featured terraces, water features and areas for relaxation.

(opposite page, top) A detail of the colour garden surrounded by formal clipped hedging.

(opposite page, left) The 'archetype' of the enclosing, protective hedge.

(opposite page, bottom right) A sketch showing the improvements for the ponds and surrounding woodland.

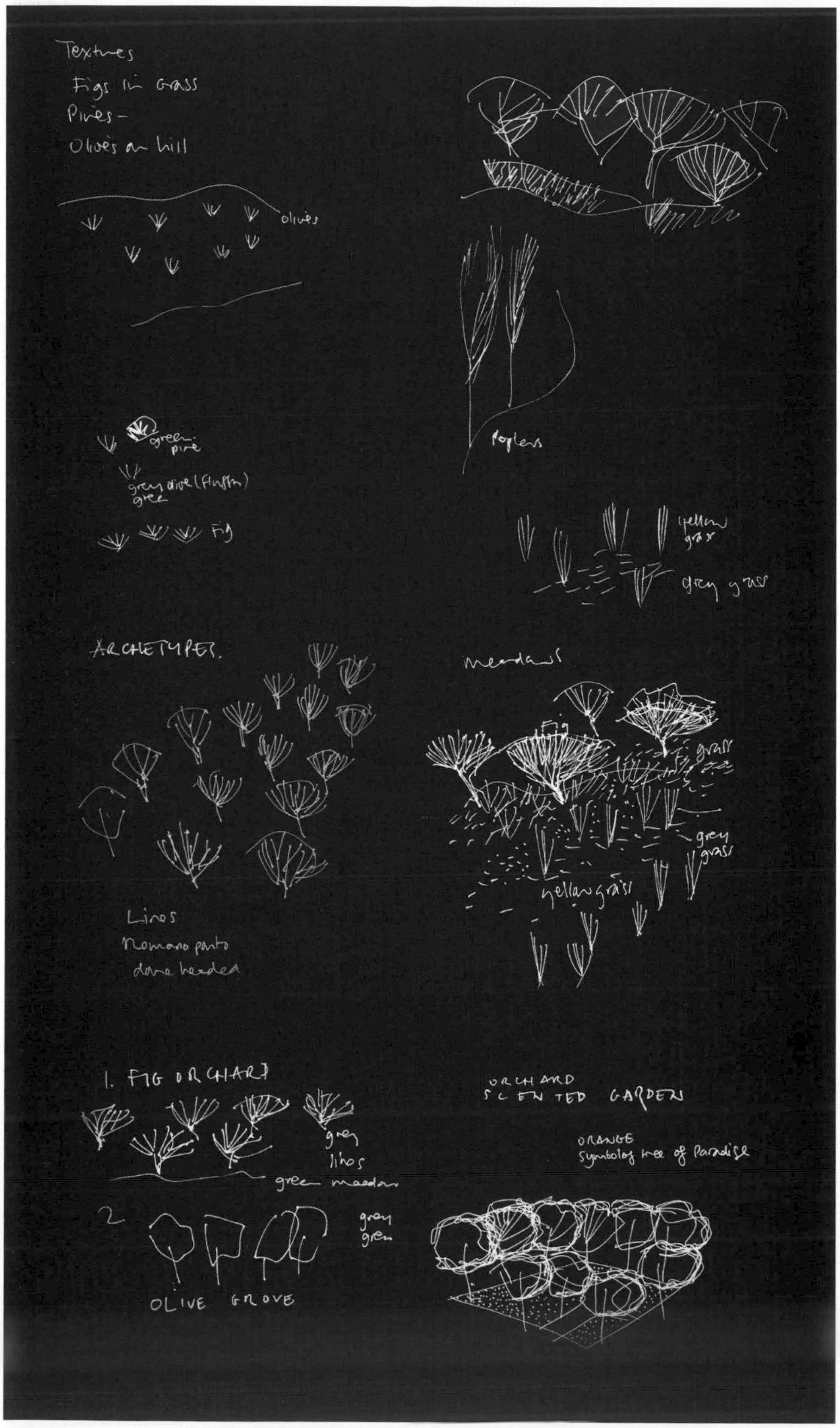
Textures
Figs in Grass
Pines -
Olives on hill
olives
poplars
green pine
Fig
yellow grass
grey grass
ARCHETYPES
meadows
grass
grey grass
yellow grass
1. FIG ORCHARD
grey
green meadow
ORCHARD
SCENTED GARDEN
ORANGE
tree of Paradise
2
grey
green
OLIVE GROVE

Fountain

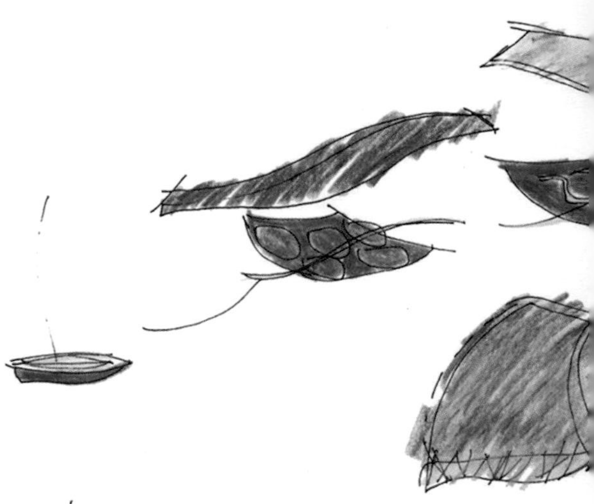

(left) A series of 'archetypes' was developed to illustrate to the client the retention and development of inherent characteristics of the site.
(above) A conceptual drawing to show the flower area within the valley garden.
(below left) A series of gardens, each with their own protective hedging grows the spa organic produce.
(below right) Further to the south of the spa and near the river the productivity gardens were to be created.

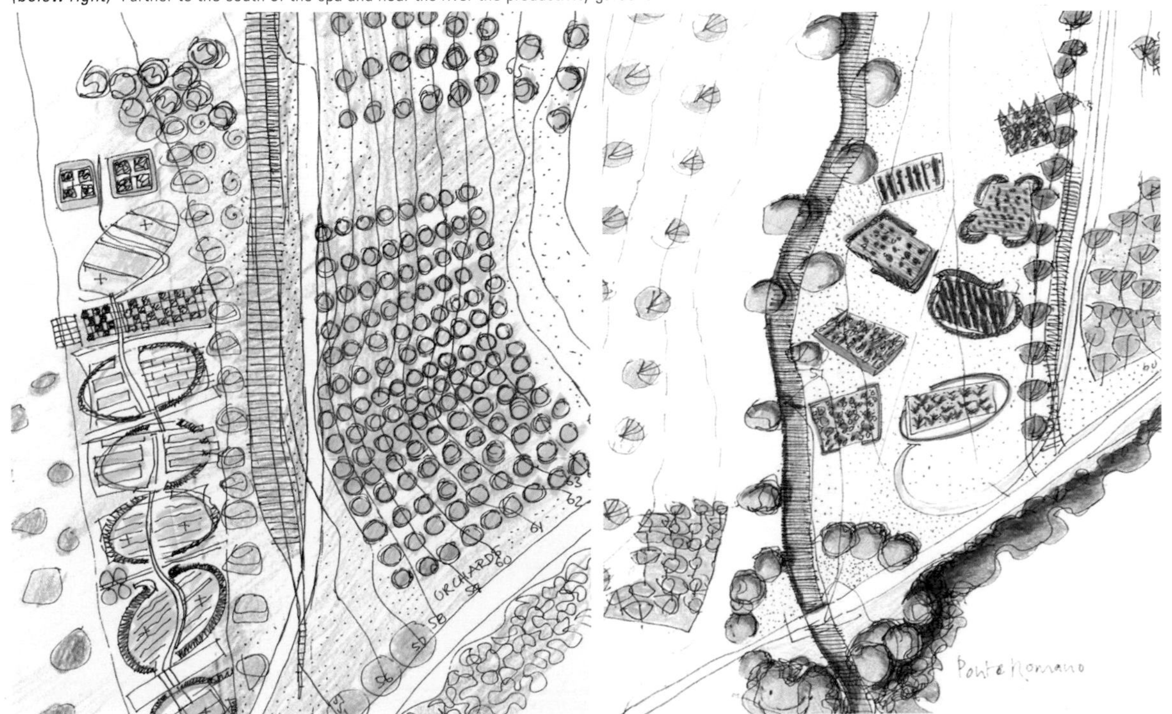

City Spa Retreat, Bangkok

It is the first series of international city spa retreats. The gardens are located on the tenth and eleventh floors of a former office block. The gardens set over three levels are an integral part of the spa experience and a sanctuary from the bustling city below, created to allow rest, repose and relaxation. The entrance to the spa is through the atrium with open views of the roof garden above. The lush planting of bamboo, tropical trees, provides shelter and shade, while the water lily pools and orchid garden are traditional Thai garden elements. The brief allowed us to specify high quality materials and planting with a number of unique features using a sophisticated palette of materials, colours and planting.

(below) The upper tier of the spa enjoys spectacular views over central Bankok.

(opposite page, top left) A seating pod set within the lush and verdant planting.

(opposite page, top right) A large lightweight pierced copper wall with a leaf motif disguises the car park area on the lower terrace, terraces were created to offer areas for guests to relax and unwind.

(opposite page, middle left) Elaborate clipped hedge pods echoing the hardwood seating pods featuring elsewhere.

(opposite page, middle right) A design proposal for a plant area on the terraces.

(opposite page, bottom) The formality of the terraced hard landscaping softened by the planting.

KEY
1. timber deck
2. trees and hedge
3. swimming pool
4. sphere pool with glass rill
5. copper fountains with colored pools
6. water lily pool
7. onyx / alabaster with lights in stone paving
8. ramped planting
9. path though garden with seating
10. copper panels
11. inset glass lights
12. raised garden

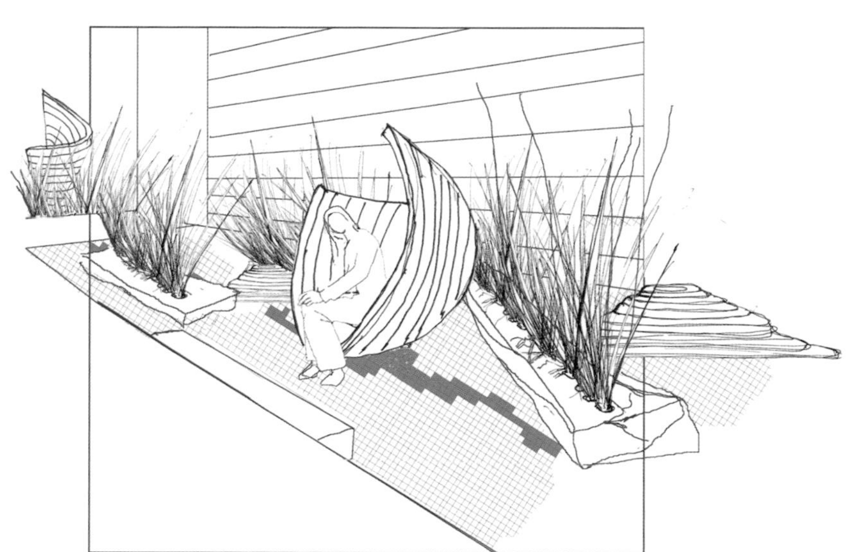

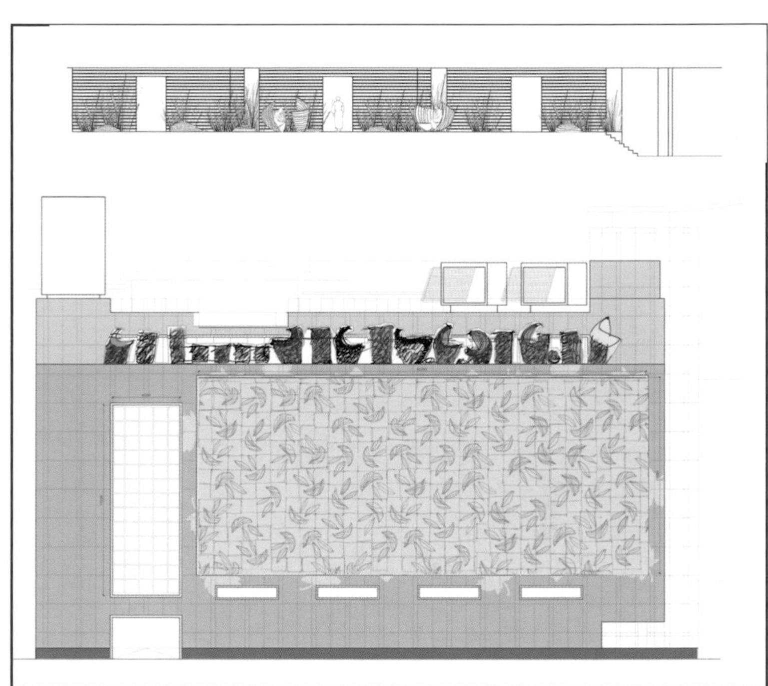

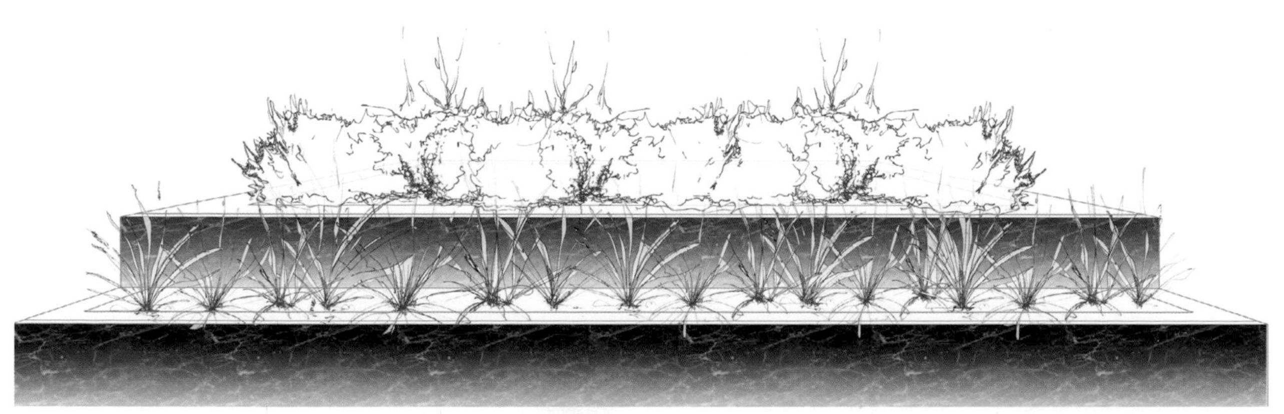

printed metal screen
engraved glass back lit
bamboo
cast glass rock pools
textured ground pattern

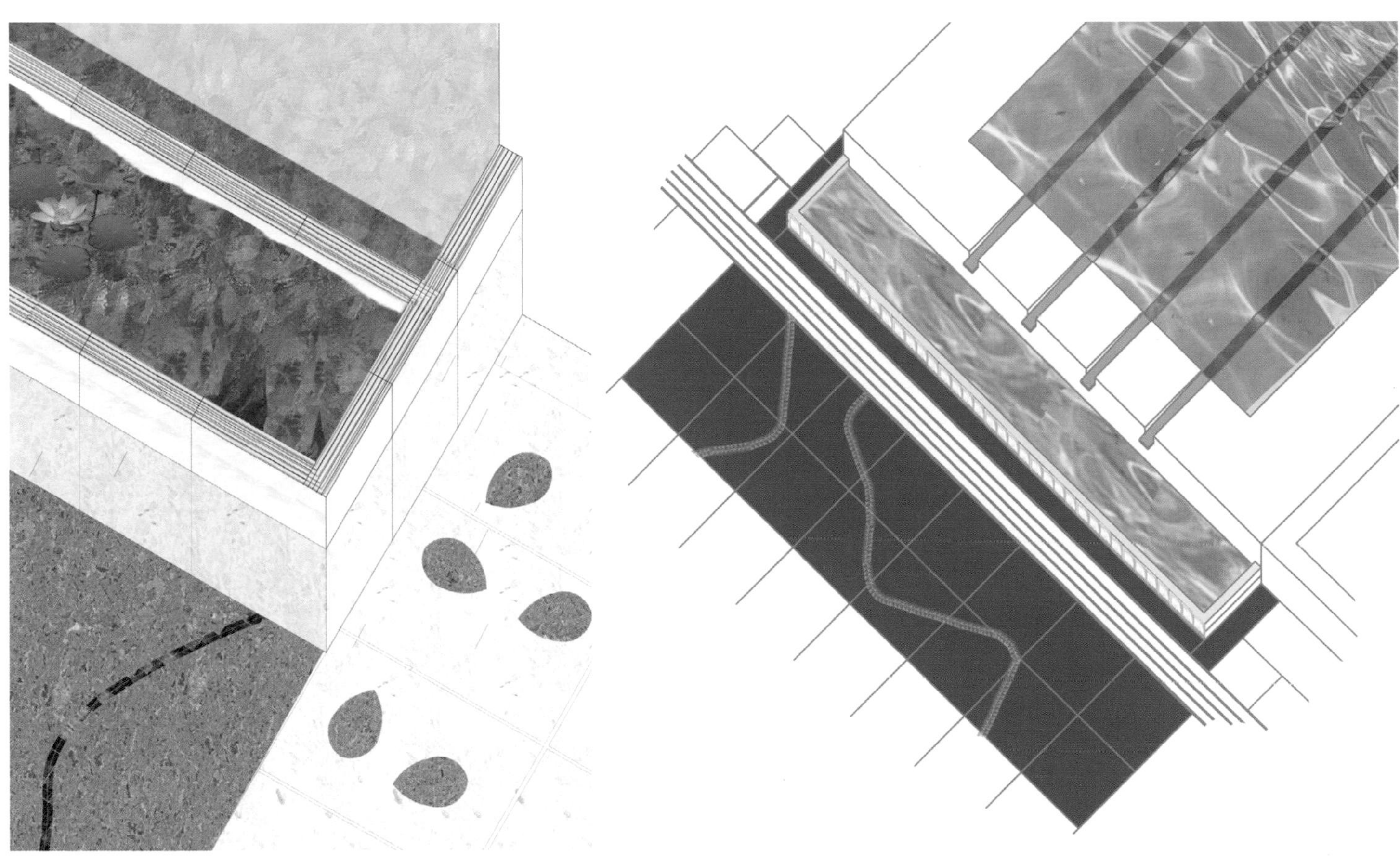

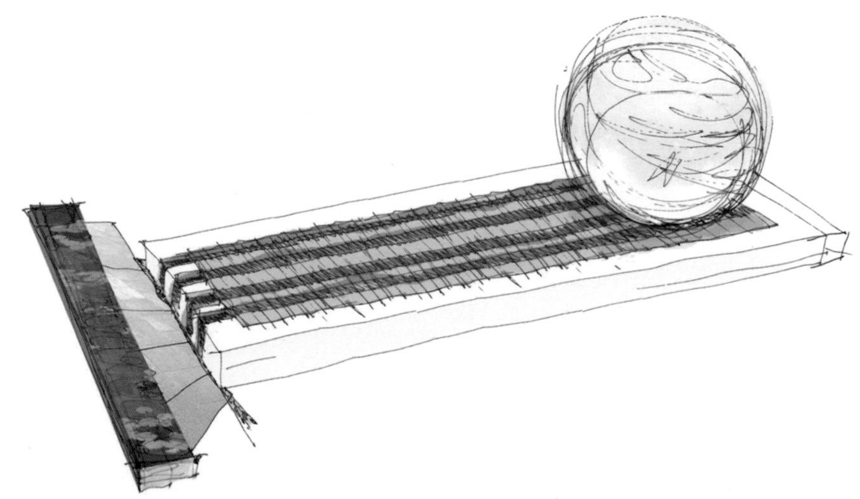

(above left) Detail of the Lily Pool.

(above right) Detail of the edge of the Sphere Pool.

(right) Sketch detail of the Sphere Pool. The sphere is the source of the water.

(opposite page, top) A swirling wall in copper and stone.

(opposite page, left) Many of the features used common materials to link the design. Copper was used throughout.

(opposite page, right top) The approach from the Level 10 gardens to the spa interior.

(opposite page, right bottom) This water feature wall had copper inserts as a decorative motif, one of the main focal points for spa guests on arrival.

Parks, Gardens and Memorials

Enviropark, North Harbour, Portsmouth

The Paulsgrove landfill site has blighted the entrance to the Portsmouth for over 30 years. However, with tipping and capping to be completed by 2008, there is now an unrivalled opportunity to create a landmark park at the gateway to the city.

Under existing planning obligations, the landfill operator is to restore the area to grassland with path routes and 30% woodland before handing the site back to Portsmouth City Council as public open space. The bold new landform's 'greening' can only be seen as an excellent improvement on the previous tip and will instantly provide a 5% increase to this densely populated city's open space. The scheme is, however, felt to be unambitious and could waste a once-in-a-lifetime opportunity to create a project of far-reaching vision and benefit.

In early 2001 the Portsmouth and South East Hampshire Partnership (an organisation set up specifically to link local businesses and local government in the pursuit of regenerating the city) turned its attention to the wider locality and the possibilities of a major gateway park with a vision to put Portsmouth on the map.

Early concepts envisaged innovative new technology and energy-efficient buildings for education and commercial uses, in a community parkland that could itself be a showcase for environmental sustainability and technology.

The ability to meet the needs of the local community and also aspire to being of wider importance is a key starting point to the Enviropark vision. The site is set out in the local plan as public open space and has to fulfill objectives for a multi-functional park allowing a variety of amenity use, nature conservation and help in reduction of social exclusion and poverty. Taking it up a notch to becoming a wider attraction must not exclude these objectives. The theme of environment and sustainability in the 21st Century is appropriate to underpin such multilayered proposals, applicable as it is to all society. The options that then open up for such a theme become endless and provide opportunities for a massive variety of uses. A diverse landscape of hills, valleys, waterbodies, woodland and open fields provides a variety of habitat and opportunity for recreation, walks, trails and meeting and performance space. There are also opportunities for inspiration, education and research, woodland crafts, sculpture and art trails, wildlife trails, fitness trails, adventure play, integrated sustainable energy and drainage systems, variously managed grasslands and outdoor educational and exhibition areas.

Built facilities within the park could offer points of arrival and major amenity hubs. Distinct opportunities for built elements offer the opportunities for exemplary state-of-the-art environmentally friendly technology buildings.

Although boundaries need to be secured in the interests of safety and management, entry should be free for all the purposes of both peaceful and active recreation, but it is felt there is no harm charging for the car parking in an Enviropark. Revenue would come from building uses, activities and special events. The park's position at the city gateway, and the water's edge ensures an aspect that is bound to attract visitors. Its immediate proximity to the leisure hub of Port Solent, local hotels, industry and transport network can only enhance its location, giving a new focus to the northern part of the City balancing the recent southern harbour regeneration of Gunwharf, with the Spinnaker Tower.

The Partnership and the design team are committed to inclusive community involvement in designing, implementing and managing elements within the park and the Enviropark project has been through a long periods of consultation, with local authority officers, politicians, local community groups, schools, environmental interest groups and local press. Nearly all who are consulted are excited by the opportunity, and eager to back the scheme, with the MoD offer of increased access to the shoreline and a waterbody for occasional aquatic events.

The main issue is funding. While there are numerous avenues for small amounts, this size of project requires substantial input. There is no money available from Council sources. The National Lottery Living Landmarks project, offering funding up to £25 million and keen to reward community consultation and outcomes, was announced in 2005 seemingly fitting the scale and aspirations of the Enviropark well. However the bid was unsuccessful despite a strong, robust presentation.

This has been disappointing and other funding sources will need to be pursued with equal vigour. The scheme could have a significant effect on the landscape of one of the south's leading cities and financial backing must be generated elsewhere to turn vision into reality.

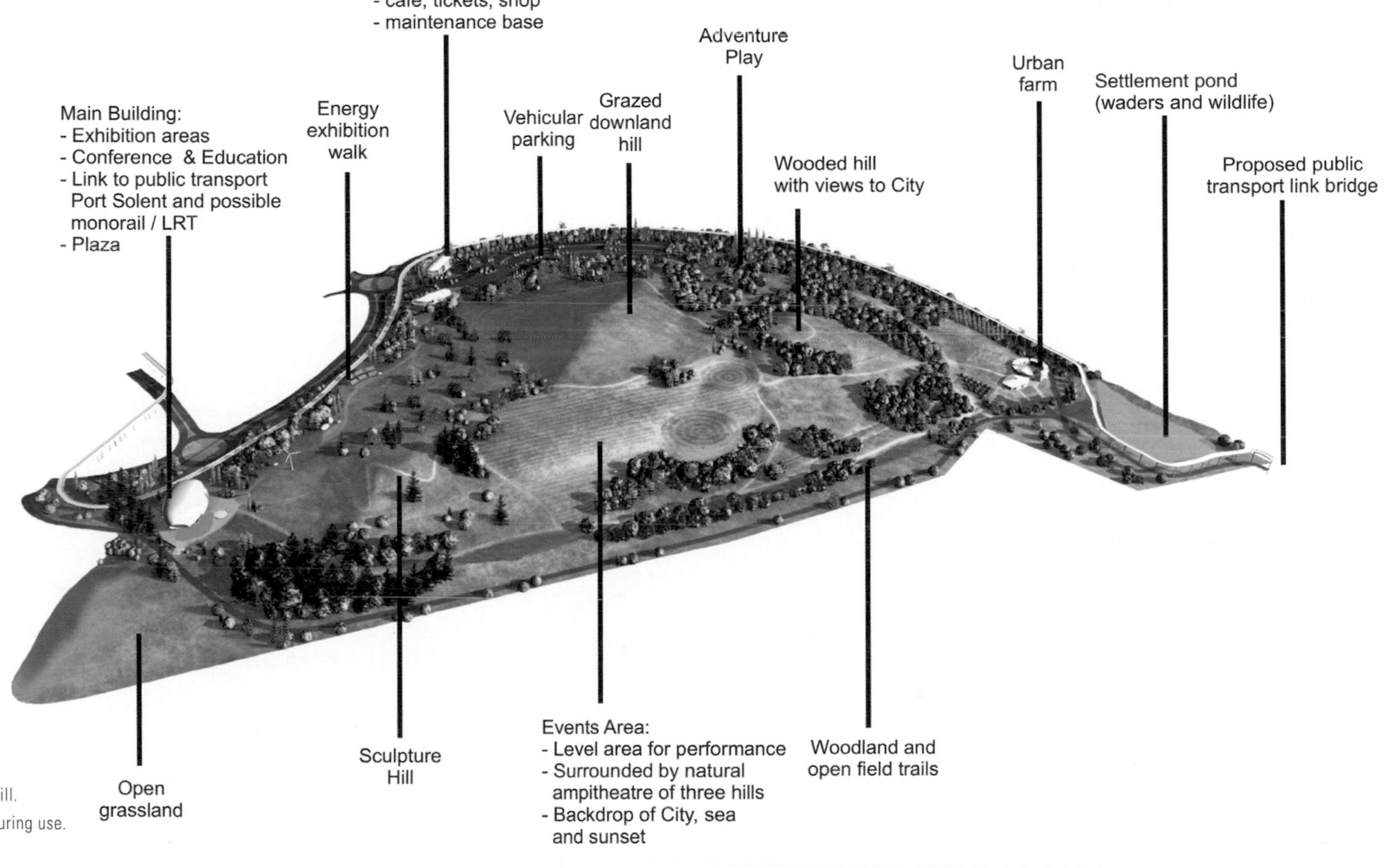

(left top) Photomontage top of hill.
(left bottom) Image of landfill during use.
(this page) The new park.

(top) The master plan.

(left) Zoning plan.

(opposite page top) Photomontage route through park.

(opposite page bottom) The new park in context.

Canberra Central Parklands (Int'l Design Competition), Canberra

Reinterpreting the Griffin Legacy for Canberra — New Directions in the Australian landscape

Canberra is a city whose prime generator has been the natural landscape. Developed from a winning competition of 1912, the Griffin Plan for Canberra has been inspirational in the development of planned cities throughout the 20th century. Griffin's plan for Canberra illustrated a city for the future, one which he saw as an ideal designed city fitting into the landscape.

Oxigen's first prize winning scheme for the Canberra Parklands (2007) builds on to Walter Burley Griffin's legacy and the contribution by other notable landscape architects including Dame Sylvia Crowe through a new landscape layer. These parklands occupy an area of 115 hectares focused on Lake Burley Griffin which lies as the central key point to the Canberra Plan within the Parliamentary Triangle.

The proposal leads to a new direction in the understanding of the Australian landscape, life and its future. The scheme responds positively to the principles of the site — revealing the historic layers inherent in the Griffin Legacy, building on to the existing positive qualities and attributes of the site, celebrating the local distinctiveness of the place, maintaining scale, resolving car parking, traffic and pedestrian movement, and encouraging activation during the night as well as the day. Equally valuing art and science, nature and culture, the design amounts to a poetic desire to develop an Australian design ethos, one that transcends the visual to contribute to an overall environmental agenda. The scheme:

- incorporates filtration of the broader City's urban stormwater before it enters the lake;
- adopts appropriate materials choice;
- formally resolves and promotes comfortable pedestrian and cycle movement supportive of principles for healthy cities; and
- minimizes energy production as well as generating energy back into the City's grid.
- transforms the park through many minor moves, building onto the existing site assets and infrastructure, rather than by grand gesture.
- responds to the greater landscape context: the natural context including and Griffin's designed city with major land axis aligning the city within the landscape

The vision for the park to connect within the larger urban context is formally resolved and promotes comfortable pedestrian and cycle movement supportive of principles for healthy cities.

A cohesive palette of materials, textures and finishes were proposed for environmental sustainability, to reduce life-cycle costing and to reflect Canberra and Australia's sense of place. The proposal of introducing new materials into a landscape integrated with innovative ways of using existing materials supports the educational and interpretive role of the park.

This is a contemporary interpretation and a new direction in landscape architecture in Australia — the landscape as a contributor to environmental sustainability at all scales of the city, an energy producer, rather than consumer. Just as Griffin designed Canberra as a city for the future, this scheme proposes a future for Australia's urban parklands.

Since the announcement of the winning scheme, Oxigen has been engaged by the National Capital Authority to develop the Master Plan for the Central Parklands. In conjunction with this, The RG Menzies Walk along the lake edge, has been identified as a project that can be designed and implemented in parallel with the development of the Master Plan. This component is currently in design documentation and is anticipated to be completed in mid 2008.

client / owner
National Capital Authority, Australia

location
Canberra, Australia

awards
First Prize, Canberra Central Parklands International Design Competition

(top) The master plan is a transformation of the site through a series of parkland experiences derived from archetypal Australian landscapes. It sees the new landscape as a contributor to environmental sustainability at all scales of the city.

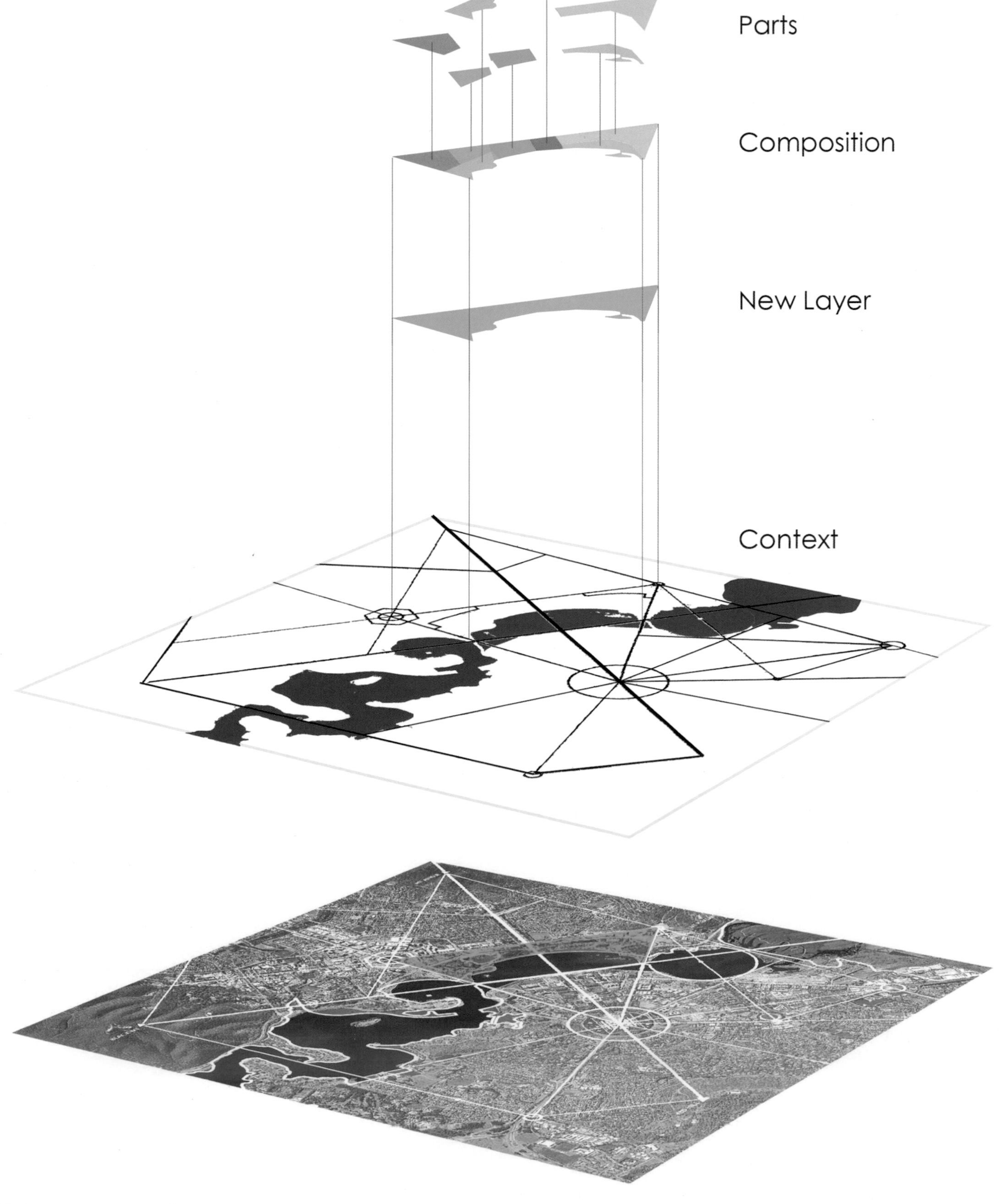
Parts
Composition
New Layer
Context

(left) A new layer for the park is proposed responding to contemporary concerns, whilst celebrating the social, historic and symbolic life of the capital. The parts represent the future implementation strategy for the park.

(top) The scheme proposed a subtle transformation of the park by a staged removal of moribund and inappropriate species and replacement with new local native species whilst retaining a proportion of exotic trees to reflect Canberra's European settlement and cultural identity.

(middle) Nerang Pool — a new layer of landscape detail is added to Nerang Pool, retaining the existing edge and stone wall but introducing 2 new islands and extensive aquatic planting with increased water filtration qualities. Nerang Pool assumes the landscape qualities of a new place, visually diverse and environmentally sustainable.

(bottom) Water Room — water quality achieved through filtration and extensive aquatic planting becomes a key principle for the transformation of the parks. New water rooms are introduced adjacent to the stream entering Nerang Pool, cleaning stormwater runoff from Civic and Parkes Way. The existing stone walls edging the stream are retained and opportunities for water play and education introduced.

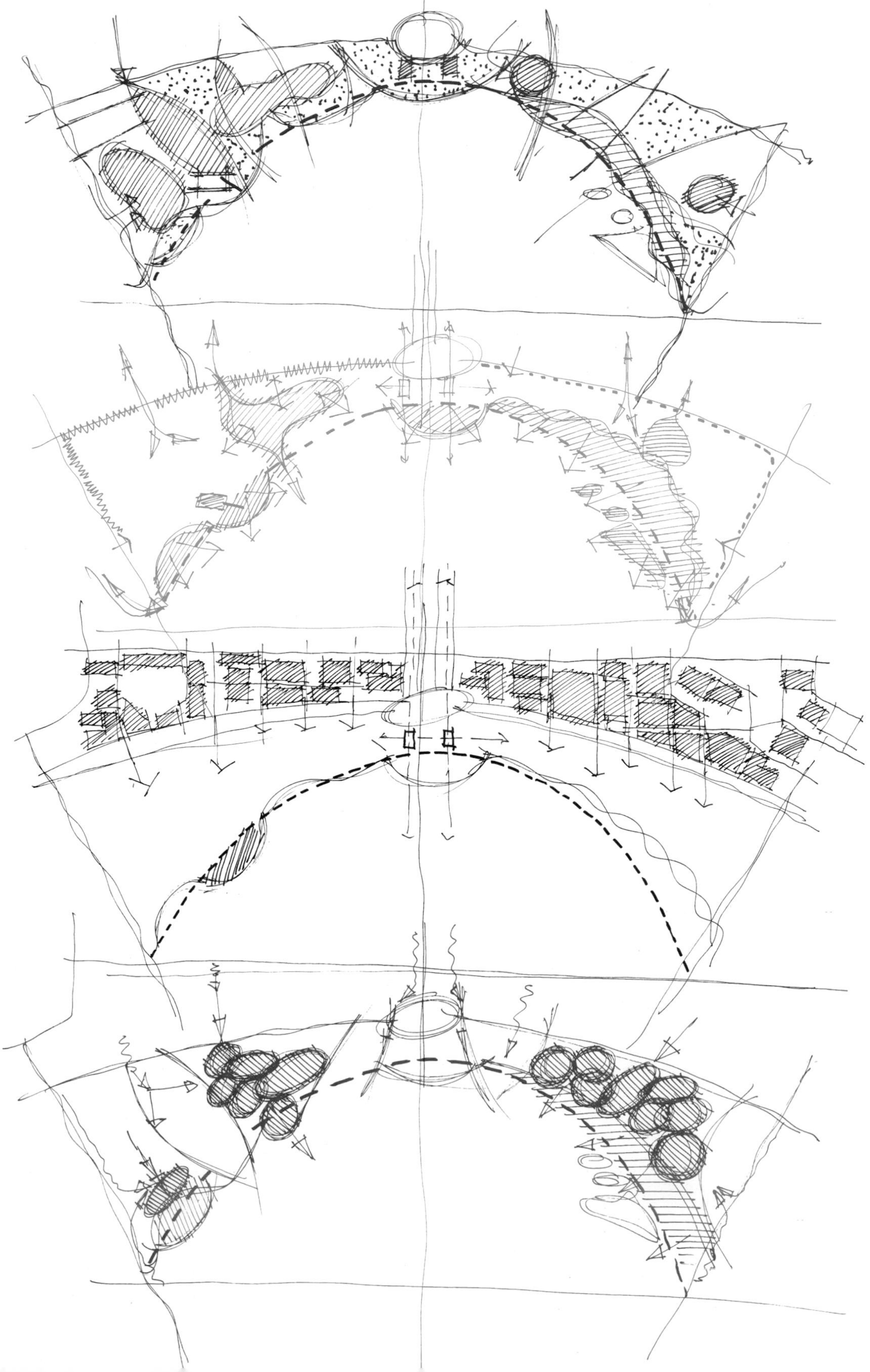

(left) The proposed master plan builds on existing site qualities and explores spatial interaction and structure as well as looking at the park as an energy producer.

(right top) Meadows — the rich diversity of the original Limestone Plains grasslands is displayed in the parks, eventually replacing Floriade with an Australian Floriade —— a sustainable display of colour, textures and forms that celebrates our native flora. This display will increase the tourism potential of Commonwealth Park and its attractiveness as a destination.

(right middle) Beaches — beaches along the Murrumbidgee River between Tharwa and Casuarina Sands are repeated at the lake's edge, reflecting an Australian way of life and love of the outdoors. As well as being the visual focus of Canberrra's plan, Lake Burley Griffin becomes more of a venue for activity and active participation, also working with the Jerrabomberra wetlands to collect and clean central Canberra's stormwater run-off. Interactive interpretive kiosks line the lake edge, celebrating the life of former Australian Prime Minister Robert Menzies.

(right bottom) Water garden edge — the lake margins are transformed by introducing water gardens into Lake Burley Griffin. The gardens improve the lake's water quality as well as the aesthetics of the lake overall. The gardens are accessed from the RG Menzies Walk onto boardwalks set just above the water surface leading to partly submerged expanded metal deck walkways. Solar collectors within the gardens power lighting mark the original Griffin lake edge.

(left top and top) The proposed RG Menzies lake edge walk explores the use of local materials and creates a variety of experiences along the 1.9km walk. A series of 'breakout spaces' along the walk mark viewpoints, rest areas and incorporate existing memorials. This stage of work is due for completion in mid 2008.

(left bottom) A new environmental ethos — a new aesthetic transforms Kings Park, replacing the extensive areas of exotic grass with a contemporary Australian landscape design ethic. The spatial arrangement of the park is retained with new layers demonstrating environmental sustainability through urban stormwater collection and filtration, bio-diversity and energy production.

(bottom) Celebrating the Griffin Legacy — the original line of the lake drawn on plan by Walter Burley Griffin is expressed by lighting. Definition of this edge is a powerful reference to the Griffin Plan over-riding subsequent incremental interventions and corruptions to his clean Beaux Arts lines for the Central Basin.

Confluence Park Master Plan, California

The Confluence Park Master Plan is proposed in response to a request by the City of Pleasanton to develop a comprehensive master plan for a 520 acre parcel of land and to address the role of urban parks in this new century. The primary objective was to create a unique place in this growing city that would set it apart from any other city in the world. Confluence Park is conceived as a continuous and inter-connected matrix of topography and infrastructure that provides for the movement of people and water to the advantage of wildlife, habitat and plantings, which respond and are designed to change throughout the seasons. Our objective was to redefine the Urban Park's role as an environmentally responsive partner, one that is both fiscally self-sustaining and curative in the long term — a gift, of this generation to future generations.

The Master Plan is the culmination of numerous programmatic aspirations synthesized into a Living System. Confluence Park is an evolving park — capable of absorbing and responding to future program elements that have yet to be imagined.

The Site:
The park land, surrounded by suburban development, is located approximately 40 miles east of San Francisco, between downtown Pleasanton and the Arroyo de la Laguna and is divided into three areas by I-680 and the Union Pacific Railroad tracks.

Planning:
The Confluence Park Master Plan is the alignment of energies and resources to gradually fulfill a three-pronged goal towards sustainability:

PEOPLE + WATER + HABITAT = SUSTAINABLE PARK

People will build the Park over time. Through neighborhood and civic interventions, the Master Plan proposes that each expenditure

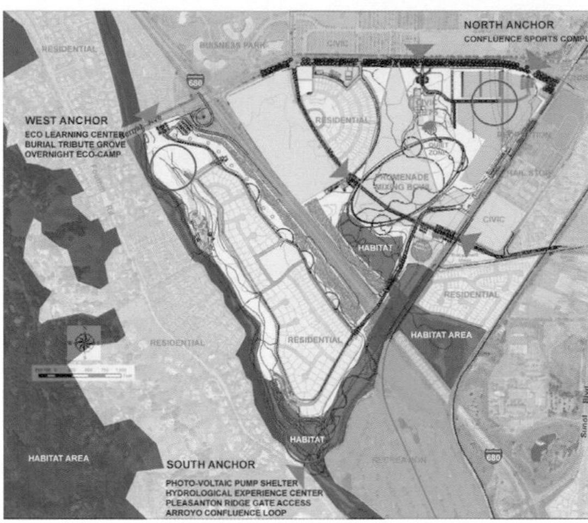

Site Concept

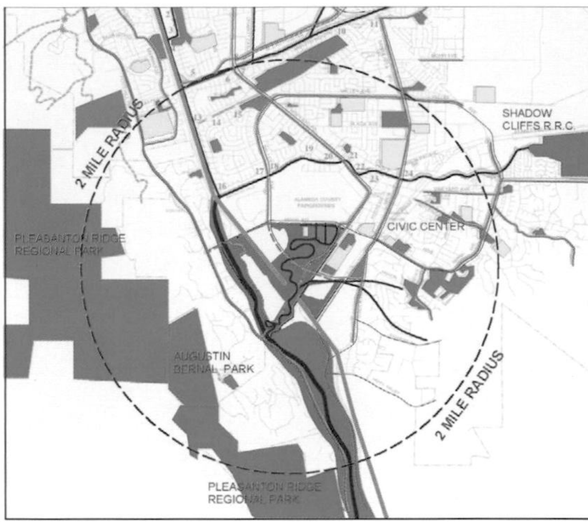

Regional Context

and infrastructural piece is a step towards building an asset. Most civic infrastructures decrease in value over time. Pleasanton's Confluence Park will increase.

Water is the departure point for an intelligent infrastructure. We propose to convert the existing developed areas to the Park's advantage; to reverse-exploit them as rain catchers for this larger living system. By catching, holding, and re-circulating water the Park will recharge the depleted ground water, while providing a sustainable annual supply that does not rely on external sources.

Habitat and ecological processes are able to re-establish themselves and replenish the park as it becomes an indispensable cultural, recreational, educational and economic resource for the city. While most infrastructures diminish, this approach will ensure a new infrastructure that will actually increase the parks land value over time.

The Living System is engendered through the unity of the park. The fact that it works as one is the cornerstone of our thinking about the park as a synthetic whole. People and water are choreographed to the advantage of wildlife, habitat and plantings, each responsive and designed to change and evolve throughout the seasons and centuries to the final advantage of Pleasanton. The Consolidation of intensive recreational program to the north allows the park extensive un-programmed open space at its core. This in turn, permits existing habitat corridors to permeate deep into the park from the South and West. This infrastructure is phased early to ensure the three embedded long-term goals:

1. To maximize connectivity within the Park.
   Regionally: through the larger natural ecosystem and the regional park system.
   Locally: by resuscitating and remediating the hydrological system.
   Specifically: by re-distributing grades to minimize the intrusion of the free-way.

2. To establish a pervasive storm-water strategy to slow, store and improve water quality on site. Using renewable energy sources to effectively: replenish groundwater, alleviate flooding, provide for habitat replenishment, and long-term amelioration and repair of the entire Park Site over the next century.

3. To establish an invaluable educational institution for future generations to learn from using the Park itself as the laboratory for the study of native emergent ecologies.

client / owner
City of Pleasanton, California, USA

other key consultants
Team at Interstice Architects
Project Principals: Zoee Astrakhan and Andrew Dunbar;
Design Team: Tim Bragan, Ivan Valin, Michael Acosta, Sa Kim;
Civil and Hydrological Engineering: Arup Engineers, Grant McInnes and Phillip Rogers.

location
Pleasanton, California, USA

awards
Northern California ASLA Award for Design Merit in Planning 2006

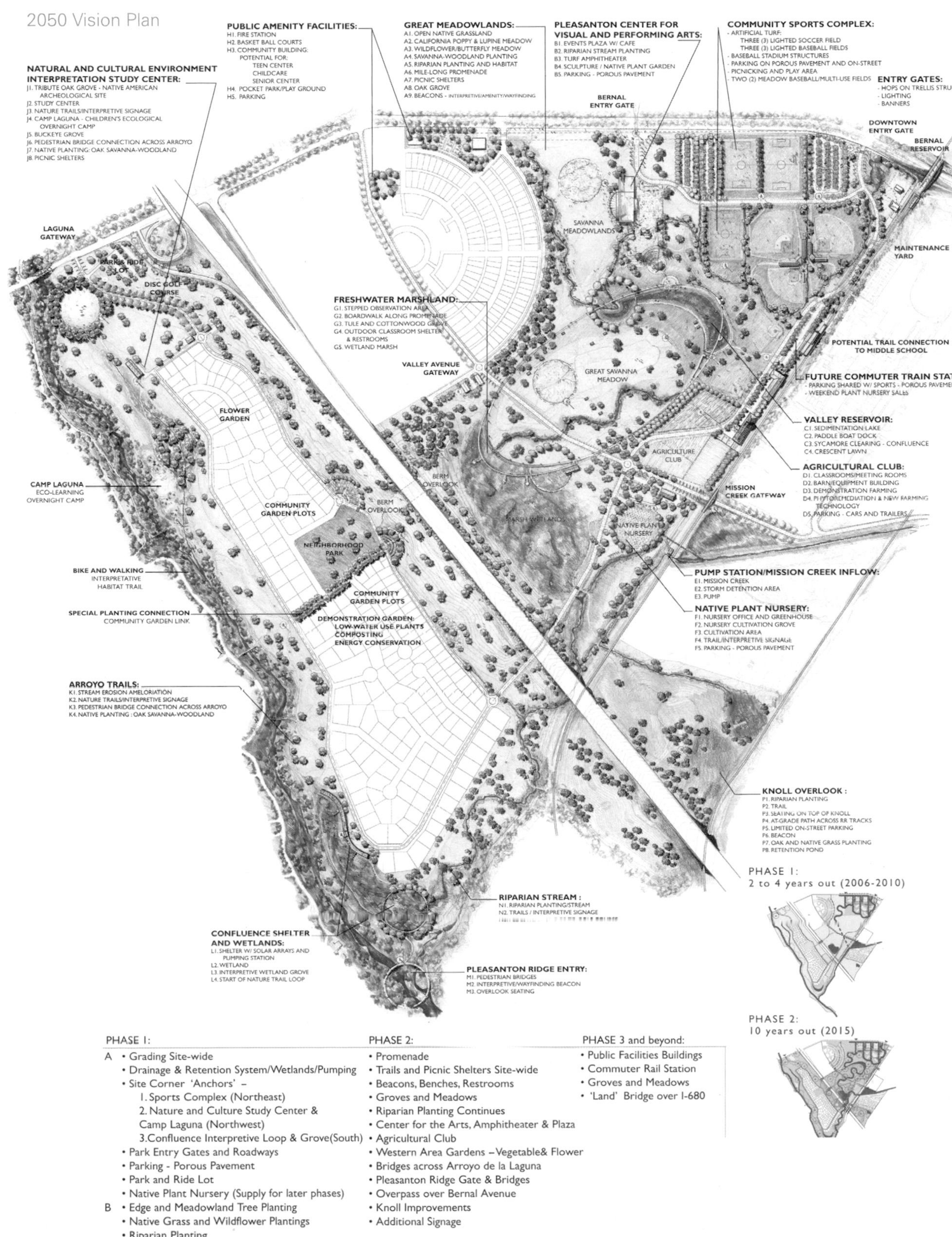

(left) The Park holds future opportunities and hydrological potential to create a Living System, linking regional open spaces.

(far left) Plan diagram showing planning relationships including land-use, adjacencies, and the three 'anchor' entry points. Concept diagrams list the objectives and implementation strategies to establish Park use by people, plants and animals.

(right) Master Plan strategy shows the potential deployment of program in the Park, where the hydrological system provides opportunities for activities, facilities and uses.

(top) Early phase grove planting by community volunteers of a 2-acre parcel, gridded and planted with acorns collected on site. The groves are located to frame views to features in the surrounding landscape, are encircled by a path of stone fines, and are under-planted with native bunchgrasses raised in the on-site nursery.

(bottom) The Tribute Grove, at the West Anchor, is the cultural and historical heart of the Park. A wide-open field framed by Valley Oaks, designates the sanctity of ancestral burial grounds at the Arroyo De la Laguna entry.

Oak Grove on Planting Day — Autumn 2005

Mature Grove Early Summer 2050

Tribute Grove of Valley Oak - Late Spring

Tribute Grove of Valley Oak - Summer

Site Sections

(top) Sections through the landforms define the vegetated riparian drainage ways and the experience of the wetlands. Section at the landform mitigation of I-680, where earth, extracted to re-grade the water system, is used to create a new horizon to unify the site across the 680 freeway divide.

(bottom left) Serial sections through the one-mile Promenade linking open spaces, facilities, and the various emergent ecologies: a sycamore grove at the Confluence, the crescent reservoir, lush riparian areas, the understory of woodland canopies, agricultural fields and wetland ecosystem.

(bottom right) Serial sections through the Promenade linking: the Savanna Woodlands, butterfly meadows, and active and passive use areas. Along the margin are the species of flora and fauna that will repopulate the Park.

Promenade Sections

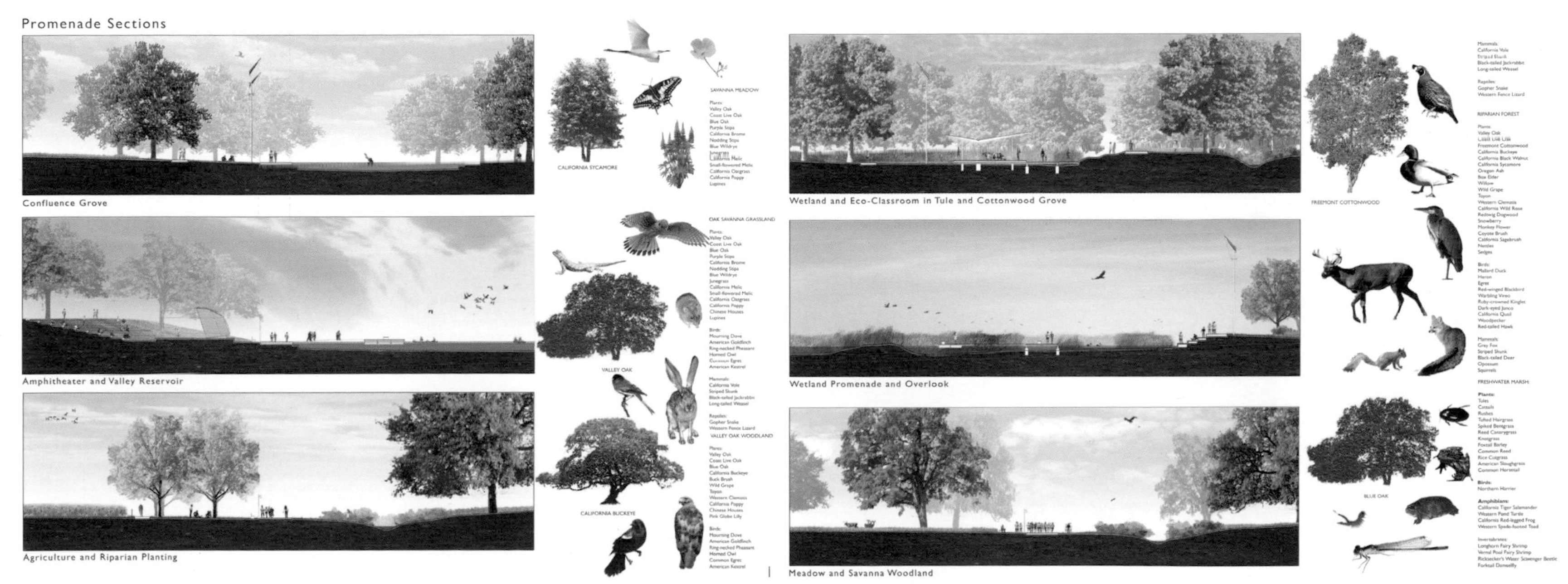

Promenade and Confluence Grove View

SEASONAL GREAT MEADOW VIEWS

Meadow View in Winter

Meadow View in Early Summer

Meadow View in Late Summer

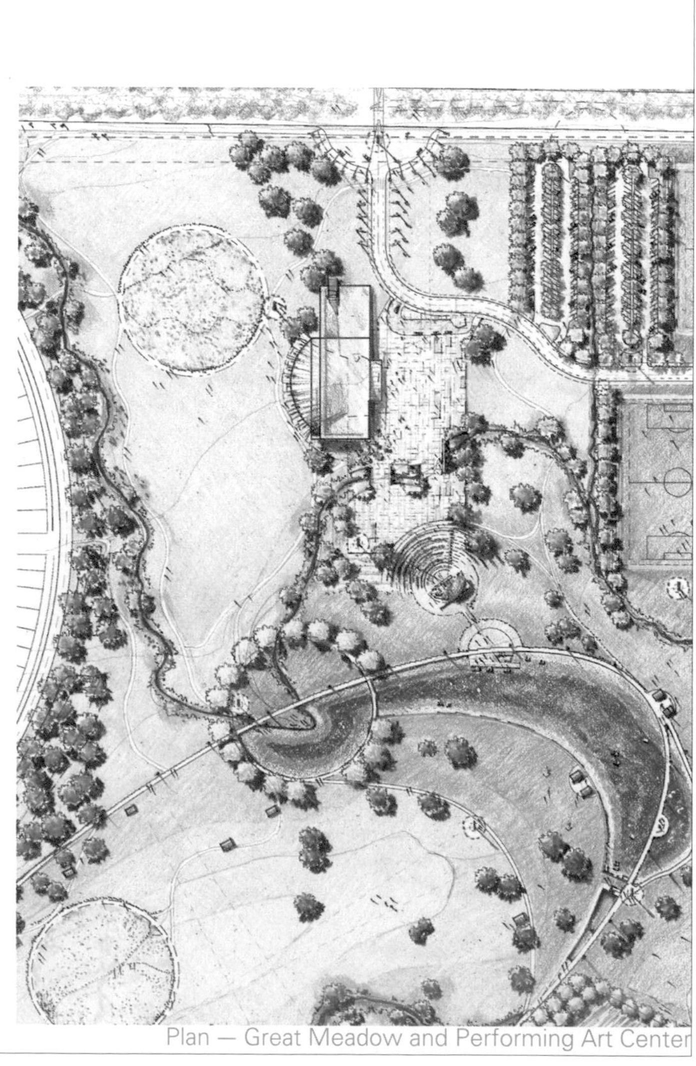
Plan — Great Meadow and Performing Art Center

Reservoir View

(top left & right) Views along the Promenade and adjacent to the reservoir show its recreational potential. The Confluence Grove is where the two forks of the storm-water collection and riparian system join to form the headwaters of the reservoir.

(left) Seasonal and diurnal views across the native bunch grasses of the Great Meadow Savannah are framed by the Visual and Performing Arts Center and perimeter Oaks. In the foreground is a wildflower and bunch grass-butterfly meadow changing with the seasonal availability of water.

(below) The wetlands are the heart of the ecological and hydrological system, ensuring sustainability and longevity. One can sit on the terraced steps looking out over the marsh, study the habitat through the interpretive signage or walk out into the marsh on stretches of boardwalk.

Wetlands and Promenade Boardwalk in Early Summer

Wetlands and Promenade Boardwalk in Autumn

Meadow Night View from Bernal Avenue

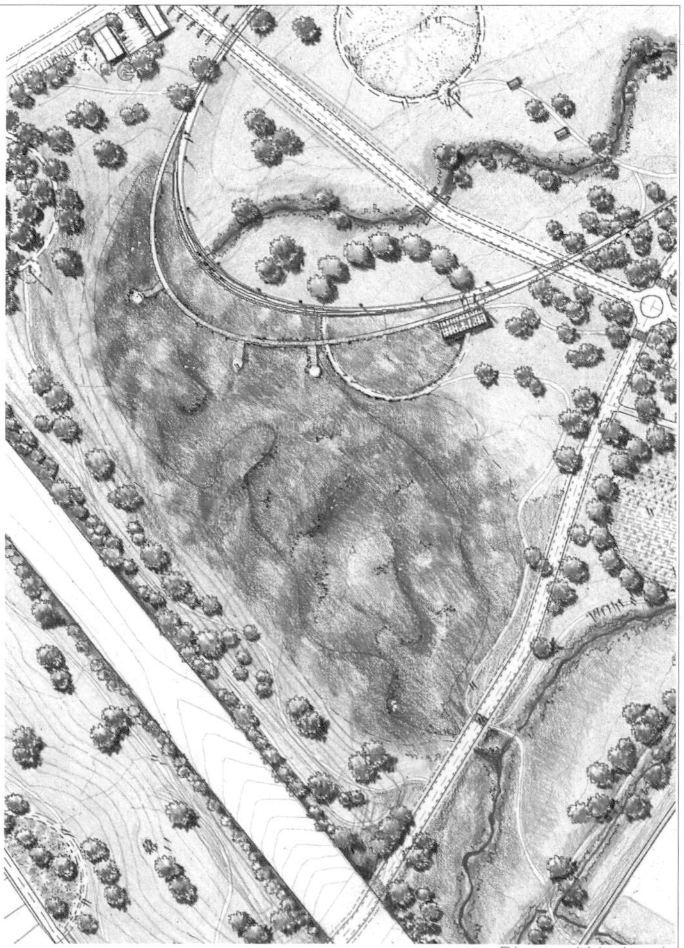

Plan — Wetlands

Reassembling Ecologies — Gateway National Recreation Area, New York

The Reassembling Ecologies proposal for Envisioning Gateway is based on an intense understanding of existing conditions and in-depth knowledge of optimal conditions for strengthened aquatic and terrestrial ecologies in and around the Gateway National Recreation Park. Running parallel with this is the need for a stronger definition of programs and activities for park users and an enhanced structure that allows for sensitive ecologies and recreation to coexist. Reassembling Ecologies attempts to repair and rebuild the deteriorating aquatic and terrestrial ecologies in and around Gateway through the rethinking and reorganizing of territories and infrastructures to better accommodate future uses and ecological flows.

The concentration and intensification of active recreation along a central spine in Floyd Bennett Field, utilizing the existing historic central runway, is the reorganizing strategy. The goal is to liberate vast tracts of land that currently have sprawling, ill-defined, uses. Intensifying activity and concentrating its footprint enables larger tracts of sensitive terrestrial and aquatic ecologies to flourish with minimal disturbance. The central spine of activity is reinforced with a linear landform. The landform, constructed of material relocated from on-site (primarily the asphalt and concrete from the retired airstrips), performs multiple functions including: gateway to park on a local and regional scale, sound barrier, viewing platform, seating, link through site and as protection from future sea-level rise.

Reassembling Ecologies strengthens both recreational and ecological functions and provides a precedent setting rethinking for Gateway National Recreation Park such that intensive recreation can exist within flourishing ecologies.

Proposed Strategies and Programs: Vegetation / Habitats

- Continue habitat restoration projects and research
- Use Floyd Bennett Field as a nursery to vegetate NYC
- Sell plants at a discount to increase vegetation on private property
- Monitor invasive species and reduce distribution when advantageous for ecological health
- Concentrate active programs to open up more areas for ecological restoration
- Connect even the smallest areas of habitat and continue to expand them
- Restrict access to sensitive areas and provide ample education opportunities
- Involve adjacent communities as habitat stewards

History / Program

- Implement Lenape tribe settlements walking tours and archeological demonstration digs
- Institute a heritage seed program on available lands of old Lenape cultivated fields
- Mark old trails on streets
- Provide ferry loop tour to historic military sites within Gateway
- Celebrate airfield history through a variety of programs
- Condense programming strategy such that all amenities can be maintained at the highest standards
- Develop private partnerships to help fund restoration efforts if necessary
- Take down old, non-designated, buildings that cannot be adapted for new use and store materials on site for future building projects
- Use Gateway as a precedent to initiate a new era of design and building in National Parks through Zero Footprint constructions

Flooding

- Implement Best Management Practices
- Create bio-swales along streets (particularly those prone to flooding)
- Foster school yard greening programs
- Green highway medians
- Provide incentive for Industrial Eco-Parks
- Consider a federal strategy for purchasing shoreline due to sea level rise
- Incorporate these new lands as part of Gateway NRA

Access

- Provide more buses and more frequent stops
- Construct future subway link with a stop at the heart of Floyd Bennett Field
- Build pedestrian bridges to link neighborhoods to Gateway
- Create better bike routes and connections, and provide bike rental
- Provide more places to dock a boat and more self propelled boat rental
- Implement all year ferry service with local ferry taxi between the various parts of Gateway NRA

Water Health / Toxicity

- Re-engineer connection through Breezy Point to allow saltwater flow into Bay (water with higher salt content will reduce rampant growth of Phragmities)
- Mandate constructed wetland creation at JFK airport to detain and phytoremediate toxic runoff into bay
- Continue to improve water pollution control plants
- Phase out combined sewers
- (Re)Construct wetlands at every available water's edge
- Use cut from these projects to level aquatic borrow pits
- Phytoremediate with bio-islands (floating mats of vegetation) and on land with plants able to remediate toxins in bay (see list of some suggested plants)
- Create new phytoremediation facility at Floyd Bennett Field to dry, compost, or ash plants that have accumulated toxins
- In the case of plants that have accumulated metals, recover metal and sell for profit

(right) Gateway Master Plan.

client / owner	other key consultants	location	awards
National Parks Conservation Association, USA	Van Alen Institute, Columbia University; The Tiffany & Co. Foundation (Sponsor)	New York, New York, USA	Second Place in Envisioning Gateway International Design Competition

PROPOSED
Pedestrian Links
Gateway Entrances
Bus Stops
Subway Stops
Ferry Stops
Ferry Lines
Gateway Parcels to Acquire in Far Future
Gateway Parcels to Acquire in Near Future
Aquatic Phytoremediation Focus Zones
Salt Water Connection
Wetlands
Bio Swales
Public Ecology Programs (School Greening)
Eco-Industrial Parks

EXISTING
Lenape Settlements
Lenape Trails
Lenape Cultivated Fields
Historic Forts and Lighthouse
Gateway Entrances
Bike Routes
Bus Routes
Subway Station
Roads
Shore Parkway
Ferry Stop
Ferry Lines
Airports
Water Pollution Control Plants
Wetlands
Significant Water Ecologies
Significant Land Ecologies
Significant Anthropogenic Habitat
Forest/Shrub/Grassland
Bathymetry
Bird Nesting Ground
Rare Bird Species Program

N

0 2.5 5 10 miles
1 inch = 2 miles

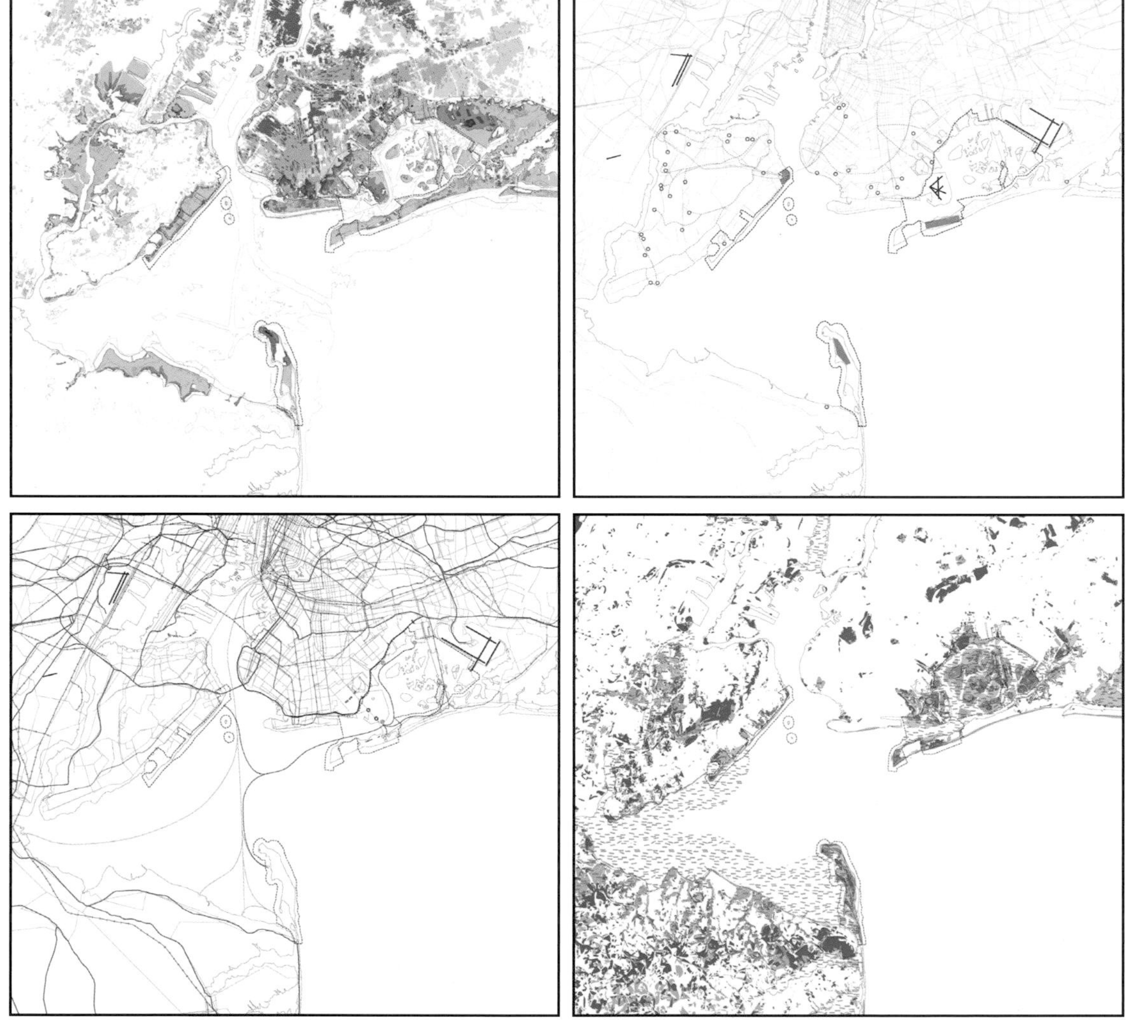

(top left) Projected flooding due to sea level rise.

(top middle) Rich cultural layers, including Lenape tribes and military structures, are scattered within GNRA .

(top right) Toxins are serious issue that require remediation, particularly in Jamaica Bay.

(left) Ailing terrestrial and aquatic habitats need to be connected and expanded.

(far left) Public transportation to and within Gateway needs to be increased.

(below) The increase of shoreline wetland ecologies will clean the bay and allow for passive recreation.

(right) Plan for Floyd Bennett Field concentrates active programs along a central spine allowing for ecologies to develop in remaining areas.

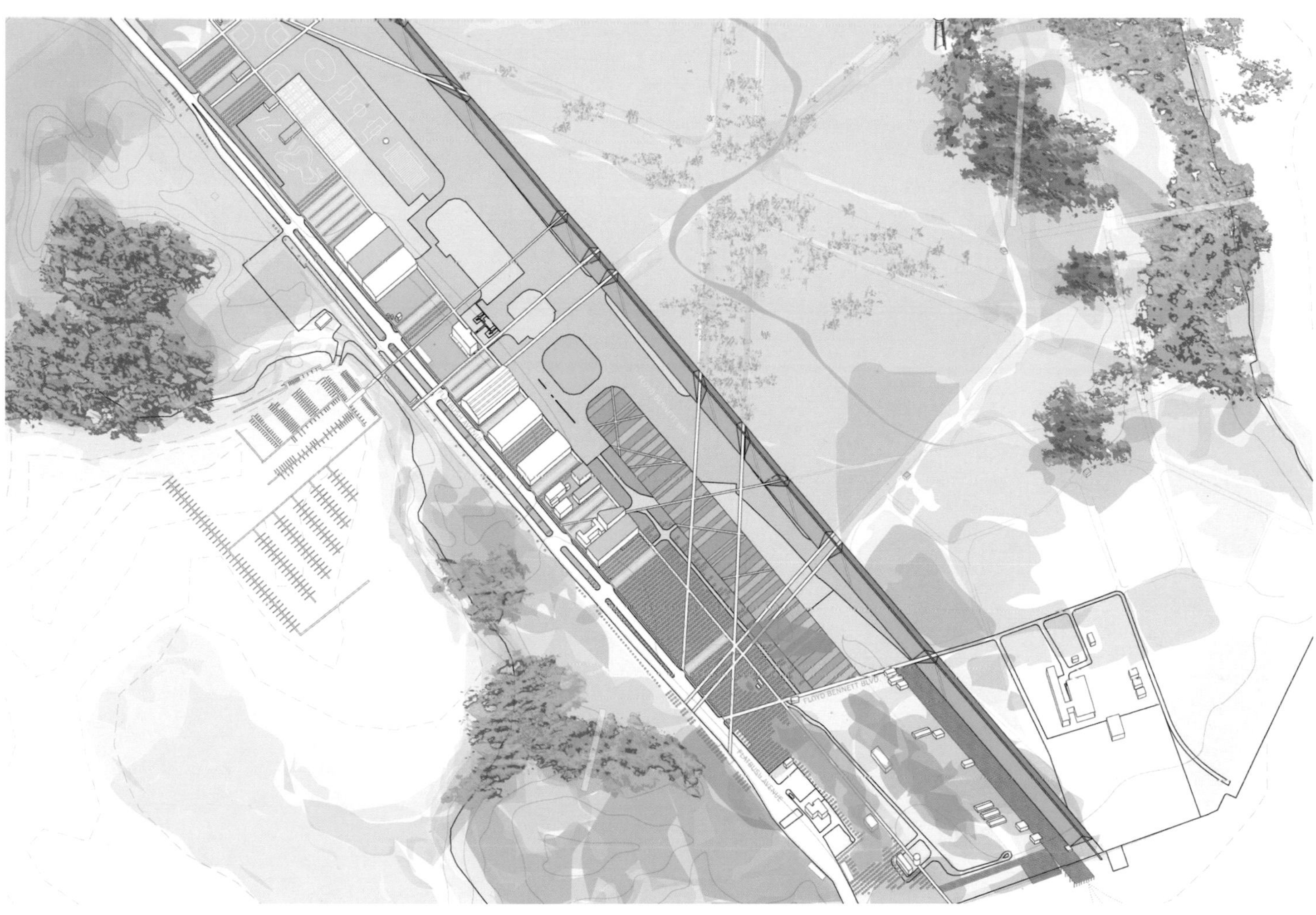

(left top) A new pier conects the park to the harbour and provides for multiple transportation connections.
(left bottom) The original runway is preserved as the central programmatic spine.
(above) Detail of the central spine of activities proposed for Floyd Bennett Field.
(below) Scattered programs should be concentrated to provide large tracts of land for ecologies to flourish.

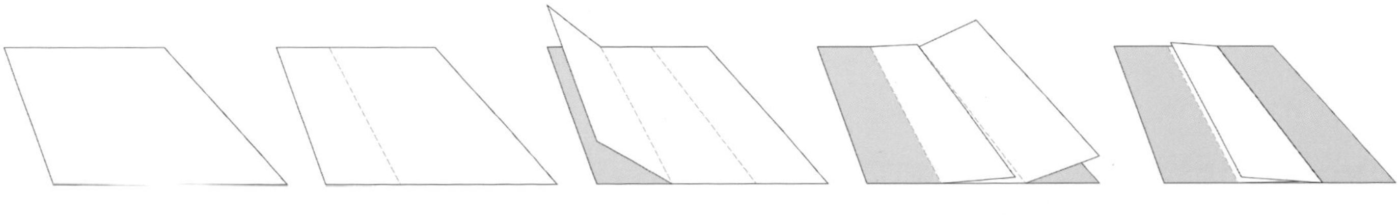

Canberra International Arboretum and Gardens (Stage 2 Design Competition), Canberra

In the 21st century, a public arboretum is a place where people are touched by the eternal inspiration of nature and experience principles of sustainability that can be emulated in their communities and homes. Canberra's vision after the fires of 2003 to create an International Arboretum and Gardens is in this vein: to create a place of 'lasting beauty', that is, a place that can be sustained to inspire future generations.

Inspiring Place's 2nd Stage competition entry conceives of the Canberra International Arboretum and Garden as a place that expresses: the powerful capacity of the community to create a beautiful and sustainable landscape based on nature's processes; the intrinsic potential of the landscape to tell the story of the cycles of life, from the transformation of a seed to the epic of the earth's evolution; and the powerful human need for forests and gardens to provide a soulful and inspiring refuge from the challenges of life in our times.

A number of core principles underpin Inspiring Place's design for the Arboretum: the nature of the Canberra landscape, an engaging personal experience for the visitor, sustainability and the harnessing of community passion, research and education.

The Arboretum strongly responds to the nature of the site: ridgelines and catchments are used as organising elements for planting and activity; the central valley, becomes an active flexible space suited to easy access and gatherings and the Saddle Visitor Centre at the head of the valley, is the start of the journey of discovery. High points elsewhere are sites for personal reflection and flatter areas for demonstration gardens.

At the centre of the experience is the 'Plaisance', a 'cultured core' in a 'wild exterior'. This is the activity core of the site and includes the 'Garden of Seasonal Delights' and the 'Great Lawn'. Surrounding the Plaisance are the informal, 'wild' areas where the emphasis of the experience is on personal exploration of each zone including demonstration gardens, feature plantings, sculptural elements and 'seeds' of contemplation.

At the global sustainability level, the Arboretum incorporates applied principles of sustainability including water cycle management, energy efficiency, materials recycling and landscape rehabilitation. At the site level, the initial development is focused within a core area yet provides seed funding for projects across the whole site. Maintenance activities are rationalised through the grouping of species by climatic zones and the general clustering of 'gardening' activities within the Plaisance.

The plan identifies the possibilities for the community to be involved in the creation of the Arboretum through volunteerism, in-kind contributions and/or monetary donations. Volunteer participation will not only build the Arboretum but will also add to the well-being of Canberra and provide opportunities for the personal fulfillment of volunteers. Chief amongst the in-kind opportunities identified at this time is that to engage with established groups working to preserve local regional vegetation types.

The plan firmly embeds research and education within the Arboretum from the macro scale of the Australian National University's research facilities to the micro scale of individual interpretation nodes, from the public interactive experience to the private contemplative level.

GRIFFIN'S SPATIAL TYPOLOGY

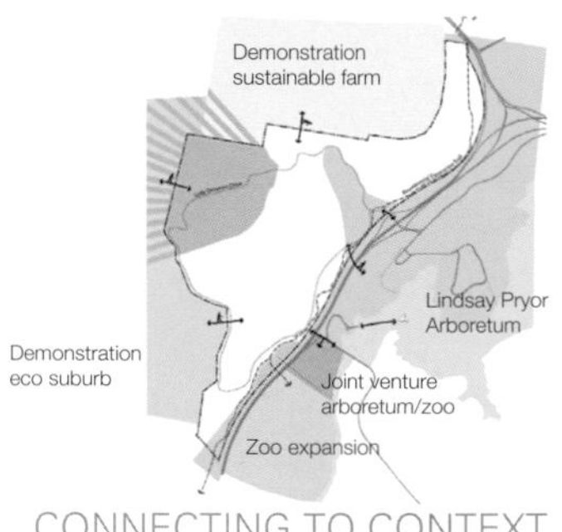

CONNECTING TO CONTEXT

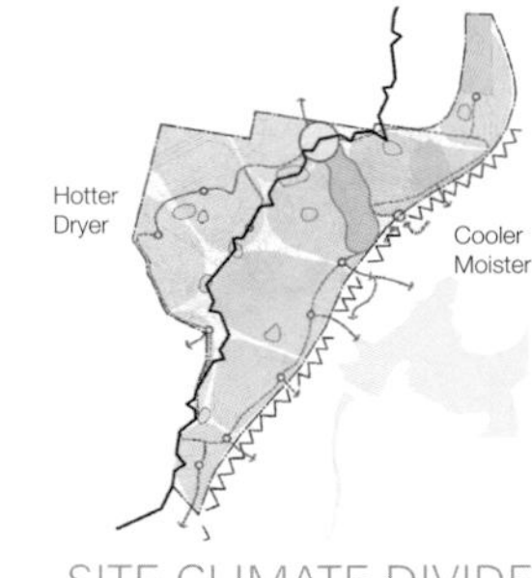

SITE CLIMATE DIVIDE

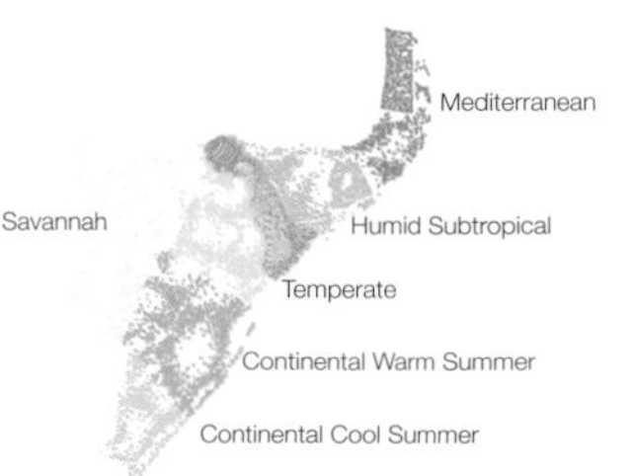

CLIMATE ZONES ON SITE

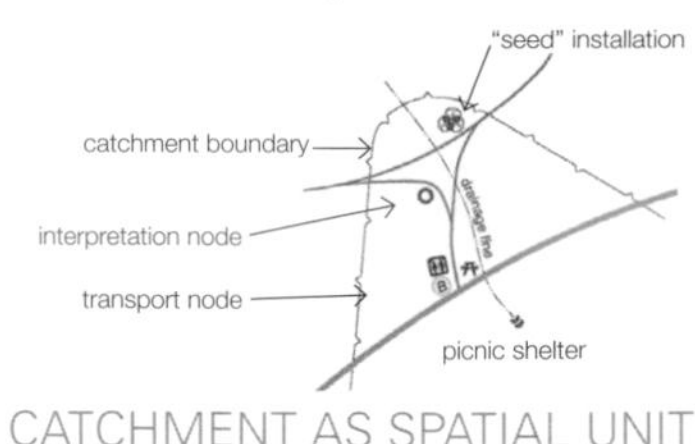

CATCHMENT AS SPATIAL UNIT

client / owner
ACT Government, Australia

other key consultants
Jacob Allom Wade, Bill Guy and Partners, Mark Fountain, Anna Housego, Horizons3, Wilde and Woollard Group, Peter J. Olin

location
Canberra, Australia

(left) Design Drivers.
(this page) Master Plan.

KEY FEATURES

THE PLAISANCE

1 Entrance
2 Car park and drop off
3 The Saddle Visitor Centre
4 The Springs Plaza
5 The Cascades
6 The Garden of Seasonal Delights
7 The Great Lawn
8 The Rock Hop
9 The Ornamental Pond
10 Temperate catchment seed node
11 Pedestrian bridge
12 Weston Lookout
13 1:20 path
14 Lindsay Pryor Arboretum and Lookout
15 Jetty and car park
16 Car park for events on the Great Lawn
17 Bonsai garden
18 Topiary garden
19 Service compound
20 Balancing pond
21 Sewage treatment plant
22 Museum of Natural History
23 Amphitheatre and sound shell
24 Dairy Farmers Cafe & Griffin Lookout
25 ANU research forests
26 Future service depot
27 Green waste recycling
28 Aviary
29 Education and Research Centre
30 Hotel
31 The Cork Oaks Wedding Chapel

TYPICAL ELEMENTS

a Transport node
b Seed site
c 1:20 path network
d Secondary path network
e Wetlands

(left) The Plaisance.
(bottom) Typical Catchment Planting.
(right) The Saddle Visitor's Centre & Garden of Seasonal Delights.

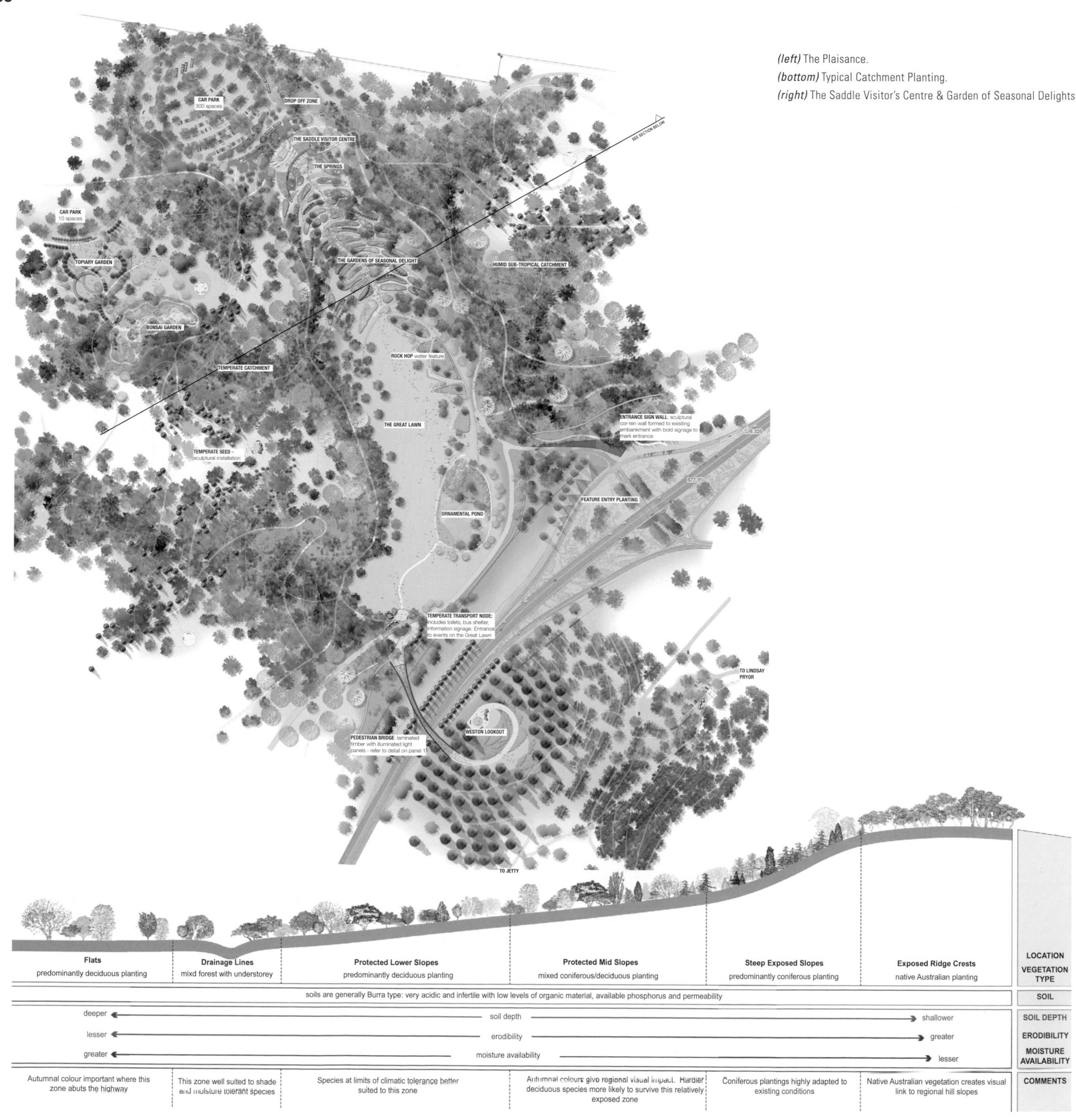

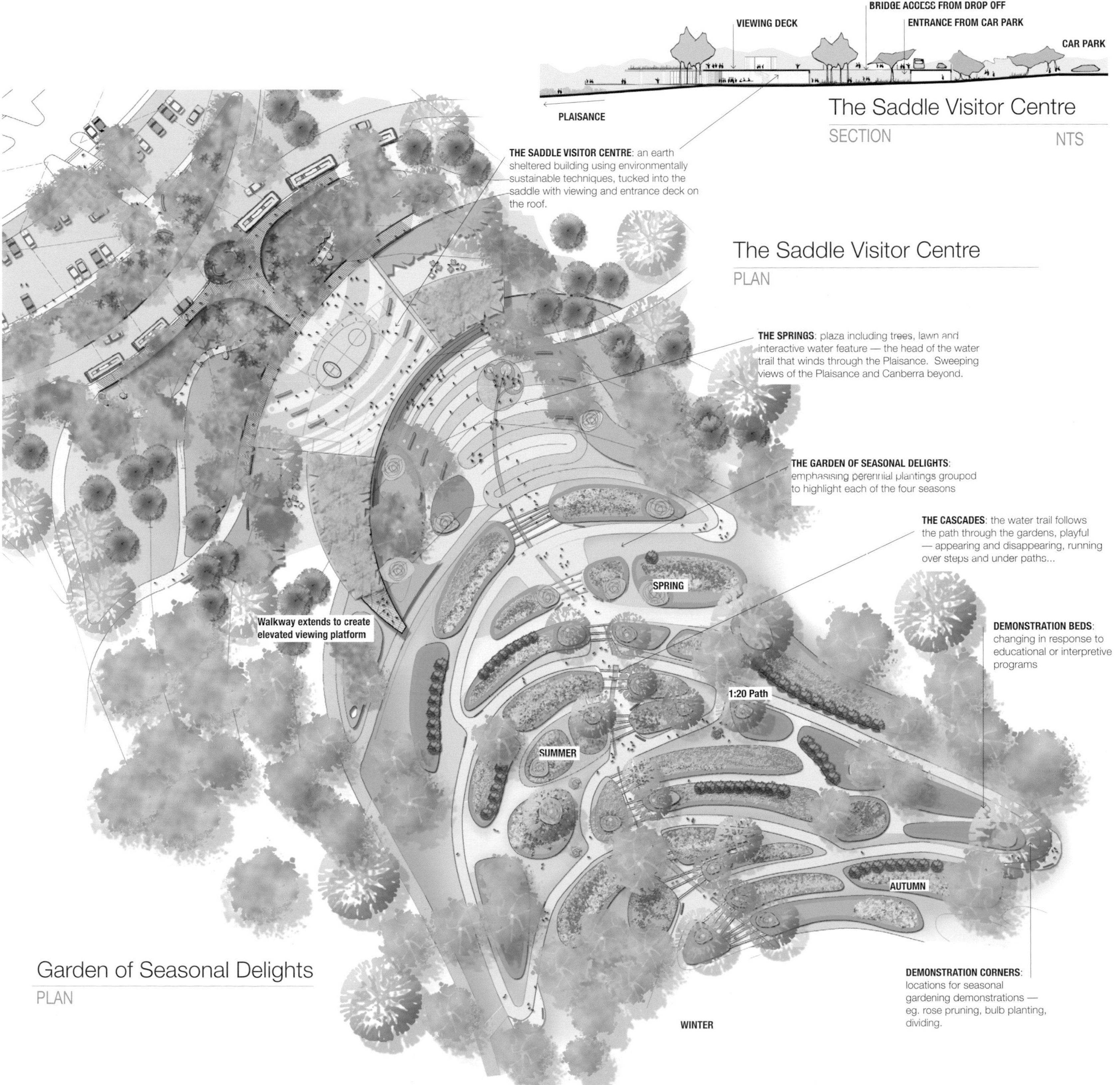
BRIDGE ACCESS FROM DROP OFF
VIEWING DECK
ENTRANCE FROM CAR PARK
CAR PARK
PLAISANCE
The Saddle Visitor Centre
SECTION
NTS
THE SADDLE VISITOR CENTRE: an earth sheltered building using environmentally sustainable techniques, tucked into the saddle with viewing and entrance deck on the roof.
The Saddle Visitor Centre
PLAN
THE SPRINGS: plaza including trees, lawn and interactive water feature — the head of the water trail that winds through the Plaisance. Sweeping views of the Plaisance and Canberra beyond.
THE GARDEN OF SEASONAL DELIGHTS: emphasising perennial plantings grouped to highlight each of the four seasons
THE CASCADES: the water trail follows the path through the gardens, playful — appearing and disappearing, running over steps and under paths...
SPRING
Walkway extends to create elevated viewing platform
DEMONSTRATION BEDS: changing in response to educational or interpretive programs
1:20 Path
SUMMER
AUTUMN
Garden of Seasonal Delights
PLAN
DEMONSTRATION CORNERS: locations for seasonal gardening demonstrations — eg. rose pruning, bulb planting, dividing.
WINTER

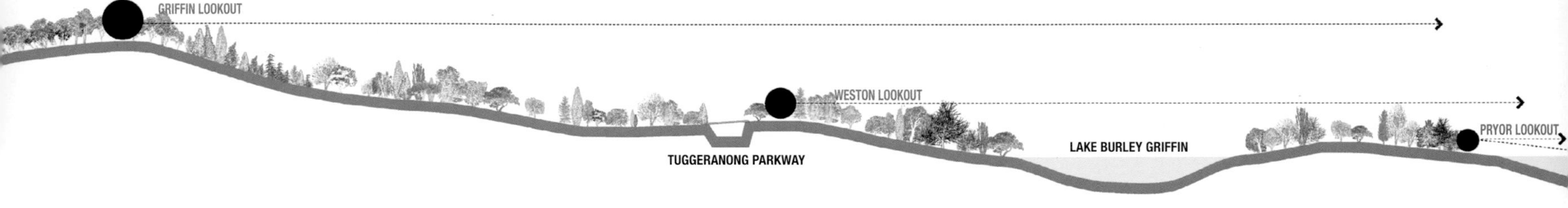

(top) Section: Three Lookouts.
(right top) Section: The Plaisance.
(below) Looking south over the Plaisance with the hills of Canberra beyond.
(bottom) The Garden of Seasonal Delights – a core element of the Plaisance.
(right) The Arboretum evolves.

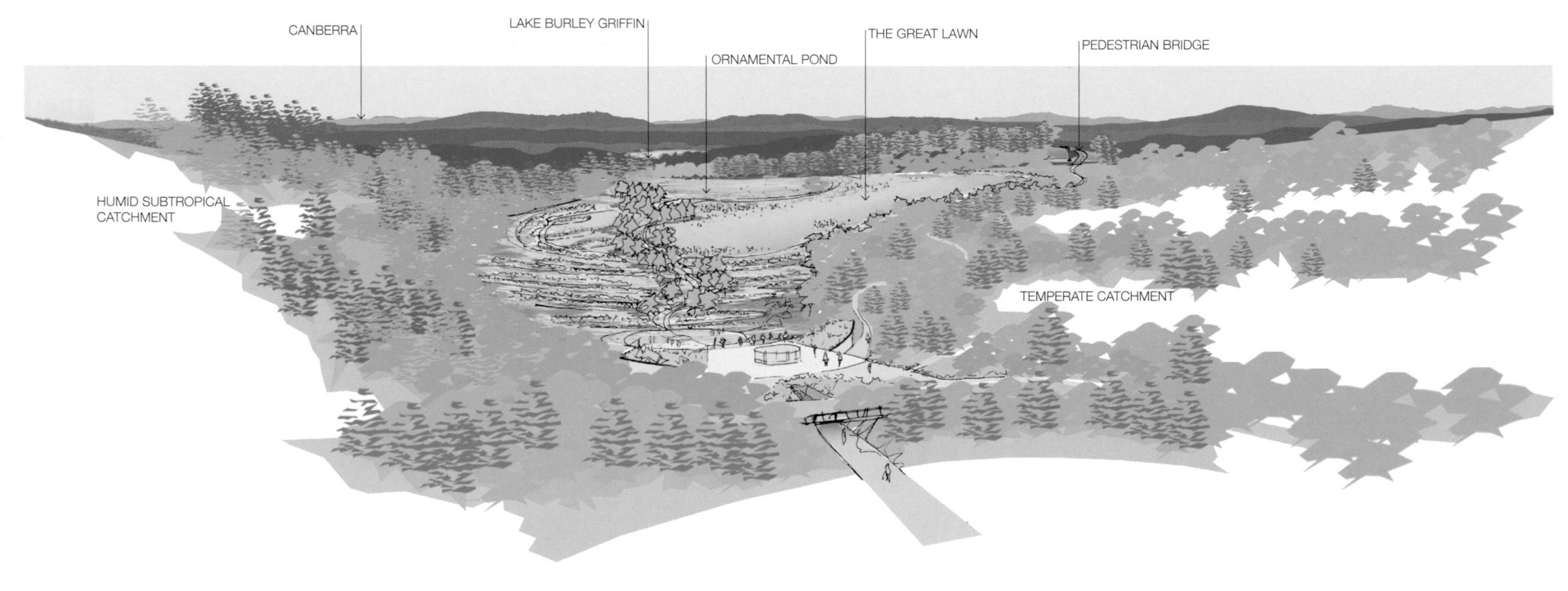

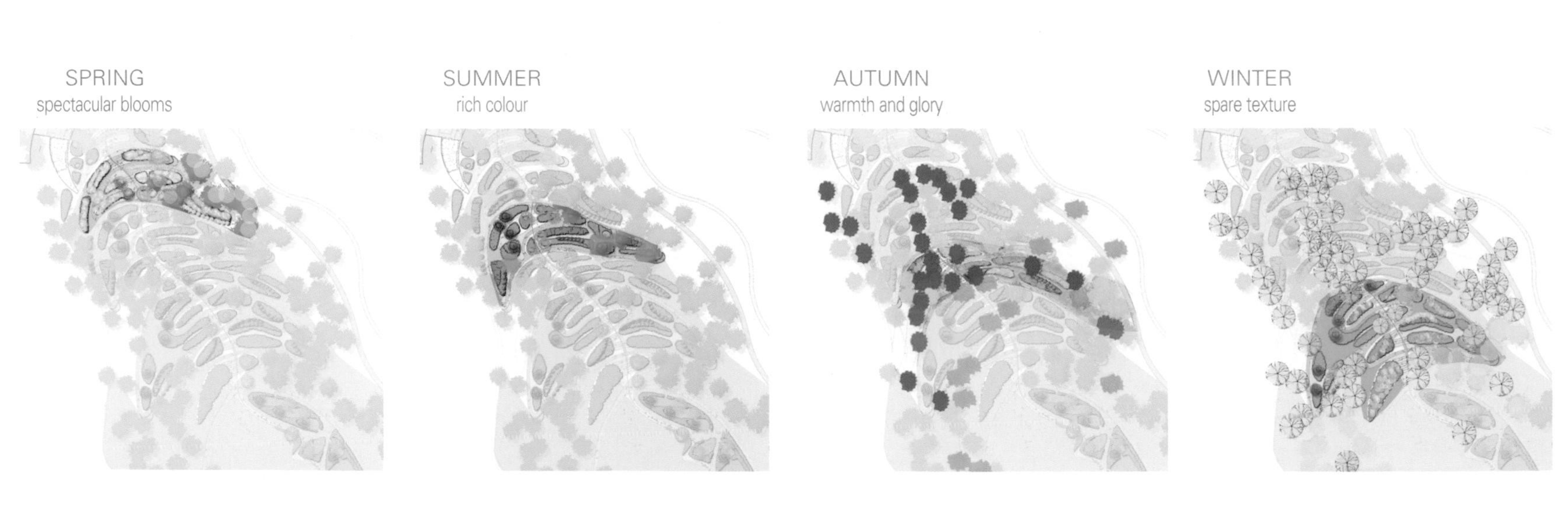

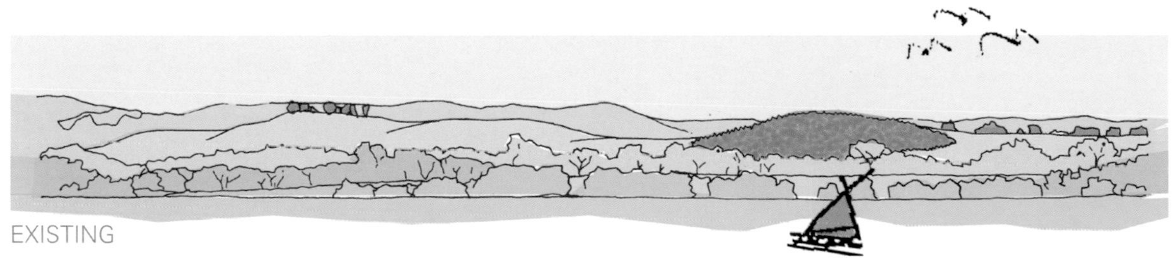

EXISTING

STEP 1: PLAISANCE AND DRAINAGE LINES

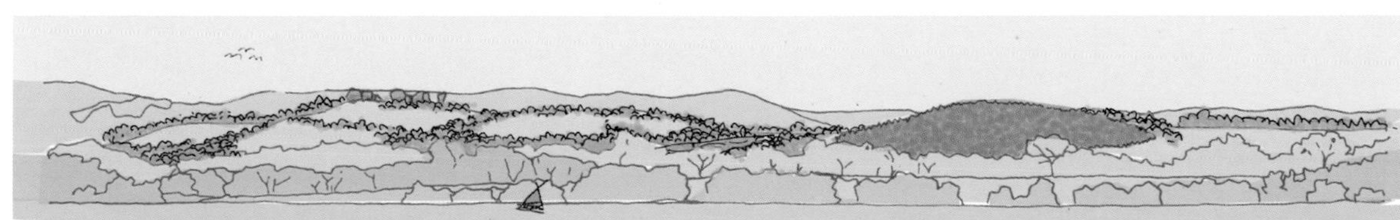

STEP 2: RIDGE LINES

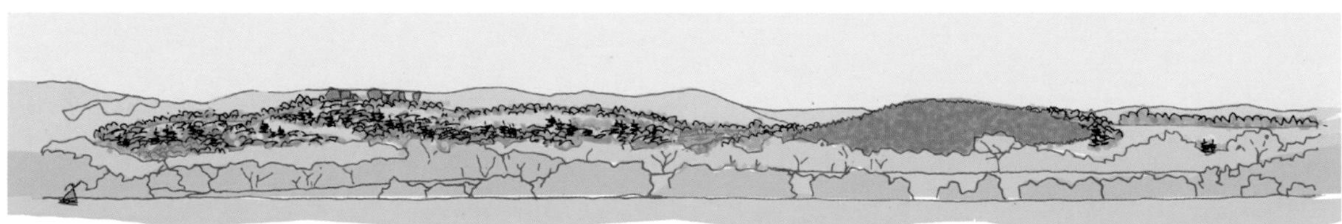

STEP 3: REMAINDER OF SITE

Diianchi Chaohai Wetland Masterplan, Kunming

The site is situated at the north eastern (Cao Hai) reaches of the Dianchi lake adjacent to the city of Kunming. The lake adjacent to the site is highly polluted with nitrates from agricultural out-wash and by effluent discharge from adjacent small holdings. A stream, with even higher levels of pollution runs to the east of the site entering the lake at the southern boundary. The land is generally low lying and cultivated with paddy or fish ponds, apart from an area of abandoned land reclamation, which sits approximately 1-1.5 metres higher than its surroundings, which is occupied by a tree nursery. The site area is designated as 'green' in the new Kunming Structure Plan.

The design objective was to provide a public park, but one that would make a positive contribution to the environment and residential communities that were planned around the lake.

The design was developed to be environmentally, as well as aesthetically functional. The Wetland Park is essentially a concept module that can be repeated around the lake as a system of 'green kidneys'. The wetland uses sustainable low technology to continuously take polluted lake water and treat it through natural processes to provide clean fresh water for parkland lakes. Clean water is continuously released back into the lake, which coupled with antipollution policies, will eventually lead to a 'dilution' of pollutants and ultimate cleansing of the main lake itself.

The flat nature of the site posed some issues for how water could be made to flow through the system. Gravity is the optimum force but requires a 'head' of water. Three major wetland cells were designed. The first and second took advantage of the higher reclaimed land while the third would be re-graded using excavated material from formation of the clean back-water ponds. The first cell is designed as a subsurface flow wetland (which is the most efficient for water treatment); the second and third cells are open channel wetlands for further pollutant 'reduction' and water oxygenation. Each main cell is divided into sub-cells and graded so that water will flow through it under gravity and each sequential cell is surcharged with water from the preceding cell.

The next challenge was devising a mechanism of elevating water from the lake into the first cell and from each main cell to the next to ensure a constant flow. The fantastic winds that continuously blow across the lake offered the ideal solution. Using the Dutch Polders as inspiration, banks of windmills are located at the top of each major cell to lift the water and supplying 'races' that then evenly distribute the water into the cell to create the 'head' required to generate the flow.

The wetland cells are located adjacent to the lake. Treated water flows into a 'clean water' pond network that is surrounded by traditional parklands with boardwalks, lawns, forest belts and waterfront meadows.

The northern end of the site is dominated by a more traditional formal park with public amenities and parking.

In the centre of the site there is a Wetland Interpretation Centre which includes the park management office.

©ICN Design International

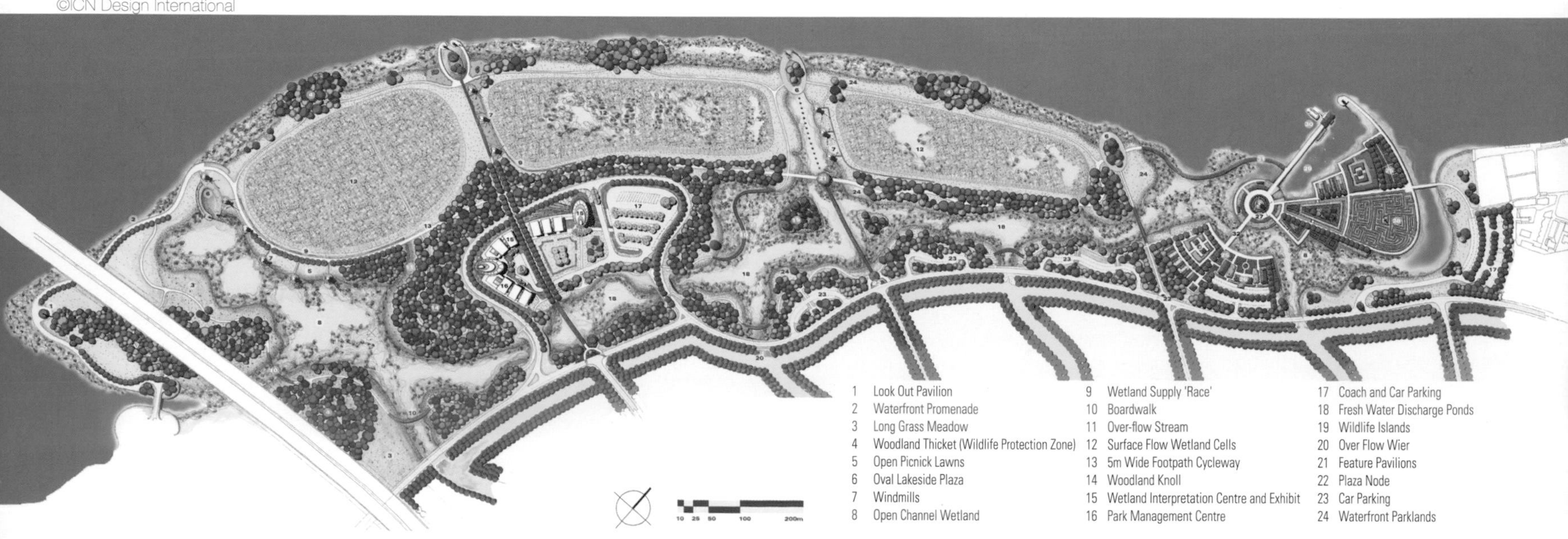

client / owner	other key consultants	location	awards
Kunming Nam Fatt Dianchi Development Co. Ltd.	Masterplan: Julien Hodson-Walker; Hydrology and Civil Engineering: Angkasa Consulting Services; Ecology: Wetlands International (Malaysia)	Kunming, China	Gold Award: Masterplanning Category – Singapore Institute of Landscape Architects (SILA) Awards 2005

©ICN Design International

(left) Masterplan.

(top) Windmills form an integral part of the park iconography.

(right) The hydrology is designed to create a continuous flow through the wetland system to provide 'clean water' amenity ponds that discharge back into the lake.

(bottom) The layout and landscape massing is designed to channel and maximize the effects of the predominant lake winds.

©ICN Design International

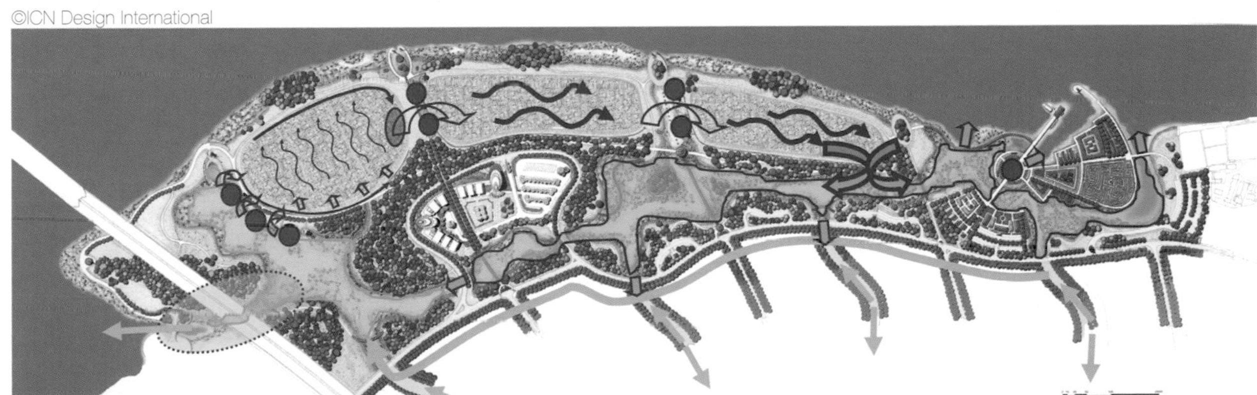

©ICN Design International

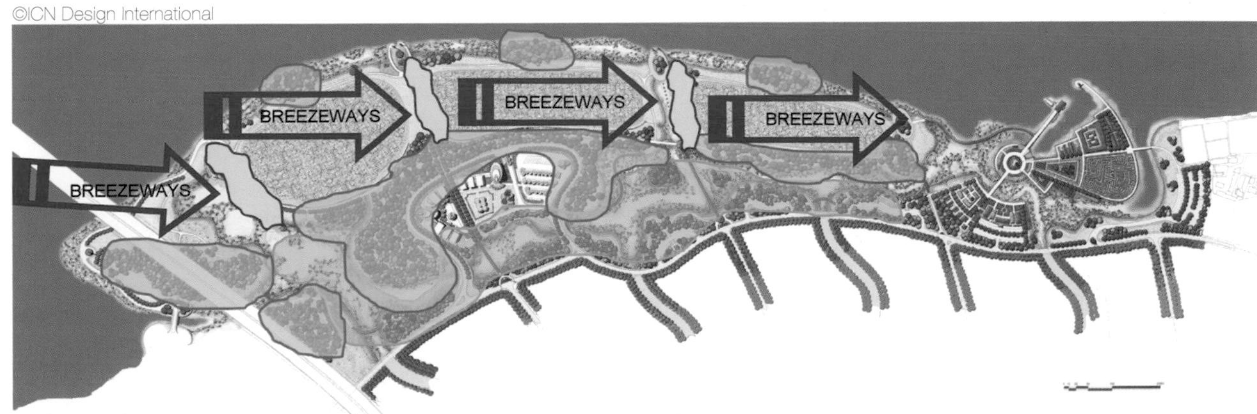

©ICN Design International

©ICN Design International

©ICN Design International

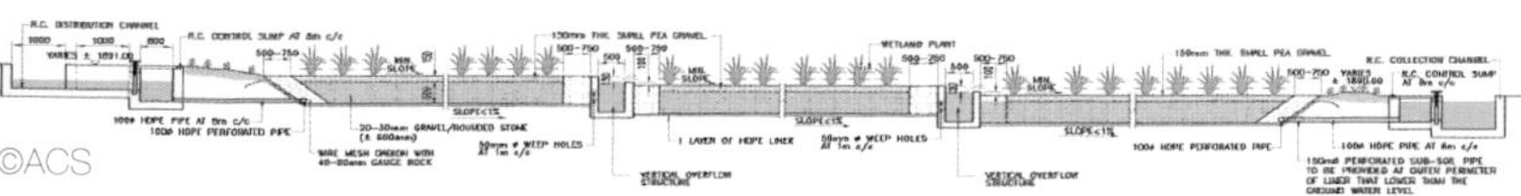

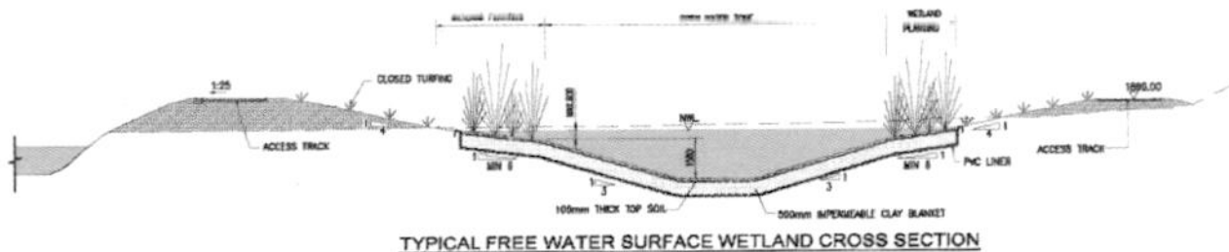

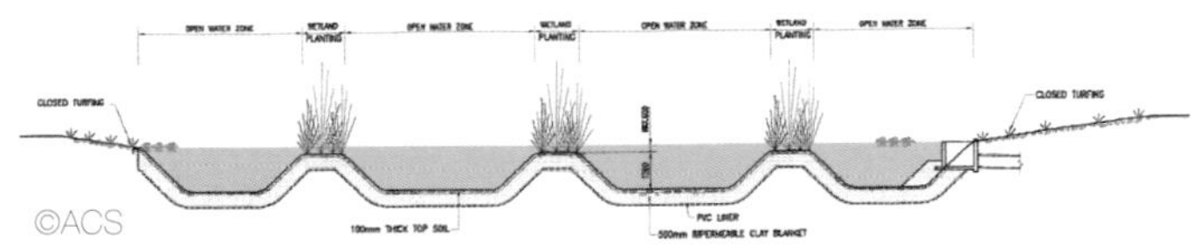

(top left) The interpretation centre is located in the centre of the park on a man made woodland knoll. The elevated location provides panoramic views from the roof top viewing deck.

(middle left) Access to the wetland environments is facilitated by traversing boardwalks.

(bottom) Bird's eye view.

(top) Subsurface flow system.

(top right) Freewater system section.

(right) Exterior berm.

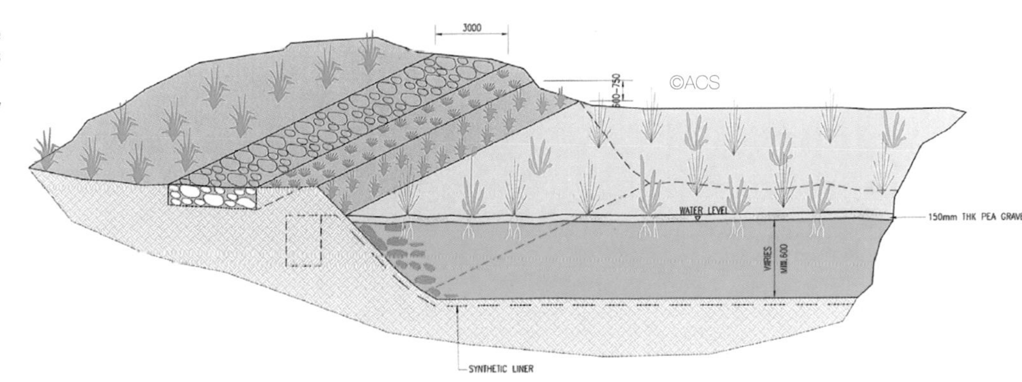

Essen Masterplan — Free Space City, Essen

In collaboration with landscape architect Andreas Kipar, the city of Essen puts a cumulative urban concept themed 'open space creates urban space' to test. This concept is aimed at establishing green connectivity - to link and develop green and open spaces throughout the city. In this process, existing inner-city streams are defined as ideational leading lines. Along these lines ('rays'), small-scale open landscape architectural projects and new linear vistas ('expose') help establish new open spaces. The 'open space creates urban space' concept is in the development and testing stage, and its results will be included in the new land use plan for the city of Essen. Due to its extensive community involvement and new urban spatial strategies, the project is a suspenseful concretion of the ELP 2010 Master Plan for the city of Essen.

Due to its classification as a public-private partnership project, it can be an important 'touchstone' for the strategic development of urban landscapes. The innovative way in dealing with the potentials of two local streams — the Berne and the Schwarzbach, as well as the treatment of available but not yet identified open spaces within the urban area raise expectations for the development of novel projects.

The Process:

Step 1: expose

— uncover existing streams

— create new open/green space and visible connections

Step 2: Highlight

— public related presentation

— 'Land-for-free' projects as initiatives for further projects

Step 3: Projection

— redevelopment of urban areas and creation of locations for investors and citizens over former industrial zones.

— upgrade of open space as 'soft location factor'

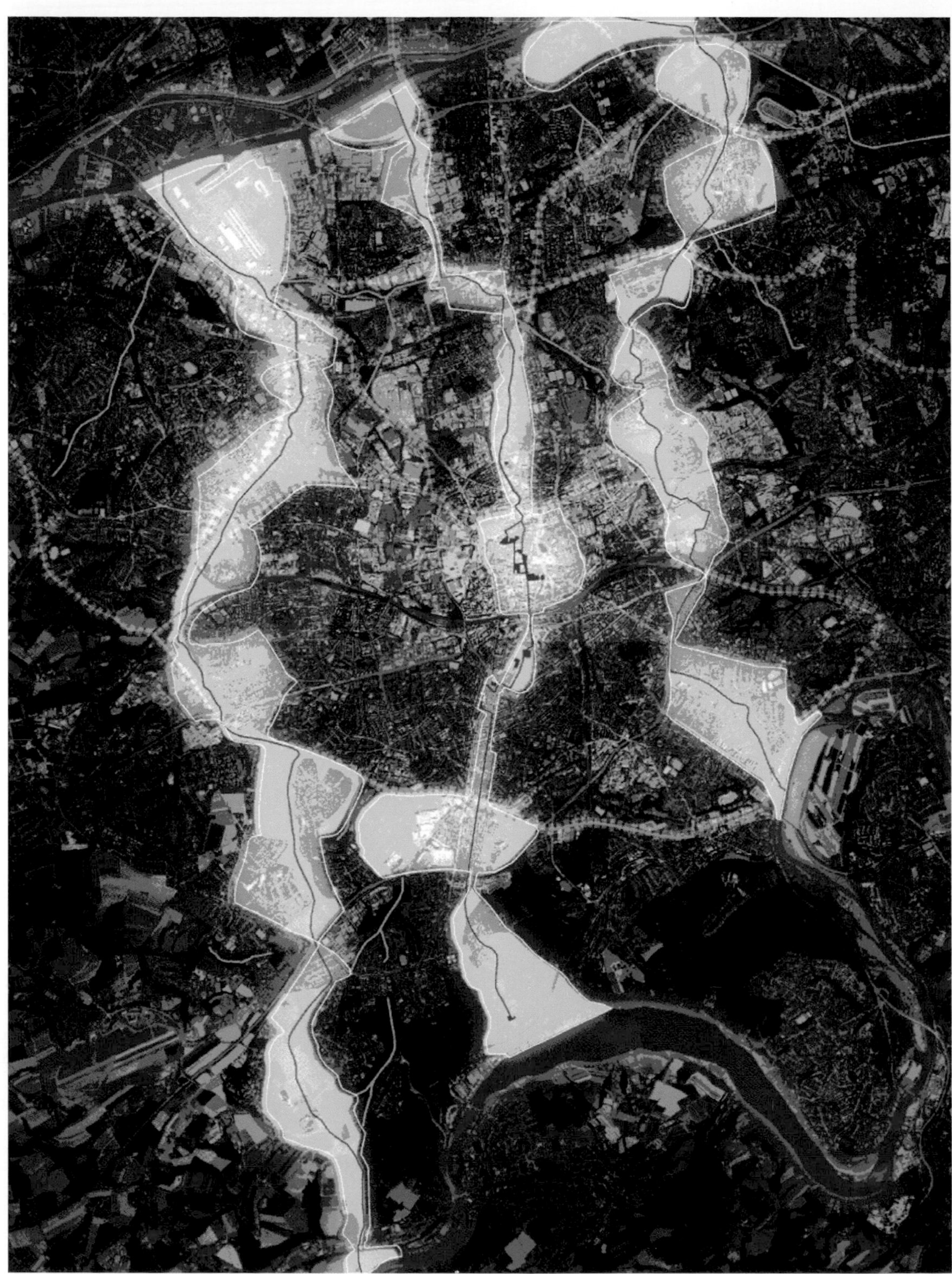

(above) 'Essen's modell of Rays' - Connection and relationship between green and open space within the municipal area, it balances existing differences in quality and quantity between Essen's North and its South concerning recreation areas. The planned regeneration of the river Emscher and its streams was the origin of this masterplan. It uses the inner-municipal streams as leading components ('rays') to link up the existing green space as well as develop visible connectivity.

(right top) Exposing the 'Schwarzbach'— valley as a designed area.

(right bottom) Realisation and upgrade of urban space (Borbecker Mühlenbach)

client / owner

City of Essen, Germany

other key consultants

Stadt Essen, Grün und Gruga;
KPMG;
Emschergenossenschaft;
Essener Arbeit Beschäftigungsgesellschaft – EABG;
Essener Wirtschaftsförderungsgesellschaft mbH;
EWG;
Universität Duisburg / Essen;
Allbau AG;
Agentur für Arbeit Essen

location

Essen, Germany

(top) Regeneration of river Emscher and its streams along Emscher street.
(bottom) Artist impression of See Altenessen.
(opposite page, top) Artist impression of regenerated Im Segerothpark and the existing situation (inset photo).
(opposite page, bottom) Artist impression of regenerated Am Bückmannshof and the existing situation (inset photo).

Fresh Kills Landfill (Int'l Design Competition), New York

Fresh Kills Landfill is located on the western shore of Staten Island, one of the five boroughs of New York City. Approximately half the 2,200-acre landfill is composed of four mounds, which are the result of more than 50 years of landfilling. Two of the four garbage mounds are fully capped and closed; the other two are being prepared for final capping and closure. Fresh Kills is a highly engineered site, with numerous systems put in place to protect public health and environmental safety. However, roughly half the site has never been filled with garbage or was filled more than twenty years ago. These flatter areas and open waterways host everything from landfill infrastructure and roadways to intact wetlands and wildlife habitats. The potential exists for these areas, and eventually, the mounds themselves, to support broader and more active uses. With effective preparation the city can, over time, transform this controversial site into an important asset for Staten Island, the city and the region.

Rios Clementi Hale Studios' proposal (chosen as one of three finalists for the competition) for the re-making of the Fresh Kills Landfill in Staten Island, to be re-named rePark, intends to make change itself the theme, experience and lesson of the place. We propose to do this by extrapolating a series of diverse "ecologies" from the differing regions of the site, and then projecting upon these a changing array of programs, or "transects". The transects, of which there would be many at any given time in the life of the park, are conceived of as both temporary and longer term sites of events and programs, not unlike installations at a museum or art gallery. The result is that the ground above the landfill cover becomes a programmable surface whose occupants — plants, animals, people — and appearance might change according to evolving conditions.

rePark attempts to work with, even expose, the continually changing nature of the site itself, and the political, economic and cultural climate that surrounds it. The design and land use constraints posed by the dynamic nature of the landfill defined both the emergent and renewable nature of our approach. The ecologies, one of the two principal organizing devices of the design, continuously transform over time, both physiologically and in appearance, rather than being cultivated and maintained to look the same year to year. Similarly, their counterpart the transects (along with the programs they carry) also change as they appear and disappear from different locations around the site in response not to ecological but to cultural change. Also, the construction of the transects, despite their dramatic visual impact, is conceived of as provisional in nature. With few exceptions, they lightly occupy the land in a way that can easily flex with the geological action occurring beneath. While most are dedicated to accommodating specific events or activities, a few are designed to act as instruments which gauge that movement, recording in different ways the secondary compression of the mounds, reminding us that the latter are as subject to the vagaries of time as the transects themselves. One not only gains an awareness of the dynamic nature of the landfill, but can also see over time the dramatic effect this has in transforming the appearance of each mound, and, by extension, the park as a whole.

(opposite page, left) Initial 2007 plan.

(opposite page, right) Full 2042 plan.

(top) View of park looking south towards Woodland ecology.

(middle) View of park looking north towards roadside ecology.

(bottom) View of park looking west towards roadside ecology with New Jersey shoreline in the distance.

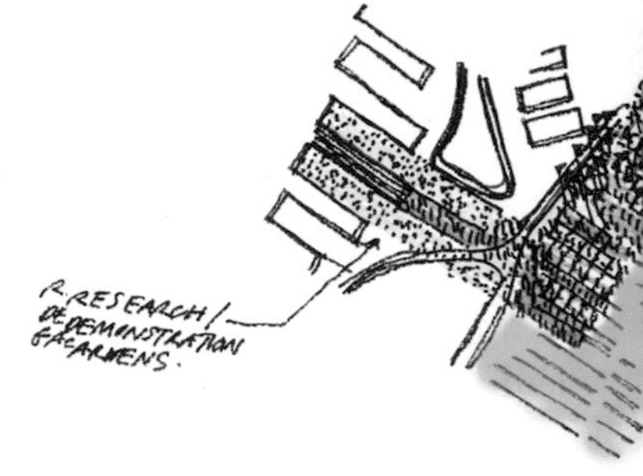
RESEARCH /
DEMONSTRATION
GARDENS.

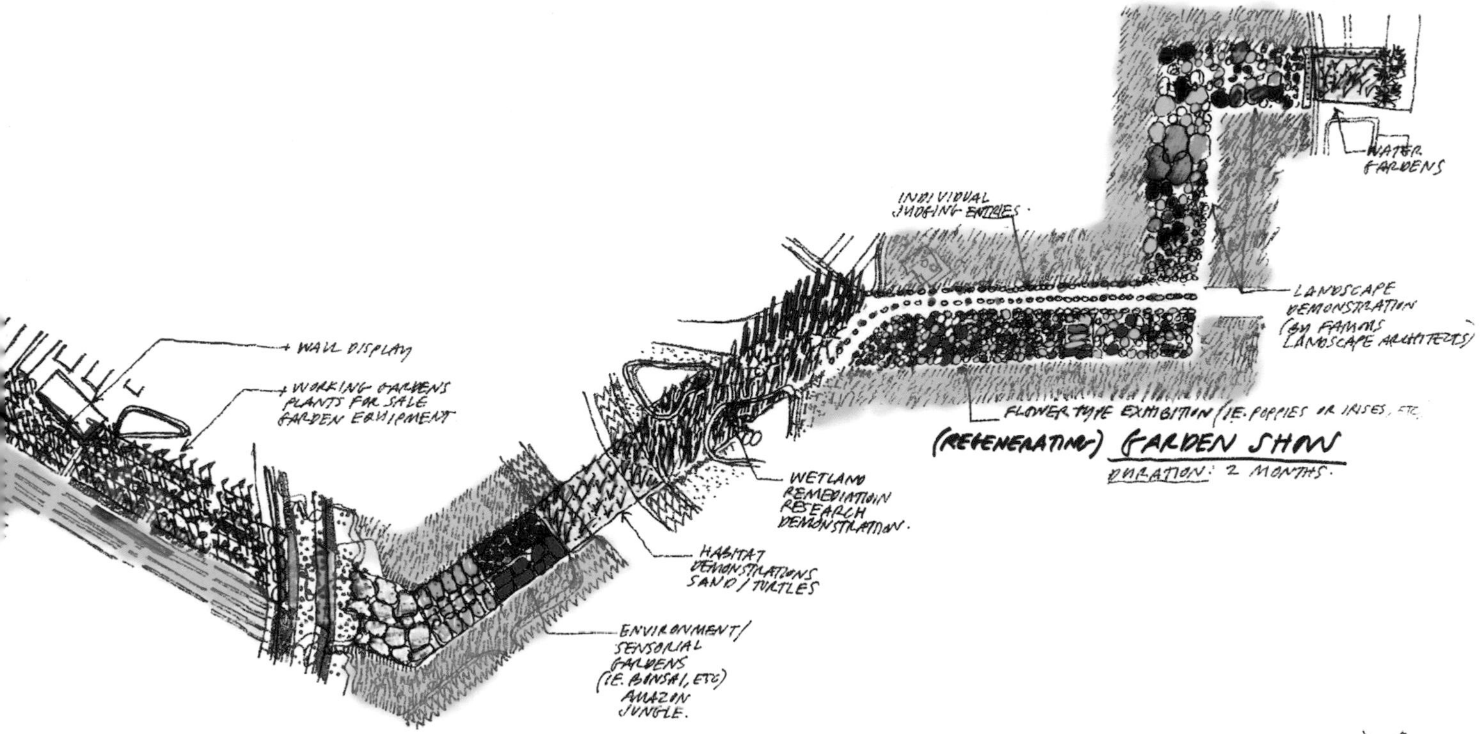

WALL DISPLAY
WORKING GARDENS PLANTS FOR SALE GARDEN EQUIPMENT
INDIVIDUAL JUDGING ENTRIES
WATER GARDENS
LANDSCAPE DEMONSTRATION (BY FAMOUS LANDSCAPE ARCHITECTS)
FLOWER TYPE EXHIBITION (IE. POPPIES OR IRISES, ETC.
(REGENERATING) GARDEN SHOW
DURATION: 2 MONTHS.
WETLAND REMEDIATION RESEARCH DEMONSTRATION.
HABITAT DEMONSTRATIONS SAND / TURTLES
ENVIRONMENT/ SENSORIAL GARDENS (IE. BONSAI, ETC) AMAZON JUNGLE.

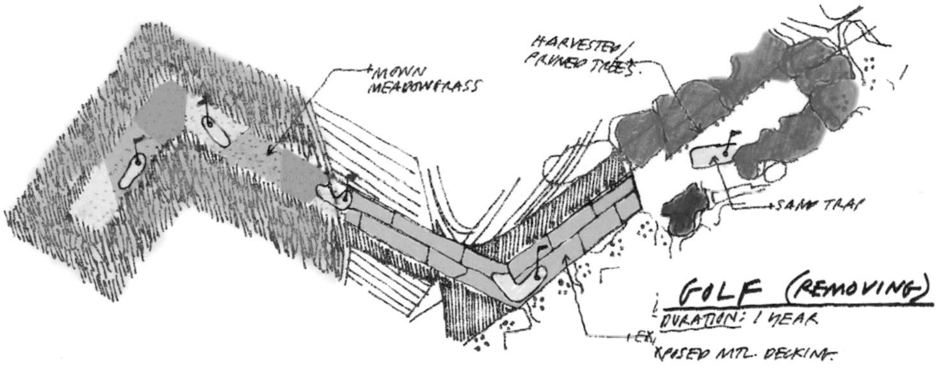

MOWN MEADOWGRASS
HARVESTED/ PRUNED TREES.
SAND TRAP
GOLF (REMOVING)
DURATION: 1 YEAR
EXPOSED MTL. DECKING

1 Walking wetland
2 Roadside
3 Woodland
4 Tidal wetland
5 Freshwater wetland
6 Commercial berm
7 Landfill mounds
8 WTC memorial forest

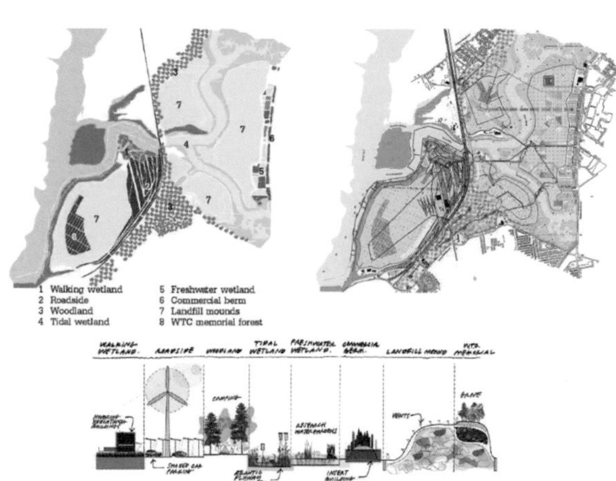

(opposite page, top) View of potential event transects: (from left to right) Garden Show, Historical Trash Walk, Water Park, Extreme Golf.

(opposite page, bottom) Overview of model.

(top) Enlarged plan of Garden Show transect illustrating localized adaptation at each ecology.

(middle) Enlarged plan of Extreme Golf transect illustrating localized adaptation at each ecology.

(bottom) Enhanced "Ecological" zones.

Mangere Gateway Heritage Avenue, Manukau

INTRODUCTION

The Gateway Heritage Avenue route is defined as the area broadly bounded by the Auckland International Airport to the south, the Manukau Harbour to the west, Mangere Mountain to the north and George Bolt Memorial Drive to the east. It is proposed as a uniquely Manukau alternative route for visitors traveling north from the airport into the city.

The work is part of a wider Manukau City Council initiative called the Gateway Heritage Project (GHP), as outlined in the Stafford Group report (Strategy for the Gateway Heritage Project, December 2004);

"The Gateway Heritage Project is currently a concept, which could act as an umbrella framework to incorporate a number of culturally diverse projects...Manukau has the widest and most diverse ethnic and cultural mix of any local government area in New Zealand."

Three key projects have been identified as anchor projects to take the GHP from a concept into a cultural tourism precinct. They are the Otuataua Stonefields, the Villa Maria winery centre and Mangere Mountain.

The Mangere Gateway Heritage Avenue project has the potential to link all of the GHP projects, including the three anchor projects. It also has the opportunity to showcase the area's rich culture and environmental assets to international, national and regional tourists.

An important aspect to understand in the design and creation of all the GHP projects is outlined in the Stafford report;

"Tourism New Zealand has identified the Interactive traveler as the generic form of preferred visitor for New Zealand. This type of visitor/holiday maker is a 'culture-vulture', wanting to not only view magnificent scenery but more importantly to understand how the land was formed, the various communities that have inhabited the land, and its strategic value and importance."

VISION

The objective of the Mangere Gateway Heritage Avenue project is to promote Manukau City's heritage resources, both natural and built, in the Mangere/Puhinui area, while providing recreational opportunities to residents and visitors for driving, biking and walking.

Rather than simply being a straightforward way-finding project there is the potential to develop the Gateway as a Heritage Learning Environment, where storytelling plays a key role in understanding different cultures and their relationships with particular places. The aim is to bring the stories to life in a manner, which enables the community to celebrate the unique character and heritage of this area.

With this approach, we hope to increase our understanding of who the people of the area are, where they came from, and some of the more complicated relationships between different people of different cultures and their respective relationships with the landscape.

STRATEGY

One of the strategies for a project of this complexity and scale was to identify, develop and implement three key areas, rather than tackle the entire route in one go.

The suggestion is that after each of these areas have been built, Council will send out a community information flyer and prepare public information boards requesting feedback and comment from the community. This will mean more people will be made aware of the overall Mangere Gateway Heritage Avenue project, so that future stages can be improved and developed with wider community input and buy-in.

In creating the designs Chow:Hill explored a series of "interventions" that could be used consistently along the entire route to develop, reveal and build character in a way that told of the unique history of the place. These involved sculpture, environmental interaction, built form, streetscape, wayfinding, vegetation, structures/furniture, connections and activity nodes.

In creating an overall concept to tie together the numerous cultural strands and stories, we developed an aesthetic of "found objects"; working spaces and features up as an eclectic mix of materials and forms, almost as though they had washed up along the coast. While appearing random, a strict design approach has been applied to each feature to ensure a tidy and cared-for aesthetic. While individually, the materials and forms appear random and scattered, they are arranged to form a consistent design language along the route.

IN SUMMARY

The overall objective of our proposals is to encourage residents and visitors to engage with the specialness of Mangere and its people.

The design of the Mangere Gateway Heritage Avenue is to be more than simply a place name, a directional sign, a bench seat, or a light. It is to be an experiential journey made up of interconnected elements of discovery, providing opportunities for residents and visitors to connect and reconnect with this unique part of Manukau City.

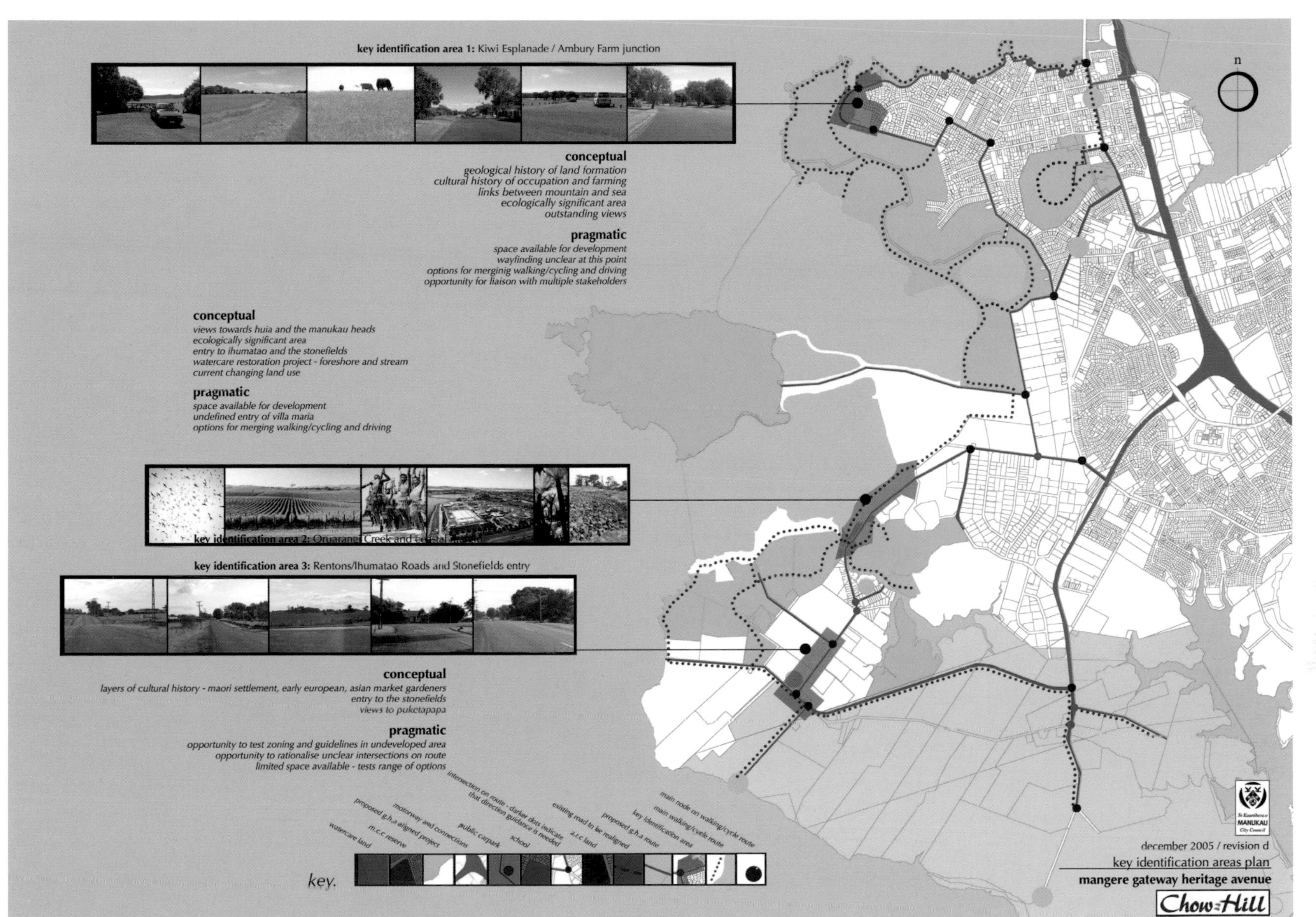

The three key identification areas were selected at key points along the route, based on their ecological, cultural or planning attributes.

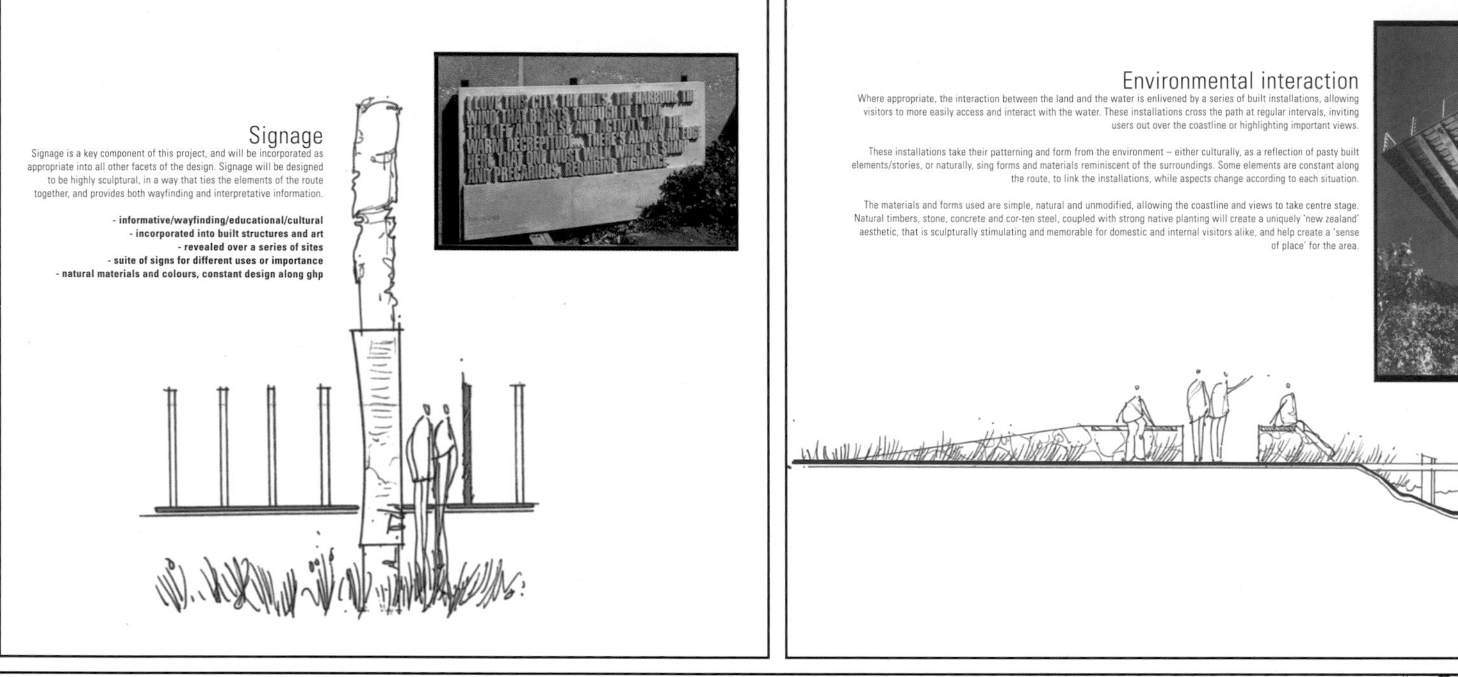

n

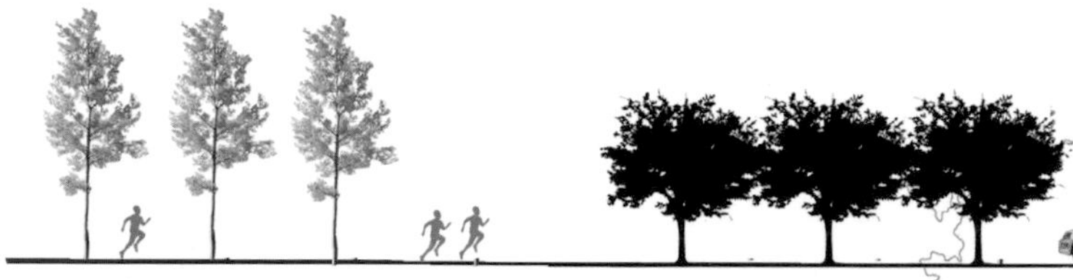

long section [pohutakawa/poplar]

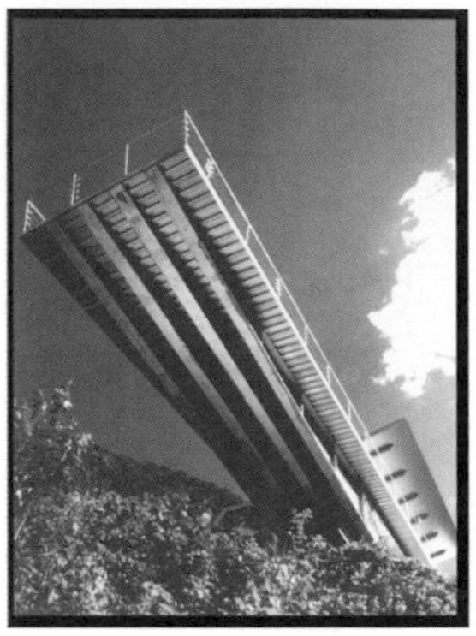

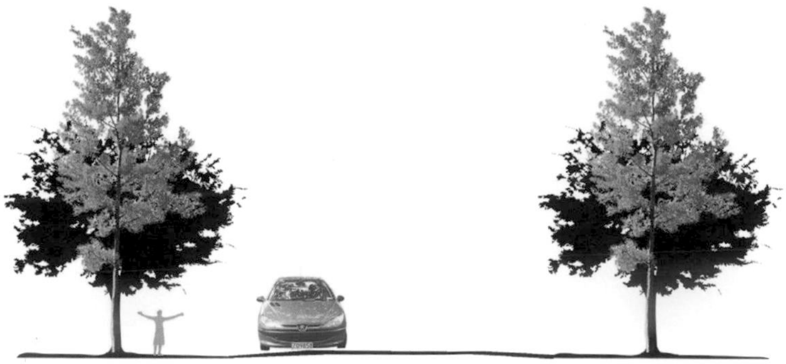

cross section [pohutakawa/poplar]

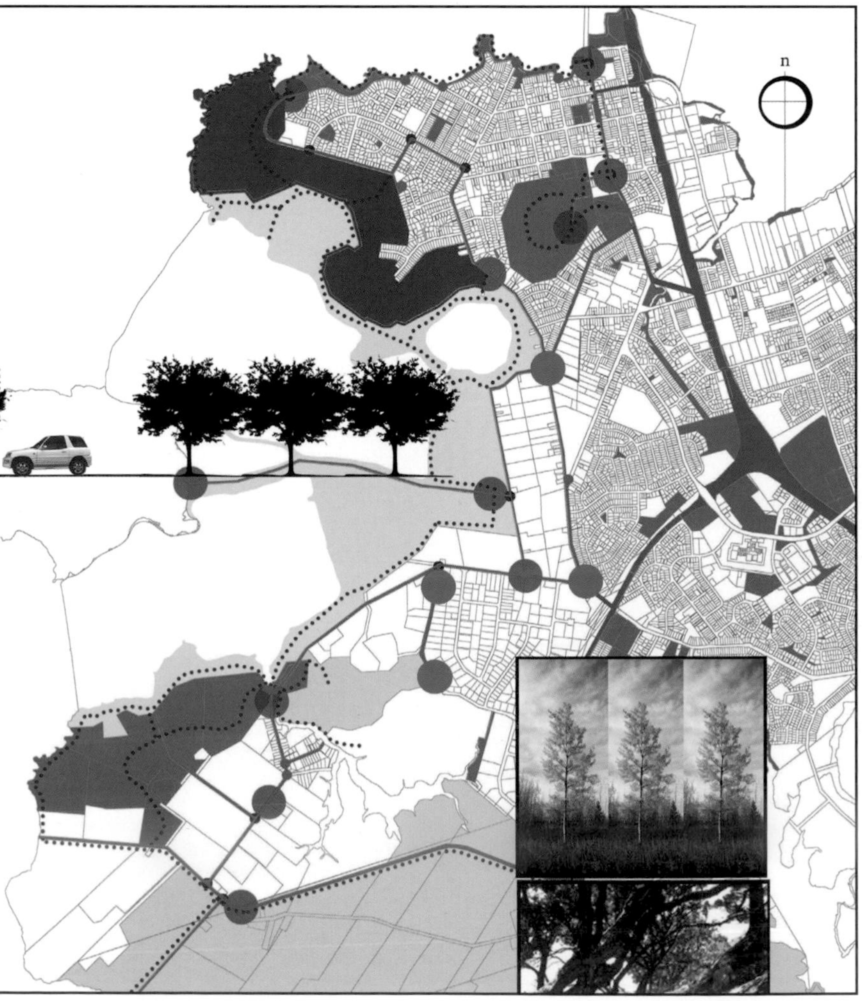

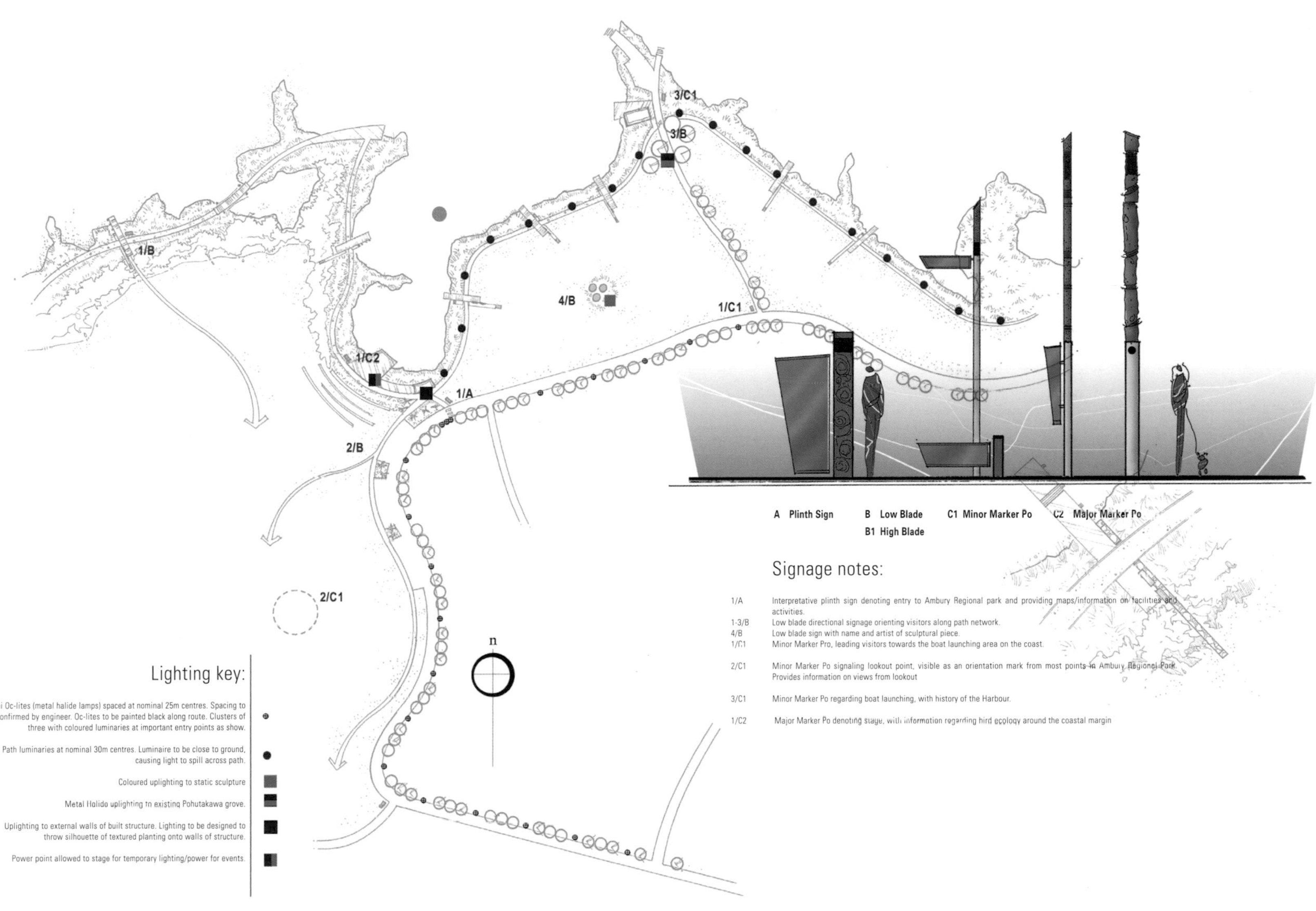

(top) The first key area was selected as it is a major site for viewing native bird species and features significant views across the Manukau Harbour.

(opposite page, top left) Signage was developed to incorporate local carving, telling stories of the area's importance to the local Maori.

(opposite page, top right) Built features were created to allow visitors to access and interact with the natural assets of the region.

(opposite page, bottom) Pohutakawa were used as the base tree species, offset by groups of accent trees as visitors move along the route.

enlarged view of seating along coast

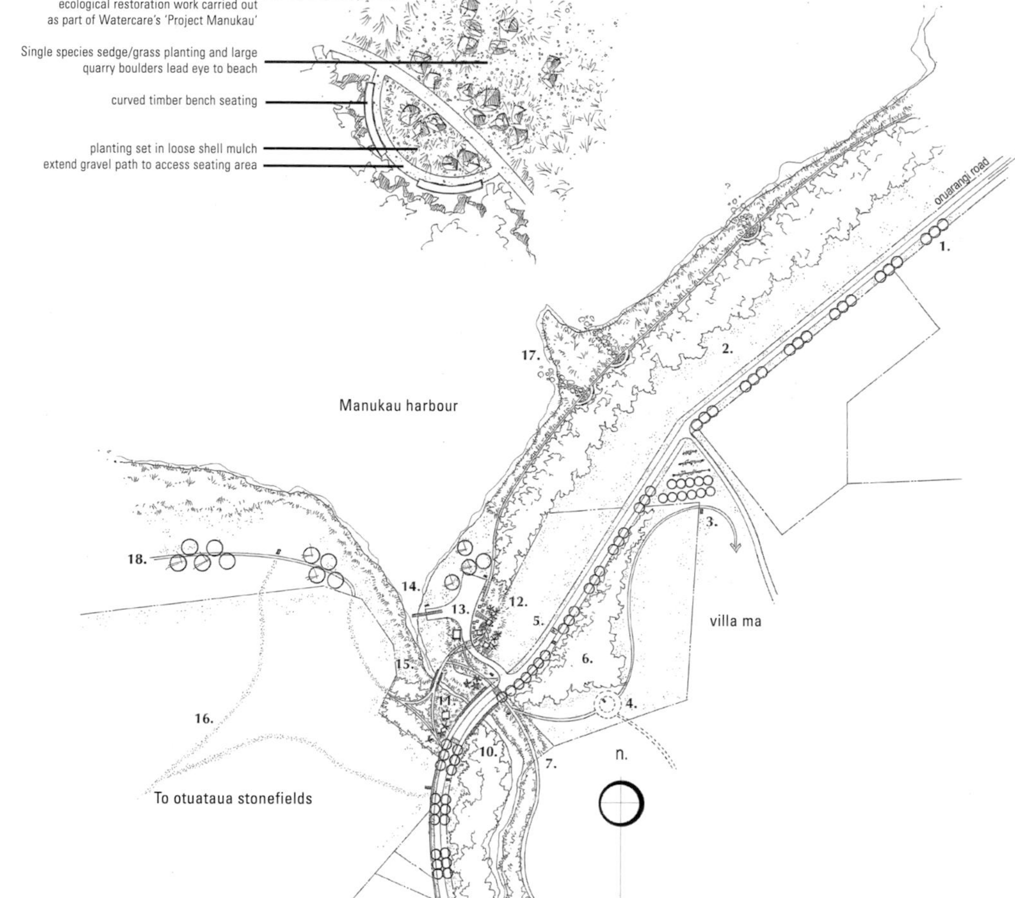

notes:

1. Street trees grouped in threes denote route and continue planting theme along vehicular route, while maintaining views to harbour. Powerlines to be undergrounded.
2. Flat land to northwest of Oruarangi Road remains a grazed paddock to retain views to Manukau Harbour.
3. Entry to Villa Maria to receive sculptural planting treatment denoting the winemaking processes on the site. Possibility of using native plants with a vineyard aesthetic, design to be confirmed with Villa Maria. Maria entry remains off Montgomerie Road.
4. Sculptural mound reflective of pa fortifications that existed on this site provides lookout over Harbour. Interpretative signage explains history of pa. Including details on fortifications and tactics. Network of paths leads to Villa Maria and the proposed "Foodbowl from this point – exact layout to be confirmed with Villa Maria.
5. Paving bands in road and signage (refer signage drawings) alert drivers to upcoming turnoff to carpark and waka launching area.
6. Revegetated slope frames Oruarangi Creek and draws the eye towards the foreshore.
7. Track along Oruarangi Creek opens up access to proposed "Foodbowl". This has the potential to become a very scenic track with views over the creek and village, and possible future link to Ihumatao village across the creek.
8. Existing vegetation along Oruarangi Creek
9. Road linking Ihumatao Village and Marae to waka launching area receives grouped trees to both sides of the road to continue the theme of the route, and a footpath along the eastern edge. This route also links into the informal track network that runs through the stonefields.
10. Existing bridge to receive sculptural lighting, with the possibility of changing colour for night events.
11. Proposed 'Hide' lookout structure frames views to Puketutu Island, and provides interpretative signage on the 'Foodbowl' concept that will be created in planting around the stonefields (the traditional food gathering area of the people that have lived in this area)
12. Regional playground created, based around the arrival of the Tainui waka. This playground will be a series of informal elements set within the existing vegetation and slope, and explore a unique New Zealand aesthetic, with materials chosen to reflect the construction of a waka. Learning elements to include waka navigation and food used on the journey.
13. Existing carpark and toilet.
14. Existing waka launching jetty, with new interpretative plinth signage as per the signage drawings.
15. Proposed bridge to be built by Watercare on the existing historic abutments.
16. Informal grass tracks to stonefields, located with a series of marker po's. These po's will feature maps and art as per the signage drawings.
17. Seating bays to be set at regular intervals along the cycle/walkway, with swathes of shell, stone and bird-attractive low planting to bring foreshore elements up to the path, and encourage visitors out to the coast. These swathes are to be designed in consultation with ARC to ensure that the Watercare consent conditions are met.
18. Existing Watercare planting supplemented by groves of native plants that were historically used for food by Maori. Associated interpretative signage makes this story accessible to visitors.

Note: All activity proposals over archaeological sites in this area will require an "Authority to Modify" from the NZHPT. It is recommended that an Archaeological survey is carried out on both K1A1 and K1A2 to determine the extent. Some modification of conceptual elements may be required following this survey.

(top) The second key area is based around Oruarangi Creek, which was recently reopened to the ocean after being sealed off for decades.

(opposite page, top) A comprehensive signage suite was developed to allow for local artistic input into the forms and shapes. All forms relate back to a large carved marker 'Po'.

(opposite page, bottom) An eclectic mix of materials was used in working up the individual sign detailing, to represent found elements washed up on the shore.

Minor marker po.

Minor marker po to be formed from a circular galvanized steel base and a rolled Cor-ten steel top Banding pattering to be in the form of black strips, designed to reflect the banding/patterning of the Major Marker Po. One 'Major' strip to be coloured in the nominated colour for the area. Fibreglass panel with vinyl adhesive mounted to the pole provides information as required for each area.

Major marker po.

Major Marker Po to be formed from a rolled Cor-ten base, with a carved timber top. All dimensions and design to be consistent throughout the route, with the point of difference being the carved top, which varies for each Key Identification Area. The purpose of these markers is to add character and identity to the route. No supplementary information is included on this sign.

High directional blade.

High blade sign to be formed from a galvanized steel pole with a rolled Cor-ten top. Coloured band forms separation between metals and 'brands' each distinctive area. Blade to be formed from painted galvanized steel with black lettering, blade colour to match pole banding.

Plinth sign.

Plinths approximately 2m in post height, with a blade of 1.8m maximum height. Post to be Cor-ten steel sheet with an etched/engraved artistic pattern. Patterning to be created by a local artist, and may vary slightly from area to area. Banding at the top to be a colour constant to each key identification area.

Plinth to be fiberglass sheet with vinyl adhesive at both sides. Generally, one side would contain a map of the surrounding area including attractions, activities, stories and other points of interest. The second side would have a more in depth description and illustrations/diagrams of a selected story from the area.

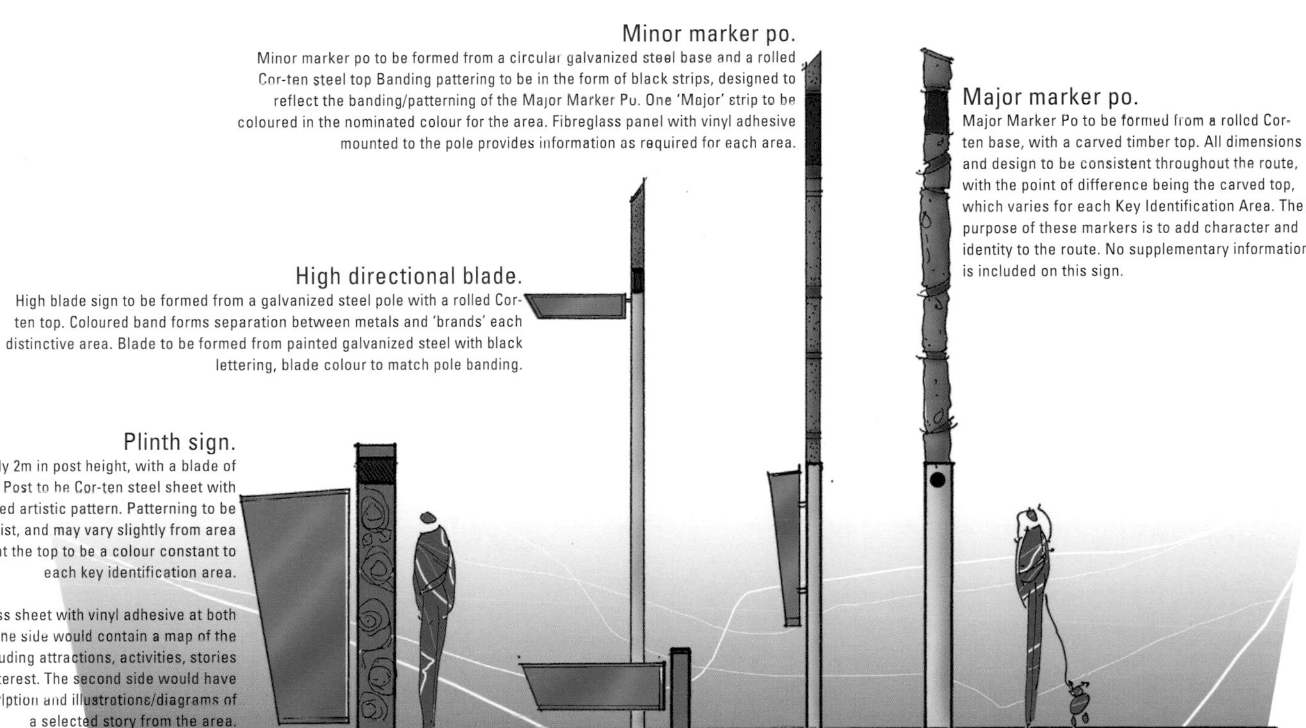

low directional blade.

Low blade sign to be formed from Cor-ten sheet with a top band painted to match nominated colour for the area. Blade to be formed from fiberglass sheet with vinyl patterning/wording to match the large plinth signs.

Gardens by the Bay, Singapore

Gardens by the Bay is an ambitious plan by the National Parks Board of Singapore to create over 100 hectares of new public gardens centred on Marina Bay. The objective is to create a world class leisure destination featuring leading edge tropical horticulture, showcase garden buildings, including over 2 hectares of Cooled Conservatories, and a permanent home for the Singapore Garden Festival. The project is of particular importance to Singaporeans and the Gardens are planned to become the premier outdoor leisure resource for local people. They will form a garden focus to the new developments growing up around Marina Bay, including the Integrated Resort and associated high rise hotels, commercial and residential buildings.

The team led and assembled by landscape architects Grant Associates from the UK were joint winners of an international design competition to master plan the Gardens. The Grant Associates team is working on the designs for the 54 hectares site of Marina South. This provides the focus for the whole project and includes the Cooled Conservatories. The emphasis is on innovation in technologies and design in Tropical Horticulture linked with a serious approach to environmental sustainability. Colour in planting displays is a key theme to the project alongside the intention to set out a wide variety of educational attractions based on the ethnobotany of the region. The Conservatories will be the first in the world to place cooled environments of this scale into a tropical climate. One Conservatory will allow the growth and display of seasonal flowers from the Mediterranean regions of the world whilst the other will have a dramatic display of the biodiversity of cool Tropical Montane areas such as Borneo cloud forests. Innovative technologies are being used to ensure these attractions not only maintain the conditions for the plants but how they achieve this in an energy and resource efficient way.

The main features within the Gardens are the tall 'Supertrees' that rise above the existing tree canopies and create a distinctive new silhouette for the area. They are clustered into several groups and provide the framework for extraordinary vertical tropical gardens and support essential elements of the environmental systems of the project such as air exhausts, solar collectors, rainwater harvesting features and a high level exhibit. A high level walkway will link two of the central cluster of trees.

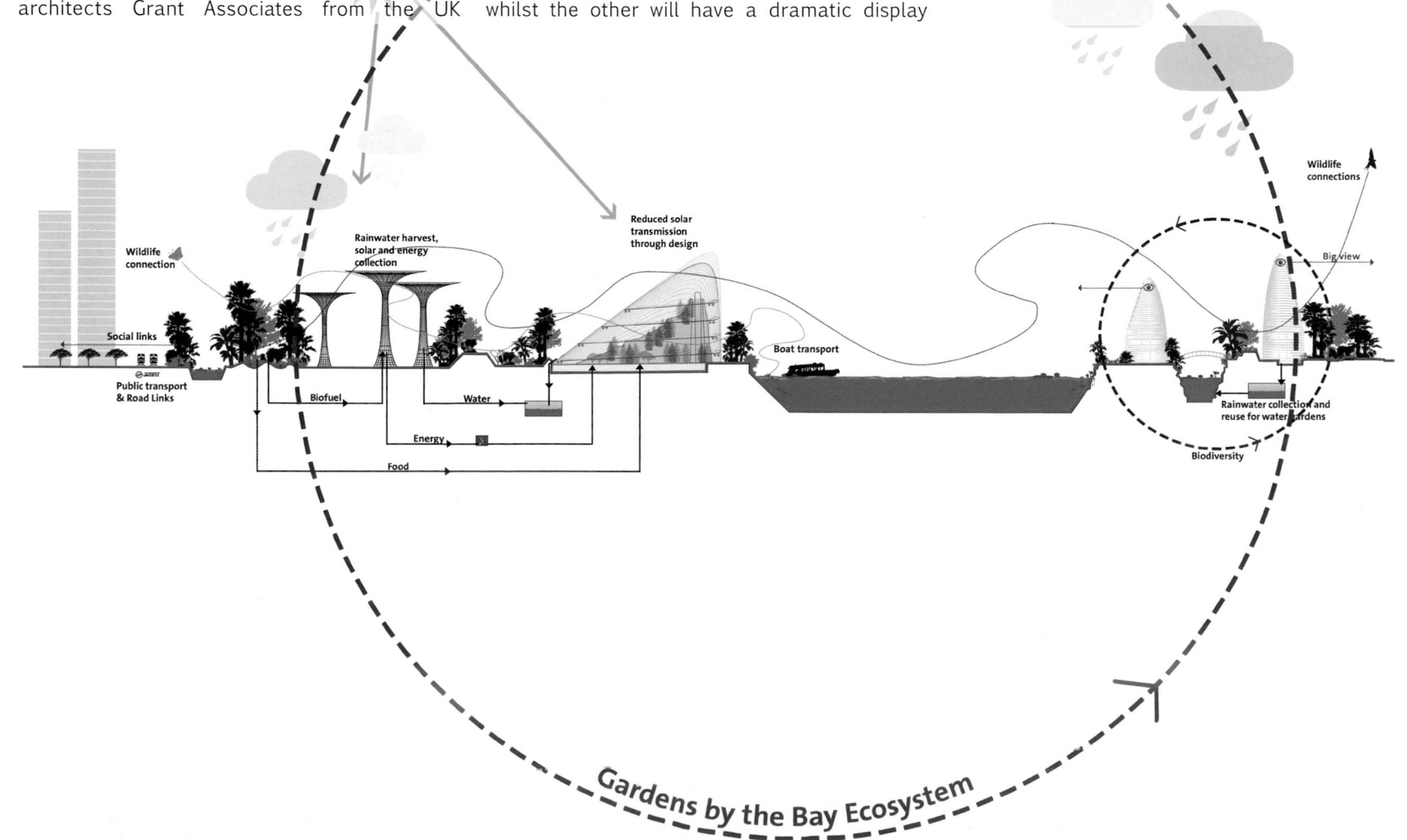

client / owner	other key consultants	location	awards
National Parks Board of Singapore	Grant Associates; Wilkinson Eyre Architects; Atelier One Structural Engineers; Atelier Ten Environmental Engineers	Marina South, Singapore	Winners, International Design Competition

Legend:
1. Cool Dry Conservatory (Theatre of Plants)
2. Cool Moist Conservatory (Cloud Mountain)
3. The Hub
4. Support Biome & Nursery
5. Garden Offices
6. The Flower Market
7. Events Stage & Canopy
8. Conference of Plants
9. Pride of Singapore
10. Orchidetum
11. Lion Grove- Supertrees & Aerial Walkway
12. Arbors
13. Languid Lake
14. Tea House Island
15. Jellyfish Refuges
16. Water Taxi Landings
17. Marina Inlet
18. Below ground Car parking & Surface Coach Parking
19. Arrival Hub & Supertrees
20. Filter Ponds
21. The 'Fragile Forest'
22. Pump House
23. Animal Exhibit
24. Observation Tower/Mast
25. Information pavillion
26. Future Themed Pavillions
27. The Scented Walk
28. Aerial Bridge from Integrated Resort
29. Floating Gardens
30. Service Road
31. Play Space

Singapore Flyer
MARINA CHANNEL
Marina
Marina East (Design by Gustafson Porter)
Integrated Resort
Baytront MRT Station
Barrage Visitor Centre
Barrage
MARINA COASTAL EXPRESSWAY (MCE)
Curved Road

National Parks Board Singapore
Gardens by the bay
grant associates
Wilkinson Eyre.Architects
atelier one
atelier ten

Scale: 1/2000@A0
0 50 100 200 300 400 500m

Marina South : Masterplan
SING 218 SK 000_02 27.02.2007

(left) Ecosystem diagram.
(top) Masterplan.
(below) Orchid masterplan concept diagrams.

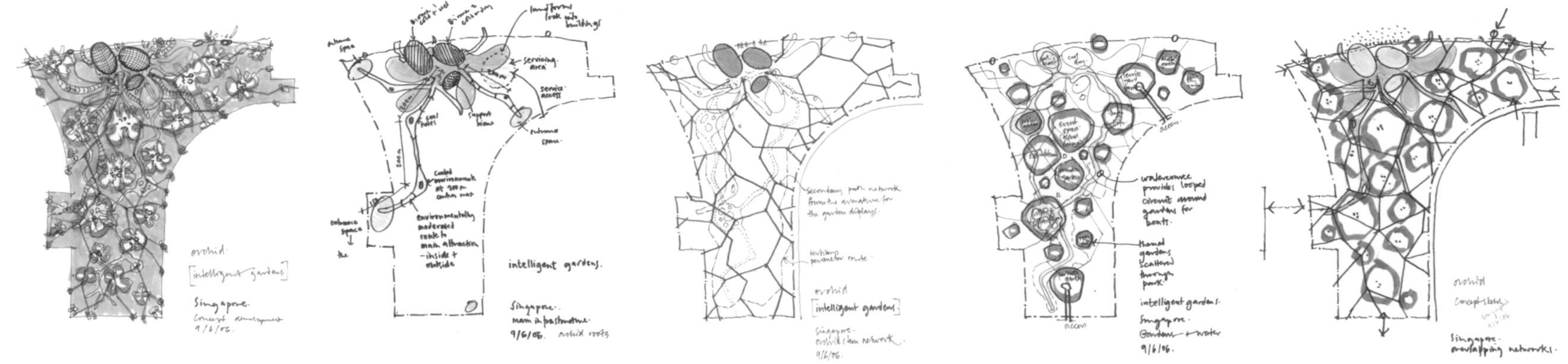

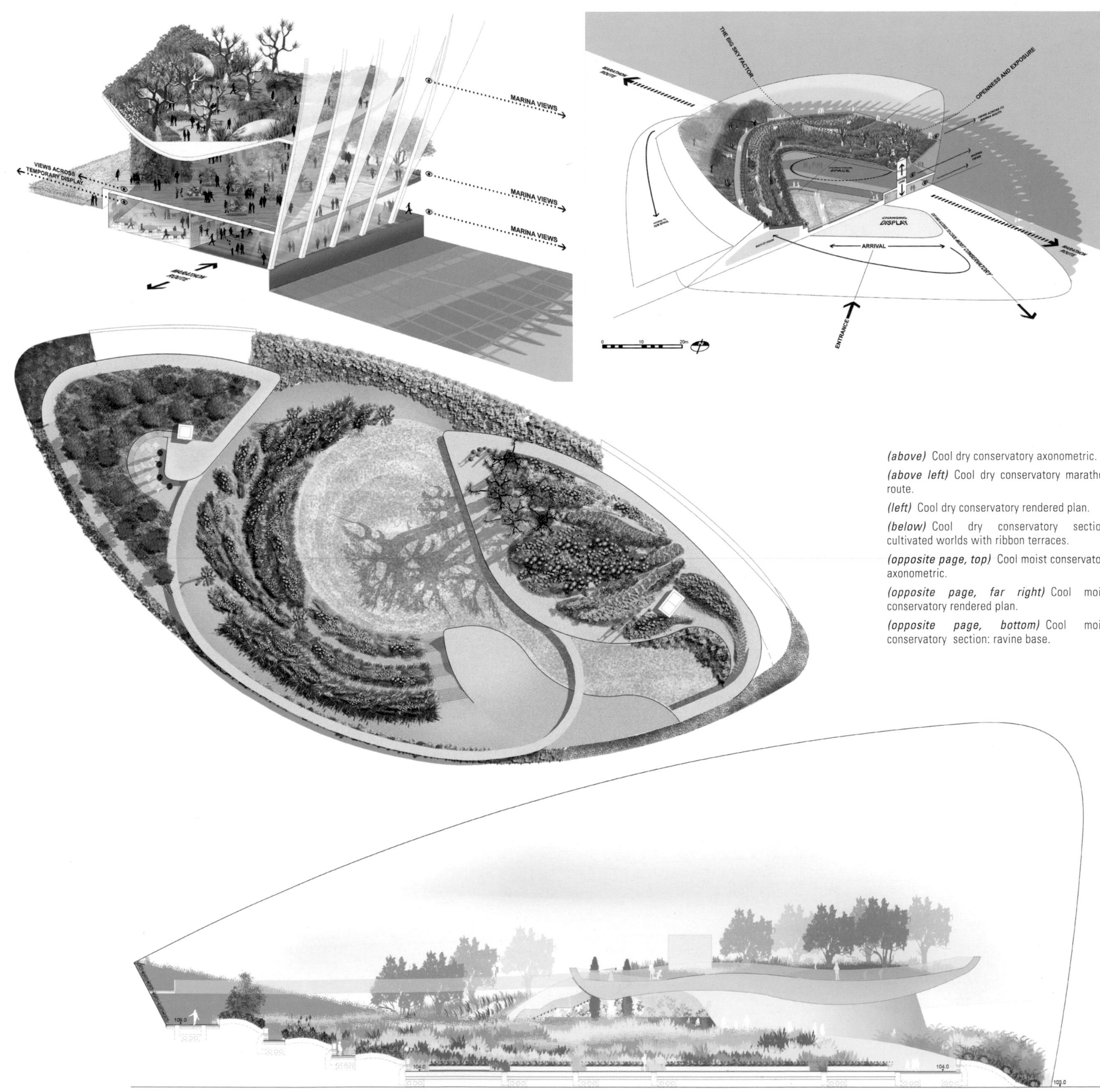

(above) Cool dry conservatory axonometric.

(above left) Cool dry conservatory marathon route.

(left) Cool dry conservatory rendered plan.

(below) Cool dry conservatory section: cultivated worlds with ribbon terraces.

(opposite page, top) Cool moist conservatory axonometric.

(opposite page, far right) Cool moist conservatory rendered plan.

(opposite page, bottom) Cool moist conservatory section: ravine base.

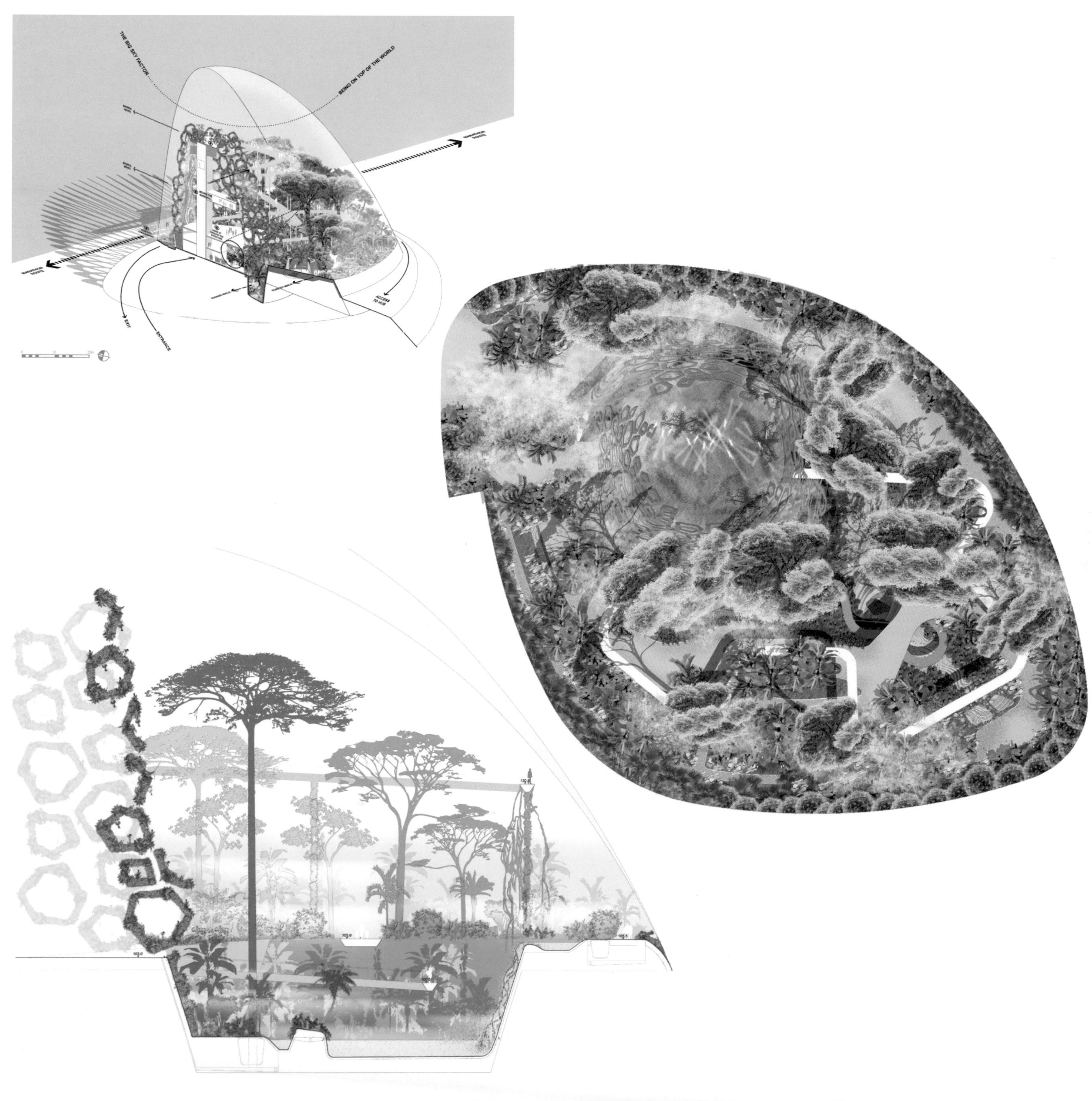
THE BIG SKY FACTOR
BEING ON TOP OF THE WORLD
ACCESS TO HUB
EXIT
ENTRANCE
0
10
20m

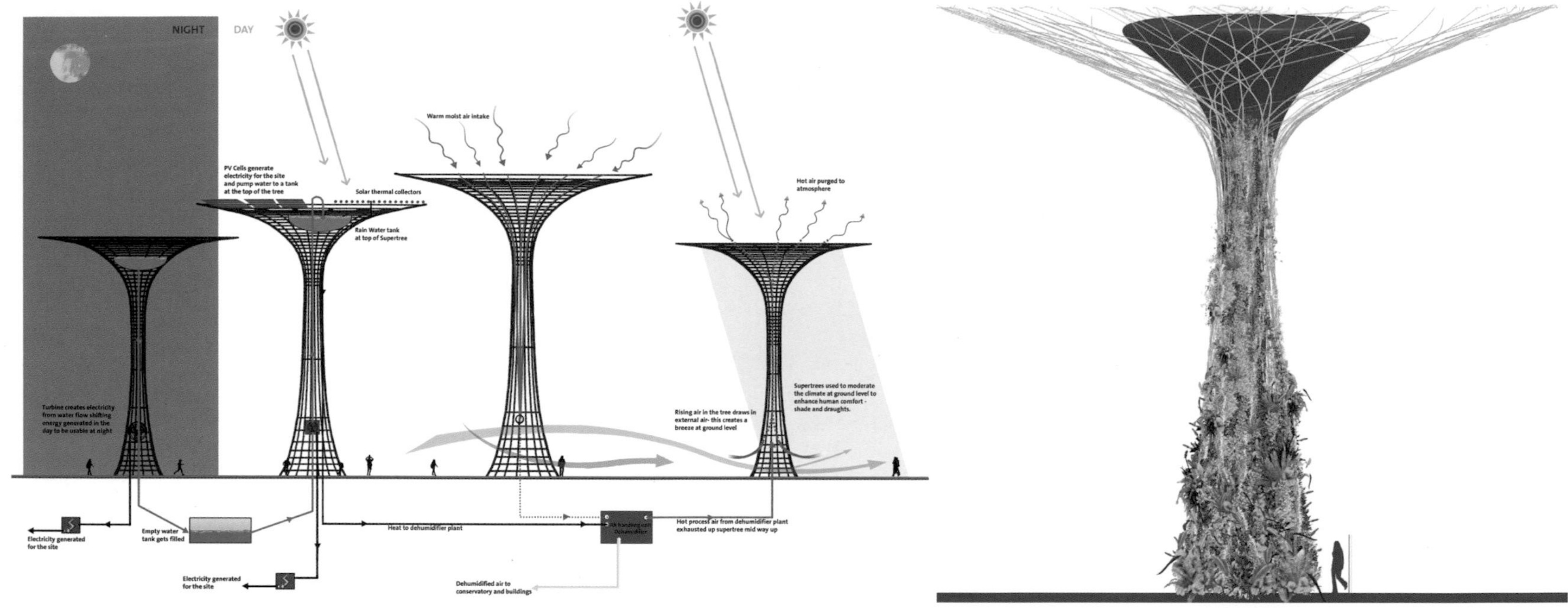
NIGHT
DAY
PV Cells generate electricity for the site and pump water to a tank at the top of the tree
Solar thermal collectors
Rain Water tank at top of Supertree
Warm moist air intake
Hot air purged to atmosphere
Turbine creates electricity from water flow shifting energy generated in the day to be usable at night
Supertrees used to moderate the climate at ground level to enhance human comfort - shade and draughts.
Rising air in the tree draws in external air- this creates a breeze at ground level
Electricity generated for the site
Empty water tank gets filled
Heat to dehumidifier plant
Hot process air from dehumidifier plant exhausted up supertree mid way up
Electricity generated for the site
Dehumidified air to conservatory and buildings

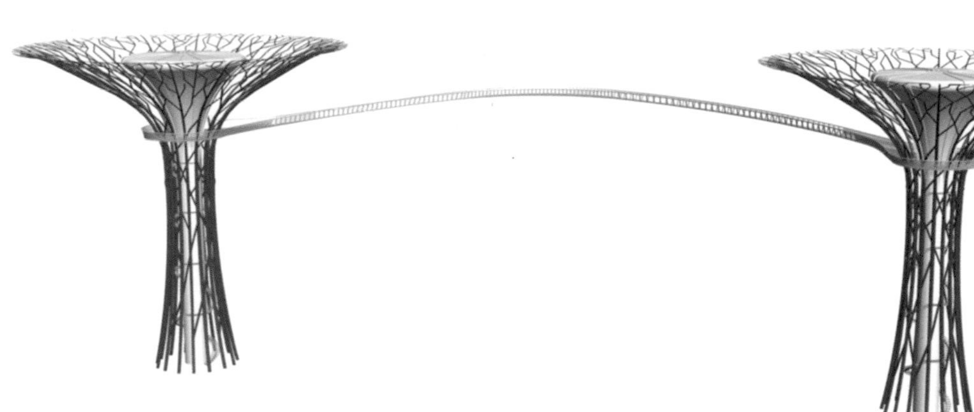

(opposite page, top left) Supertrees environmental strategy diagram.
(opposite page, top right) Supertree elevation with planting.
(opposite page, bottom) Lion grove daytime by Squint Opera.
(above) Perspective of aerial walkway.
(right, bottom right) Supertree plant attachment options.
(bottom) Competition sketch of Supertrees in lion grove.

(above) The Dragon Fly Bridge.
(left top) Gardens concept: moody valley perspective.
(left) Gardens concept sketch.
(bottom) View of conservatories across the bay (Squint Opera).
(right) Lake general arrangement plan.

AVENUE
AVENUE
SHEARES
KEY
Lake Extents with water depths greater than 600mm
Bioremediation filter beds
Green carpet planting zone to southern end of lake
Shallow lake benches with water depth 0 - 600 mm
Existing Trees to be retained
Proposed boat landing zones
Boardwalk
Water run off from higher garden areas

Providence Waterfront Park, Rhode Island

In November 2006, Brown, Richardson & Rowe was selected as the winner of the Providence Waterfront Design competition sponsored by the City of Providence, Rhode Island for two prominent parks along the east and west banks of the Providence River. The eight-acre total parkland is currently the site of an interstate highway overpass which is being demolished and built in a new location further away from the downtown. A six-acre park will be on the west side of the river and a two-acre park on the east. The City plans to connect the parks with a pedestrian bridge that will be supported by the stone piers that originally supported Route 195. The construction of the parks will begin once the overpass has been removed, which is anticipated to be 2010.

The City's Beaux Arts architecture and its charming scale inspired the landscape architects. Providence is a very walkable city with beautiful streets that lead to the waterfront. The parks will continue those important ties, with numerous entries from the surrounding neighborhoods, beautiful views and elements to draw people down to the river.

On the west side of the river, Dorrance Street, a significant city street leads to the park. A tree's promenade will extend this important urban axis through the park, down to the river's edge. At the end of the promenade is the proposed Ember Summer House, a free-standing open-air structure inspired by the city's Beaux Arts architecture and Waterfire Providence®, an award-winning art installation featuring ritual bonfires in the middle of the Providence River. The Ember Summer House will be illuminated to complement Waterfire® and serve as a beacon visible from both the downtown and the eastern side of the river. Other elements of the western park include a terraced amphitheatre, a sculpture garden and an open lawn framed by trees.

Proposed for the smaller park on the east side of the river are a tree-lined park featuring a riverwalk and a one-of-a-kind playground. The fish-themed play equipment, wave slides, turtles and shells interpret the aquatic life of the river.

The proposed pedestrian bridge will provide an important connection between the two parks and the existing Providence Riverwalk. It will also serve as the new terminus for Waterfire®. Five illuminated globe-like sculptures, inspired by Waterfire® and the molecular structure of water, would be mounted on the bridge piers.

Durable and sustainable materials will be used in the construction of the parks. The Ember Summer House will be constructed out of finished, recycled mill steel and architectural wire fabric. Granite facing and blocks from the former highway abutment walls will be reused. Park walkways will incorporate recycled glass aggregates in concrete mixes. Native woody and herbaceous plant species that can tolerate existing urban, exposed waterfront conditions and require minimal maintenance will be planted to provide habitat for animal communities.

The parks will provide a much needed green oasis in the heart of the City and are being heralded as a defining feature of the waterfront for future generations.

(bottom) View to west and east side parks.
(right) West side park.
(right bottom) Ember Summer House during the day.

client / owner
City of Providence

location
Providence, Rhode Island, USA

awards
Brown, Richardson & Rowe won the competition which awarded this project.

©Alison Richardson

©Alison Richardson

©Alison Richardson

©Sung Tae Cho

(top) East side park.
(left) Water molecules sculpture.
(bottom) Shell slide.
(right) Park locus map.

©Joanne Hiromura

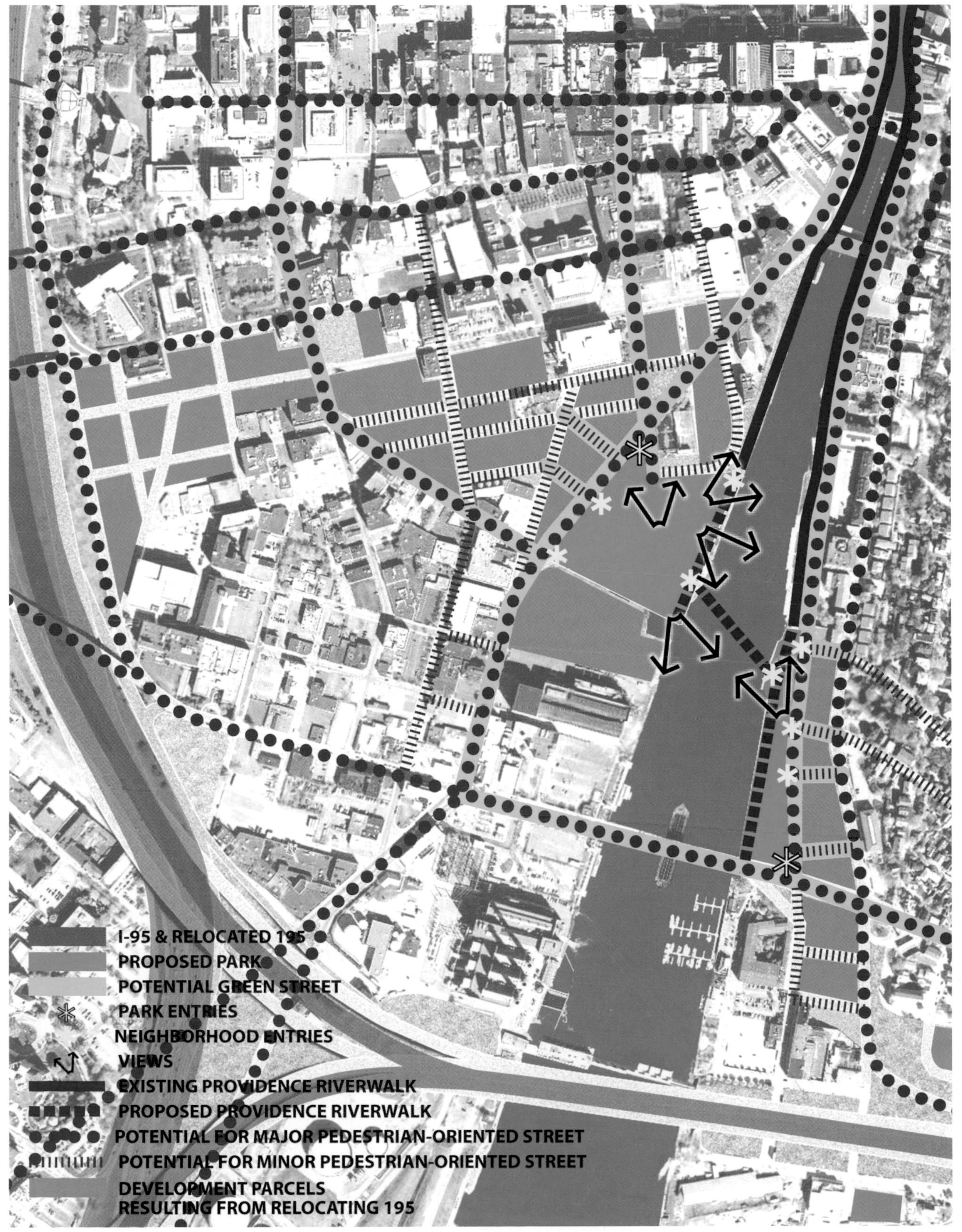
I-95 & RELOCATED 195
PROPOSED PARK
POTENTIAL GREEN STREET
PARK ENTRIES
NEIGHBORHOOD ENTRIES
VIEWS
EXISTING PROVIDENCE RIVERWALK
PROPOSED PROVIDENCE RIVERWALK
POTENTIAL FOR MAJOR PEDESTRIAN-ORIENTED STREET
POTENTIAL FOR MINOR PEDESTRIAN-ORIENTED STREET
DEVELOPMENT PARCELS
RESULTING FROM RELOCATING 195

Jinsha Ancient Capital, Chengdu

Jinsha Ancient Capital is a world class heritage attraction celebrating the richness and diversity of regional people. It aims at inspiring visitors to appreciate the culture and ecology of Sichuan. In this context, the park combines the best techniques in historical planning and the highest quality of recreated physical environments. There are several examples of these unrivalled tourist developments around the world such as Williamsburg, in Virginia where the term "Living Museum" originated. In these places, people work within a real micro-economy thriving on ancient trading techniques, businesses, crafts and creative cultures. In Jinsha Ancient Capital, our goal is to bring the ancient dynasties "alive" — visitors will be completely immersed into the life experiences of people centuries ago.

Landscape Principals

Mountain Ridge, River Valley, Fertile Landscape

The master plan is to portray the overall characteristics of landscapes in Sichuan province: from dramatic mountain ridges with cascading water and natural sculptures, to lush green river valleys with terraced agricultural landscapes, villages and crops. Along the North Park boundary, a mountain ridge emerges as a strong visual backdrop to the project. At the foot, a serpentine river valley inspired by the Jinjiang River, sweeps through the Park creating many different pockets of landscapes, villages and spaces. Together, the river and the rock ridge create a fantastic variety of distinctive spaces where 5 historical villages are located.

Open Space Strategy

Lush green landscapes are carefully integrated around the architectural massing as a unifying element, blending building styles and features from many different historical periods into one cohesive park. Landscape "fingers" are extended as buffer zones between each historical zone to provide a sense of visual transition, open space and garden beauty.

The centre zone of the park is free of any architecture except for the main signature observation tower. The zone within the central park is reserved for spectacular landscape shows, light and sound, and dramatic staged events. The space forms a pure circle, encompassed by the Ancient Bird Walk, to become the symbol of the rising "Sichuan" Culture.

Sichuan Tower — Story of a Rising Culture

The heart of the park is marked by a 100m observation tower. Visitors enter the Main Entrance Plaza which resembles the 20th century architecture, and move towards the tower along a dragon axis. They are taken to the time when history begins. A large subterranean show hall exhibits ancient artifacts of the region in large display cases. Subtle lighting and sounds of wind and water create a magical atmosphere. The story of the soil, water, and earth explain the agricultural and geographical origins of Sichuan culture. Visitors then enter into a circular room which slowly turns and rises. A 3D multimedia show explains the evolution of Jinsha society, along the timeline of the various dynasties. At the top, the spectacular views over the park and surrounding Sichuan province are suddenly unveiled through the clear (Liquid Crystal Effect) windows. Here, visitors are brought back to the present day, and will be inspired to look into the future.

client / owner
Chengdu Zhixin Industrial Group Co., Ltd.

location
Chengdu, China

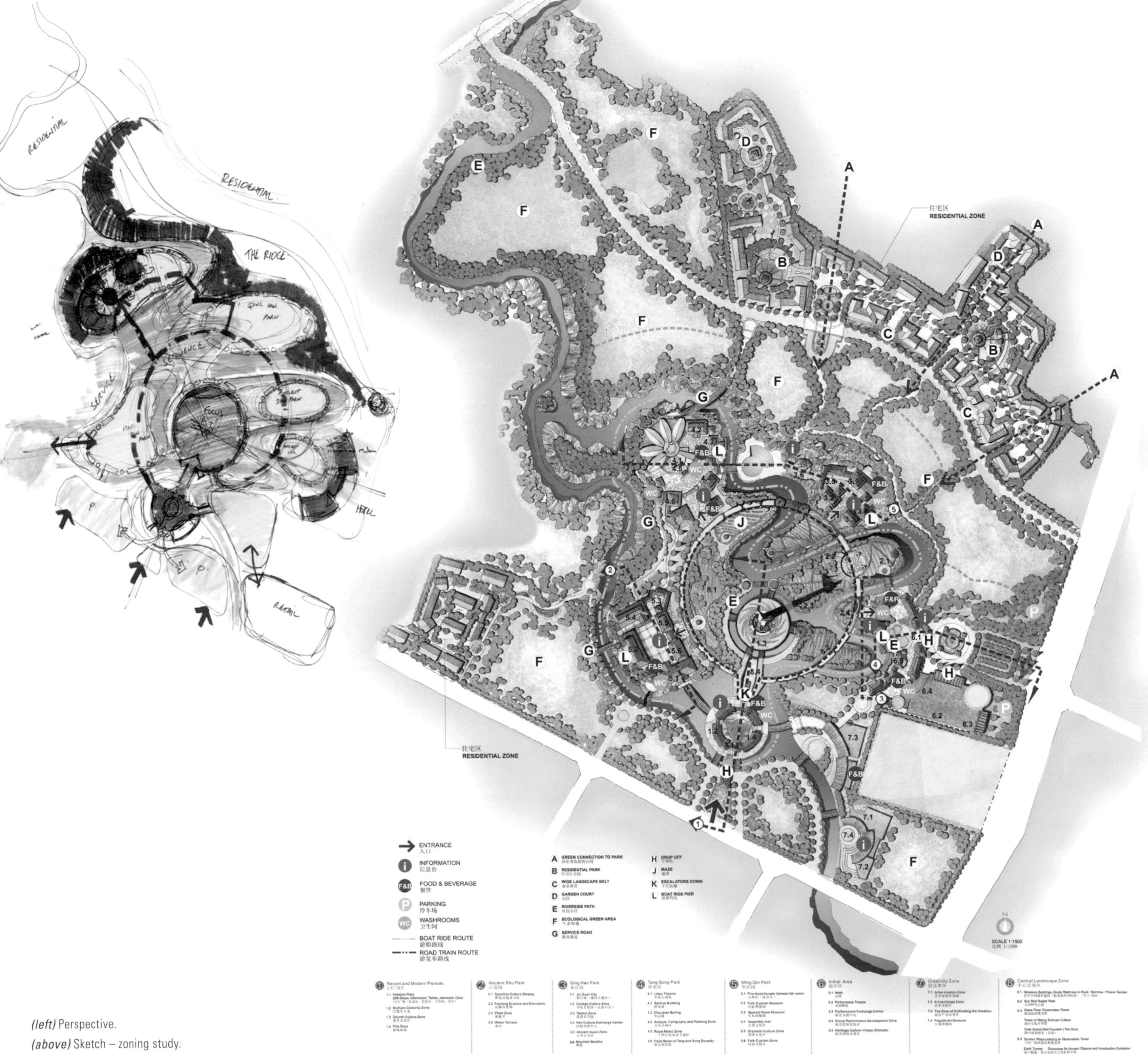

(left) Perspective.
(above) Sketch – zoning study.
(right) Master plan.

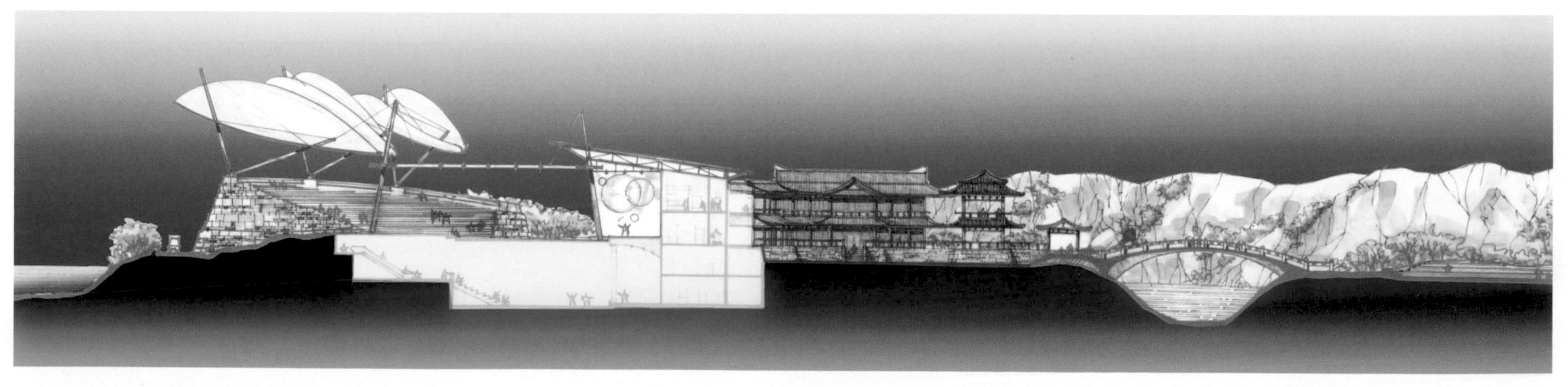

(left top) Perspective.
(left bottom and blow) Elevations – Qin Han Park/Tang Song Park.
(top left) Perspective.
(top right) Night view.
(above) Elevation —— Ming Qing Park.

(this page) Sichuan Tower — rendered axonometric view, plan and section.

(left top and bottom) Sichuan Tower — perspectives.

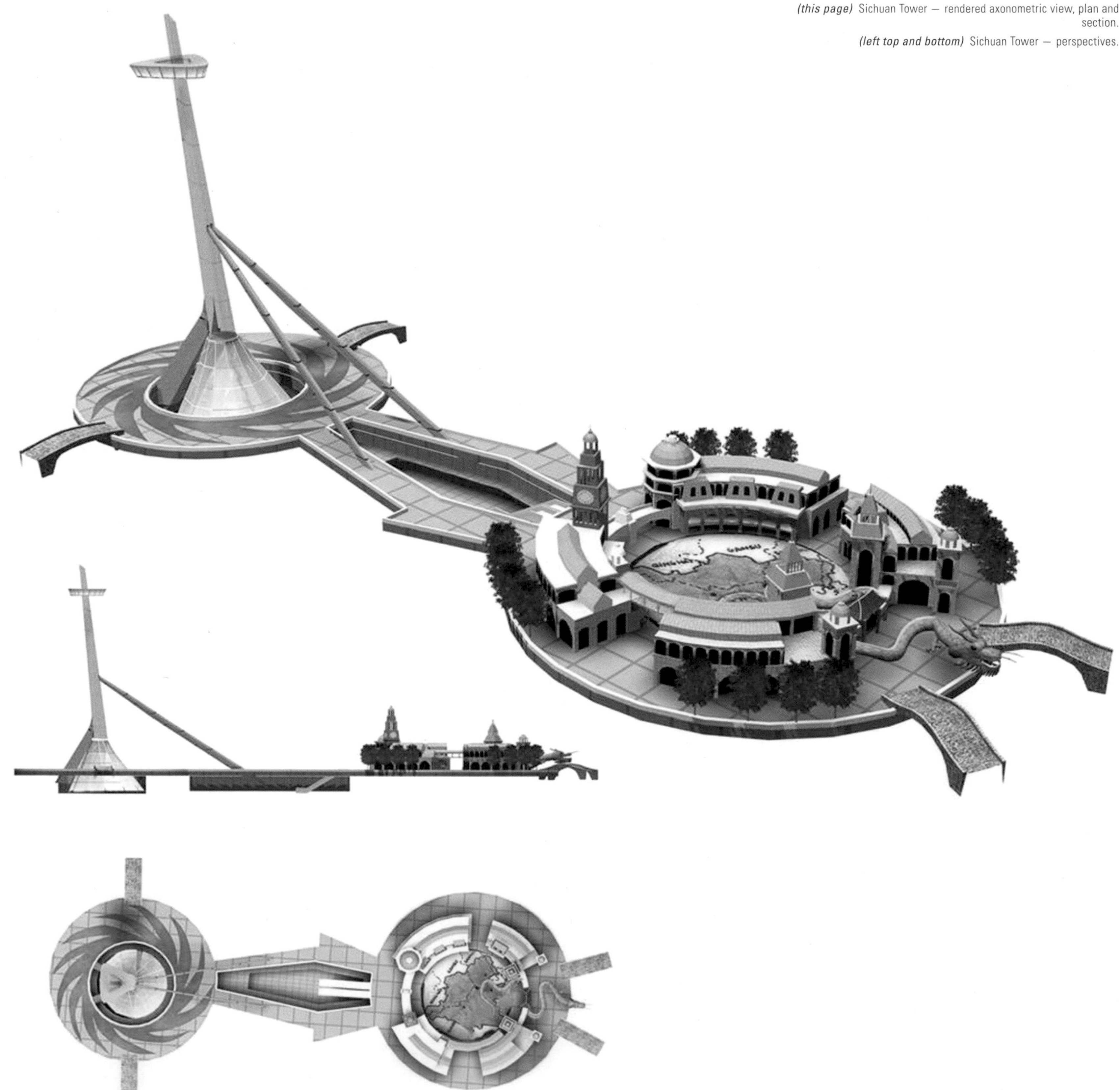

South Waterfront Greenway Development Plan, Portland

This section of the Willamette River is being transformed into a vibrant environment for people, plants and wildlife.

In a rare move, the design team was able to work closely with the City of Portland, developers, and natural resource advocates to strike a balance between development, recreation and re-naturalization of this neglected post-industrial waterfront. Extensive public outreach and charrettes with the community, natural resource advocates and developers revealed conflicting goals between the extent of development and re-naturalization, public access and habitat continuity of views and upper habitat. Over a two year period, the designers conducted extensive research and analysis, and public meetings to reach a consensus on a framework for the Greenway.

The schematic design together with design guidelines, is a comprehensive guide to the incremental development that will follow. The park is first and foremost dedicated to the restoration of a post-industrial waterfront to a naturalized river edge and riparian habitat. The dense mixed-use development planned along its edge, as well as pedestrian and bike trails, placed the need for access at odds with the habitat. Working closely with environmental advocates, the design team devised a rational plan for the park, which strategically places access and activity in "moments" and nodes without compromising the newly-formed habitats. These spaces range from dramatic cantilevered pier overlooks, boat launches and active civic plazas to quiet, sloping lawns meadows and terraces. All are intended to serve the park's diverse constituency and are connected to the city's bikeway, tramway and light rail systems.

The design celebrates a rich, Native American and industrial logging and ship building heritage with a landscape narrative of cranes, ship's bows, terraces, log overlooks and bargeways; all expressed in the design language of our current culture. While South Waterfront Greenway is unique to Portland's cultural and historical heritage, it is a model for new urban waterfront parks across the country. It demonstrates that our 21st Century environmental, cultural and urbanism goals can find common ground and be met in ways that also sparks the public's imagination.

client / owner
City of Portland Parks and Recreation

key consultants
Thomas Balsley Associates
Thomas Balsley, FASLA - Principal/Lead Designer
Steven Tupu - Project Manager/Designer
Michael Koontz
Walker Macy
Michael Zilis, Principal/Landscape Architect
Wayne Stewart, Project Manager
Mauricio Villarreal, Project Landscape Architect
Miguel Camacho
Lisa Town
Wendy Bell

location
Portland, OR, USA

awards
2006 Award of Excellence – ASLA Oregon
2007 Honor Award - NY ASLA

(left) The proposed development and new greenway.
(top) View of Barge Ramp transformation into park and urban beach.
(bottom) The Greenway Master Plan.

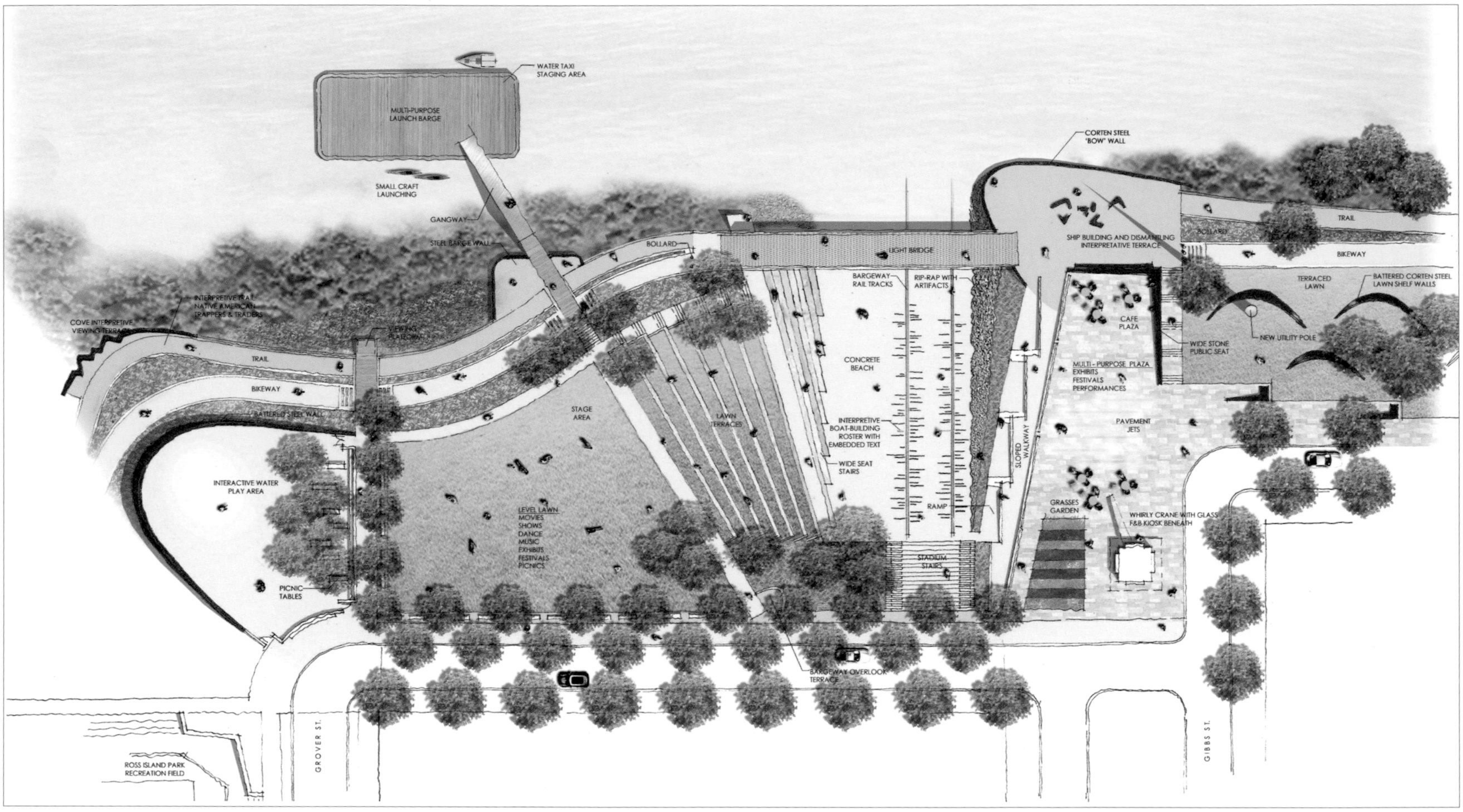

(top) Plan of park node at Barge Ramp.
(bottom left) Section of Bird-blind overlook in north end.
(bottom right) Sloping lawn with corten terraces.

(top) Perspective of southern activity node pier and habitat area.
(bottom left) Log burner sculpture.
(bottom right) Overlooks at southern grasslands.

Bass River Park, West Dennis

The project is modest in scale and scope, a 2.5-acre waterfront parcel in a town on Cape Cod, Massachusetts, known as a summer resort destination and more recently as a home for retirees. The community is interested in a primarily passive-use park which enhances the public's experience of the river — an experience newly attainable after the demolition of a two-storey restaurant and an outlying commercial building.

The site is filled with salt marsh — compacted and deadened. The ambition is to re-ignite social and ecological dynamics.

The strategy looks to establish a varied landscape field — an earthen carpet of hillocks — that supports short- and long-term competition among four vegetal communities characteristic of the region: red cedar meadow, sand plain, wet meadow, and salt marsh. Circular landforms — some convex, others concave; some conical, others offset; some whole, others severed — form a continuous landscape mat across the site. The physical differences in elevation, slope, and aspect create an almost unlimited variety of conditions upon which vegetation may grow, adapt, and compete. Long-term environmental changes, short-term disturbances, and even use or maintenance practices can subtly or radically shift the balance among vegetal types, allowing one or another community to establish predominance — if only temporarily.

Human activity is accommodated straightforwardly, yet flexibly. A thirty-foot-wide arcing boardwalk is situated along the river, mimicking the constructed but now ecologically fragile shoreline; its edges are interrupted by existing natural features (a lonely dune, a stand of cedars) as well as by intruding hillocks, rendering it a varied wooden ribbon that contracts and expands along its length. Planted concrete pavers enter the site as a driveway from the adjacent road, but quickly expand as a broad field that spreads to touch the nearby hillocks; in doing so, they create a permeable yet reinforced field that alternately or simultaneously hosts parking and public events. A network of stabilized earthen paths threads its way among the hillocks, offering a vast array of circulatory and experiential opportunities. And a series of land-based structures (showers, changing screens, restrooms, shade structures, kayak rental hut) and water-based structures (docks and piers) are scattered across the site, momentarily intensifying the landscape field.

In many ways, the project is an extension of the firm's interests in constructed ecologies and robust topographies. Yet it also represents a shift away from more complex and articulated formal vocabularies in favor of simpler, repetitive and modulated forms whose size and shape are as influenced by construction equipment and technologies as they are by ecological or programmatic considerations.

(right) Overview of the park context, with the Bass River to the bottom, a conservation area to the left, and a state road — which contributes substantial stormwater runoff — to the top.

(left and right bottom) Images of the existing site, a filled wetland, and the proposed field of landforms from the river.

client / owner
Town of Dennis

other key consultants
Architecture: The Galante Architecture Studio;
Civil engineering: Nitsch Engineering;
Structural engineer: Richmond So;
Marine engineer: Child Engineering

location
West Dennis, Massachusetts, USA

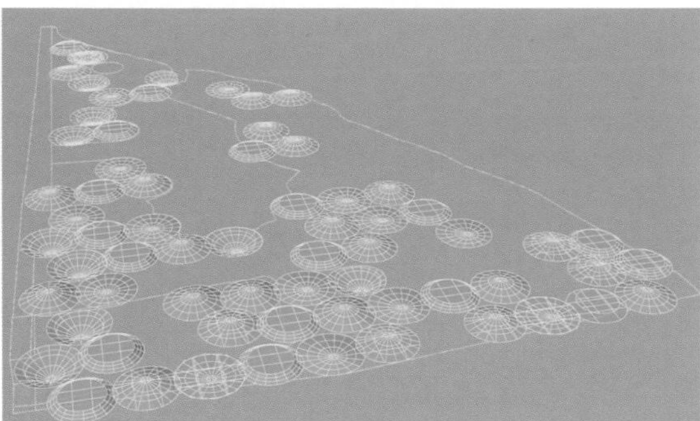

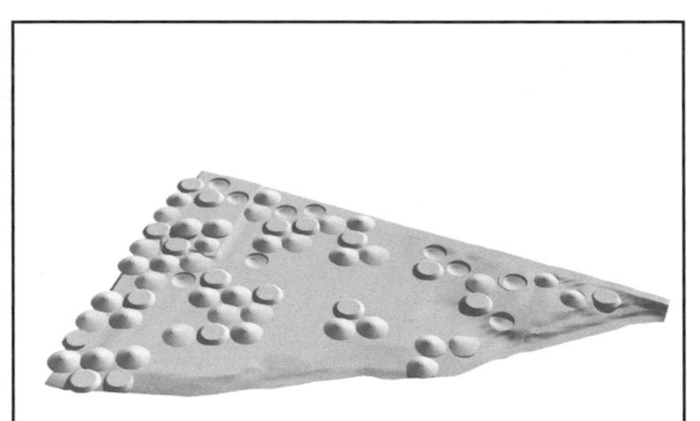

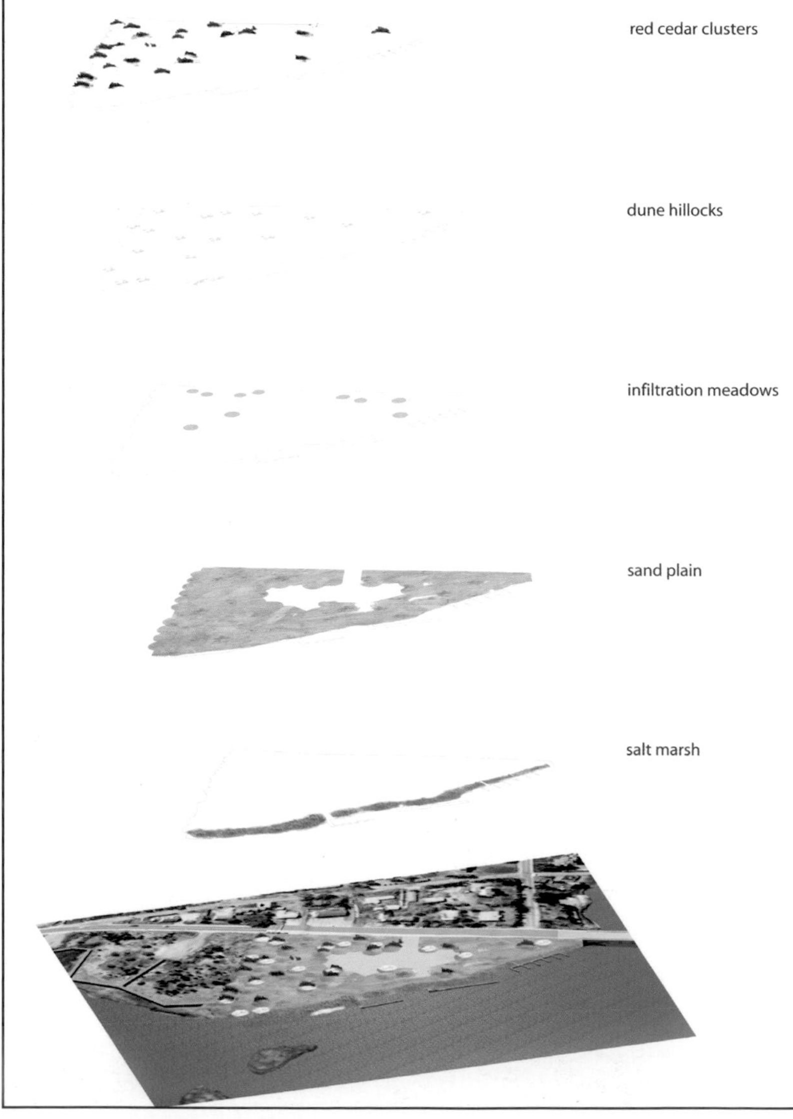
red cedar clusters
dune hillocks
infiltration meadows
sand plain
salt marsh

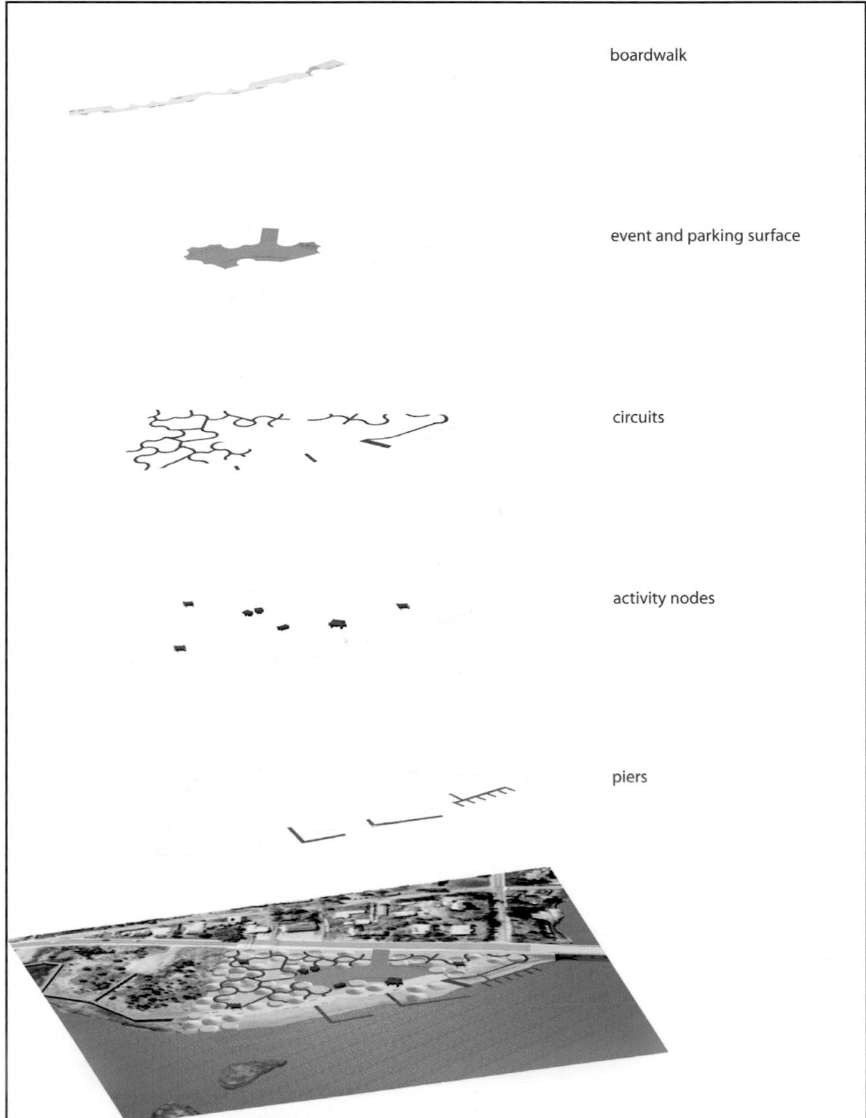
boardwalk
event and parking surface
circuits
activity nodes
piers

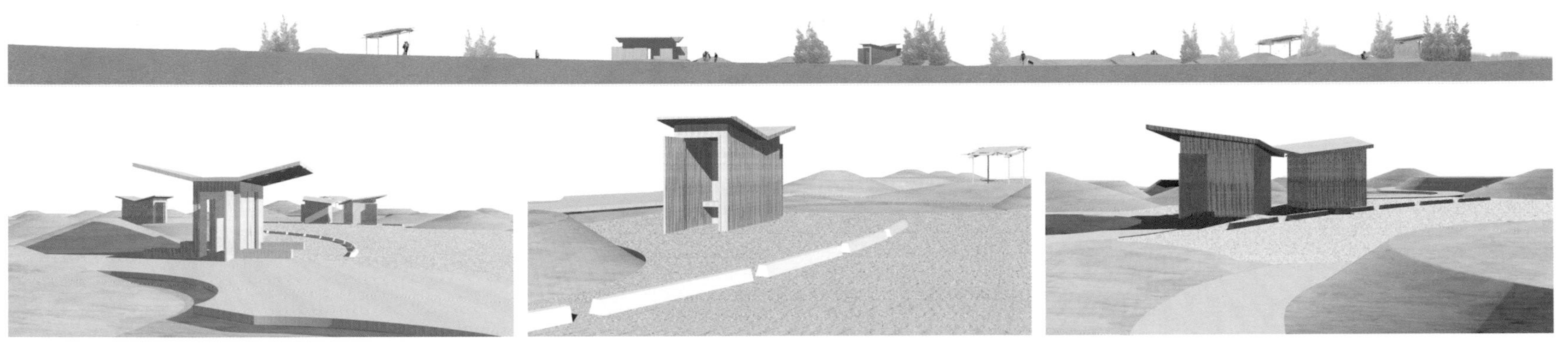

(opposite page, top) Field of hillocks and depressions mimic regional glacial topographies.
(opposite page, bottom) Park components.
(top) Wood structures distribute activity nodes across the park and play off landforms.
(below) View from nearby bridge.

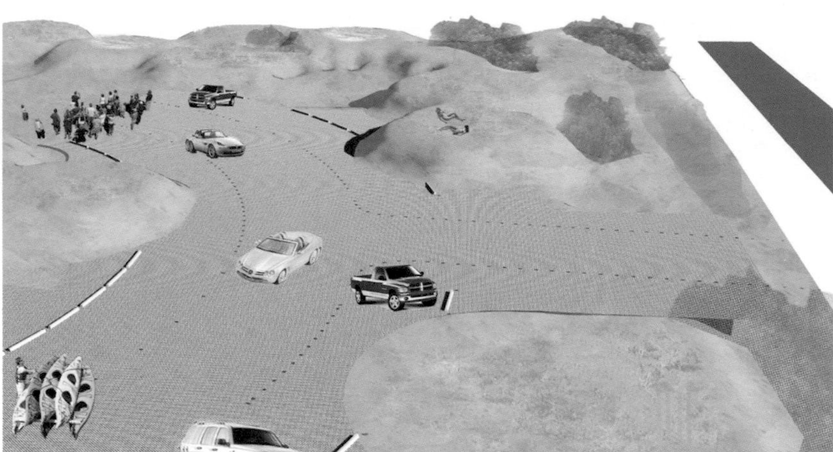

river's edge/salt marsh

key species

- salt water cordgrass (Spartina alterniflora)
- salt meadow cordgrass (Spartina patens)
- beachgrass (Ammophila breviligulata)
- spike grass (Distichlis spicata)
- quack grass (Elymus repens)
- alkali grass (Puccinellia maritima)
- red fescue (Festuca rubrum)
- northern bayberry (Myrica pensylvanica)
- sea lavender (Limonium carolinium)

dune/sand plain

key species

- beachgrass (Ammophila breviligulata)
- salt hay (Spartina patens)
- little blue stem (Schizachyrium scoparium)
- poverty grass (Danthonia spicata)
- bearberry (Arctostaphylos uva-ursi)
- bayberry (Myrica pensylvanica)
- low bush blueberry (Vaccinium angustifolium)
- Queen Anne's lace (Daucus carota)
- goldenrod (Solidago spp.)

red cedar meadow

key species

- Eastern red cedar (Juniperus virginiana)
- pitch pine (Pinus rigida)
- bearberry (Arctostaphylos uva-ursi)
- bayberry (Myrica pensylvanica)
- low bush blueberry (Vaccinium angustifolium)
- American beech (Fagus grandifolia)
- beach plum (Prunus maritima)
- American holly (Ilex opaca)
- hairgrass (Deschampsia flexuosa)

infiltration meadow

Key species

- Common rush (Juncus effusus)
- Bottlebrush sedge (Hystrix patula)
- Porcupine sedge (carex hystericina)
- Wild Iris (Iris shrevei)
- Monkeyflower (Mimulus ringens)
- Ironweed (Veronica Fasciculata)
- Purple coneflower seed (Echinacea purpurea)
- Blue Vervain (Verbena Hastata)
- Nodding pink onion (Allium cernuum)

(left and far left) Parking field doubles as event space.

(bottom left and bottom) Proposed vegetal communities and potential future scenarios.

(right) Concept model of riverfront; views of upland and riverfront.

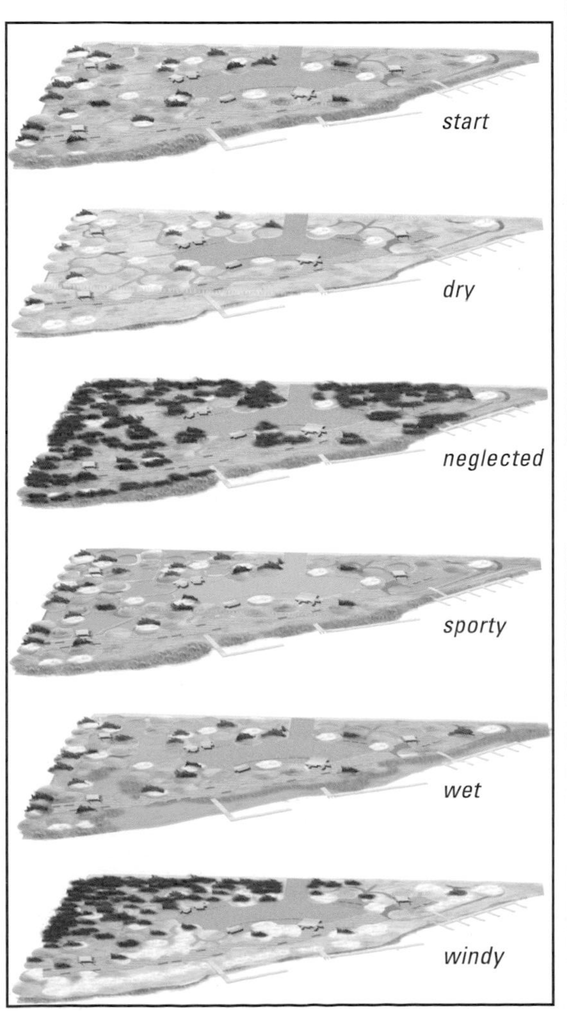

Pedestrian and Cyclist Bridge for the Tamar Valley World Heritage Site, Tamar Valley

In October 2005 Studio Bednarski, collaborating with the bridge engineer Flint and Neill Partnership, emerged as the winner in a limited competition involving a new bridge for the then proposed new world heritage site. On the competition shortlist were also Clash Associates, Wilkinson Eyre Architects, and a local practice, which in the end did not submit. The competition was judged on the basis of past track record and a design approach statement.

2006 was the year of 200 anniversary of the birth of Isambard Kingdom Brunel, one of the most inspirational engineers of the 19th century, designer of the Royal Albert Bridge on Tamar at Saltash. Also in 2006 UNESCO declared the Tamar Valley Mining District a World Heritage Site. The mines of this district worked an important group of tin and copper lodes whose outcrops can be traced from Callington and Kit Hill eastwards to the fringes of Dartmoor, crossing the Tamar Valley between Luckett and Calstock and centred on the settlement of Gunnislake.

The new bridge will cross the Tamar Valley and link Gunnislake with the mining areas. It is a unique structure based on the stress ribbon principle, with a Y-shaped plan, linking three abutments at different ground levels.

The Y-shaped plan form of the bridge resulted from an analysis of the desire lines on the east side of the river, with two different paths and levels needing to be connected to the bridge, and is based on a practical and logical consideration of the problem of flooding. The Y-shape provides excellent resistance to lateral loads during an extreme flood, with upstream branch of the Y acting in tension to resist the flood loads and prevent high transverse bending effects in the bridge deck.

A special saddle shaped element, the main visual attractor of the otherwise very low key bridge, forms a link that joins together the main span and the two arms of the Y over an inclined prop. Its flowing shape provides a gradually changing stiffness and thus 'softens' a structural 'hard spot' and reduces peak stresses in the deck.

While reviewing the various options for the bridge different types of construction have been considered and evaluated. Thus various forms of arch, stayed and beam bridges were analysed, taking account of the particular characteristics of this site. In addition to the potentially dominant visual intrusion that many of these options would have created in what is a sensitive rural environment; there were several practical reasons why they were rejected in favour of the stressed ribbon.

It was considered that any solutions which required the felling of a significant number of trees and the formation of a major temporary access road, resulting in a significant change and damage to the sensitive woodland environment would be unacceptable. Thus

client / owner	other key consultants	location	awards
Tamar Valley AONB Partnership	Bridge engineer: Flint & Neill Partnership	Gunnislake, Tamar Valley, UK	Winner of an invited competition

the nature of the site and the difficulties of access by large vehicles made solutions involving large cranes or heavy equipment very disruptive and uneconomical.

The construction of a stressed ribbon bridge would require only lightweight components and correspondingly lightweight equipment with no heavy craneage.

The stressed ribbon form is one of the purest and simplest in bridge structures. With its origins in ancient rope suspension bridges in mountain passes which sway and wobble as users cross a precarious ravine, the modern stressed ribbon is by contrast a robust and well engineered structure providing a safe and stable platform for pedestrians, cyclists and even heavy vehicles. A hanging ribbon of concrete or steel is draped across a river and pulled tight, anchored into solid, firm abutments. The tighter it is, the flatter the profile. A straight line profile requires an infinite tension (or a weightless deck!) and is of course unachievable, so design developments over the years have settled on an optimum range of sag profiles to achieve the appropriate balance between structural performance and cost.

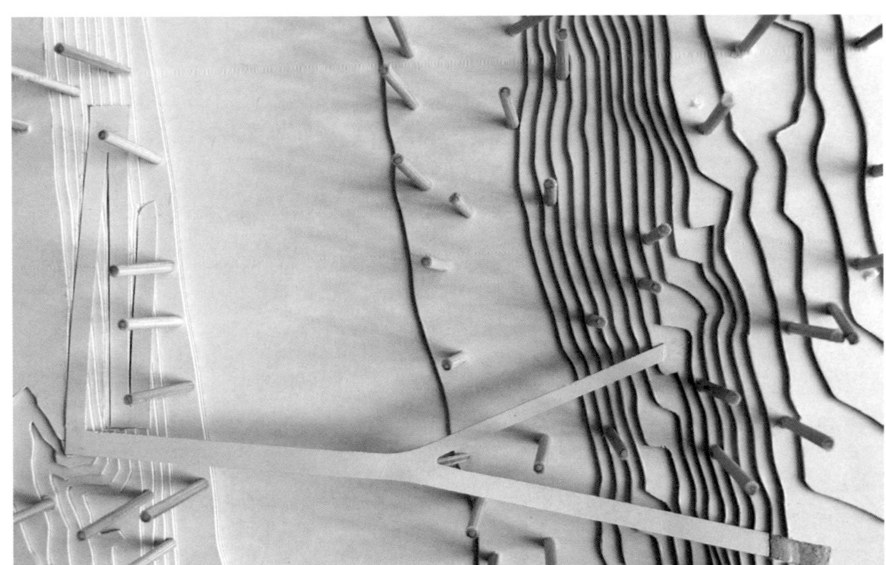

(left) Collaged view along the Tamar River.
(top) Working model
(bottom) Bridge elevation.

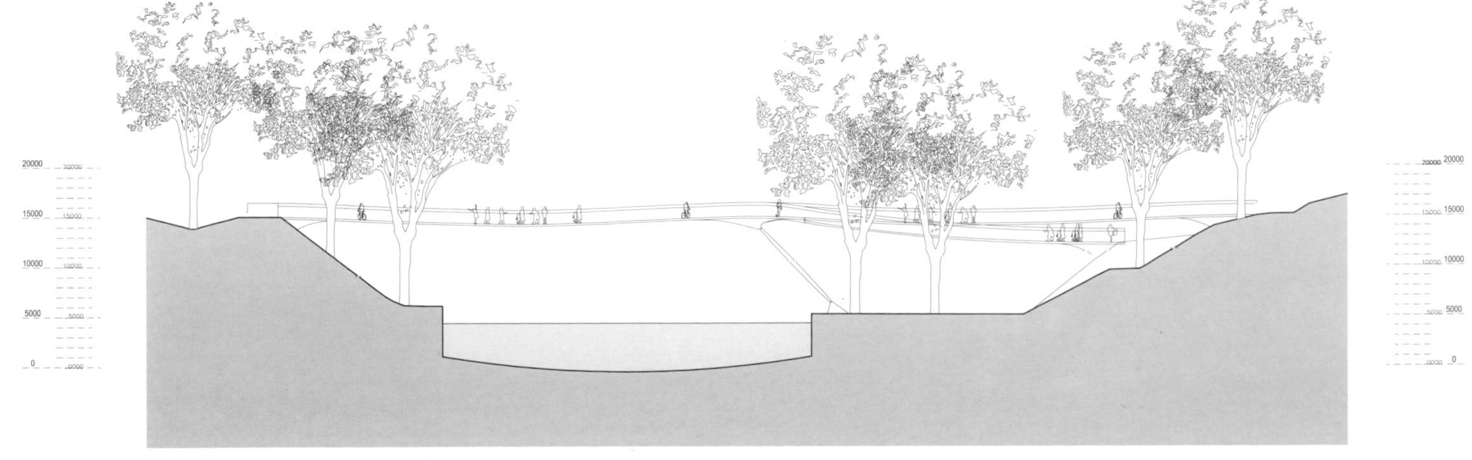

Flight 587 Memorial, New York

The design proposes three towering limestone columns, reaching up to embrace the sky creating a soaring chapel-like space. As you enter the sculpture, designed by artist Donald Lipski, the names of those who lost their lives in the tragedy are etched into the stone, and the upper portion of the walls are covered with mirrored stainless steel. Looking up, there are infinite reflections of the surroundings, and of yourself, creating a miraculous kaleidoscopic sphere with facets reflecting the ever-changing sky.

Framing the sculpture is a garden, which bestows upon the memorial an internal court for reflection, tranquility and dignity. The garden is planted with a seasonal grove of serviceberry trees and privet hedges. Meyer + Silberberg sited the sculpture to purposely shelter it from its immediate context and to give it a sense of enclosure. However, the densely planted trees are open to the ocean, letting the horizon act as a vast, infinite, and promising backdrop to the towering columns.

©Donald Lipski

©Meyer + Silberberg

(left) Site model from southwest.
(top) Perspective – View looking up inside the memorial at the kaliedoscope.
(right) Perspective – Detail of memorial.

client / owner	other key consultants	location	awards
City of New York, USA	Artist: Donald Lipski	Queens, New York, USA	Finalist

©Meyer + Silberberg

©Meyer + Silberberg

(left) Site model from south.
(right top) Perspective – memorial in winter.
(right middle) Perspective – memorial in summer.
(right bottom) Perspective – memorial in fall.

©Meyer + Silberberg

©Meyer + Silberberg

©Meyer + Silberberg

RSA Memorial, Manukau Memorial Gardens, Auckland

2006 was a particularly special year for the Royal New Zealand Returned and Services' Association (RSA). It was the RSA's 90th Anniversary, the "Year of the Veteran" and the year that funding was approved for this project, the RSA Memorial.

The memorial is intended as "*... a permanent reminder of those who gave their all to preserve our freedom and way of life*".

The project is led by the South Auckland RSA's Cemetery Committee and in particular, the Manurewa and the Papatoetoe RSAs. It is a collaborative project, supported by Manukau City Council, numerous RSA groups, as well as a number of local community groups.

Chow:Hill's involvement started in 2000 when working with the RSA, we prepared the preliminary concepts. In 2006 Chow: Hill were engaged to further develop the original concept, and put together a team of consultants to carry the project through to implementation. The project team includes Chow:Hill (landscape architecture), RDT Pacific (quantity surveying), Fraser Thomas (engineering), StoneWorkz (design build engraving) and LDP Ltd (lighting).

The site for the RSA Memorial is located within the Manukau Memorial Gardens and is an extension of the Servicemen's area.

The concept has three key aspects:

- The first is an area for Commemoration (Gathering)
- The second is an area for Remembrance (Contemplation)
- The third is an area of Education (Learning)

The commemoration (gathering) space is an open paved area, edged by columnar trees which focuses on a flagpole. The area is primarily intended for Remembrance ceremonies.

The remembrance (contemplation) space is a semi-enclosed area for remembrance and quiet contemplation. It is semi-enclosed by four sculpted granite panels.

Each of the panels will represent one of the four services: airforce, army, nursing and navy. The panels are to be sculpted to appear as if "real-life", full size people are walking out of them. It is intended that the remembrance, the memories be brought 'alive'. This area also includes seating, bold poppy and rose planting, a reflective water feature and a single Cherry Tree.

The education (learning) area is a diagonal axis featuring four large vertical panels, with a combination of text and imagery. These panels reveal some of the "real" stories and experiences of New Zealand's servicemen and women. They are intended as highly graphic panels illustrating the various "Theatres of War". The exact design of these panels is currently being developed in consultation with the Auckland War Memorial Museum.

Together the sculpted and educational panels are intended to bring the memorial alive, especially for younger generations removed from the time, events and people for whom this memorial represents.

All of the elements of the RSA Memorial are protected, bounded by grass mounds and tall trees. The simplicity of the design, with appropriate detailing and quality materials will result in an elegant setting that is both respectful and welcoming. The suite of hard and soft materials has been carefully chosen with restraint to support the memorial panels. Hard materials are unadorned, featuring shades of grey and pure white with deep red Jarrah timber as support, while the planting is a strong mix of red and green.

The memorial will bring many benefits to the community including:

- Remembrance and a place of healing;
- Commemoration – past, present and future;
- A place of quiet contemplation for those visiting the cemetery;
- Potential to be an important teaching aid for schools;
- A place of cultural heritage;
- Strengthen the relationship between the RSA and the wider community;
- Establish a unique point of focus for Manukau.

The design team are currently engaged in the preparation of Contract Documentation. It is estimated that construction of the project will start in November 2007.

It's been over eighteen years in the making.

It's an opportunity to be part of a unique project, the creation of a very special place, a place to bring generations together, a place to share stories, to celebrate.

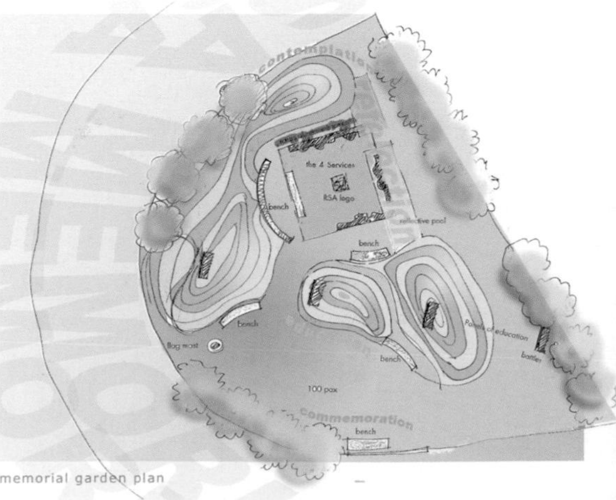

memorial garden plan

client / owner
RSA and Manukau City Council

key consultants
Quantity Surveying: RDT Pacific;
Lighting and Electrical: LDP Ltd.;
Design Build Granite Panels: Stoneworkz;
Civil and Structural Engineering: Fraser Thomas.

location
Manukau Memorial Gardens, Papatoetoe,
Auckland, New Zealand

(top) The developed design plan strengthened the forms and selected materials.

(left) The early concept plan featured the memorial surrounded by organic grass mounds.

(right) View towards inner memorial space, with reflective pool surrounded by grass mounding.

(bottom) The initial sketch concept showing the four granite memorial panels cutting through the site.

As the stars that shall be bright when we are dust,
Moving in marches upon the heavenly plain;
As the stars that are starry in the time of our darkness,
To the end, to the end, they remain.

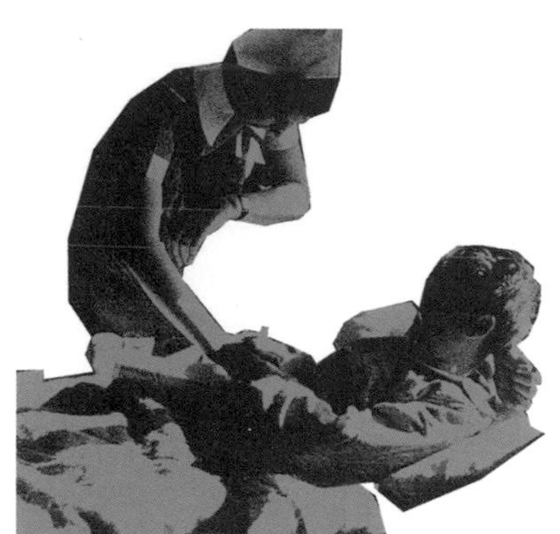

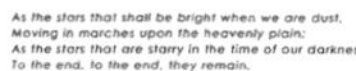

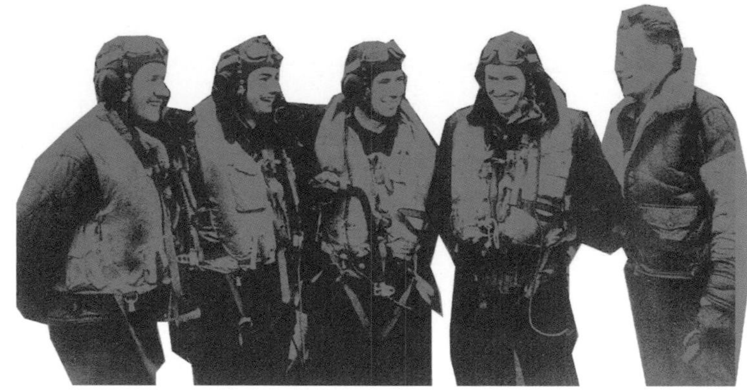

They mingle not with their laughing comrades again;
They sit no more at familiar tables of home;
They have no lot in our labour of the day time;
They sleep beyond England's foam.

But where our desires are and our hopes profound,
Felt as a well-spring that is hidden from sight,
To the innermost heart of their own land they are known
As the stars are known to the night;

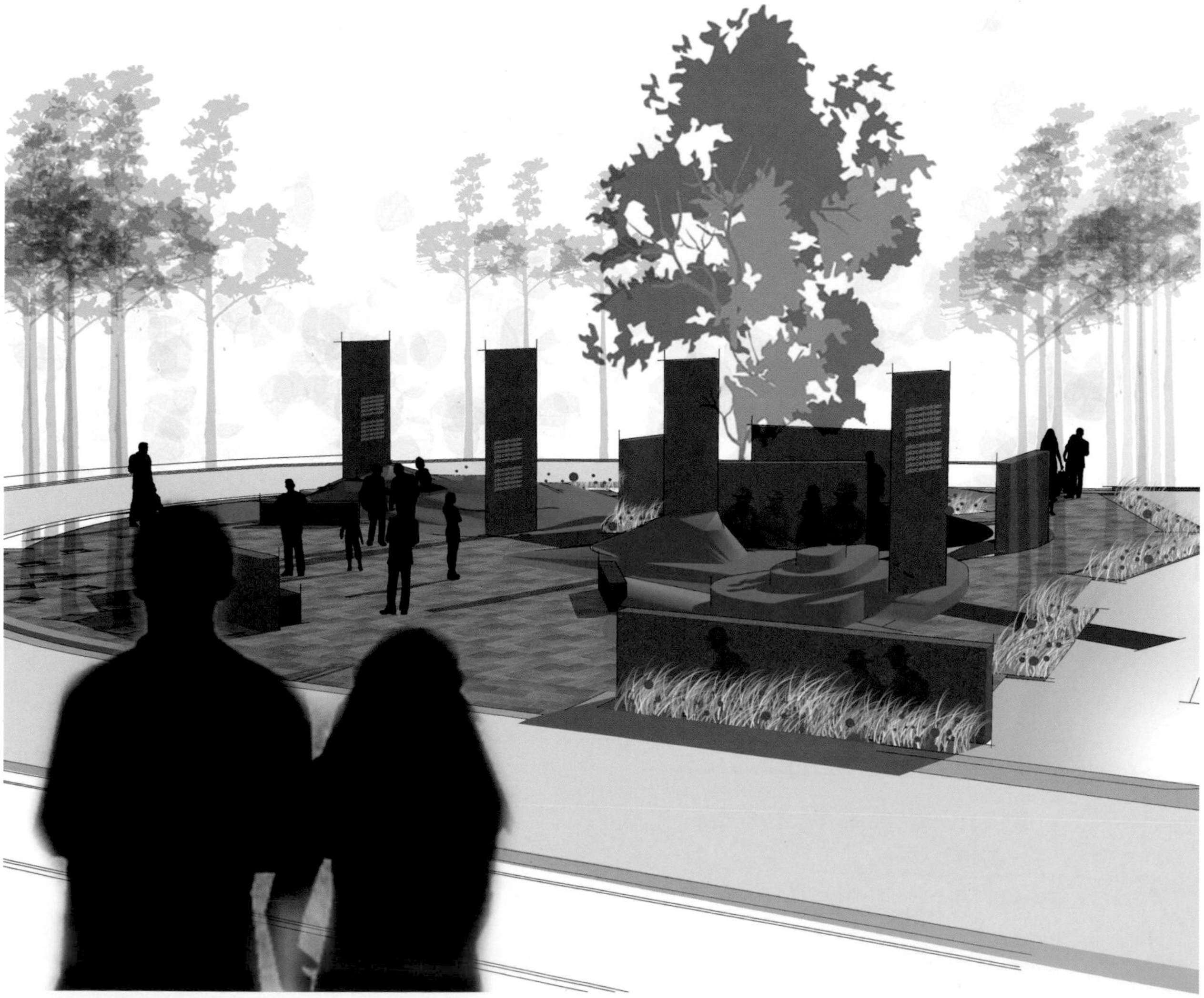

(top) Each of the four memorial panels features 3D images with inscribed text .

(left) View of commemoration space to be used for ceremonies.

(right top) Planting is a strong blend of red roses and red poppies with vivid green support foliage.

(right bottom) View along the axis of educational panels rising out of the grass mounding.

a Path a Muse taken — Trudeau Memorial Park, Toronto

The Trudeau Memorial Park is the City of Toronto's commemoration of the life, contributions and legacy of the late Right Honourable Pierre Elliott Trudeau who served as the Prime Minister of Canada from 1968 to 1979 and from 1980 to 1984. Considered one of Canada's most outstanding citizens, Trudeau passed away in the year 2000.

'*a Path a Muse taken*' is the selected scheme in a Canadian art competition that was held in 2003. The site for the Memorial is a 0.2 hectare parcel of land located at the City's waterfront. It is positioned between the Yo-Yo Ma inspired Music Garden to the west, with it's cultural theming and geometrically derived spiral forms, and the Spadina Wetland to the east, with it's emphasis on nature and ecological restoration. Similar to Trudeau's combined interest in the cultural and natural make-up of Canada, the Memorial draws together essential qualities of these two adjacent sites.

The existing site is an open lawn in the shape of a rectangle that slopes gently to the south. The site is bounded by Lake Ontario and the Waterfront Promenade to the south, Queens Quay West sidewalk/road to the north, a concrete walkway and wall to the east and a raised concrete walkway/ belvedere to the west.

The proposed Memorial includes large sculptural objects that are discrete symbolic elements, though as a park, the Memorial is embodied within the overall site and offers contemplative places for rest and reflection. The experience of the entire site and its many varied features will reconfirm the individual and collective memory of the spirit of Trudeau. The site is boldly articulated with alternating naturalistic, linear patterns of contrasting planting beds, walkways and open turfgrass. The patterns of the park are a reminder of Canada's dynamic, multi-cultural mosaic. This flowing mosaic includes a dominant path, the '*path=way*', characterized by an overall organic quality and imbued with river related imagery. The shape of the path takes its inspiration from the St. Lawrence River near the Island of Montreal and Canoe Lake located in Algonquin Park. Trudeau is associated with both of these. In addition, these water bodies are two natural geographic features that have a key place in the psyche of Canadians. The '*path=way*', the diverse site elements and the overall composition of the site reminds us of Trudeau's love of Canada's natural landscape as well as his critical role in enhancing Canada's cultural mosaic.

Within the park, the numerous discrete, interpretive elements are visually powerful and rich with symbolism. The individual art objects are carefully arranged as integrated parts of the rigorously designed, memorable landscape. This reflects the rigor of Trudeau's intellect. The locations of the iconic sculptural elements, mostly along the '*path=way*', acknowledge that Trudeau altered the 'flow' of Canada's development substantially, uniquely and permanently.

In addition to the '*path=way*', the primary interpretive elements include a polished granite 'canoe' constructed in thirteen segments that correspond to the total number of Canadian provinces and territories; a '*T Stone*' composed of a singular, Canadian, granite boulder; the stone '*Sussex Pier*' that is a literal reference to the entrance piers of 24 Sussex Drive, the residence of the prime minister in Ottawa; the '*tableau*', a contemplative sitting area embraced by a dynamic arrangement of Niagara Escarpment limestone and Canadian Shield granite; and the '*Isle Tree*' that casts a multi-faceted shadow evoking the presence of Trudeau.

The memorable quality of '*a Path a Muse taken*' is not one based on a singular, bold architectonic form, but stems from its conceptual basis as a moving tapestry or a garden of discovery in fluid balance. The Trudeau Memorial Park manifests the true dynamic quality of Toronto's urban environment, the intricate make-up of Canada and the complexity of Trudeau's passion and intellect.

(left) Model of 'tableau', a contemplative sitting area.

(opposite page, top) Aerial view of the 'Trudeau Memorial Park' looking north-west.

(opposite page, bottom) Diagram of 'canoe\arc', composed of thirteen colours of granite.

client / owner	other key consultants	location	awards
City of Toronto, Canada	Artist and Collaborator: Stephen Cruise Aerial Illustration: Ken Nice	Harbourfront, Toronto, Ontario, Canada	First Place, Trudeau Memorial Public Art Competition

©Ken Nice

Canoe\arc
total length: 7.8m
13 polished granite sections
(mid-section: l.: 1.4m, w.: 0.6m, ht.: 0.6m)

Section w\example of sandblasted lettering
'Diversity Our Strength'

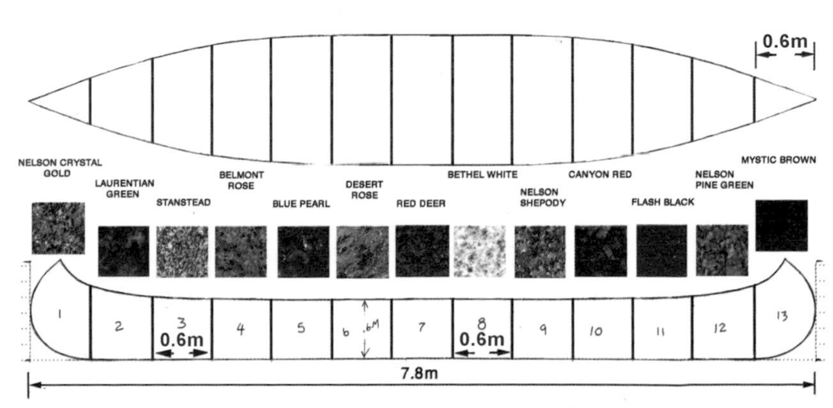

Legend
1 Existing East Walkway
2 Reinstated Pergola
3 Existing Street Walkway
4 Existing West Walkway
5 Existing Lookout
6 Waterfront Promenade
7 North-East Entrance
8 West Entrance Walk
9 South Entrance
10 East Entrance Walk
11 South-East Greenspace
12 Sussex Pier
13 Tableau
14 Canoe
15 Isle
16 Path=Way
17 T Stone
18 Isle Tree
19 Typical Bench
20 Typical Boulder
21 South-East Sitting Wall
Lake Ontario
North

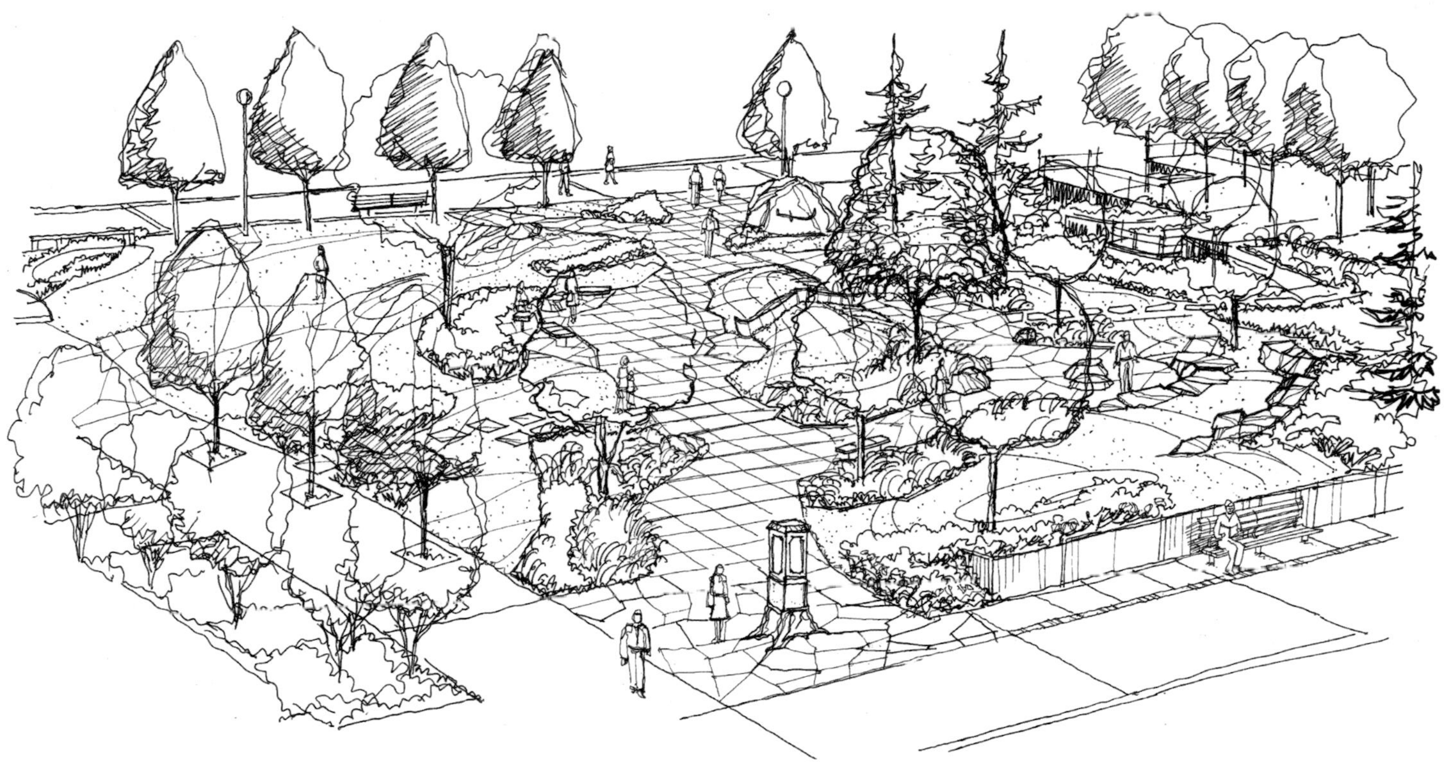

(opposite page) Site Plan of the 'Trudeau Memorial Park'.
(top) Aerial sketch looking south-west along 'path=way'.
(bottom left) 'Sussex PIER' is an entrance sculpture and information kiosk.
(bottom right) View looking south from 'tableau'.

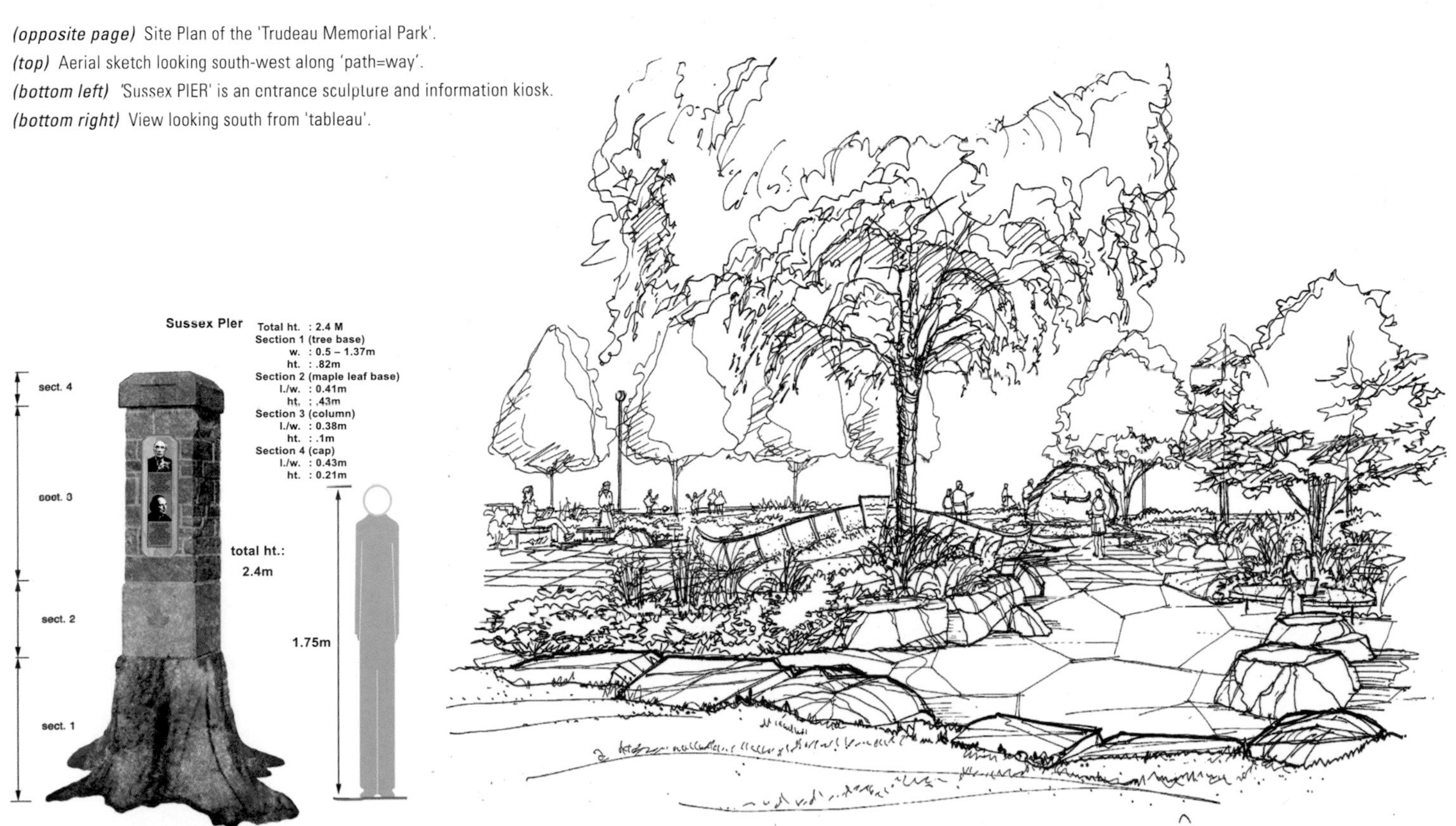

The Living Wreath — Veterans' Memorial, Toronto

The objective of the Veterans' Memorial was to create a new place for commemorating Canada's armed forces veterans. The site for this submission to a national memorial competition was the Legislative Grounds, Queen's Park, Toronto, Ontario, Canada, directly in front of the Province of Ontario's Legislative Building. Numerous existing memorials are located in Queen's Park. On the grounds of this place for public discussion, remembrance and commemoration, the Memorial signifies the critical contribution of Canadian veterans to the protection of the democratic foundations of Canadian society.

'*The Living Wreath*' respects the existing honoured grounds of Queen's Park, engages the open lawn while resting quietly among the existing, majestic grove of trees. It is prominent yet it does not challenge the ambience of its setting.

The spirit of the Veterans' Memorial is based on the idea of a living wreath. It is circular in shape and speaks of unity, global understanding, and eternity. From the central circular gathering space, '*The Living Wreath*' reaches out to embrace the existing trees, visitors and the spirit of the veterans. Together these layers form a wreath as a growing and learning memorial environment, a process all are welcome to become part of it. We join hands with the spirits of the veterans to complete the wreath. We feel the eternal existence of the veterans who have served. It is a place for rest, for reflection, for remembrance.

Garden plantings form part of the wreath to create a 'living' place of contemplation and refuge. As the older trees die and are replaced with newer native species, and the gardens age and flourish, '*The Living Wreath*' will continue to grow and evolve. The torch will be passed to future generations of Canadians. The Veterans' Memorial is a sacred place as all of life is sacred. The veterans' sacrifices have given us freedom and the life we know today. It is a place of life and growth. The Veterans' Memorial is a place to show our love and appreciation for our veterans.

A curved, ceremonial, entrance path connects the Veterans' Memorial to two existing walkways and is the beginning of the journey of understanding. The '*Walk to Remember*' is a linear space for contemplation, a path of interpretation. Symbols and elements located along the path, such as the 11 circles and benches for reflection, direct us gently between the mature trees and toward '*The Living Wreath*'.

At the centre of the Veterans' Memorial is an inviting, open green space that fills with life where visitors and the spirit of the veterans collectively mingle. It is a slightly mounded, circular lawn surrounded by a swirl of granite pavers. Together the lawn and ring of pavers form the basis of the central gathering space, the '*Circle of Remembrance*'. Three garden-like rooms radiate from this central space. Within each of these rooms we experience a different and new understanding of our veterans and their experiences.

The Veterans' Memorial is a place that combines the beauty of enduring art with the intimate and large spaces. It is a memorial combining monuments and places. Large and small bronze figurative sculptures combine with the landscaped rooms as places for collective and individual remembrance. Red stone walls, including the granite plinth for the central sculpture, complement the warmth of the red stone façade of the Legislative Building. Upon these mending walls, interpretive and didactic artwork, in the form of images and inscriptions, convey the experiences and sacrifices of our veterans and their contribution to Canada and world harmony.

Like the existing sacred grove of trees that the Veterans' Memorial embraces, '*The Living Wreath*' will 'grow' in relevance with the passing of each year and will renew its presence with the change of seasons and each new generation of visitors.

client / owner	other key consultants	location	awards
Government of Ontario, Canada	Artist: Adrienne Alison; Landscape Architect: J. Andrew L. Wilson	Queen's Park, Toronto, Ontario, Canada	Finalist, The Veterans' Memorial at Queen's Park Competition

(top) Working model illustrating relationships and character of the three primary figurative sculptures.
(bottom left) Preliminary design sketch illustrating the relationship of the Memorial to the existing site features.
(bottom middle) Preliminary sketch of 'Silver Cross Mother' in the 'Sanctuary of Loss and Lament'.
(bottom right) View toward 'I Will Remember' in the 'Garden of Hope and Peace'.
(opposite page, left) View toward the Legislative Building from the Memorial site.
(opposite page, middle) Preliminary sketch of 'A Moment of Truth'.
(opposite page, right) Military storage container with material samples.

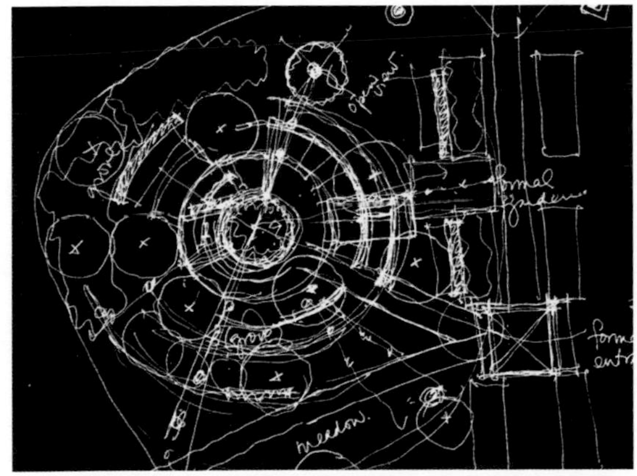

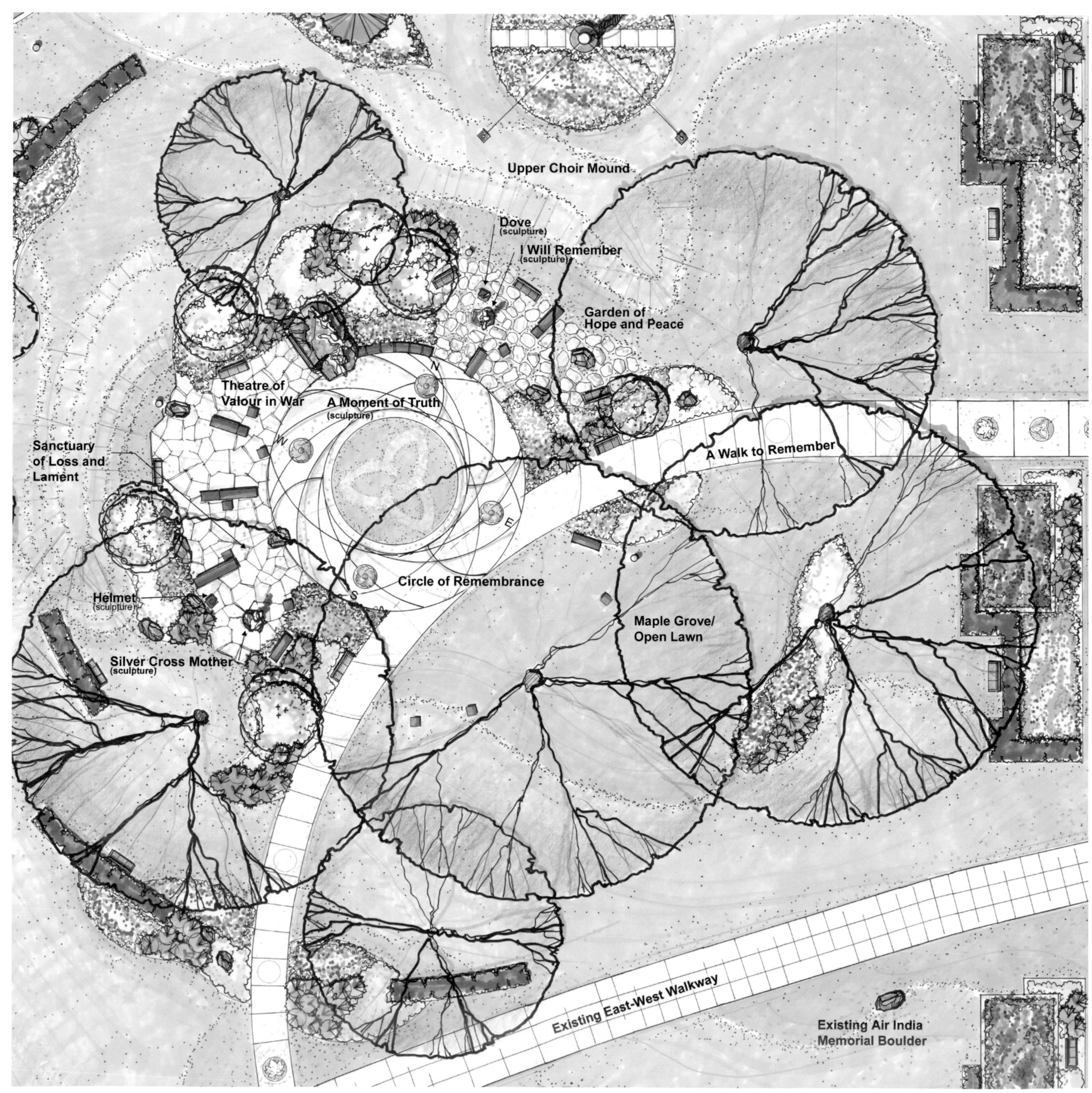
Upper Choir Mound
Dove
(sculpture)
I Will Remember
(sculpture)
Garden of
Hope and Peace
Theatre of
Valour in War
A Moment of Truth
(sculpture)
Sanctuary
of Loss and
Lament
A Walk to Remember
Circle of Remembrance
Helmet
(sculpture)
Maple Grove/
Open Lawn
Silver Cross Mother
(sculpture)
Existing East-West Walkway
Existing Air India
Memorial Boulder

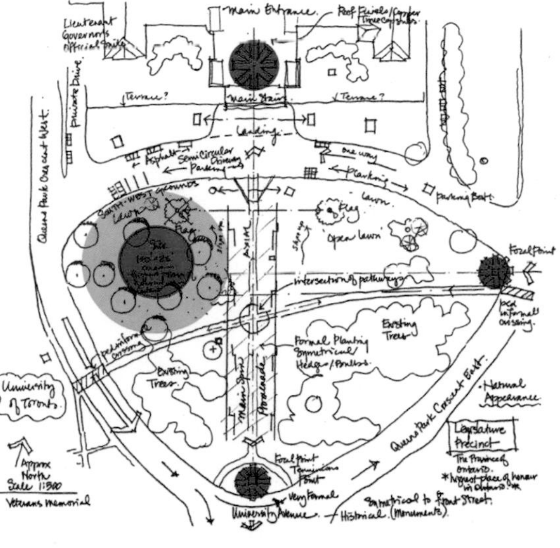

(top) Aerial view looking west along 'A Walk to Remember' toward 'The Living Wreath'.

(bottom) Site analysis diagram illustrating the location and relationships of the Memorial site within the Legislative Grounds.

(opposite page) Site Plan illustrating 'The Living Wreath' carefully nestled between existing trees.

The Greater Rochester 9–11 Memorial, New York

The Greater Rochester 9-11 Memorial must acknowledge the great loss and tragedy in America and overseas to the events of September 11th, 2001.

The design of the memorial utilizes a new walkway, situated between the First Universalist Church and the Frontier Building, which connects the Clinton Avenue sidewalk to a public walkway. The 9-11 memorial is located along this pathway which gently carves into the earth providing spaces at this site for circulation, contemplation, and assembly. Through non-directional, entering the memorial from Clinton Avenue a curved wall seeks to embrace and engage the visitor while integrating with the existing planters and gardens. Rather than an image of descent, the design works to create an image of the earth rising up around us to embrace, nurture and shelter.

The first element we encounter along the path is an open circular space along the path for small gatherings. This round open room is a symbol that can be found in all of the religions of the world. This space may be used for public gatherings supporting the memorial, as a meeting space for the adjacent office building, the church and the Rochester community. Further along the pathway, we observe seventeen openings with paths engaging the grass lawn. This design element symbolizes the interrupted lives of those lost from the Rochester, New York community. Seventeen paths broken–ended — merge into the landscape. The overall view is that of unfinished, incomplete foundations — illustrating to us our loss of what their lives could have been.

The memorial is constructed of cut Indiana white limestone for the walls and pavers. The highest point of all construction was chosen at twenty-seven inches (27") above the sidewalk — creating a comfortable height for seating — while preserving the sight lines of the First Universalist Church and the Frontier Building. Architectural elements which could significantly rise above the ground plane celebrate human achievements and were deemed not appropriate for this proposal. The low structure allows for the public's safety at the memorial and level pathway meets for barrier free accessibility. The memorial with the exception of subtle base cove lighting will employ all natural materials. Consideration of a low maintenance memorial is a priority. In the realization of the memorial, three existing trees would need to be relocated on the site. New trees, indigenous to Rochester would be planted, which over time would create a canopy sheltering the memorial pathway.

The Greater Rochester 9-11 Memorial recognizes and includes all faiths and seeks their participation in the commemoration process. After the completion of necessary approvals, a public fund raising for resources will be conducted to facilitate the design and construction of the memorial.

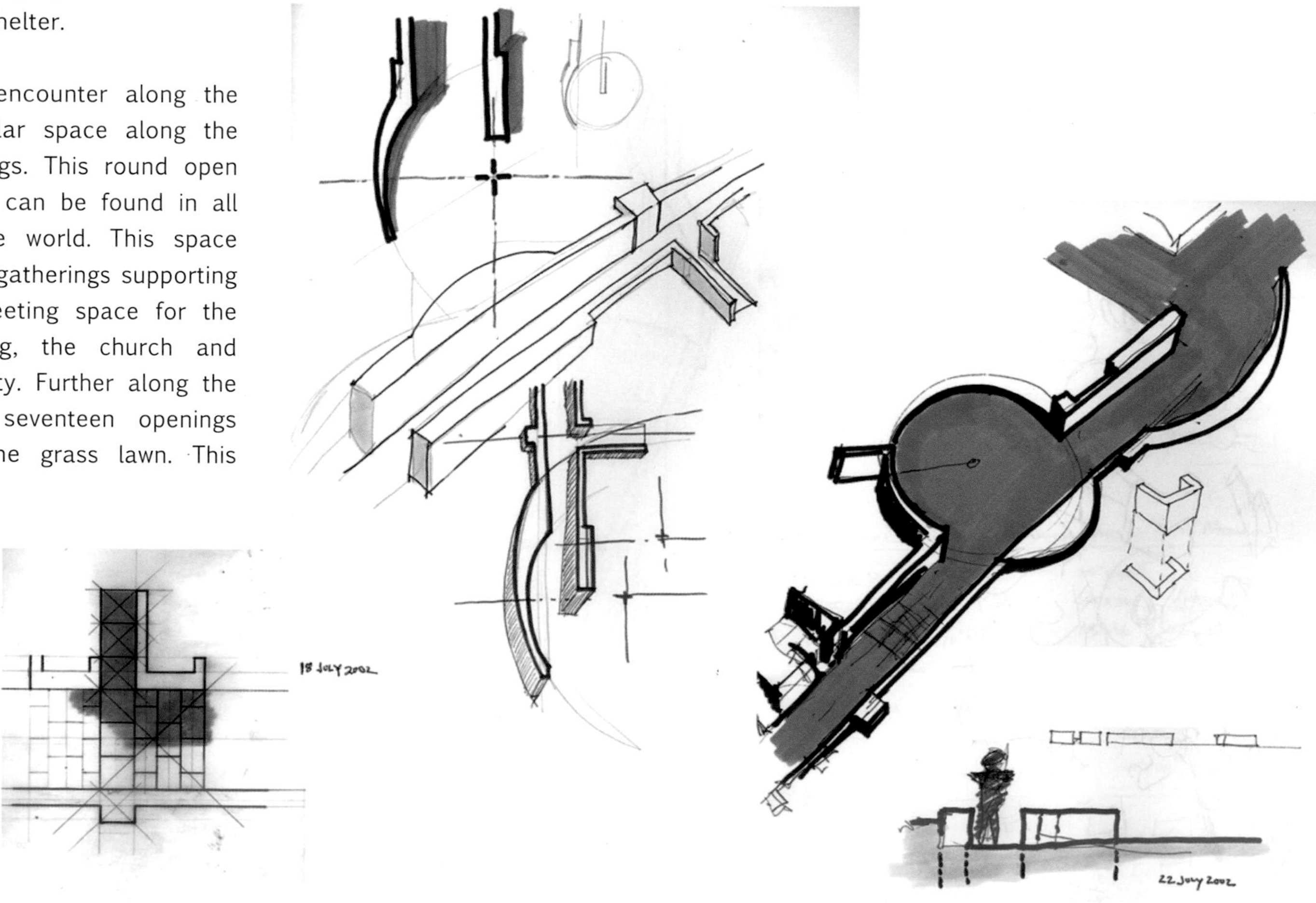

client / owner
City of Rochester, New York

other key consultants
Rachel Martin;
Christopher Romero;
Lindsey Folger;
Alexandria Rabuffo;
Jon Dolinar

location
Rochester, New York, USA

awards
Awarded 2003 Design for Excellence,
AIA Rochester

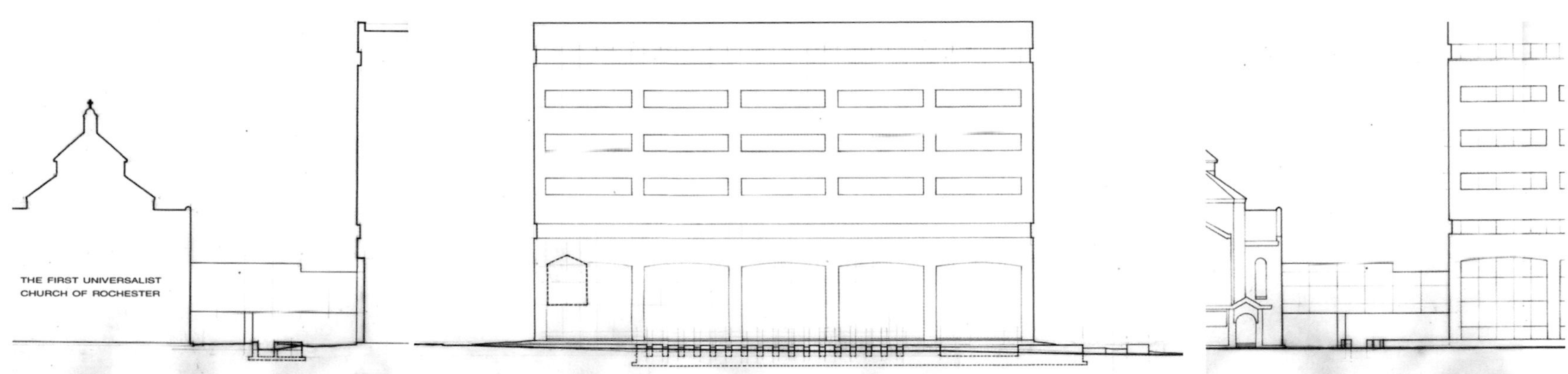

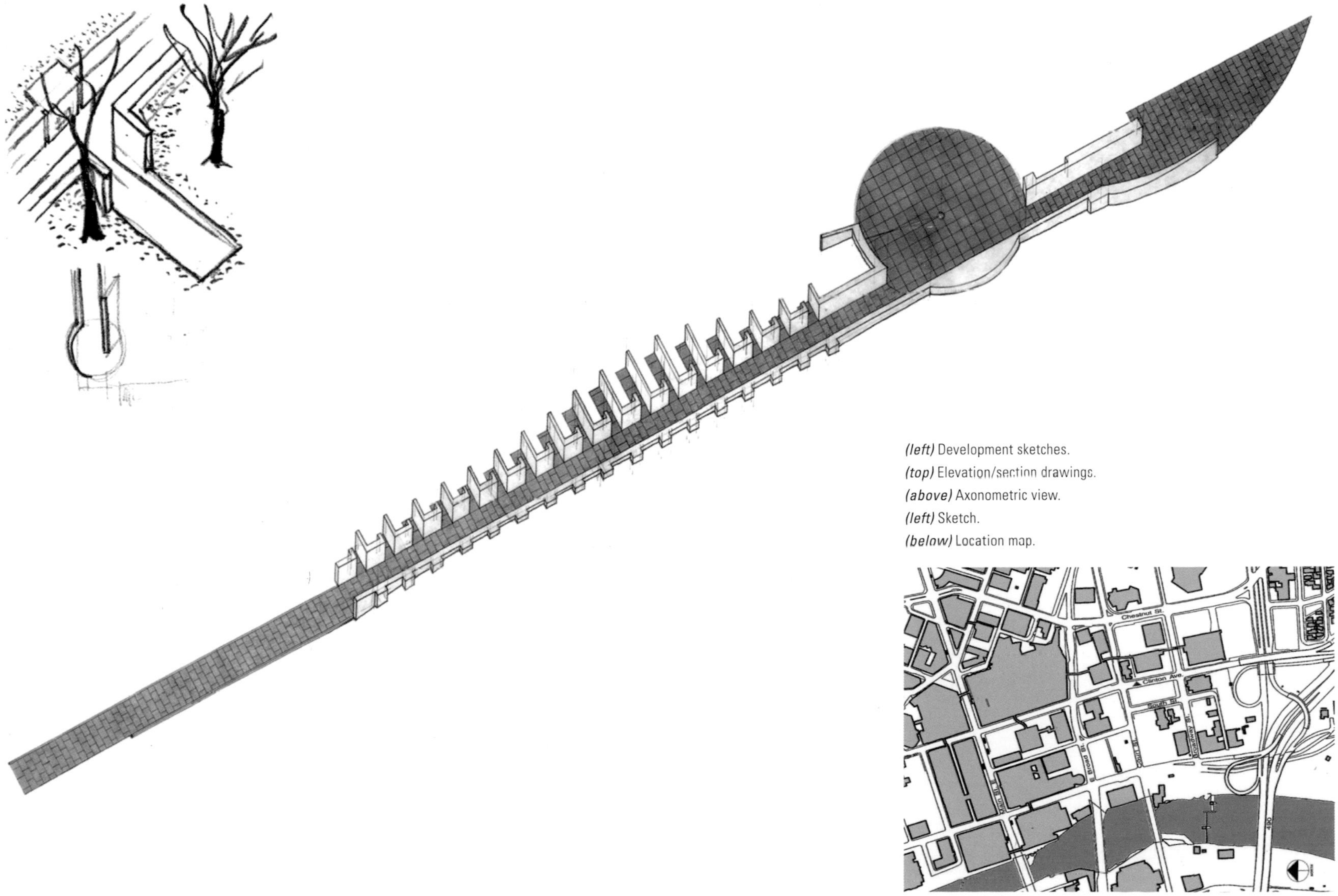

(left) Development sketches.
(top) Elevation/section drawings.
(above) Axonometric view.
(left) Sketch.
(below) Location map.

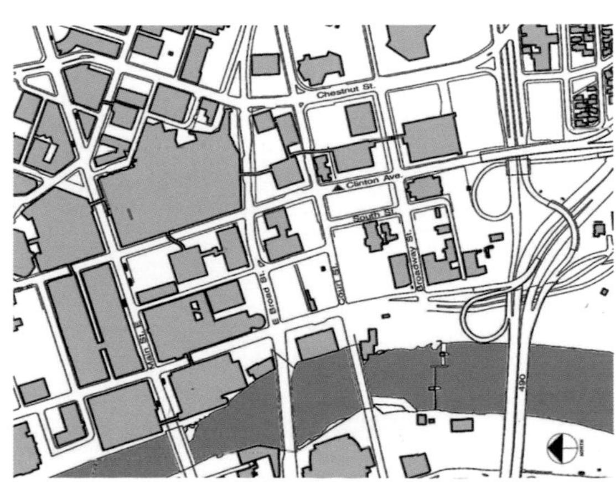

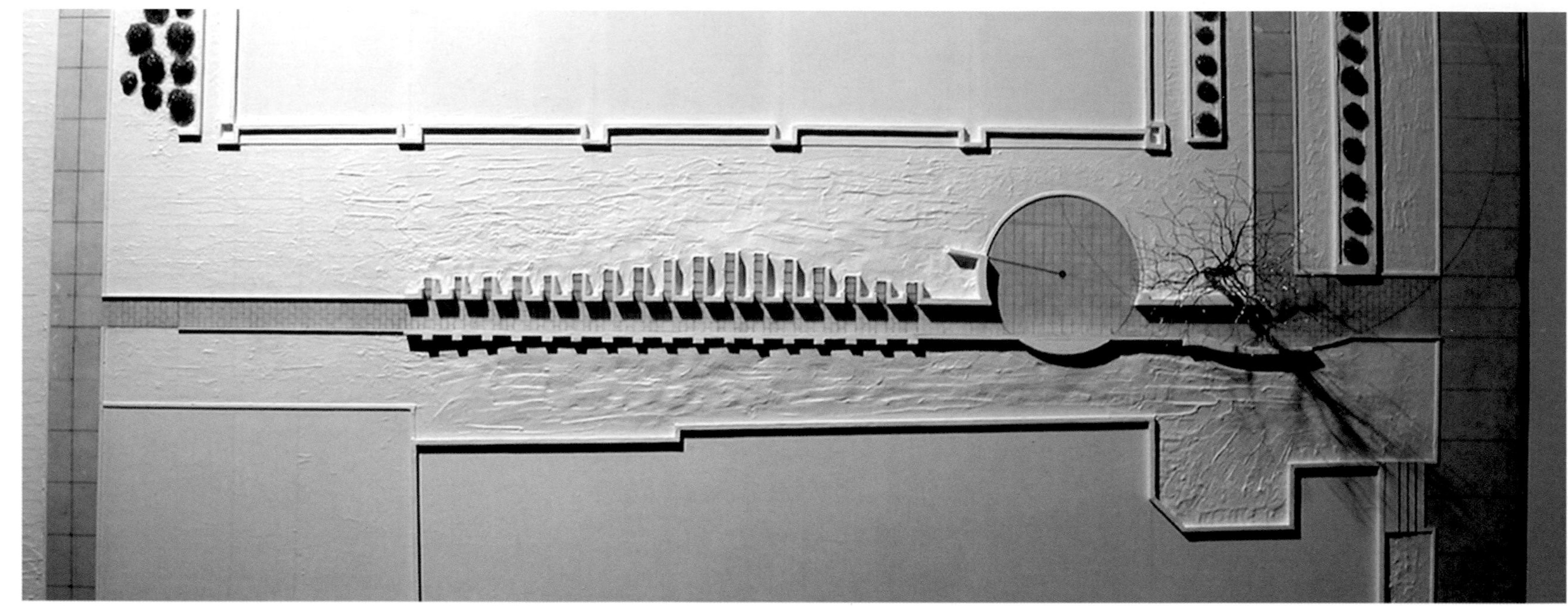

(opposite page & right) Model views.
(bottom) Geometry drawing.

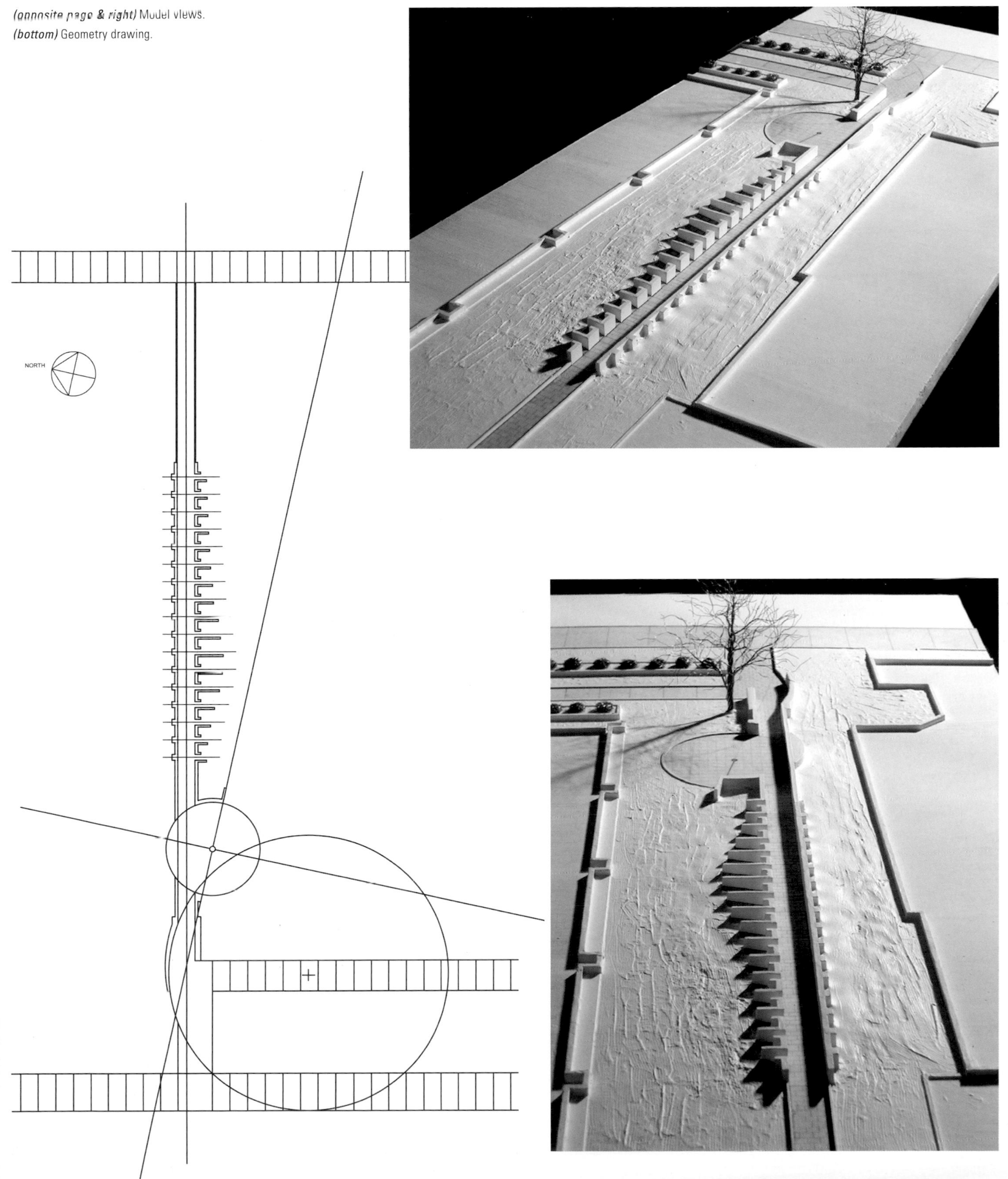

Kent State May 4th Memorial, Ohio

The Kent State May 4th Memorial must acknowledge the great loss and injury, a recourse for reconciliation and a hope that such a tragedy should never occur again.

The design solution utilizes a level version of the existing location of the walkway and allows the path to gently carve into the earth providing circulation for places of contemplation and assembly. Through non-directional, entering the Monument from the north a large wall seeks to embrace and engage the visitor. From the south and from the Prentice Hall parking lot one encounters the Memorial along a campus walkway. Rather than an image of descent, a conscious effort has been made to create an image of the earth rising up around us. Architectural elements which could rise above a ground plane celebrate mankind and technology and were deemed not appropriate for this solution.

Subtracted from earth are four circular rooms representative of the absence of Allison Krause, Jeffery Miller, Sandra Scheuer, and William Schroeder. These sanctuaries nestled in the Hillside are places for reflection and contemplation: a container, refuge or home for spirits scattered many years ago in the parking lot. The acts of violence are reflected in nine gashes and four wounds in the earth elements opposite the round rooms. Further along, the path widens to reveal a square open air room for assembly meetings. A large stair steps up from the meeting room, out of the memorial and on to the hill suggesting from communication we can ascend to a higher plateau.

The earth enclosing the walkway rises from level with the path to a maximum of six feet opposite the assembly room. Earth surrounding the four round rooms graduates from a height of two feet six inches to four feet. At the foot of the stairs in the square room the earth is approximately two feet in height. The walkway remains eight feet wide. Three trees are lost in the realization of the design and would be replaced / relocated on the hillside slope. Finished materials textures would create the effect that the memorial was craved from existing rock below the grass surface with vines, greenery, and ground cover attempting to heal the wound. The Memorial, with the exception of subtle base cover lighting, would employ all natural materials.

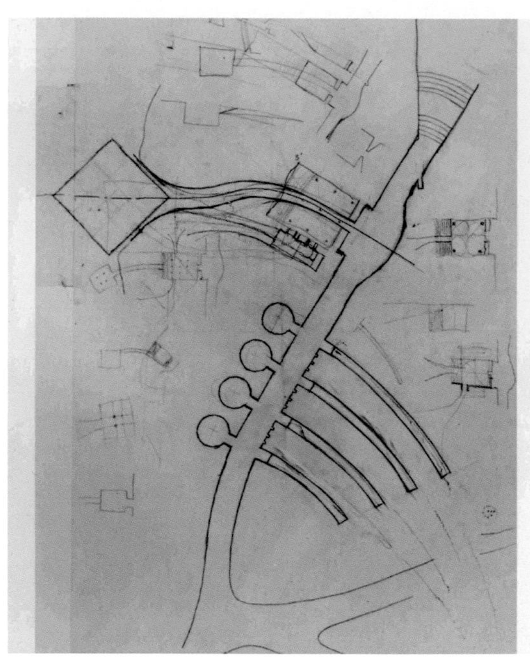

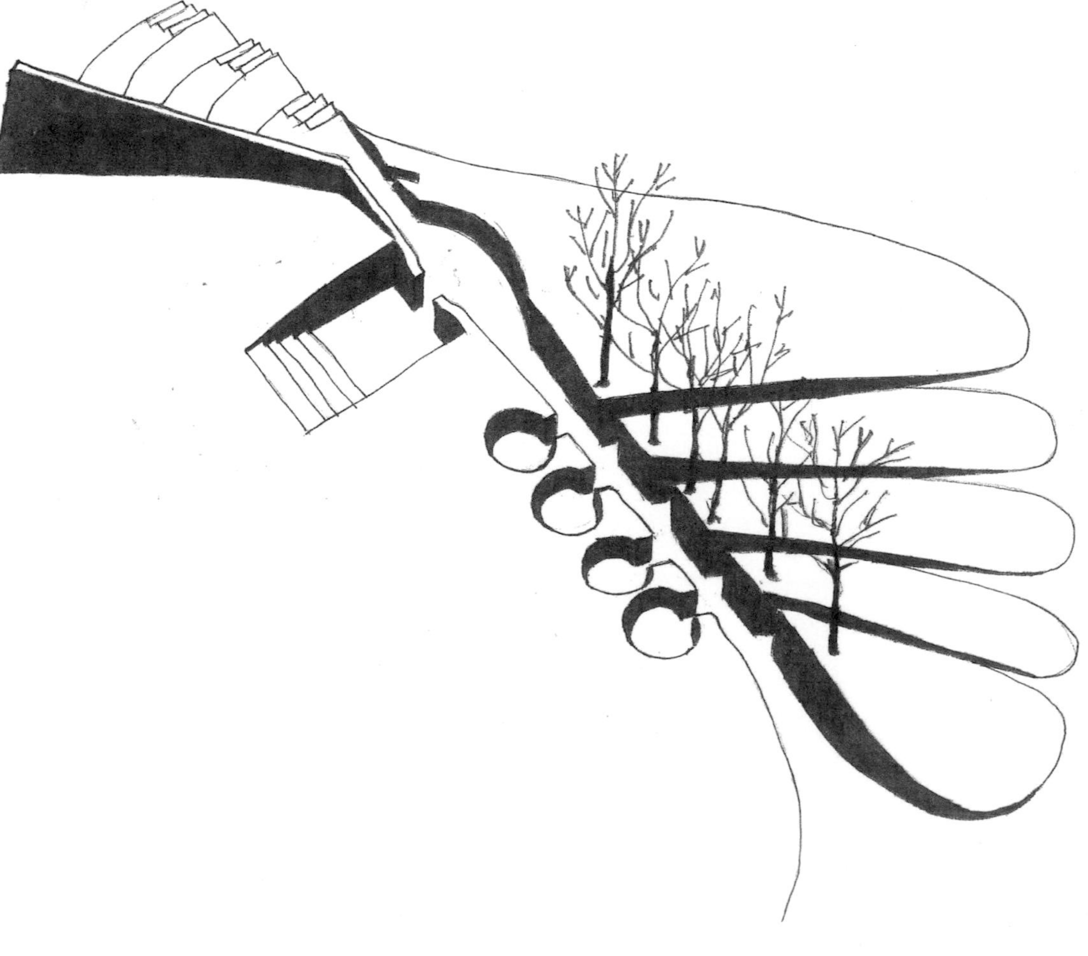

client / owner
Kent State University, Kent, Ohio

other key consultants
Lynn Chang;
Mark Krecic;
Lester Fader;
Jon Paddock;
Michael Fahey;
Photographer: George Laetz;

location
Kent, Ohio, USA

awards
Competition Entry, Awarded First Place, disqualified as author was not a US Citizen

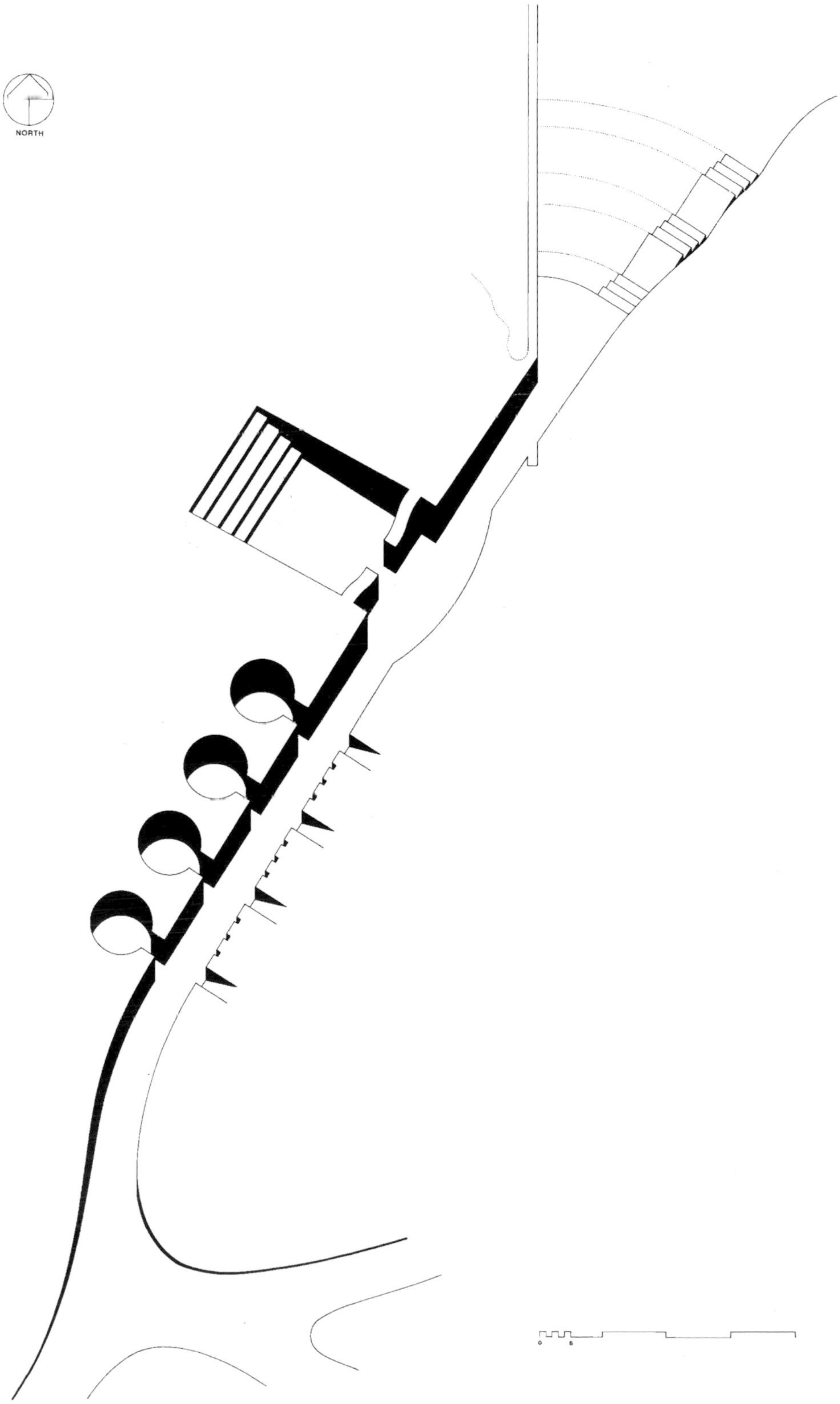

(left) Concept sketches.

(above and right) Axonometric Drawings.

(left) Site plan and schematic diagram.
(bottom left) View at night.
(bottom) View from above.
(right) View from north.
(far right) Geometry drawing.
(bottom right) Overall view from above.
(bottom far right) Detail view of open air classroom.

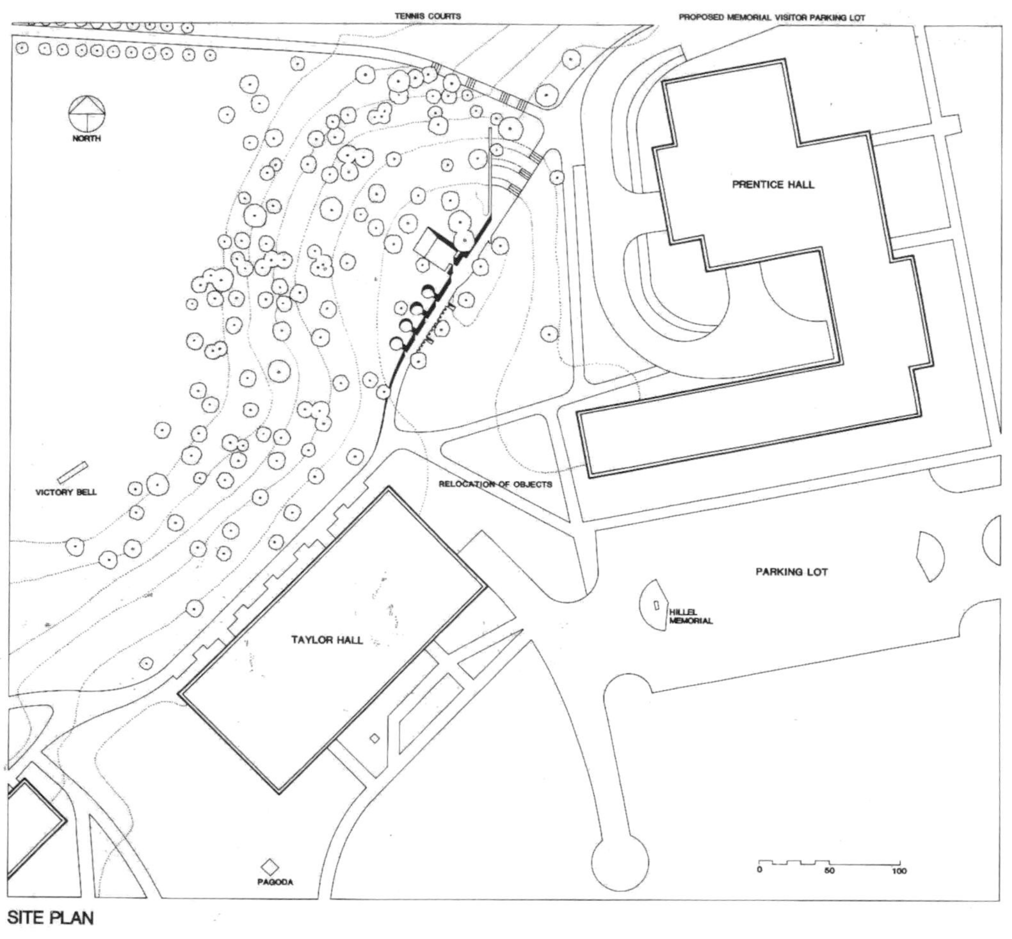

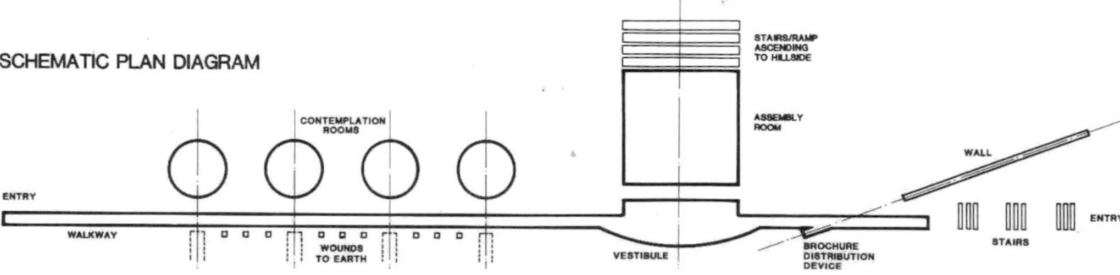

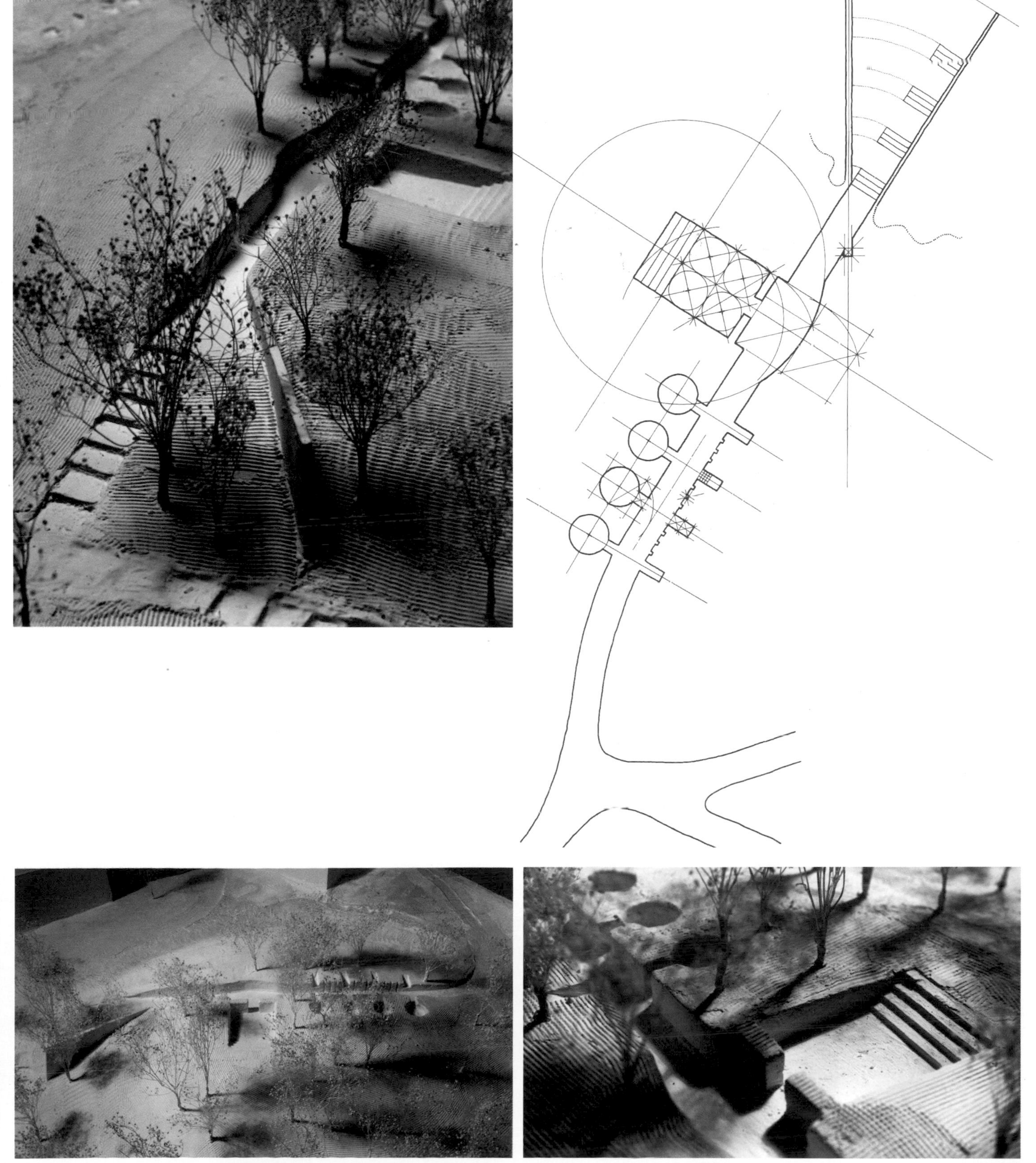

Residential

Hualong Lake, Chongqing Tiandi Development, Chongqing

Urbis Limited was commissioned in April 2007 by developer Shui On Development Limited (SOL) to design the Hualong Lake, located at the heart of the Chongqing Tiandi Development, a "signature" comprehensive development by SOL in various major cities in China. Construction will commence in the beginning of 2008 and the lake will be open for public use in fall 2009.

The overall Hualong Lake development consists of two inter-connected "lakes", which are visually dissected by Mid-Level Road that runs east-to-west. The north lake is a man-made lake, while the south lake is an existing floodplain basin, surrounded by hundred-meter high hillsides. Thus the two water bodies are commonly referred to as "North Lake" and "South Wetland".

To the north of the North Lake is the commercial and office district, separated by Jialing Road, a major arterial road. To the east, the North Lake is directly attached to a future five-star hotel development. A high-end dining and entertainment hub is situated along North Lake west. And as noted, Mid-Level Road bounds the south edge of North Lake.

The South Wetland is bounded by Mid-Level Road to its north, and natural hillside topography surrounds the other three sides. However there are several note-worthy structures within its boundary, including the heritage address of Xin Hua Publishing House; an existing railway superstructure, elevated from its base some 50-meter high; and a new light-rail overpass approximately at a similar elevation, planned just to the north of the historic Publishing House that will run across the valley.

Given the distinguishing functions of the two lakes, the design intent of the whole project is two-fold. Firstly, the landscape design of North Lake provides a one-of-a-kind leisure amenity to the public. With the long axis at 500-meter long and stretching as wide as 140 meters, the lake provides a variety of activities along its periphery. Steps away from Chongqing Tiandi Shopping District, the careful design of a performance stage and its surrounding viewing terraces creates a unique venue for special occasions. Residents and visitors alike will enjoy a casual mid-morning walk along the lakeshore promenade of Jialing Road. Approaching lunch hours, people will walk towards the high-end restaurants on the opposite side of the lake, while pausing at the iconic New Hualong Bridge to take 360-degree panoramic postcard pictures around the lake. During the afternoon, organized school groups will visit the cultural centre for creative educations and explorations. Hovering along the community arts corridor at North Lake's southwest area, more scenic hotspots are discovered as couples strolling and seniors exercising in the sunset. A five-star hotel makes a strong visual terminus at the east, while the stage is set for night-time partying in the well-lit landscape plaza.

In contrast, the South Wetland takes on a completely different design approach, in which a "wetland story" is being told as it moves farther into the valley. A Wetland Exhibition Centre is planned close to Mid-Level Road. Coming in either from the road entrance or through the pedestrian tunnel under the road, various wetland demonstration ponds will be passed by and observed. Access to the major portion of the functional wetland, however, will be restricted, so as to maximize its environmental contribution and value. Nonetheless, for bird-lovers and environmental enthusiasts, a well-protected jogging trail with observation stations is designed along the mid hill. In summary, the project aims to provide the public not only an exciting place to be, but it also creates a strong connection to nature.

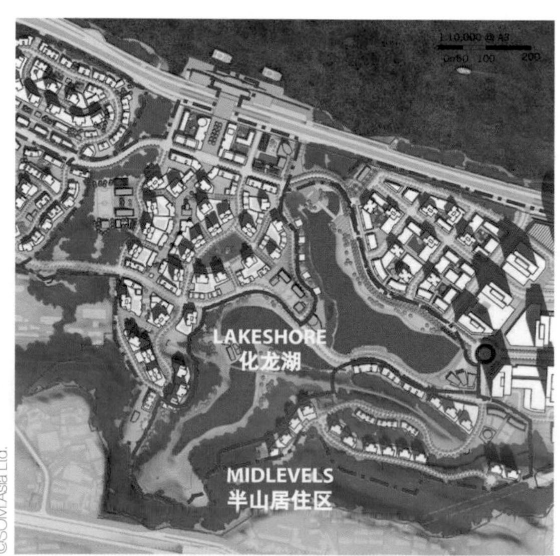

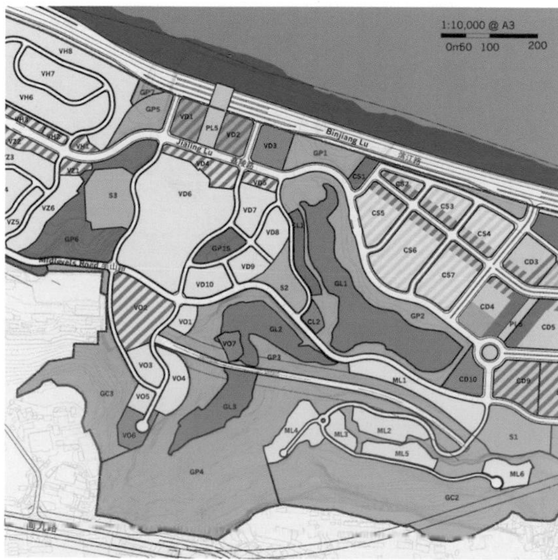

(far left) Comprehensive Development Masterplan, showing Hualong Lake and its surrounding communities in the future.

(left) Comprehensive Land Use Plan of the overall development. Hualong Lake, marked with dark blue, is zoned as Green Open Space.

(right) Overall Landscape Conceptual Masterplan with indication of major landscape attractions. Hualong Lake development consists of two distinguishing water-body types. The North Lake, a man-made lake, is primarily a recreational hot-spot while its volume of water sustains heating and cooling pumping system of the adjacent downtown core. The South Wetland, improved on an existing floodplain, will provide busy city dwellers a naturalistic environment where wildlife habitat can be observed and enjoyed.

client / owner
Shui On Development Limited

key consultants
Project Manager & Landscape Architect: Urbis Limited;
Electrical / Mechanical / Structural Engineer: Maunsell Consultants Asia Ltd.;
Comprehensive Masterplan Consultant: SOM Asia Ltd.;
Sustainability Consultant: Ove Arup & Partners Ltd.

location
Chongqing Tiandi Development, Chongqing, China

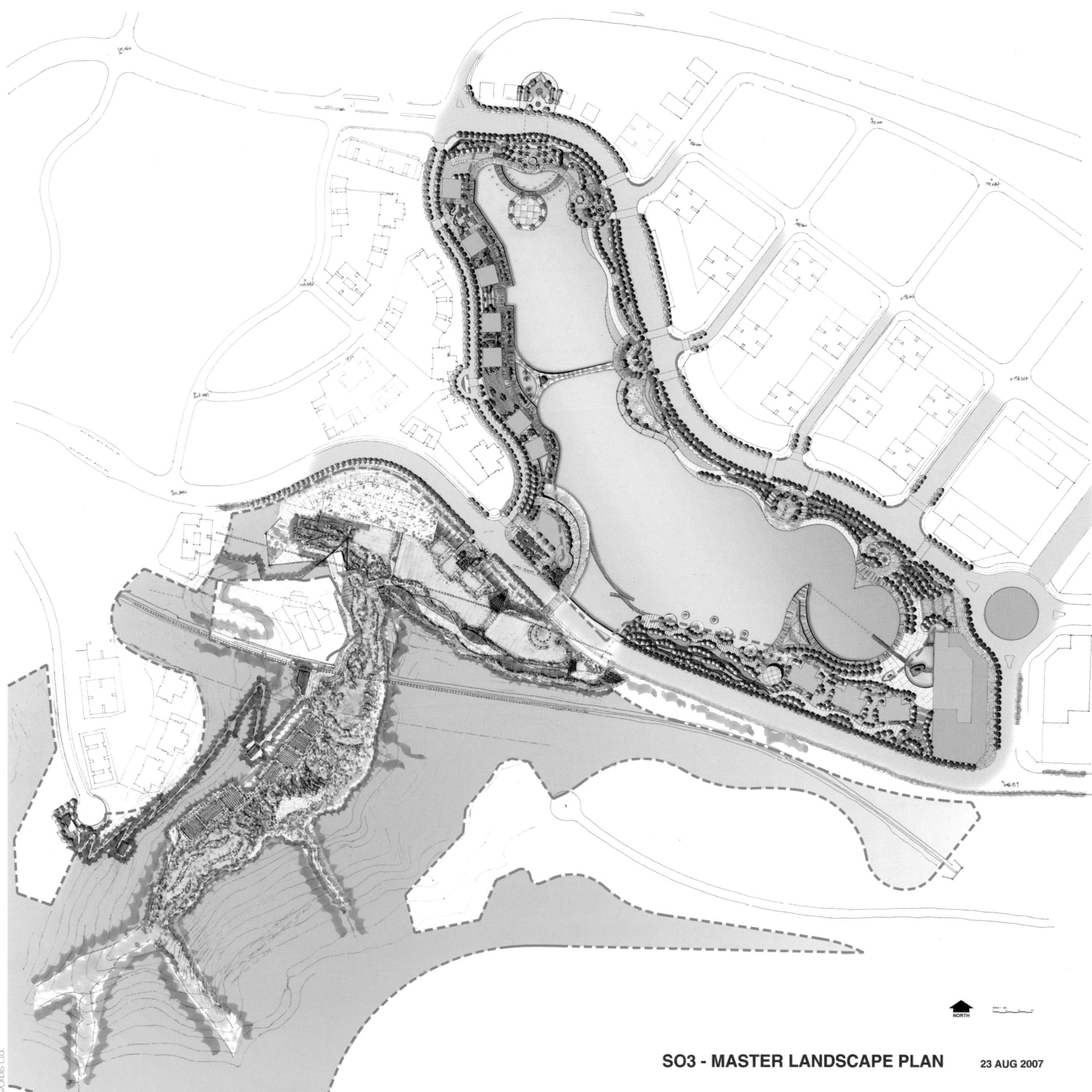

©Urbis Ltd.

(right) An artist's rendering of the wetland after construction. The primary function of the South Wetland is to serve as a stormwater retention and biofiltration pond. Water collected will be recycled for landscape irrigation use within the whole site.

(middle) A typical section of the wetland demonstration area, located in front of the Wetland Exhibition Centre.

(bottom left) A conceptual sketch of the South Wetland, which is formed by several small ponds cascading down the existing valley.

(bottom right) A typical section of South Wetland, indicating essential wetland components.

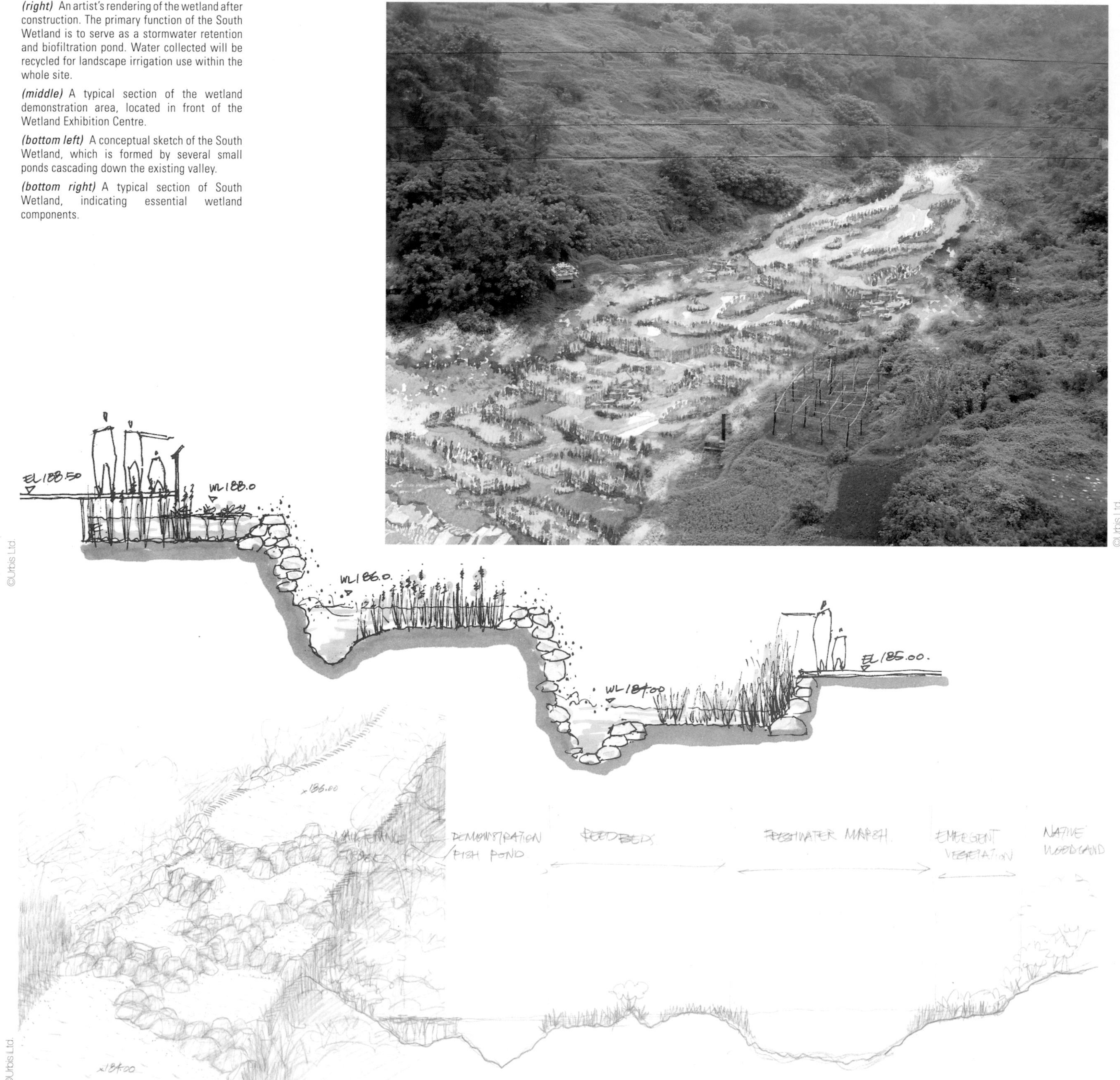

©Urbis Ltd.

©Urbis Ltd.

©Urbis Ltd.

©Urbis Ltd.

©Urbis Ltd.

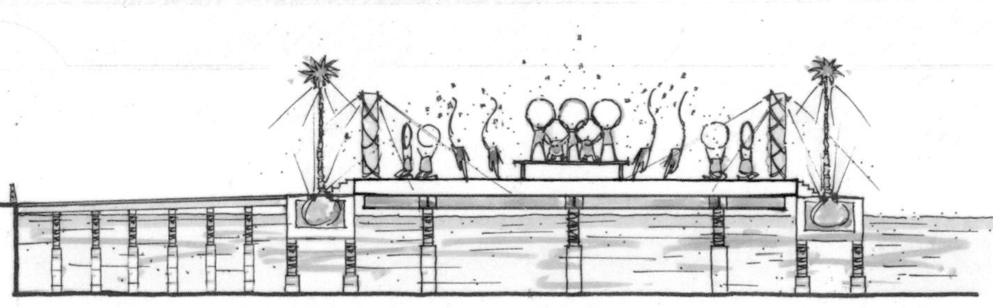

SECTION A2 HUALONG LAKE PERFORMANCE AREA
— DURING PERFORMANCE/FESTIVAL. SCALE 1:200.

©Urbis Ltd.

(top left) Artist's rendering during a celebration event at the performance stage island. Situated at the north tip of North Lake, the island is designed to be surrounded by topographic viewing stages, forming a natural amphitheatre.

(top right) Artist's rendering at the east tip of North Lake in a sunny afternoon. The animated lakeshore promenade provides a wide variety of interests to tourist groups, downtown working class and local residents.

(middle) A cross-section at the performance stage area. Note the surrounding topography provides an excellent viewing opportunity for a vast number of audience during special events, such as New Year's countdown.

(bottom) A typical section across Jialing Road indicates a grandiose boulevard feeling created along the major arterial road along the north side of the project site.

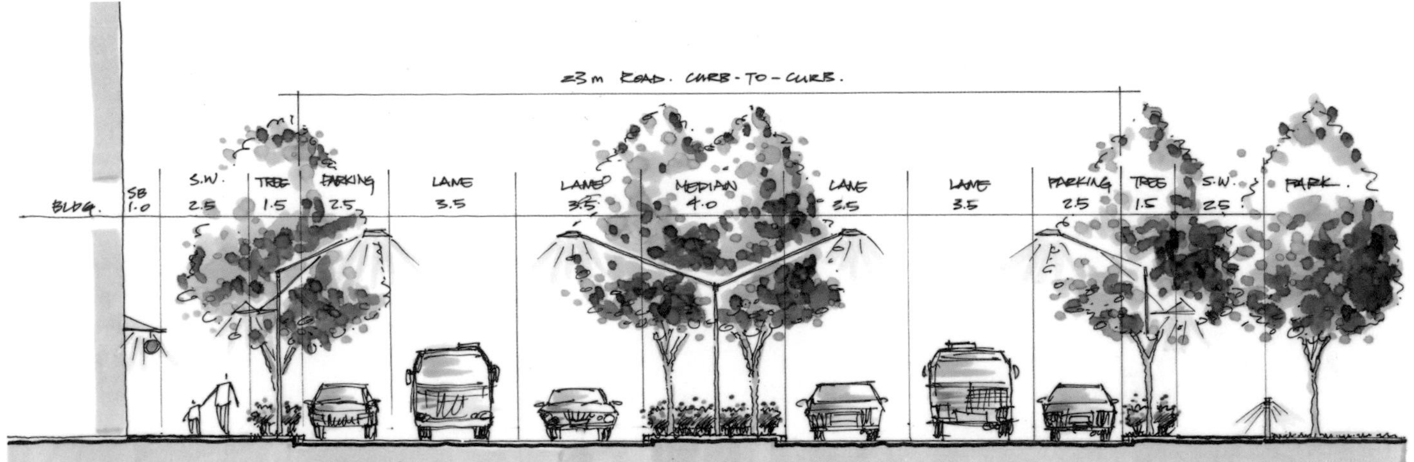

©Urbis Ltd.

Dongshan International New City — Luxi River Revitalising Project, Chengdu

ASPECT was invited to provide landscape design for Luxi River, by Chengdu Longquanyi District Land Preparation Company. The river had suffered from pollution and erosion over several decades and required rehabilitation, bank stabilization and removal of all sewerage flowing into the creek. Following reconstruction of a new sewerage main along the river, the proposed design for the rehabilitation of Luxi River included 2.2 kilometres of waterway and a wetland that incorporated water sensitive urban design principles. A 10,000 square metre wetland with gross pollutant and sediment traps were integrated into the design at the head river where it enters the development site to treat urban water runoff and increase the quality of the river water entering the site. Each internal development stage has been designed with grassed water treatment swales and recharge strips to capture urban storm water runoff and roof top drainage to ensure that water entering the river from the residential development is of the highest possible quality.

In addition to the above the water treatment solution put in place a CoMag™ sewerage treatment system of approximately 10,000 square meters was installed to treat the entire site effluent load from Stages A to E. Domestic sewage, and industrial wastewater of the entire Dongshan development will be collected and treated in the treatment plant where CoMag™ is employed to achieve high levels of particulate contaminant removal with a small footprint and low capital and operating costs. CoMag™ excels in meeting or exceeding the particulate removal standards for water for reuse whether the standards are for irrigation, aquifer re-injection, industrial processes, or even for drinking water production plants.

The project is now under construction and should be completed in early 2008. These initiatives are ensuring that the Luxi River will become a green waterway for people to escape city life and enjoy a natural river landscape again and have been supported by the local government and the developer.

The ongoing efforts and initiatives on the Luxi River include:

1. Developing an ecological plan for the river's waterfront residential communities and the creation of a river parkland tying the new Dongshan development areas together through improved open space along the river;
2. Reducing pollution loads, restoring ecological integrity, improving fish passage, increase in wetland area, expansion of forest coverage and increase in public and private participation and stewardship of the land with increased recreational opportunities.

The restoration of the Luxi River provides a unique opportunity to live in an ecologically designed waterside living environment promoting ecological values and recreational and cultural pursuits.

client / owner
Chengdu Longquanyi District Land Preparation Co. Ltd. and Sino Trust Grand Wealth Real Estate

location
Chengdu, Sichuang Province, China

(left) Path and submorgod water margin planting.
(top) Aerial view of Luxi River.
(bottom) Sports court.

(opposite page, top left) Fish weirs.

(opposite page, top middle) Pedestrian bridge and stormwater outflow from development.

(opposite page, top right) Timber pedestrian promenade.

(opposite page, bottom) Constructed wetland outflow.

(bottom) Amphitheatre.

Crossharbour, London Docklands

The London Arena on the Isle of Dogs has been demolished to make way for a new mixed use development of 25,500m², which will provide a total of 1,098 apartments. The development site is 2.55ha and it sits between Millharbour Dock on the west edge and the elevated Docklands Light Railway (DLR) on the east edge. Two courtyard gardens will be created for the enjoyment of new residents and the local community. New east/west links through these courtyards will be opened up and they will provide visual and physical connectivity between Limeharbour and Millharbour Dock. A central boulevard will be the main pedestrian thoroughfare with a linear water feature linking the two edges of the site. However, the most significant changes to the local context will be the improvements to the DLR corridor. The existing 2.5m high stone clad berm which encases the support structure will be removed to open up views and to provide pedestrian permeability to the dockside. Sculptural glass cubes will wrap around each of the columns to create a striking new elevation and provide a memorable landmark at the point of arrival.

It is intended that the cubes will be backlit to create a dynamic and responsive element that can change to reflect times of the day, seasons and special events.

All of the external soft landscape and public realm will be built on a podium slab over parking. The development will provide for a population that will include an estimate of 370 children. Whilst there will be an area dedicated to play with specialist equipment, most of the play provision will be integrated throughout the external public realm in a variety of multipurpose sculptural elements, upstands, water features etc. These elements will also provide meeting places and places to sit for other members of the community.

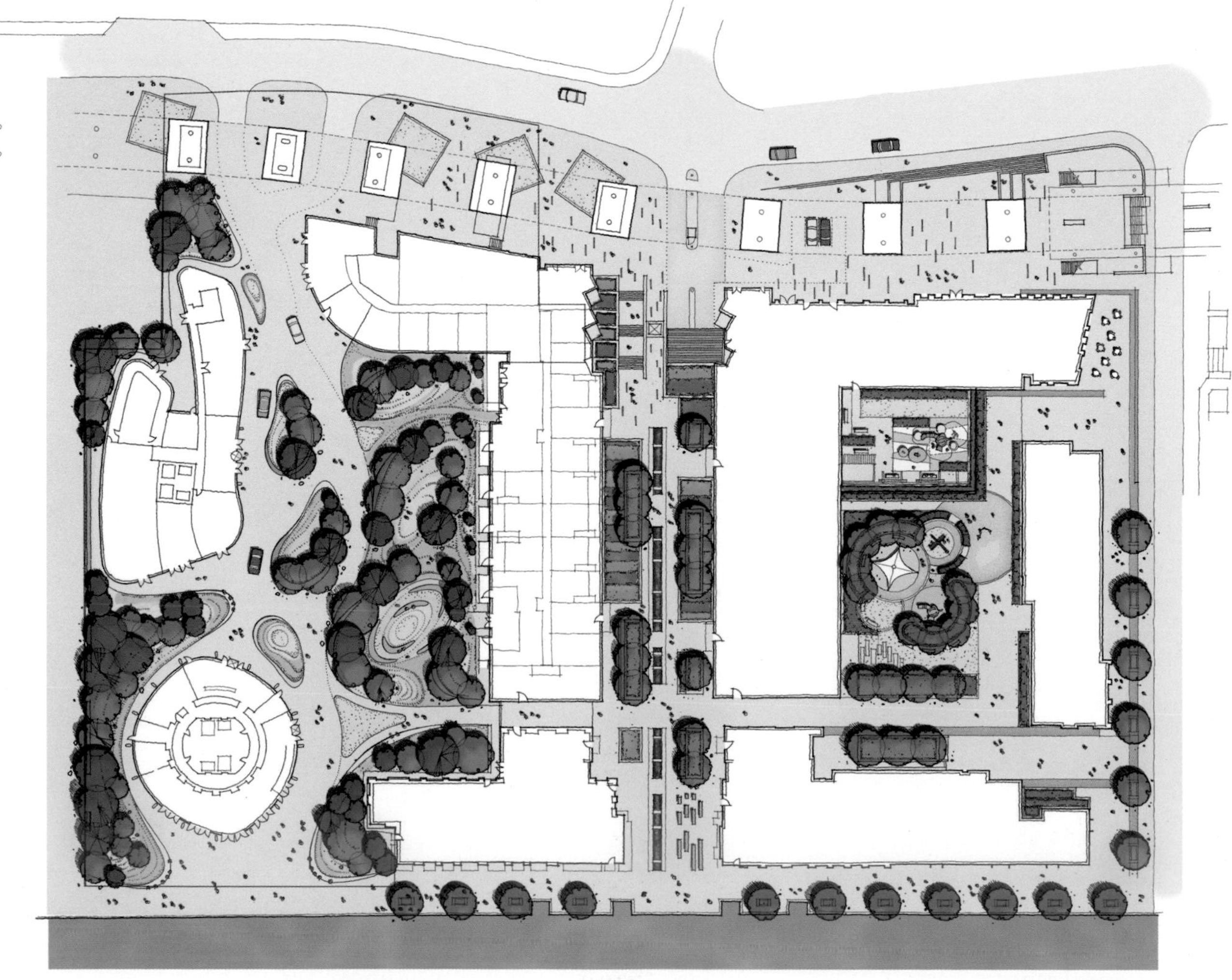

(left) Landscape Masterplan.
(opposite page, top) Crystal Cubes.
(opposite page, middle) DLR detail.
(opposite page, bottom left) Millharbour.
(opposite page, bottom middle) Crossharbour DLR.
(opposite page, bottom right) Dock Edge.

client / owner	other key consultants	location
Ballymore, London, UK	SOM, Hilson Moran, GVA Grimley, WSP, Indigo PA, Environ, Johnson Naylor, Willerby Landscapes	Docklands, London, UK

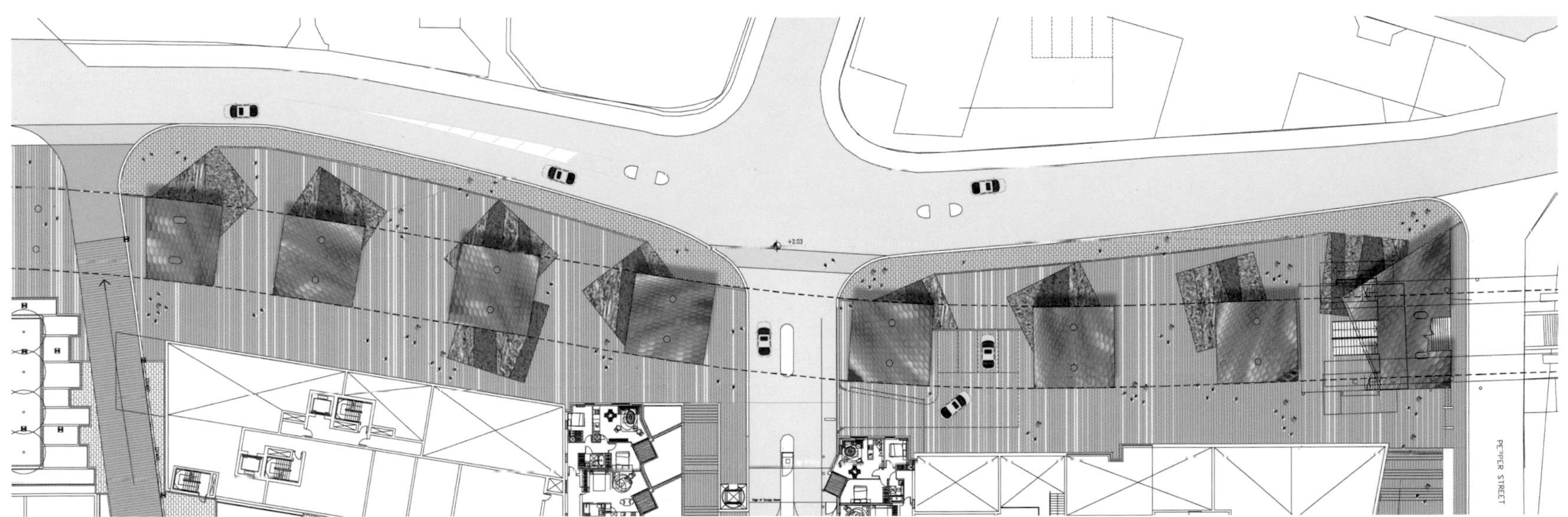

(top) Boulevard view.
(top right) Courtyard view .
(bottom) DLR section.
(bottom right) Panoramic of site.

West Southall Landscape and Public Realm, London

Introduction

This 34 hectare former gasworks site in west London is to be re-developed as a new quarter to the existing town of Southall. The site which is bordered by a canal, country park, residential streets and railway will provide some 3500 homes along with shops, school, cafes, restaurants, community facilities, town square and a central park.

Place making is at the heart of the masterplan which has been designed around a distinctive public realm hierarchy of connected streets, squares and parks. Responding to both its physical and social context the masterplan seeks to create a new 'place' to both complement and enhance the existing community in this part of west London.

Southall currently presents a rich and diverse culture with a strong identity and character. As an extension of the town West Southall seeks to build on this and to further enhance amenity and opportunities both for existing and new populations.

The landscape and public realm strategy draws on its context and aspires to provide a high quality environment for a thriving new community to enjoy with ease and safety. The diversity of the landscape and the quality of both private and public space seeks to encourage respect and understanding of the environment both at a local and global scale.

The Public Space

The public realm environment creates a diverse range of spaces that provide for differing functions and sections of the community. There will be flexible open space for festivals and events, spaces for social activity with cafes and restaurants, a tree-lined shopping street, safe and secure play areas for varied age groups, sports and recreation space, areas for wildlife and wetland areas for bio-diversity and as educational resource.

The nature and character of these spaces will vary in response to the functions and activities that will be taking place. Some will have a busy and contemporary urban feel whilst others may provide more reflective and intimate quiet informal space. The provision of a high quality public realm and amenity that is accessible and inclusive will make the West Southall a focal point for the wider community and a destination in its own right.

Central Park

In the heart of the site will be a large Central Park and urban retreat arranged around a primary circular space, the village green and cricket pitch. A variety of open spaces are created of varying scale and character to provide for wide ranging recreational activities for the local community. The primary areas of the park around the village green/cricket pitch are the wetlands, the sports grounds, the ornamental garden and the community gardens.

Town Square

The creation of a vibrant new Town Square will form the urban heart of the West Southall development and assist in the promotion of its civic status. The pedestrian and public transport orientated square of contemporary urban character will provide a flexible space that can facilitate a range of community events and activities from morning to evening, throughout the seasons. As such, it is a place to informally meet and gather, relax, watch or participate in organised events and festivals.

©Make

client / owner
National Grid

other key consultants
Architects: Make;
Sustainability: Beyond Green;
Transport: Savil Bird & Axon;
Environmental: White Young Green

location
Southall, West London, UK

©Lovejoy London

©Lovejoy London

(left) Aerial photo showing site.
(top left) View looking south-west along canal edge.
(top right) View looking west along southern site boundary.
(right) Central park and civic square analysis diagram.
(bottom) Landscape Masterplan.

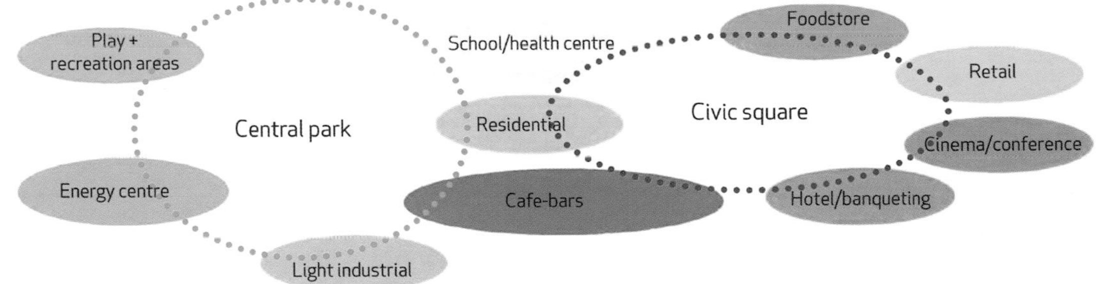

©Make

©Lovejoy London

(left top) View of patio showing proposed sitting area and trellis construction on house façade.

(left bottom) View of patio showing proposed entrance situation.

(Above) View from doors towards feature area.

Olin Partnership www.olinptr.com

106 University of British Columbia (University Boulevard Competition), Vancouver

Oxigen Pty Ltd. www.oxigen.net.au

146 Canberra Central Parklands (Int'l Design Competition), Canberra

plancontext landscape architecture www.plancontext.de

86 Redevelopment of "Spielbudenplatz" Hamburg

Planet Earth Ltd. www.planet-earth.co.uk

66 Bury Mount and the Mill Stream, Towcester

Rios Clementi Hale Studios www.rchstudios.com

180 Fresh Kills Landfill (Int'l Design Competition), New York

RMP Stephan Lenzen Landschaftsarchitekten www.RMP-Landschaftsarchitekten.de

92 Rhine Boulevard, Koblenz
118 Festival Hall, Messe Frankfurt, Frankfurt

rush\wright associates www.rushwright.com

96 Monash University Caulfield Campus Landscape Masterplan, Melbourne
102 Deakin University Rainforest Courtyard, Melbourne
122 Hargreaves Mall, Bendigo

Sander Design www.sanderdesign.ca

266 Toronto East End Residential Back Yard Design, Toronto

Stoss Landscape Urbanism www.stoss.net

52 Erie Street Plaza, Milwaukee
212 Bass River Park, West Dennis

Studio Bednarski Ltd. www.studio-bednarski.com

24 Overhead 400kv Electricity Transmission Towers — Vertical and Horizontal Formation
90 Tram Spaces and Places - Mornington Crescent, London
218 Pedestrian and Cyclist Bridge for the Tamar Valley World Heritage Site, Tamar Valley

Suzman & Cole Design Associates www.suzmancole.com

262 Rancho Petaluma, California

Sweeny Sterling Finlayson & Co. Architects Inc. www.andco.com

34 Kaohsiung Waterfront Master Plan — Floating Hills, Living Islands, Kaohsiung

The Terra Firma Consultancy Ltd. www.terrafirmaconsultancy.com

142 Enviropark, North Harbour, Portsmouth

Thomas Balsley Associates www.tbany.com

208 South Waterfront Greenway Development Plan, Portland

Tom Barratt Ltd. www.tblla.com

74 Whistler's Mountain Square, Whistler

Urbis Ltd. www.urbis.com.hk

246 Hualong Lake, Chongqing Tiandi Development, Chongqing

van der Zalm + associates inc. www.vdz.ca

114 Abbotsford Cultural Centre, Abbotsford

Walker Macy www walkermacy.com

208 South Waterfront Greenway Development Plan, Portland

West 8 www.west8.nl

30 Toronto Central Waterfront Innovative Design Competition, Toronto

INDEX by Country